RICHARD BANGS

THE ART OF LIVING DANGEROUSLY

TRUE STORIES FROM A LIFE ON THE EDGE

LP
LYONS
PRESS

Essex, Connecticut

*To all with whom I have plotted and conspired to color in the map,
and to Laura Hubber, my loving partner in grime,
and my two pathfinding sons, Walker and Jasper.*

An imprint of Globe Pequot, the trade division of
The Rowman & Littlefield Publishing Group, Inc.
4501 Forbes Blvd., Ste. 200
Lanham, MD 20706
www.rowman.com

Distributed by NATIONAL BOOK NETWORK

British Library Cataloguing in Publication Information available

Library of Congress Cataloging-in-Publication Data available

ISBN 9781493074297 (hardback) | ISBN 9781493079667 (ebook)

∞™ The paper used in this publication meets the minimum requirements of American National Standard for Information Sciences—Permanence of Paper for Printed Library Materials, ANSI/NISO Z39.48-1992.

CONTENTS

INTRODUCTION

DYING TO EXPLORE

Men go out into the void spaces of the world for various reasons. Some are actuated simply by a love of adventure, some have the keen thirst for scientific knowledge, and others again are drawn away from the trodden path by the "lure of little voices," the mysterious fascination of the unknown.

—Sir Ernest Shackleton

In the metaphysics of identity, the ship of Theseus is a thought experiment that raises the question: If a boat, battered by storms, rotted by salt and barnacles, reaches the state that all its original components have been replaced, is it then the same object?

If but a safe voyage is sought, the boat should never leave the harbor.

Yet if the ambition is discovery, or telluric wisdom, or the evolution of consciousness, or even the crasser quests of religious, political, or economic booty, then sails must billow, waves must be crested, risks assumed, and boats broken. The risk/reward minuet comes with the note that one might not come back.

In the Age of Exploration adventurers were most often sponsored souls willing to trade limb and life in search of plum for their backers. This was closer to war than romance, in that participants often lived in mortifying dread; supped on hard biscuits, sawdust, and rats; and slept lonely on hard surfaces in hopes of returning to a better life, a bit richer, perhaps with a promotion and some fame. More often than not, these adventures were distinguished by their accidents, either in geographic discovery, disappearance, or loss of life; they were, in essence, well-planned trips gone wrong. Leif Erikson was blown off course during a voyage from Norway to Greenland around 1000 CE and knocked into North America. Nearly five centuries later, Columbus imagined he had arrived in the Indies, when he was half a world away in the Caribbean.

Richard, age eleven, makes his first raft trip down the Potomac River on a self-made boat. LOUISE BANGS

Almost thirty years later Ferdinand Magellan was looking for a western trade route to the Spice Islands when he came to a sticky end in a local skirmish in the Philippines; likewise, Ponce de Leon, Étienne Brûlé, Captain Cook, John Gilbert, and Jedediah Smith were killed by indigenes during their explorations. Vitus Bering died of exposure navigating the northern sea that would bear his surname; Henry Hudson disappeared in his namesake bay after he was put adrift in a small boat by a mutinous crew; and Scottish doctor Mungo Park vanished while navigating the Niger River. John Franklin lost his entire expedition, two ships and 129 men, when he became icebound trying to negotiate the Northwest Passage. And while Henry Morton Stanley survived his 999-day journey across the malarial midriff of the Dark Continent, half of his 359 men did not. Robert Falcon Scott may have been a last of a breed, sacrificing himself and his party to an Antarctic storm for the sake of science (he dragged rocks and specimens across the continent to within eleven miles of a resupply depot) and of British boasting rights to be the first to the South Pole (Norwegian Roald Amundsen beat him by five weeks).

The point is, these adventures were decidedly dangerous, and, like enlisting to battle, those who volunteered had the grim expectation they might not return. These were individuals willing to go where only dragons marked the map, and to tender lives for queen, country, or God, or the trading company. They were saintlike only as martyrs to their own ambitions. If there was any personal gratification or growth that came from the exercise, it was tangential . . . the central goal was to survive and come home with bounty, be it new colonies, converted souls, slaves, spices, or knowledge.

First descent of the Alas River, Sumatra, Indonesia. Richard greeting the day. BART HENDERSON

The next historiographical trend in exploration had its archetype in Richard Burton, who, though commissioned by the English East India Company and later the Royal Geographical Society, really set about exploring to satisfy his own insatiable curiosity about foreign life, languages, and exotic sex. He was a new-fashioned adventurer who sought out perfectly unnecessary hazards in the name of inquisitiveness and pursued the unknown not for empire or some larger good, but for his own love of discovery.

Ernest Shackleton was another early executant of this sensibility. For his ill-conceived plan to cross the Antarctic, he had major backers and promoted his "Imperial" expedition as scientific, though he had no interest in science, even scorned it . . . the real reasons for the extreme endeavor were personal: He loved a good adventure; loved the romantic notion of searching for fortune; and loved to sing, jig, and joke with his mates in the field. Everything else was an excuse.

Others came to personify this type of adventure in a more direct way, such as New Zealand beekeeper Ed Hillary, who clearly had a vast enthusiasm for climbing and was able to parlay it to membership on a high-profile British Himalayan expedition; and Wilfred Thesiger, who loved the desert and spent forty years exploring its inner reaches, including a crossing of Arabia's Empty Quarter. When Teddy Roosevelt decided to explore the River of Doubt in Brazil, he said, "I had to go. It was my last chance to be a boy." It was his passion for adventure that took him to the Amazon, where he picked up the malaria that led to his premature death.

More of late, Arne Rubin, who made the first canoe trip down the Blue Nile; Naomi Uemura, the first to reach the North Pole solo by dogsled; and Robyn Davidson, the first woman to cross the Australian desert by camel, personified this indomitable spirit of exploration, those who followed some irresistible inner call to find terra

Richard flying with the Blue Angels. LOUISE BANGS

incognita and the light that illumes the ground within. They took the curves of risk with two wheels hanging over the abyss. The catalogue is Homeric with those who did not come back, from George Leigh Mallory to Amelia Earhart, Ned Gillette, murdered on a glacier in Pakistan, and Doug Gordon, drowned while attempting a first descent of the Tsangpo Gorge in Tibet.

Like all, these adventures needed to be financed. Some used the glossy pretexts of flag planting or coloring in the map and found patrons; others paid their way as journalists, photographers, filmmakers, or shills for commercial products or services. And some had the family pocketbook to underwrite the passion for adventure. One of the first of this class most certainly was the pipe-smoking Englishman Samuel Baker, who spent the early 1860s on a stylish self-financed expedition exploring the watersheds of Abyssinia, camping on Persian rugs beneath double-lined umbrellas as hyenas whooped nearby; a little over a century later New Jersey native and self-styled adventurer Joel Fogel financed a first raft descent of the crocodiled lower Omo in Ethiopia with family monies. Not long after, the media fawned over the various self-financed balloon adventures of doughboys Richard Branson and Steve Fossett.

In early readings of these accounts, I sought to unpack the minds of the men and women who unsuccessfully resisted the temptation to leave the safe harbor, who became inexorably caught in the spiraling steel coils of exploration. Many harbored a deep tan of conviction that humankind has become too remote from its beginnings, too remote from Nature, too remote from the innocent landscapes that lie within us. The adventures they undertook offered a chance to pluck at the strings of simplicity again, to strip the veneer of dockside worldliness and sail to some more primitive, if more demanding, state of grace; and though the world is sometimes better for the discoveries made in their bold forays, sometimes their searches proved folly, and they didn't come back.

I once sailed by rubber boat down the Grand Canyon of Asia Minor, the Kemer Khan of Türkiye's Adiyaman Plateau, a spectacularly striated gorge of sedimentary and volcanic rock through which the upper Euphrates cut and purled for tens of thousands of years. It was such a stunning passage, it hurt my eyes and stole my breath away. Yet, when a few years later I planned to return with friends, I was shocked to discover this vault of history, the Grand Canyon of the Euphrates, had been dammed in a styptic blink when nobody was looking, and the river flowed no more.

In 1770, the Scottish explorer James Bruce, in his search for the source of the Nile, came across the 150-foot-high Tissisat Falls in Ethiopia. He described it thusly:

> The river . . . fell in one sheet of water, without any interval, above half an English mile in breadth, with a force and a noise that was truly terrible, and which stunned and made me, for a time, perfectly dizzy. A thick fume, or haze, covered the fall all around, and hung over the course of the stream both above and below, marking its track, though the water was not seen. . . . It was a most magnificent sight, that ages, added to the greatest length of human life, would not deface or eradicate from my memory.

Yet when I scrambled to this magnificence last year, a thin ribbon of water scraped down the cheek of a dark cliff. The immense cascade was gone, 90 percent diverted into a power scheme built by Chinese and Serbian contractors, erected without knowledge or critique from the rest of the world. The river was redeposited a few hundred yards downstream after pouring through penstocks and turbines, but it had left the great falls bald and sallow.

In 1989 I rafted the Amu-Darya that flows from Kyrgyzstan into Uzbekistan, ending in the Aral Sea, once the fourth-largest freshwater lake in the world. Now it is but a puddle, with scores of huge iron fishing trawlers tipped and partially buried in the surrounding desert, as though tossed miles inland by a massive tidal wave, a ship cemetery with no water in sight. The once free-flowing rivers that fed the Aral were siphoned to irrigate new lands and produce higher cotton yields. The same story played with the Jordan River, which feeds the Dead Sea, now shrunk to a third the surface area of a half century ago. An Israeli resort I visited after navigating the upper river had fallen into a sinkhole and was now too far from the water for me to walk to it.

This has been a subtheme to my travels and explorations over the past fifty years. So often I would stumble to spectacle so bravura, it would speed the blood and validate existence, but then upon return discover it was less so, or gone, because of non-sustainable commercial concerns set to exploit the earth. There is no waterway on the planet uncoveted for diversion or damming; there is no forest that is not lusted over for felling and development. It is a paradoxical and pestilential notion that the places we wish to remain protected and wild cannot become so unless visited and appreciated.

Over the decades, I witnessed many special places preserved and many lost like snowflakes in the sea. The critical vector in survival or demise was more often than not the number of visitors who trekked the landscape or floated the river and were touched deeply by their unique beauty and keening spirit. When such a space became threatened, there was a constituency for whom the place was personal, a collective force ready to lend energy, monies, and time to preservation. The Colorado still dances through the Grand Canyon largely because those who rafted this cathedral rallied against a proposed dam. The Tatshenshini, a river I pioneered with Sobek colleagues in the 1970s, runs through one of the wildest and most inaccessible corridors in North America, through the three-mile-high St. Elias range, and is host to more grizzly bears and bald eagles than anywhere else in the world. Nobody lives here; there is no evidence of man. It belongs to wildlife, wildflowers, and wildness. The only intrusions are from the occasional rafters who float down the river during the summer months. Yet, when a giant open-pit copper mine was proposed in the British Columbia section of the river, it was in such an obscure location the backers never expected opposition. But the rafters saw what was happening and discovered that the mine, besides scarring the impeccable face of a wild place, would leak sulfuric acid into the water table, which might poison the salmon and, as part of the food chain, then the eagles and bears who ate them. It was the rafters who grew incensed with this arcane project, and who built a grassroots movement to stop the project. They brought the issue to the pages of *National Geographic, Life, Sierra, Audubon*, the *New York Times*, and millions now saw the rare and special beauty that had been the privilege of a few rafters. Finally, the plug was pulled, and the region was declared an international park, due in no small part to the adventurer travelers who passed through, were affected by what they saw, and chose to act. Culturally intact Dyak villages in Borneo and throughout the tropics sustain because visitors who witnessed their magic made public battle against timber and oil companies otherwise poised with bulldozers.

Yet in my sleep there is sometimes a lament that falls drop by drop upon my heart. I am haunted by the losses and question if I could have done more to entice people to come and see. In the 1980s, I explored the Alas Basin in Sumatra, running through the largest orangutan reserve in the world. Timber poaching has reduced the once luxurious habitat to a scrawny shadow, and the "men of the forest" are on the brink of extinction. In the late 1970s, I led the first descent of Chile's Rio Bio-Bio, a tumbling gem that offered up some of the finest whitewater in the world. I tried to persuade as many folks as possible to come glide this limpid course, but not enough, as a local power company rolled over resistance and broke the wild water with a series of dams.

In 1981, I joined President Kenneth Kaunda at a function in Lusaka to help save the last of the black rhinos of Zambia. I pledged to motivate more to experience and engage, but I never really made good on the promise. When I returned in 1983, all the rhinos were gone.

A recent census estimates the lion population in Africa has decreased 95 percent since the 1950s. In the 1960s, the Luangwa Valley was home to 100,000 elephants, the largest concentration in the world. Today, because of poaching, an estimated 15,000 remain. In Madagascar, 90 percent of the forests are gone. Scientists warn we are in the middle of a firestorm of species reduction, a mass extinction event. Between 1970 and 2020, the planet lost 70 percent of its populations of wild mammals, fish, birds, reptiles, and amphibians. Today, roughly one million species are threatened with extinction.

If the source rivers of the Okavango Delta in Angola are dammed, diverted, or developed, as some have proposed, one of the richest wildlife basins in the world could become bankrupt. And as we gaze about the world, it is not just trees, rivers, and animals vanishing. The Dead Sea is drying up; variegated coral reefs are bleaching; glaciers are retreating. There is no Planet B.

Not the only one, but a bona fide solution to saving the extraordinary, but sometimes distant, natural assets of our world is to hearten enough people to see and tap and be tapped, as then the concept becomes real and personal, not pedantic, and the value of wonder becomes patent. It is the realization of the nineteenth-century German philosopher G. W. E. Hegel's declaration of humanity's most advanced thought, the idea that recognizes itself in all things.

I've spent a career designing and conducting adventures with purpose, travel that is expectantly meaningful and hopeful. But the graveyard of my own sacred places gone speaks to regrets and quests not fulfilled.

So, this book is an invitation, a summons to come and hear the raw, deep voices of nature and behold architecture supported by the brilliant beams of rainbows. By making that step beyond the equipoise of provisional comfort, there is the chance to be swept away by glorious displays of flocks and herds, to be baptized into the marvels of the natural life. And then I hope when the time comes for volunteers to save what they have seen, hands and voices will rise to the sky.

CHAPTER 1

CRY OF THE OKAVANGO

For every problem there is one solution which is simple, neat and wrong.
—H. L. MENCKEN

JUNE 2022. THE OKAVANGO-ZAMBEZI WATER TOWER, ANGOLA. EMOTIONS SWIRL AS the current at my feet. Everyone looks so young, so charged, so immortal. I was once at such a place, standing on the banks of an unrun river, wild with anticipation, vested with a feeling of launching into something exceptional, something archetypal, beyond normal lives, discovering as the nineteenth-century seekers of the source of the Nile. Downstream, so many wonders, so many dangers, so many moments of sublimity; and then the shock and gloom of injury and death. It was like volunteering to go to war, with full expectations that we would win, but with reality sometimes different. "Hope is the last thing to die," goes a popular Angolan saying. I was awakened last night by the shrinking of history's clock, but here the eyes are glazed with hope, the same optics through which I stared at so many beginnings.

I have entered the museum of my youth. I mingle with the expedition members: Brits, Americans, Germans, South Africans, Namibians, Botswanans, Angolans, researchers, scientists, a social media manager, an Emmy-nominated film producer/director, a Zimbabwean river guide who rafts the Zambezi below Victoria Falls, a sketch artist along the lines of Thomas Baines, who accompanied David Livingstone on this exploration of the Zambezi in 1859. They have sponsors, some of transparent intent—National Geographic, the Wild Bird Trust, and the HALO Trust (the organization that clears land mines)—others perhaps opaquer, such as Rolex and De Beers, with its past complicity in apartheid and blood diamonds. But at Sobek we had a similar range of supporters, from the Sierra Club to RJR Nabisco, the Smithsonian to the CIA.

The river at which we are standing is the Lungwevungu, and the team hopes to rewrite Wikipedia, which claims the source of the Zambezi is in North-Western Province, Zambia. They intend to make the first descent of what they believe is the true source . . . the farthest contributing stream from the mouth in Mozambique on the other side of the continent. There is no universal agreement on what defines a true source. Some argue it should be the tributary that offers up the greatest volume, as the Blue Nile does when it confluxes with the White Nile in Khartoum, where the combined flow becomes the Nile proper. Others crown the White Nile with the title, as its waters bubble up hundreds of miles farther away than its sister stream.

But this expedition is part of a larger scope, called the Okavango Wilderness Project, which intends to survey the many lakes, streams, swales, and rivers in the Angolan Highlands that make up the life-nurturing watershed for both the Zambezi and the Okavango River, which decants into the Kalahari Desert in Botswana, finally sinking into a sea of sand. The Okavango Delta is one of the greatest cradles of biodiversity on earth, with hundreds of species of birds, plants, and wild animals. It is Africa's last remaining and largest intact wetland wilderness. The greatest concentration of elephant thrives here, 130,000 by some estimates. There are towers of giraffe, dazzles of zebra, bloats of hippo, crashes of rhino, confusions of guinea fowl, flamboyances of flamingo, and more than a million humans who depend upon these waters. UNESCO recognized the Delta as the thousandth World Heritage Site in 2014.

If the upstream spigot were to be turned off, the results for all life in the Delta would be devastating. Not to mention the economic consequences, as tourism and its supporting networks make up some 11 percent of Botswana's GDP (gross domestic product).

A derelict T-55 Russian tank left from the near-thirty-year civil war in Angola.
RICHARD BANGS

The goal then is to champion a network of protected areas that create a corridor from the Angolan sources to Botswana's Okavango Delta and Zambia and Zimbabwe's Zambezi. Tourism could be a key.

The Water Tower is about the size of England, and just as green, but it is a land that time forgot. Its ontogenesis is more paleolithic than neoteric. Its vast peatlands could be Scotland of ten thousand years ago. For the duration of Angola's civil war, there was little to impact the righteous flows of the Okavango headwaters. In many ways this was a proxy war, democracy versus communism, the Soviet Union and Cuba versus South Africa and America. Battles were fought across its banks and bogs; an estimated 500,000 Angolan lives were lost. And an unknown number of land mines were scattered throughout the watershed. By some twisted piece of fate, the land mines kept development and human interference at bay, and the water ran full and clear into the cupping hands of the Delta.

In the midst of Angola's civil war, the HALO Trust began its clearance work. Princess Diana lent her presence and influence to the cause in 1997, just months before her death. Wearing a protective head visor and anti-armor vest, she walked through an active Angolan minefield. She pushed a button and detonated a mine in front of the press. "One down, seventeen million to go," she honeyed to the cameras. The UN at the time estimated some twenty million land mines in Angola. Others who have been on their knees on the ground deactivating mines have more conservative numbers. The Swiss NGO Fondation Pro Victimis figures up to 600,000 mines have been cleared and destroyed to date, but an estimated 300,000 remain. There may be more to be found, in line with Donald Rumsfeld's "known unknowns" and "unknown unknowns." HALO publishes maps of the cleared areas, and much of the Okavango watershed is now safe to wander . . . or develop.

My presence in this outlying piece of Africa traces to a dinner I had in 2019 in Venice Beach with Chris Boyes, who had been part of the National Geographic–sponsored survey expedition that made the first descent of the Cuito River, which spills from the coy source lake that is farthest away from the inland Delta. His older brother, Steve, a South African conservation biologist, conceived and led the expedition, which identified several new species in this little explored plat of Africa.

Chris came to me to describe threats to the Okavango Delta that seemed to be fermenting up in the Angolan Highlands, everything from accelerating deforestation to giant agro-schemes to mining to poaching to hydro projects backed by the Chinese. Angola has been battling corruption since its independence, and, for some, exploitation of the vast untouched watershed in the southeastern swaths of the country is irresistible.

An economic alternative that could indeed help preserve the Water Tower region is tourism. When I cofounded Sobek with my high-school friend John Yost in 1973, we did not imagine our little idea to explore and share the remote wilderness areas of the world would become a force in tourism. But many of our excursions into unknown waters, deserts, rain forests, and mountains became iconic, and today

There were no roads in Eastern Angola, so our only transport was a Bell
407 helicopter from Botswana. RICHARD BANGS

millions annually commit the sins of adventure travel, many following in Sobek's
footsteps. Our first descent of the Zambezi from Victoria Falls to Lake Kariba in
1981, with the support of National Geographic and ABC Television, took a while to
catch on, what with land mines lining the shores and aggressive crocs and hippos in
the river, but ultimately it took off, and it is now the most popular adventure tourist
activity in the region.

So, during our meal I agreed we would try to put a trip together, bringing the
first tourists to the Water Tower, providing proof of concept that non-extractive economic alternatives could be viable. Certainly, the halls of power in Luanda know of
the hundreds of millions of dollars realized in tourism income in nearby Botswana.
Why shouldn't that be replicated in Angola?

There were, however, several challenges with this concept; the first being the
conspicuous lack of charismatic megafauna in Angola. The country once teemed
with the classics: elephant, lion, giraffe, rhino, buffalo, zebra, cheetah, and a panoply
of antelope, including the Angolan giant sable. But, as Colin Bell, co-founder of
Wilderness Safaris in 1983, told me, "All wars in Africa start in the national parks.
Firstly, the troops need to be fed, and the pickings are easy. But also, wars are expensive, and one way to finance is by selling poached ivory and endangered species." So,
after twenty-seven years of civil war, most of the wildlife was either killed or fled to
neighboring sanctuaries, such as in Botswana.

When most tourists come to Africa, they come to see the wildlife. So, for the
moment, that was off the table when designing a trip.

Another challenge was the expense. Angola, which has significant oil reserves, is among the most expensive countries in the world to visit. But more than that, there are no support services in this part of Angola: no lodges, no restaurants, no safari vehicles, no guides, no infinity pools. There are no commercial flights, and no airports at the source lakes. The only way to visit the Water Tower region in a holiday time frame would be by helicopter, and the helicopter would have to fly from Botswana almost five hundred miles to the north. And the only helicopter available for such a journey would be a Bell 407, which seats six, including the pilot, so any tourism pioneering would have to be with a small group. That put the tab per person at around the cost of a new electric car.

The last major obstacle was the two-year travel interregnum imposed by COVID-19. So, while we unpacked this plan in 2019, it was not until June of 2022 that we finally confounded the challenges and set off on an exploratory of potential consequence. There are six in the helicopter as it shudders northward: Mark Schneider, who traveled with me on pioneering trips to North Korea and Saudi Arabia; Robin and Bob Ebinger, who recently returned from an MT Sobek adventure in Sudan; Daniel Williams, our pilot, who did a hazardous stint flying miners in the Democratic Republic of the Congo (DRC); and Kai Collins, a Botswana-born conservation biologist with a special focus on threatened species and the impacts of climate change on ecosystems. He has been surveying for the Okavango Wilderness Project for the last three and a half years and was last year attacked in his tent while on survey by a rogue elephant who gored him, tossed him thirty feet, and left him near dead. Now he's back on the horse, and when an elephant approaches to within inches of our lodge deck in the Delta, Kai doesn't flinch.

As per Angolan requirement, we take our PCR tests for COVID in Maun and then wend our way up the panhandle of the Delta, stopping for exit visas in Shakawe, and then to Rundu in Namibia for refueling. Rundu is at the doorstep of the Caprivi, the narrow neck of land acquired by then German South West Africa, now Namibia, in 1860 in order to provide access to the Zambezi River and a supposed route to German Tanganyika on the east coast of the continent. Victoria Falls put paid to that navigational dream, but the strip remains and holds the wildlife-rich Bwabwata National Park. We see parades of elephant, pods of hippo, herds of antelope, and stacks of termite mounds before our border crossing.

We enter Angolan airspace and maneuver north to Cuito Cuanavale, where the eponymous source rivers meet, and where the largest tank battle in Africa since WWII took place between 1987 and 1988. From the pitch runway we can see the upper sections of a monument to the battle, a colossal black AK-47 built by North Korea. "No pictures while on the tarmac," Kai instructs.

Back in the air we turn with the glassy ribbon that is the Cuanavale, one of the major source fountains. Much of this area was known as *terra do fim do mundo*—the land at the end of earth—coined by the first Portuguese colonists. Until recently, it was as wild and unaffected as earth's first morning. But now, on all sides we see fires

burning the woodlands. With the war over and areas cleared of land mines, villagers have taken to large-scale burning. Trees regrow after natural fires, but man-made burns inhibit the natural order. Forests that once held and regulated moisture, once scorched, will no longer make the healthy feed to their rivers.

We angle and tend up to the mother lake of the Cuanavale, a glass that has tucked itself outside of time's crashing momentum. The translucent waters that percolate from this lake will arrive in the Delta six months from now.

It is here we land in a field of tall grass.

This secret heritage to the Okavango is shockingly beautiful, and more so because of its absences. There is nothing manufactured in any direction, no sign of human habitation now or ever, just a chorus of miombo trees and a little lake shimmering as though dipped in a bowl of crystal. It harbors a single chthonic crocodile, and a cryptid monster called Mukisikisi, so says Kai. It was near here in 1955 that the largest elephant ever hunted to that point was bagged, and it now stands in the center rotunda of the National Museum of Natural History in Washington, D.C. There are no signs of elephant of any size now.

We trek from the landing site down a fine-sand path inked with afternoon shade and meet a Scotland-born former British Army officer and demining expert who was the HALO Angola program manager during Prince Harry's 2013 visit to Cuito Cuanavale, Gerhard Zank. The human bonding that results from jointly stepping through land mines happened, and Prince Harry invited Gerhard to the Royal Wedding in 2018, for which he had to source attire not in his sapper closet: a proper morning coat.

Gerhard is providing support for our little groundbreaking safari, including recruiting villagers from the source lands, called the *Lisima* Landscape ("source of life," in the local vernacular). Gerhard is training them to assist this exotic species called tourists. He purchased new tents and showed the Angolans how to set them up and how to dig latrines, and he turned their cooking skills to new grubery, including English breakfast and *saignant* steak dinners (most eastern Angolans eat *funge*, cassava flour porridge, three times a day). Everything Gerhard brought to this outing is hard to find in this part of Angola, but he did, including sleeping bags, solar-powered lamps, camp chairs, peanut butter, bacon, gin and tonics, and a twelve-year-old bottle of Glenmorangie scotch.

The shuttles of a cold dawn nudge me awake. Outside the canvas tent I watch billows of mist smoke across the lake. Above the brume, hornbills wheel with elegance and bateleurs souse about as though drunk.

Gerhard piles us into a couple of Land Rovers on loan from HALO, and we trundle down a track to a rusting derelict T-55 Russian tank and a battered BMP-2 personnel carrier, casualties of the war. The Reagan administration and CIA-backed UNITA (National Union for the Total Independence of Angola) hid in this solemn assembly of trees as it made repeated well-armed attempts to seize power from the ruling Marxist-Leninist party, the MPLA (People's Movement for the Liberation of Angola). When the Portuguese hastily withdrew from their second-largest colony in 1975, they left a power vacuum that triggered an internal war for control of the country. After almost thirty years of conflict, the civil war ended in 2002 after UNI-TA's leader, Jonas Savimbi, was killed in battle in the province of his birthplace, not far from here. With weapons laid down, Angola emerged as a relatively stable constitutional republic governed by the MPLA, which remains the dominant party today.

After a quick lunch and a Cuca *cerveja*, we take flight again, crossing small knolls and hommocks into the Zambezi watershed. The flight is thrilling for the infinite sweep of first-growth forest, the green lung of Africa. Though Kai interrupts the revery by pointing out the intermittent stands of rosewood, saying the Chinese have an insatiable appetite for the dense, dark hardwood, which they use to craft classical furniture and decor. Villagers are contracted to illegally harvest, to meet the booming Asian demand. With this dialectic, a textured carpet of trees with invisible axes at their trunks, we pass over several lakes that look like human eyes glittering or brooding, as the mood strikes. The enveloping fields look young and green, as if they were breathing in the warm sun. You would never think that this land had ever been a battlefield, and the rivers tank traps.

The ride is smooth, as Daniel is the precision pilot, creasing the sky with a steady hand on the stick. Only once did he scare. We flew over a region that hosted yet another of the large battles in the civil war and looked down at the rusted hulks of blown-up tanks and the twisted remnants of two downed helicopters strewn over the peatlands. Not long after, with a sudden jolt, the helicopter pitched steeply to the right, then sharply to the left. It felt as though we were out of control or were hit by a surface-to-air missile. There were involuntary vocalizations, white-knuckle grips, and thoughts of *Almost Famous* confessions. I lamented for a second that this would be an awful way to die after a half century of hairy explorations. Then, just as suddenly, the helicopter was back upright and sailing straight. "Sorry," said Daniel. "It was a bird. A big bird. I had to dodge it. A bird like that can bring a chopper down." Calming words but words that put us all on high alert for wayward fowl for the rest of our airtime.

In the soft pool of afternoon light, we spot the yellow tents and a fleet of *mokoros*, traditional dugout canoes, at the river's edge, and we circle around a couple times and land. The team members are busy preparing for tomorrow's launch, readying to wrestle nine boats some six weeks and six hundred crooked miles to the Zambian border. But they also seem glad to see drop-ins, as they know they will be stuck with team members for the next several weeks. Dr Rutledge (Steve) Boyes, the visionary leader of the project, has been dealing with health issues and is not present, but he is reportedly on the good recovery road and plans to join downstream. In his place is Rainer von Brandis, with a doctorate degree in nature conservation, and Kerllen Costa, an Angolan biologist and environmental anthropologist whose sister was featured in the National Geographic film *Into the Okavango* and became something of a celebrity and government advisor.

Rainer and Kerllen approach Kai and Daniel and ask if they can borrow the helicopter for a short recce. They say there are rapids not far downstream, and the plan had been to portage, but some local villagers warned there are land mines along this stretch. This cautioning brings me back to our first descent of the Zambezi below Victoria Falls in 1981, just months after Zimbabwe emerged from white-minority-ruled Rhodesia. During the fifteen-year civil war, land mines were planted up, down, above, and below the Batoka Gorge of the Zambezi, a stretch sliced with huge rapids. So we recruited two former Rhodesian army sappers to join the descent, and every time we pulled into a beach to camp, they would sweep the sand first before we made a step. But there are no sappers here, so the expedition is concerned.

Hearing this I immediately offer to join the recce. "I can read water," I offer. But the offer is declined. I remember so many years ago when I set out with a Sobek team to make the first descent of the Çoruh River in eastern Türkiye. The classified topo maps we had secured from the CIA suggested a steep gradient, making large and difficult rapids likely. But as we prepared to launch, an elder from the neighboring town came to me and advised we not attempt to run his river. He had walked up and down the river all his life and he pronounced it unnavigable. "You will die," he announced, "unless you take me with you." In my own youthful arrogance, I felt I knew more than he, and we launched and spun into the muddy flux, waving goodbye to the elder on the banks. We survived (though the Çoruh did not . . . it has since been dammed). Our hubris did not kill us that time; but it would get us later.

A fish eagle is disturbed from its treetop perch, signaling the helicopter return. The machine lands gently, and the scouts jump out to announce the rapids runnable, so the team will not have to portage through a field of land mines.

I so envy the crew and their embark on a passage that might make a difference, and I hope they land buttered-side up. But I also recognize that my little six-person aerial, lake, and land tour could be the tip of the spear drawing international visitors to these wonderlands, giving policymakers and the Angolan people economic reasons to protect their vital water resources.

Now Daniel is waving me to the helicopter, as it is getting late. I take one last long look at the clear-flowing Lungwevungu. It looks so tempting. A big part of me wants to jump in a boat and head downstream.

But I turn to step up the hill to the waiting helicopter. I've traveled unsailed canyons so many times before, and I need to appreciate that, against some odds, I made it out the other side. There is a huge measure of luck in any life, but also, in some, there is an art of living dangerously.

CHAPTER 2

RAPTUROUS TERROR

Are not the mountains, waves and skies a part of me and of my soul, as I of them?
—George Gordon Byron

It was the seventh day of a trek up into the Annapurna Himal in Nepal. Some years previous, in 1978, the throne room of the mountain goddess Annapurna was the objective of the first American women's expedition to an 8,000-meter peak. On October 15, after a long and perilous climb, Vera Komarkova and Irene Miller succeeded in reaching the summit. Two days later, two members of the expedition, Alison Chadwick-Onyszkiewicz and Vera Watson, disappeared into a cloud of unknowing on the mountain, and their bodies lie entombed there still.

The weather had been unseasonable and unreasonable, and I resorted to looking at postcards to catch the grandstand views supposedly outside the tent door.

For the past several hours, my team had passed a river of trekkers retreating down the trail, shaking heads and warning in a dozen accents that avalanches ahead made it impossible to continue.

Now, at Hinku Cave, as we stopped for thrice-brewed milk tea and hard-boiled eggs. Maureen, our trek leader, looked worried. She was hunched in solemn conversation with Ngati, our sirdar and veteran of three Everest expeditions, including one with legendary British mountaineer Chris Bonington. Ngati's flat, Apache-like face was leathery and lined with the ruts of altitude and time.

Finally, Maureen turned to us and announced the plan. Even though her clients had traveled halfway around the world and paid upward of $2,500 each, plus airfare, to be guided up into the Annapurna Sanctuary, the dangers were too high. The heavy snow had created high-risk avalanche conditions in the final, narrow entrance to the sanctuary. Half a dozen major avalanches had already spilled into the gorge, and the lodge owners at the Machapuchare Base Camp had evacuated.

There was a communal sigh with the news. Most were ready to sacrifice time and money for some assurance of safety. But Maureen sensed my compulsion to con-

tinue because, just as my heart was sinking, she turned her somber brow-dark gaze on me and said, "I will allow one exception: Richard, who is the strongest, fastest hiker, can continue with the help of Ngati."

The rest of the group grew angry and questioned the preferential treatment; the group dynamic began to disintegrate. But by then I was gone, heading up the incline behind Ngati. We'd taken only a few steps when a young Englishman with a face the color of old bone came scrambling down the trail, carrying a sleeping bag under his arm. "Don't go any further," he implored. "An ice chunk came down and just missed me. My friends kept going, and they're crazy. I almost died."

Yet up we continued, into a dark cloud, and I realized I was feeling some pleasure in this stab of fear. As we approached the first swath of avalanche debris, we saw a message scrawled in the snow: "No Pass." But Ngati mentally computed the distance across, the freshness of the snow, and the angle of the sun, and he was willing to proceed. The rubble at our feet was from an avalanche a few days old, he said. It looked as if someone had rolled a bin of soccer balls off the ridge. The trail disappeared into this white riot of ice and snow.

Ngati told me to loosen my backpack so I could jettison it if another avalanche began and urged me to cross, if I could, in a *lung-gom* mode, a type of Tibetan mystic running. My passage, though, felt more like that of a pink-skinned tourist heading for happy hour.

When the trail reappeared, it snuck beneath an overhanging wall. As we started toward the overhang, a rumble split the unsullied oxygen of this space, and a spume of ice and snow spilled off the rim like a white waterfall, right onto the path. "Sir, that's where the Englishman was almost hit," Ngati said. "And two years ago, a German was caught by an avalanche here and died. But I have another way."

Ngati steered us off the trail into knee-deep snow. We crossed to the east side of the river, the Modi Khola, and up a small rise, out of the immediate way of the avalanches that slide down from Hiunchuli, the dripping mountain we couldn't see that towers over the western walls of the Modi Khola valley. As we waded upward, we could see and hear lethal spears of ice dropping on the path not taken.

After a couple of hours of hard trekking, we could see Bagar and its one building, the Gangapurna Lodge, named for the 24,458-foot-high mountain that looms directly to the north, which in turn is named for another Hindu goddess.

At last, we crossed the river and stepped our way up to the red-lumber lodge, the last outpost before the sanctuary. We were at 10,825 feet. At half past noon we opened the door and discovered two other visitors and the innkeeper inside. The foreigners were Nick and Nicolette, both from England, both students in English literature, and both terribly unprepared for a mountain expedition. They had no gaiters or waterproof outerwear, and Nick had made it to this outpost wearing shorts. Still, our little den had a vaguely exclusive air, dark and sumptuous with plight.

As we settled in for milk tea and cold yak cheese pizza, we heard what sounded like the low peak of organ music outside. Another avalanche. The weather was getting nastier. Faint crow's-feet nested under Ngati's chocolate eyes as he announced we wouldn't continue farther that day. In fact, he said, he must head back to the main group. "You're an experienced mountaineer. Why don't you stay with us?" I appealed. "I'm sorry, sir," he answered. "I have four children now. I do not take risks anymore." And with that, Ngati, as lean and brown and hard-muscled as a snow leopard, disappeared into the whiteness.

We tried to relax in the little way station and prayed for better weather tomorrow. We settled back for an afternoon of hot lemon, card games, and small talk. Nick and Nicolette seemed delighted with the predicament. They told me they had been spending holidays in Switzerland, following in the footsteps of some of the great English romantic poets who had found inspiration among the Alps. Seeing the mountains through the eyes of Byron and Shelley motivated them to seek ever higher ground and ultimately brought them here. I confessed I didn't pay much attention to the musings of the mountains in my literature schooling. I grew up in the boggy flats of the Eastern Seaboard and went to college at the edge of Lake Michigan. The highest peak at the time was Mount Trashmore, an artificial slope in Chicago fashioned from landfill. There was nothing elegiac to be found in that heap.

With the dark we stepped outside for the short walk to the frigid meat-locker barracks of the Gangapurna Lodge. There was no electricity, so no reading lamp. I pulled an egg-shaped novelty candle from my pack and lit it to postpone the day's finish, and to read a card unrolled from my sleeping bag. It was from my wife, and it read: "Have a safe, sublime, sweet, serene, sure, and sacred trip." The alliteration notwithstanding, I sensed none of those qualities at that moment.

The morning didn't look much prettier, the sky like underexposed film with a bit of snow buzzing around. Aspersions were cast my way as I wolfed down a three-egg omelet. Three days ago, we passed the rock shrine to Pujinim Barahar, the powerful mountain goddess who protects the Annapurna Sanctuary. Beyond the shrine no impure person should pass, nor any polluting foods, such as eggs. Violations risk the anger of the goddess, whose revenge will be sickness or death. In 1956, when Col. James O. M. "Jimmy" Roberts became the first outsider to enter this sacred ground, he left fifty eggs behind at the shrine. Between bites I reminded myself I didn't subscribe to such myths. "These eggs are sublime," I said with a grin to Nick and Nicolette, who recoiled at my words and choice of breakfast. Nick stared out at the snow, vigorously cutting his bread as though demonstrating the murder of Julius Caesar.

Our plan was to see if we could march the two hours or so through the pinched gateway of the sanctuary to the Machapuchare Base Camp. We knew the camp was abandoned and closed, but it was where we might rest before heading west another few hours through waist-deep snow to our ultimate target, the Annapurna Base Camp.

So we whiled away the skin of the day with more card games and talk. Then, around noon, the sun finally broke through, and the world briefly bent toward us. We rushed outside to witness the scene, a view up valley of Gangapurna's triangular, snow-and-rock face. Pastel waves of light cascaded off the sharp walls, and the world pulsed with possibilities. This was our chance. We hoisted our packs and headed out into the snow, up to where the mountains blush, toward the vestibule of the otherwise impregnable sanctuary.

After forty-five minutes trudging through the snow, we stepped over a lone black feather from a cinereous vulture, a bird seemingly as out of place at this altitude and landscape as we were. Minutes later we reached the remains of a colossal, recently triggered avalanche. It was several hundred yards wide, and, like a huge, pocked arm, it reached all the way across the Modi Khola to the far wall of the ravine. Upstream, less than a mile away, we could see the point where the trail squeezed through the steep-walled pass to Annapurna Sanctuary's restricted precincts. The Gurungs, the Sino-Tibetan ethnic group that has lived in the shadows of the Annapurna for centuries, believe this is the abode of Pujinim Barahar, the goddess who protects the Annapurna Sanctuary. The Tibetans, who view the range from the other side, say this is the home of Tara, the savioress of Tibetan Buddhism.

Then, as we stared into the chalky abyss of the avalanche, something roared behind us. We turned to see a shower of snow spraying off the east rim directly above us. Nick ran in circles with the noise and then made a series of superhuman flying leaps through the snow. I couldn't tell whether he was scared to death or in some state of exalted joy.

The avalanche never materialized; it petered out a hundred yards short of us, and Nicolette laughed out loud at the spectacle.

When the sounds and snows settled, I took stock. The sky had darkened and boxed us in, and the Himalayan wind was whistling. It seemed as if we were standing at the threshold between the ordinary universe and the bardo, a sacred realm, but to continue was courting death. Many have died on Annapurna, most from avalanches. A porter died recently right at this stretch. Nick and Nicolette agreed, though reluctantly, and so we retreated to the little lodge.

At nightfall I lit my egg candle and lay awake for hours, wondering why the attraction to the flame of risk. What was it about the mountains that kittled and drew so irresistibly to some? I had no answers. At last, the candle flickered and went out.

When I got up to relieve myself around midnight, I stepped outside and listened to the furtive plops and flurries that are the language of snow. I titled my head up and saw a sky so clear the starlight cast shadows on Machapuchare. So many sparkles and glitters and glints appeared above me, it looked as if an expensive bauble had been dropped and shattered above this redoubt. I stood transfixed, shivering in silent wonder. The flatlands never inspired this.

In the pre-dawn dustiness of consciousness, I awoke to the ear-rending explosion of a plane crashing. And then another. And another. The clamor seemed to be coming from down valley, toward the Himalaya Hotel, where the rest of my group was camping, waiting for me. It was next to the Himalaya Hotel in the spring of 1989 that three Sherpa kitchen boys died when an avalanche rolled over their tent in the middle of the night. I got up to relieve myself once again and stepped out into the bracing shock of a blizzard. The sky had shut, flakes were flying, and a foot of fresh snow smothered the landscape. I cast about for the skyline, an outline, any line, but there was only whiteness in the roaring dark.

An hour later we gathered for a breakfast of frisson, but while I was solemn, Nick and Nicolette seemed positively blissful, in some sort of agreeable kind of horror. The owner of the lodge said that two years ago an avalanche from Machapuchare had rolled down and ripped off the roof. I retreated to pack. I heard the door creak as someone stepped outside.

Minutes after the owner's story, there was another cataclysmic roar, and a blast of wind pushed its way through the cracks. It lifted the side of the roof a few inches, powdering me with snow and forcing me to shut my eyes. A scream followed outside. In ran Nicolette, pasted with snow, looking like the abominable snowwoman.

"That was sublime!" she announced, an arch smile across her face, white as an arctic bear. Nick nodded in rigorous approval.

"How's that?" I asked. But Nick and Nicolette weren't forthcoming. We all finished our packing in silence and headed down to safety and our own separate lives, a groove of wonder now carved in my mind.

Not long afterward, I went snowshoeing in the Cascades with my son Walker and a friend, Anna Bezzola, an alpine guide of Swiss descent. After stepping through the fresh snow for a spell, we cleared a spot and sat down to a Swiss lunch of thick-crusted bread, Appenzeller and Gruyère cheese, and a rack of Toblerone chocolate. It was a perfectly beautiful day, but I was in a crevasse of a mood. I was in midlife and had many of the aspirational trappings—a beautiful home, a beautiful wife, a good job at a large corporation. Everything was proportional and predictable. But there was a dullness inside, as though all the beauty muted the real colors. I never shared these feelings, but rather let them simmer beneath the surface. At one point I took a big bite of Gruyère, and it was so smooth it poured down my throat like a light mead. "This is sublime," I oooohed to Anna. She didn't respond, her face blank with the moment. Then, behind us, higher up the valley, we heard a sudden peal, a question turning over in the sky's mind perhaps. We looked up to see the cascading spray of an avalanche. Walker's eyes went wide, as, I imagine, did mine. For an instant I felt a stirring inside with the danger at a distance. "Now that is sublime," Anna corrected.

Anna went on to explain that The Sublime, as she understood it, having spent much of her life in the Swiss Alps, was not and could not be a tasteful bite, or a little moment of happiness, or even a thing of delicate beauty. That was some postmodern drivel, a vial of tincture that had lost its potency. The Sublime was large, overwhelming, and dangerous—like an avalanche. She mentioned that several of the Romantic poets and artists of the late eighteenth and early nineteenth centuries ventured to Switzerland from England and other parts of Europe and there found the inspiration for The Sublime. To these early proponents, The Sublime was greater than The Beautiful. Beauty was light, fleeting, and charming. The Sublime was profound, overwhelming, scary. Anna suggested that if I wanted to disinter this concept then I should review my adventures to this point in my life and the teleology would become evident.

While in Berkeley, California, for an American Alpine Club dinner, I found myself at the famous local bouldering site Indian Rock with John Harlin III. John, the speaker for the evening, had recently climbed the Eiger's North Face, following in the boot steps of his father, who had died, falling four thousand feet on the Eiger, thirty-nine years earlier, when John was nine. The account was featured in an IMAX film, *The Alps*; in John's own book, *The Eiger Obsession: Facing the Mountain That Killed My Father*; and on a website I developed for Yahoo! After he finished a little clamber around the rocks, he dropped down next to me. His craggy features, engraved by the mountain weather, were as calm as those of a head on a coin. John's father took him climbing for the first time when he was six years old, and he has been an axis in the climbing world ever since.

"For my dad, it was connecting with the deeper dimensions of yourself and the outdoor world through exposing yourself to dangerous, risky situations. He wanted to be a participant in The Sublime, and he succeeded."

John was the editor of the *American Alpine Journal*, so I guessed he might have encountered citations of The Sublime in various articles throughout the years.

"Today we often confuse the term with 'wonderful,' and writers and climbers do that too. But The Sublime is an appreciation for nature in its most numinous, awe-inspiring sense. It is more powerful than mere beauty; you feel like you're under the influence of something bigger than you. You feel the scale and power. It is intimidating and thrilling at the same time. It's not something that can be understood academically or through reading books; it must be experienced."

In 1735, the poet Sir Hildebrand Jacob penned an essay, "How the Mind Is Rais'd to the Sublime," in which he presaged John Harlin's evocation: "A Mind truly disposed for the Perceptions of that, which is great and marvelous, whether in nature or in art, is a product of nature and cannot be attained through study. All the vast and wonderful Scenes . . . which the Universe affords, have this Effect upon the Imagination."

Memory is a butterfly landing on your fingertips, briefly, and then fluttering away, leaving traces of itself on your hand. But scribbled records taken in the time and place can fill in the gaps and start to make sense of it all. At Anna's provocation I decided to rifle through my attic and pull out my old Baedekers and journals and see if there was a throughline, a common theme, which might help explain this life lived at the borders. What I discovered was a country rich in treasures, entertainments, and regrets, a Zeno's paradox of young features in an adult animal.

While in the arched ceiling room, I found a musty copy of *Peri Hupsos*, or *On Sublimity*, attributed to Dionysius Longinus, left over from a college philosophy course. Rereading the slim, third-century volume, I found that this original Greek enumeration of The Sublime was mostly rhetorical; its purpose was to teach oratorical devices that empowered a speaker to move an audience. The author called The Sublime "the echo of a noble mind" and argued that "intensity" was greater than sobriety, that "living emotions" are higher than "good breeding," that "speed . . . vehemence and power" compensated for lack of fluency, smoothness, and charm. He even outlined techniques, such as the "rhapsodic cadence," which includes repeating key phrases, repeating key phrases. It all sounded as if he were describing the oratorical magic of such legends as Julius Caesar, Daniel Webster, John C. Calhoun, Henry Clay, Indonesia's president Sukarno, Cuba's Castro, Malcolm X, the Reverend Jesse Jackson, John F. Kennedy, Barack Obama, and all others with the gift of open-vowel intonations. These were sublime rhetoricians who could inspire wonder, rapture, even ecstasy in a crowd.

But Anna's interpretation was somehow different. Her take was that the poets and philosophers, the artists, aestheticians, and adventurers of the nineteenth century who passed through or spent time in Switzerland took this oratorical feeling, applied it to nature, and forged a new way to regard mountains and other bold landscape features.

Under the bare lightbulb of the attic, I leafed through several old guidebooks. The appeal and satisfaction of a guidebook was in its reticence, its incompleteness— in the gap it left for the imagination to fill pending arrivals. But my journals were noisy and ill-behaved, prompting more questions than answers. Over the next weeks it became evident that cracking the doctrine of the sublime art of living dangerously was like playing Alice in Wonderland croquet, with the flamingo mallets curving around to stare at the player. There may be rules, but they bend in every direction, and there are beasts at every post.

In my box of old journals, I found one from October 1973, marked "Baro River Exploratory, Illubabor Province, Ethiopia." This was the sublime a step too far.

CHAPTER 3

LOST ON THE BARO

If we could be twice young and twice old, we could correct all our mistakes.
—Euripides

Above, the jungle was a brawl of flora and vines and roots. Colobus monkeys sailed between treetops, issuing washboard cries.

Below, three specially designed inflatable whitewater rafts bobbed in a back eddy, looking, from the ridge, like restless water bugs. There were eleven of us, all whitewater veterans, save Angus. He was in the raft with me, Karen Greenwald, and John Yost, who at last was joining a Sobek expedition, the concept we had hatched together the year before. As the leader and the most experienced river runner, I was at the oars.

Our raft would go first. At the correct moment we cast off—Angus coiled the painter and gripped for the ride. I adjusted the oars and pulled a deep stroke. For a prolonged instant, the boat hung in a current between the eddy and the fast water. Then it snapped into motion with a list that knocked me off my seat.

"This water's faster than I thought," I yelled. Regaining the seat, I straightened the raft, its bow downstream. The banks were a blur of green; water shot into the boat from all sides.

Just minutes after the start of the ride, we approached the rapid. Though we'd been unable to scout it earlier . . . its convex edge was clad in thick vegetation, preventing a full view of the river . . . I had a hunch it would be best to enter the rapid on its right side. But the river had different notions. Despite frantic pulls on the oars, we were falling over the lip on the far left.

"Oh my God!" someone screamed. The boat was almost vertical, falling free. This was not a rapid—this was a waterfall. I dropped the oars and braced against the frame. The raft crashed into a spout, folded in half, and spun. Then, as though reprieved, we straightened and flumped onward. I almost gasped with relief when a lateral wave pealed into an explosion on my left, picking up the raft, slamming it against the nearby cliff wall like a toy, and then dumping it and us upside down into the millrace. Everything turned to bubbles.

I tumbled, like falling down an underwater staircase. Seconds later, I surfaced in the quick water below the rapid, a few feet from the overturned raft. My glasses were gone, but through the billows I could make out another rapid two hundred yards downstream, closing in fast. I clutched at a rope and tried to tow the raft toward shore. Behind I heard Karen: "Angus. Go help Angus. He's caught in a rope!"

He was trailing ten feet behind the raft, a snarl of bowline tight across his shoulder, tangled and being pulled through the turbulence. Like the rest of us, he was wearing a sheathed knife on his belt for this very moment—to cut loose from entangling ropes. His arms looked free, yet he didn't reach for his knife. He was paralyzed with fear.

I swam back to Angus, and with my left hand I seized the rope at his sternum; with my right I groped for my own Buck knife. In the roiling water it was a task to slip the blade between Angus's chest and the taut rope. Then, with a jerk, he was free.

"Swim to shore," I yelled.

"Swim to shore, Angus," Karen cried from the edge of the river.

He seemed to respond. He turned and took a stroke toward Karen. I swam back to the runaway raft looking for hope, a candle seeking oxygen. It was futile: The instant I hooked my hand to the raft it fell into the pit of the next rapid, with me in tow. My heart, already shaking at the cage of my chest, seemed to explode.

I was buffeted and beaten by the underwater currents, then spat to the surface. For the first time, I was really scared. Even though I was swashed in water, my mouth was dry as a thorn tree. I stretched my arms to swim to shore, but my strength was sapped. This time I was shot into an abyss. I was in a whirlpool, and looking up I could see the surface light fade as I was sucked deeper. A sound poured in as into a bowl, and the buzz of the river's prop sliced through me ear to ear. I struggled wildly, but it had no effect, except to further drain my small reserves. My throat began to burn. I became disassociated from the river and all physical environments. Then I became aware of a strange thing. The part of me that wanted to panic began to draw apart, and then flew away. There no longer seemed any but the flimsiest connection between life and death. I went limp and resigned myself to fate. I seemed to witness it all as an onlooker.

In the last hazy seconds, I felt a blow from beneath, and my body was propelled upward. I was swept into a spouting current, and at the last possible instant I broke the surface and gasped. I tried to lift my arms; they felt like barbells. My vision was fuzzy, but I could make out another rapid approaching, and I knew I could never survive it. But neither could I swim a stroke. The fear of death was no longer an issue, for that seemed already decided. But I kept moving my arms automatically, for no better reason than that there was nothing else to do. It felt like an age passed like this, my mind stuck in the realization of my fate.

Then, somehow, a salvo of current pitched me by the right bank. Suddenly branches and leaves were swatting my face as I was borne around a bend. I reached up, caught a thin branch, and held tight. I crawled to a rock slab and sprawled out. My gut seized, and I retched. A wave of darkness washed through my head, and I passed out.

When my eyes finally focused, I saw figures foraging through the gluey vegetation on the opposite bank. John Yost was one; Lew Greenwald, another. He had been in the third boat, and seeing him reminded me that there were two boats and seven people behind me. How had they fared?

John paced the bank until he found the calmest stretch of river and then dived in; the water was so swift that he reached my shore fifty yards below his mark. He brought the news: The second raft, piloted by Robbie Paul, had somehow made it through the falls upright. In fact, Robbie was thrown from his seat into the bilge during the first seconds of the plunge, and the raft had continued through captainless. The third boat, handled by Bart Henderson, had flipped. Bart was almost swept under a fallen log but was snatched from the water by the crew of Robbie's boat.

All were accounted for—except Angus Macleod.

The date was Friday, October 5, 1973. We were thick in the region some claim hosted the first coffee trees. Our goal had been to make the first raft descent of the Baro River, a major tributary of the White Nile.

I felt I understood the reasons for everyone's involvement in the expedition, except Angus's. He was the odd person out. I met him in Clifton, New Jersey, a few weeks before our departure. We were introduced by a neighbor of his, Joel Fogel. Joel liked to tell people that he was a "professional adventurer." He had had a brochure printed up describing himself as "Writer, Scientist, Adventurer, Ecologist." Something about him seemed less than genuine, a legend in his own lunchtime, but he had hinted that he might invest in our Baro expedition, and we desperately needed money. I agreed to hear him out. In August Joel flew me from Arizona to New Jersey. I was impressed—no one had ever offered to pay airfare to hear my plans. In fact, I decided Joel was suffering from affluenza . . . coming from a wealthy family, he apparently never really worked in his life and spent his time trying to make himself famous. In exchange for what seemed like a sizable contribution to our cause, Joel had two requests: that he be allowed to join the expedition, and that I consider letting his friend, Angus Macleod, come along as well.

I was leery of bringing along anyone outside my tight-knit, experienced coterie on an exploratory, but the lure of capital was too strong. Joel, however, would never make it out onto the Baro. He traveled with us to the put-in, took one look at the angry, heaving river, and caught the next bus back to Addis Ababa. He may have been the smartest of the lot.

Portaging on the Baro River; the author is in the life jacket on the right.
BART HENDERSON

Angus was altogether different. While Joel smacked of presentation and flamboyance, Angus was taciturn and modest. He confessed immediately to having never run a rapid, yet he exuded an almost irresistible eagerness and carried himself with the fluid bounce of a natural athlete. It had struck me that Angus had the same surname as the British fatality on the 1968 Blue Nile Expedition, Ian Macleod, and I even mentioned it to Angus, but neither of us was superstitious.

He was ruggedly handsome and had played professional soccer, and though he had never been on a river, he had spent time sea kayaking the Jersey shore. After spending a short time with him I could see his quiet intensity, and I believed that—despite his lack of experience—he could handle the trip, even though there would be no chance for training or special conditioning before the actual expedition.

Once in Ethiopia, Angus worked in the preparations for the expedition with a lightheartedness that masked his determination. On the eve of our trip to Illubabor Province—a seventeen-hour bus ride on slippery, corrugated mountain roads—I told Angus to make sure he was at the bus station at 7:00 a.m. for the 11:00 a.m. departure. That way we would all be sure of getting seats in the front of the bus, where the ride wasn't as bumpy or unbearably stuffy. But, come the next morning, Angus didn't show until 10:45. He got the last seat on the bus and endured.

Later, after the accident, standing on the bank of the river with John Yost, I wondered if I'd made the right decision about Angus. We searched the side of the river where I'd washed ashore; across the rumble of the rapids, we could hear the others searching. "Angus! Are you alright? Where are you?" There was no answer. Just downriver from where I'd last seen him, John found an eight-foot length of rope—the piece I'd cut away from Angus's shoulders.

After an hour John and I gave up and swam back across the river. We gathered the group at the one remaining raft, just below the falls.

"He could be downstream, lying with a broken leg," someone said.

"He could be hanging onto a log in the river."

"He could be wandering in a daze through the jungle."

Nobody suggested he could be dead, though we all knew it was a possibility. All of us had a very basic, and very difficult, decision to make, the kind of decision you never want to have to make on an expedition: Should we stay and look for Angus, or should we get out while there was still light? Robbie, Bart, and George and Diane Fuller didn't hesitate—they wanted out. Karen Greenwald wanted to continue searching, but she seemed hysterical. Against her protests, we sent her out with the others.

That left five of us—Lew Greenwald, Gary Mercado, Jim Slade, John Yost, and me. We decided to continue rafting downstream in search of Angus on the one remaining raft. I had mixed feelings about it—suddenly I was scared to death of the river; it had almost killed me. The ambient sentiment was that we could all very well die. Yet I felt obligated to look for a man missing from a boat I had capsized; on an expedition I had organized. And there was more: I felt I had to prove to myself that I had the right stuff, that I could honor the code and do the right thing.

But the river wasn't through with us. When we were ready to go, I climbed into the seat of the raft and yelled for Jim to push off. Immediately we were cascading down the course I'd swum earlier. In the rapid that had nearly drowned me, the raft jolted and reeled, kicking Gary and me into a barroom brawl of boxing currents.

"Shit—not again" was my only thought as I spilled out of the raft into another whirlpool. But this time I had the bowline in hand, and I managed to pull myself quickly to the surface. I emerged beside the raft, and Lew grabbed the back of my life jacket and pulled me in. My right forearm was lacerated and bleeding. Jim jumped to the oars and rowed us to shore.

My injury wasn't bad—a shallow cut. But Gary had dislocated his shoulder; he'd flipped backward over the gunwale while still holding onto the raft. He was in a load of pain, and it was clear he couldn't go on. Lew—thankful for the opportunity—volunteered to hike him out.

John, Jim, and I relaunched and cautiously rowed down a calmer stretch of the river, periodically calling out for Angus. It was almost 6:00 p.m., and we were just three degrees north of the equator, so the sun was about to set. We had to stop and make camp. It was a bad, uncomfortable night. Between us, we had a two-man A-frame tent, one sleeping bag, and a lunch bag of food; everything else had been washed into the Baro.

The rude bark of a baboon shook us awake the next morning. The inside of the tent was dripping from condensation, and we lay in a kind of human puddle. I crawled outside and looked to the eastern sky, which was beginning to blush. My body ached from the previous day's ordeal. I wanted to be back in Bethesda, at my folks' home, warm, dry, and eating a fine breakfast. Instead, we huddled around a wisp of fire, sipping weak tea and chewing wet bread.

That morning we eased downriver, stopping every few minutes to scout, hugging the banks, avoiding rapids we wouldn't have hesitated to run were they back in the States. At intervals we called into the rain forest for Angus, but now we didn't expect an answer.

In the shank of the afternoon, we came to another intimidating rapid, one that galloped around a bend and sunk from sight. We took out the one duffel bag containing the tent and sleeping bag and began lining, using ropes to lower the boat along the rough edge of the rapid. Fifty yards into the rapid, the raft broached perpendicular to the current, and water swarmed in. It thrummed as though a tree an ax had struck. Slade and I, on the stern line, pulled hard, the rope searing our palms, but the boat ignored us. With the snap of its D-ring (the bowline attachment), it dismissed us to a crumple on the bank and sailed around the corner and out of sight.

There was no way to continue the search. The terrain made impossible demands, and we were out of food, the last scraps having been lost with the raft. We struck up into the jungle flange, thrashing through wet, waist-high foliage at a slug's pace. My wound was becoming infected. Unseen birds seemed to screech in pain. Finally, at sunset the light folded up on itself and we had to stop. We cleared a near-level spot, set up the tent, squeezed in, and collapsed. Twice I awoke to the sound of trucks grumbling past but dismissed it as jungle fever, or Jim's snoring.

In the sun-sucked light of morning, however, we soon stumbled onto a road. There we sat, as mist coiled up the tree trunks, waiting. In the distance we could hear the thunder roll of a rapid, but inexplicably the sound became louder and louder. Then we saw what it was: Two hundred machete-wielding locals marched into sight over the hill. General Goitom, the police commissioner of nearby Motu, hearing of the accident, had organized a search for Angus. Their effort consisted of tramping up and down the highway—the locals, it turned out, were more fearful of the jungle canyon than we were.

I remember little of the next week. We discovered that Angus held a United Kingdom passport, and I spent a fair amount of time at the British embassy in Addis Ababa filling out reports, accounting for personal effects, and communicating with his relatives. John and Jim stayed in Motu with General Goitom and led a series of searches back into the vile jungle along the river, over dark ground thick with fire ants. We posted a $100 reward—more than double what the villagers earned in a year—for information on Angus's whereabouts. With financial assistance from

Angus's parents, I secured a Canadian helicopter a few days after the accident and took several passes over the river. Even with the pilot skimming the treetops, it was difficult to see into the river corridor. The canopy seemed like a moldy, moth-eaten army tarpaulin. On one flight, however, I glimpsed a smudge of orange just beneath the surface of the river. We made several passes, but it was impossible to make out what it was. Perhaps, I thought, it was Angus, snagged underwater. We picked as many landmarks as possible, flew in a direct line to the road, landed, cut a marker on a tatty doum palm, and headed to Motu.

A day later John, Jim, and I cut a path back into the tangle and found the smudge—a collection of leaves trapped by a submerged branch. We abandoned the search. "How did I get to this point?" I wondered while bouncing in the back of a Unimog trundling back to Addis Ababa. "Where did the groove go wrong?" Starting from a tony deed-covenant suburb of Washington, D.C., a town filled with diplomats and politicians, and the legal set that supports them, I wandered away from the golf courses and country clubs and stepped down to the river.

CHAPTER 4

BEGINNINGS

BETHESDA, MARYLAND, 1967–1968

Beware of all enterprises that require new clothes.
—HENRY DAVID THOREAU

IT IS A SINGULARLY AMERICAN RITE OF PASSAGE, READING MARK TWAIN'S MASTER-piece, *The Adventures of Huckleberry Finn*. I bore the scars of a happy childhood, and the story of Huck and Jim and their raft trip down the Mississippi affected me in a way that Jay Gatsby and his silk shirts, or John Marcher and his figurative beast, or George Babbit's conformity, or even Natty Bumppo's "noble savage" ever would. Huck discovered adventure, beauty, self-reliance, peace, and equipoise by rafting down the river. "It's lovely to live on a raft," Huck said, and I believed him. I wanted to raft a river.

I lived a few miles from the Potomac, the "River of the Traders," as the seven-teenth-century Indians who bartered tobacco and catfish near my house called it. One Sunday in May my father, at my urgings, reluctantly took me on a hike on the towpath of the Chesapeake and Ohio (C&O) Canal up near Great Falls, fifteen miles above Washington, where the broad river is squeezed through an obstacle course of massive boulders and in just a half mile roars downward some seventy-five feet.

Juno, our golden retriever, saw a squirrel and made a beeline down a tight path through a welter of vegetation. I followed, leaving my father on the towpath, and found myself on the edge of a 200-foot-high cliff overlooking the Potomac.

The sight was dazzling, the fast currents spinning the reflecting light as though thousands of silver pinwheels were washing downstream. I was hypnotized, drawn towards the blazing water, and I knew I had to get on that river.

I fell in love with the Potomac that summer and wanted to know everything about her—every dimple, every curve, where she came from, and where she was going. I began to study her serpentine mysteries in my free time. She trickles forth at an altitude of 3,140 feet just downhill from the crest of Backbone Mountain in a deep fold of the Allegheny Mountains in West Virginia. There she seeps from a spring beneath a chunk of rock, called the Fairfax Stone after the colonial landowner Lord Fairfax. The fledgling river soon becomes the Maryland–West Virginia border, loops back and forth around Appalachian ridges in the region of the Paw Paw bends, and then bursts through the Blue Ridge Mountains at Harpers Ferry, where the Shenandoah joins her. Here the plunging slopes and roiling rapids make "perhaps one of the most stupendous scenes in nature," Thomas Jefferson wrote, "worth a voyage across the Atlantic." Continuing her journey, the Potomac levels off, now alive with geese and eagles, oysters and shad. She eventually becomes a seven-mile tidal giant, easing majestically into Chesapeake Bay as she stretches between the Maryland and Virginia shores.

Monday morning, I announced to Miss Hammond, my English teacher, I wanted to build a raft and journey down the Potomac just like Huckleberry Finn. She said fine, as long as I didn't miss any school. The three-day Memorial Day weekend was coming up, so I thought that would be the chance. I recruited my camping friends John Yost, Ricky Vierbuchen, and John Kramer. John Yost was something of a prodigy, two years younger than the rest of us, having skipped two grades before reaching high school. He was in the German and French Honor Societies, a National Merit semifinalist, a mathlete, and on the varsity soccer team and in the Mountaineering Club. He was also on the In-School publicity committee. I had met John at the Bethesda River Bowl, where I accused him of cheating when I looked at the scoresheet he was handling and saw that some of my strikes and spares had disappeared. He made a nervous, high-pitched laugh and put the points back, and we became friends. John Kramer was a dancer, a member of National Thespians and the swim team, and the president of the Mountaineering Club. He was a fluid athlete, nimble and long muscled as a cat, capable of boundless verve. Kramer took me caving and showed me the joys of the underground. Ricky Vierbuchen was taller, stronger, and more studious than anyone else in our circle, also a member of the Mountaineering Club, as well as the cross-country ski team, but he shared a glee for the mischievous. Together we pranked through high school, including running a fake candidate for student body president (J. H. Plumb . . . he came in a respectable third) and taking off on various outdoor adventures.

For the Huck Finn raft redux, I also brought in friends Dave Nurney, Fred Higgins, and Steve Hatleberg, and together we started gathering the equipment we'd need to build our raft and float the Potomac. None of us had ever been in a kayak or canoe, yet alone a raft. We picked out an eight-mile run through Mather Gorge, one that expert kayakers had been running for years. Though, as we talked to the experts, including a scuba rescue team who routinely retrieved drowned bodies from the river, the prognosis was we wouldn't make it through in a log raft; the rapids were too treacherous.

Word of our expedition spread like marmalade on a muffin, and the editor of the *Black and White*, the school newspaper, Dan Reifsnyder, approached me for the exclusive story. At age seventeen, Dan was already hard-boiled, and he smelled disaster in my little plan. He made no pretense of his looking for blood, or a spectacular failure, to fill column space in an upcoming issue. I said I was happy to give him the story, but I was certain he'd be disappointed: We planned to make it down the river on time, and intact.

On Friday afternoon we all set up camp not far below Great Falls and, with axes, started cutting the timber we needed. We rolled the logs to our assembly spot down by the river and began binding them with crosspieces and eight-inch gutter nails.

Our raft was about half finished when a stentorian voice echoed across the canyon. "Have you ever messed with a German shepherd?" It was a park ranger, calling from atop a palisade of gneiss on the Virginia side, a huge German shepherd at his side. "You're on national park land. You can't cut down trees, you can't build a raft, and you can't camp. Now get outta there before I come get ya."

The author, bottom left, with a lizard on his shirt, in elementary school. AUTHOR'S COLLECTION

It was the end of our dream trip. We slowly packed up and trudged back to the parking lot. On the drive out we passed a ranger vehicle coming in with a dog in the back and guessed it was our friend with the German shepherd.

We still had two days of the Memorial Day weekend left and couldn't go back home; not with everyone expecting us to have at least attempted our raft expedition. So we headed for Bear Island, a popular camping spot below Mather Gorge, and holed up there for the rest of the long weekend, swimming, fishing, and trying to forget our failure.

Monday night we were all back at my house cleaning the camping gear when the phone rang. It was Dan Reifsnyder, and he wanted the scoop on our expedition.

I put my hand over the receiver and talked to our team. "Let's tell him we did it," I proposed with a grin. "We can't," Steve Hatleberg countered. "It's not the Christian thing to do." In *The Adventures of Huckleberry Finn*, Huck had to battle with his conscience, because according to the morality of society and the church, he should have reported Jim, whom he had come to love as a brother, as a runaway slave. His final decision in Jim's favor was concluded with his famous reflection, "All right, then. I'll go to hell!" I looked around at our group, then back at Steve, and said, "All right, then, I'll go to hell!" and put the receiver to my mouth and started to tell Dan about our raft trip.

On June 9, the article appeared, entitled "Rapids Capsize Craft; Raftsmen Score First." It went on to say, "The raft had to be scrapped in the middle of Yellow Rapids. 'We scrambled for the inner tubes and kept going,' boasted junior Richard Bangs. 'You wondered if you were going to live.' 'Man, was I scared.' 'It was out of sight, like an LSD trip.' These were just a few of the emotions described by the group, all of whom made the entire passage alive."

The article gave us some fame and inspired us to form "The Raft Club," which was the seed from which would sprout Sobek, the international rafting and adventure travel company I would later co-found. Steve Hatleberg couldn't live with our secret, though, and one day he told Dan the full and true story. To Dan's credit, he never pursued it in print, but whenever I passed him in the hall, he gave me that basilisk stare editors around the world have mastered. And it made me want to make good on the Potomac.

It was still early summer when I saw an ad on the bulletin board at the grocery store. It told of a 17½-foot fiberglass Old Town canoe for sale, for $150. I called all the members of The Raft Club and asked if anyone would go in with me on halves. Ricky Vierbuchen had the $75, so we bought the canoe, painted "R&R" on the stern (we flipped a coin for top billing), and toted our new toy down to Bear Island. We launched and headed upstream, towards the crystalline mouth of Mather Gorge.

We were awkward paddlers, and the canoe crankled through the water as though drunk. We bobbed and weaved upstream and slowly picked up some proficiency as we angled towards Difficult Run Rapids, marking the end of the gorge. The white-breasted water got faster as we got closer, and my blood accelerated correspondingly.

This was exciting. We were going faster than I had ever been in anything without an engine. Then we were in the rooster tails, flung up and down on a dizzy aquatic seesaw, paddling with all our strength. "Let's go higher," I screamed over the rapid's roar, and we sunk our blades deeper and lunged forward. Then the bow snapped to its side, abruptly capsizing the canoe and precipitating us into the spume. We'd been christened as river runners.

Ricky and I spent all our free time the summers of 1967 and 1968 in our blue canoe, exploring new routes, refining techniques, scoring the bottom of our boat with a matrix of scratches and dents. We made many of the classic runs, including the coup de grace run of the Potomac beginning at the base of the Great Falls, where the Potomac spectacularly drops over the edge of the continental bedrock onto the sedimentary soil of the Coastal Plain.

Above Great Falls the river stretches to a half mile in width; below it pinches into the sixty-foot-wide Mather Gorge and then opens to a wide run with shallow rapids until reaching the Brookmont dam. Constructed in the 1950s for the city water supply with no thought for the safety of boaters, the deceptively innocuous weir is a death trap for upset paddlers, with a perpetual hydraulic that, like a black hole with stray light, sucks in boats and bodies, never to let them go. A rust-spotted sign adjacent to the pumping station stated that an average of seven people a year drowned in this area. Its nickname was "The Drowning Machine." Below Brookmont was the most hair-raising one mile of navigable whitewater along the entire 383-mile course of the Potomac, culminating in the explosive Little Falls, in which the entire river is funneled from parking lot width to a Grand Prix raceway, then spectacularly split in two by a sharp granite-slab island. It was here Capt. John Smith, in his search for the elusive Northwest Passage, was stopped in his upriver journey in 1608. Little Falls is the last whitewater—or the first, depending on which way you're traveling—on the Potomac. In the massive flood of 1936, the velocity of the water was recorded as the fastest ever in nature. Just below is Chain Bridge. A short way beyond, the river becomes tidewater, and the nation's capital begins to spread its concrete tentacles along the banks.

Ricky and I never canoed the Little Falls section; it was beyond our abilities. But that didn't mean we couldn't run it. With the money I'd saved working as a carhop at the local Kentucky Fried Chicken outlet, I purchased a yellow Taiwanese-made four-man raft from Sunny's Surplus. And with it we paddled out to Snake Island, across from the Brookmont pumping station, and slipped over the killer weir where we thought the one clear passage, down a fish ladder, was supposed to be. But we missed and were suddenly in the backwashing hydraulic, capsized, bouncing about in the aerated water along with beach balls, chunks of cooler Styrofoam, rubber sandals, branches, and other debris stuck in the eternal washing machine. I remembered reading the only way to escape a strong recirculating hydraulic was to abandon one's life jacket and dive beneath the surface, where the water makes its deepwater exit. But I couldn't bring myself to take off my floatation, which was propping my mouth just above the terrible soapy froth. I looked over to Ricky, who was choking with water splashed into his throat. "Swim towards the island," I yelled to Ricky above the weir's gargling. And though it was slow going, we found it possible to dog-paddle perpendicular to the current, along the hydraulic line, back towards Snake Island. I towed our little yellow raft, and after several scary minutes we reached the edge of the island, where a chute emptied water in a straight shot downstream. We were out, and into the next section, where the water accelerated as the river narrowed, and the waves grew thicker with each stroke.

Then the final pitch presented itself, with the river piling up onto the anvil-shaped island, spilling off either side into huge, impermeable complex rapids. We blasted straight down the middle, plowed into the saber-toothed island, spun backwards, and then collapsed over the falls on the Virginia side, the worst side. The first drop catapulted Ricky into the air. When he fell back into the bilge, the floor of the raft peeled back like a sardine can, depositing Ricky into the depths. I continued to paddle alone, my feet dragging in the current where the floor had been, my neck spinning looking for signs of Ricky. The roar of the rapid muffled as I strained to hear Ricky's cry. Hours later, or so the seconds seemed, Ricky resurfaced fifty yards downstream, slick as an eel, all smiles. Climbing back on board, we drove our paddles deep to our takeout at Chain Bridge on the Virginia side, where my mother was waiting with the 1966 Oldsmobile and a prayer. My father had stayed home to read.

I discovered the lack of floor didn't make much difference in the tiny Taiwan boat and continued to use it for runs down Little Falls the following weeks with the various members of The Raft Club, even Steve Hatleberg, who thought he saw God during one capsize. For us it was the ultimate thrill in a suburban existence conspicuously short of such.

CHAPTER 5

SHIVERING PLEASURE

The most cherished goal in physics, as in bad romance novels, is unification.
—Lee Smolin

As summer faded to fall the frequency of our trips decreased because of the cooler weather, school commitments, and a new diversion: women. Ricky and I were both taken by a tall blonde, an unwitting Circe named Arlene Wergen. The air surged with the dull clacking sound of soft young antlers in nervous ritual combat. Since he shared homeroom and some classes with her, Ricky had the advantage, and he exploited it. He took Arlene caving and camping and bought her an expensive friendship ring. I had an ace up my sleeve, however . . . the river. I just had to wait for the right moment.

That moment came mid-December. We were in the midst of an unseasonable heat wave, and the weatherman said the upcoming weekend would be warm enough for outdoor activities. I asked Arlene if she'd like to go canoeing.

I picked out a run I had always wanted to do, a stretch beginning at Bloomery, West Virginia, on the Shenandoah, running to the confluence with the Potomac and continuing below Harpers Ferry, the place where John Brown's body lies a moulderin' in the grave. The ten-mile run was supposed to be beautiful, with some challenging rapids and good camping, all-important ingredients in what I perceived to be an important weekend.

Saturday morning was clear and crisp as we loaded the blue canoe and headed downriver through a nave-like arch of sycamores and silver maples. The river here had sawed away at the mountains as they rose up beneath it, embedding itself twelve hundred feet or more in the Blue Ridge. I was wearing my new letter jacket, which I had been awarded for the dubious honor of managing the soccer team. Still, it was a badge, and I wore it proudly with hopes it would impress Arlene. It was a beautiful day, brimming with a sense of adventure and romance, and I could tell Arlene shared the thrill of a live vessel beneath us sliding silently over brawling water. An ad for Canadian Club had been running that fall showing a couple canoeing the rapids. The woman in the bow looked very much like Arlene, and though I bore no resemblance, I felt like the man in the stern in that ad.

As we eased our way down the river, the sun's rays reflected off water the color of copper, and I started to warm. I took off my letter jacket and bundled it in front of my knees. At lunch we pulled over beneath a spreading willow, and I prepared a sumptuous repast with Pouilly-Fuissé and Brie and French bread. As we took our first bites, a pint-sized bark came from behind, and a little puppy bounded into our picnic. He was a mongrel, but with the biggest brown eyes I'd ever seen and a wiggly, irresistible appeal for affection. For Arlene it was puppy love at first sight. She fed the little mutt all her meal, and then some of mine, and then asked if we could take him along. "But he must belong to somebody," I protested. "Please go check," she implored, and I got up to make a search. Sure enough, I could find no evidence of owners within a half mile of our mooring, and we came to the conclusion that the puppy was, indeed, hopelessly lost.

So we perched the puppy on my letter jacket and continued downriver.

As the day wore on it began to cloud, and the temperature dropped. The puppy was asleep, so I didn't bother to put on my letter jacket, but instead paddled harder to keep warm. By late afternoon we approached the river-wide ledge of Bull Falls, which the guidebook rated as difficult but doable, and recommended a portage for less-than-expert boaters. Checking my watch, I saw we were at least an hour behind schedule; the puppy incident had taken up precious time. The guidebook said the portage around Bull Falls took an hour, an hour we didn't have on a short midwinter day. If we portaged, we'd have to paddle the final miles after dark, a dangerous prop-osition in the cold of December.

And, after a full summer canoeing, I figured I was more than less-than-expert and could make the run. So we rammed ahead into Bull Falls. The entry was perfect, gliding between the boulders as though on a track, slipping down the drop as though by design. At the bottom I held the canoe paddle above my head and screamed, "We made it!" But I was a bit premature. The tail waves at the bottom of the rapid contin-ued to wash over the bow of the canoe, and the boat filled with turbid river water. By the time we reached the last wave, we were swamped, and the canoe phlegmatically rolled over, dispatching us into the icy river. The current was swift here, and the cold punched my breath away. With one hand I hung onto the canoe; with the other I tried to paddle, all the while yelling for Arlene to swim to shore. Then I saw my letter jacket surface a few feet away. The jacket meant the world to me, so I started paddling towards it. Then, a feeble yelp came from the opposite direction. The puppy was spinning in an area of circling water with a center like an inverted shield boss: a strong, sucking eddy. For a quick second I weighed options. I could retrieve only one. I went for the puppy.

A few hundred yards downstream I managed to grapple the canoe to shore, the puppy still held above my head with my free hand. Arlene was there, shivering violently, yet she gave the puppy a hug that would crush a bear.

Both Arlene and I had lost our paddles in the capsize, though I had one spare strapped to the center thwart. I emptied the canoe, turned it over, and tried to tell Arlene to get back in . . . but my speech was slurred; I could barely form words. I was becoming hypothermic. So was Arlene. I knew we couldn't stop here . . . we had nothing dry, and it was getting dark. We'd die if we stayed. I pressed Arlene into the bow of the canoe, and she crouched over the trembling puppy, while I pushed us off. I had just the one paddle, but I dug like an antbear. The sun dipped behind the trees, and a chilling wind blew up the valley, filling it with dusk. Barely able to see the rocks, I propelled us into the last rapids, the mile-long Staircase. We scraped, bumped, and banged every few seconds but somehow emerged in one piece at the Route 340 bridge below Harpers Ferry, where my car awaited.

My plans for a romantic campout were scrapped that night. Rather than a hero, I was a bungler who almost cost us our lives and, worse, the life of the puppy, who won the contest for Arlene's heart and became her constant companion.

Still, I remained hung up on Arlene, as did Ricky. But it was unrequited love. As the school year wound down, Arlene started dating a Young Republican, a radical act in the Vietnam era. When Ricky and I independently asked Arlene to the Senior Prom, she turned us both down for the right-wing radical.

We'd been left high and dry. Neither of us found alternative dates for the most socially significant event of a teenager's life. So we turned to each other and said, "Let's go run a river."

We picked the Smoke Hole Canyon section of the South Branch of the Potomac in West Virginia for two reasons: We'd never done it before, and it was as far away from the prom as we could get and still be on our favorite river. It was a section described by George Washington as, "two ledges of Mountain Impassable running side by side together for about 7 or 8 miles and ye River down between them." So, as the senior class was slipping into crinoline and tuxedos, we were fitting our kneepads and kapok life jackets. And as carnations were being exchanged, we were trading strokes on the upper Potomac. Mockingbirds called from the auditorium of woods through which we passed, hardly giving us solace. It was springtime, and the delicate pink blossoms of the laurel and the notched white flowers of the dogwood dappled the greening banks. We moved to music, but not the base-note Motown our peers were enjoying, rather the haunting whistle of the lordly cardinal. The river here was shallow, stinging cold from the spring runoff. Some miles below our launch we struck a moss-encrusted rock, jutting out into the current like some miniature Lorelei. The siren rock punched a hole the size of my fist into our fiberglass hull.

We didn't have the materials or the time to properly repair the hole in our boat, so we stuffed the puncture with spare clothing and continued downstream. It was slow going. We'd paddle ten minutes and then pull over the same to bail. When we emptied the canoe at camp at twilight, we discovered our neoprene duffel bag had not been waterproof; that all our gear, sleeping bags, tents, food, were soaked. We dragged everything up a knoll of weathered limestone overlooking the Potomac, erected the wet tent, and laid the rest of our effects out to dry in the waning minutes of daylight. It was quickly evident our attempts to dry the gear by natural means would not work, and that it was to be a nippy night. We had several packs of matches, but they were all saturated and wouldn't light. We gathered wood and with our knives trimmed paper-thin shavings that would light at the least spark. But we went through several packs of matches and couldn't get the spark. With nightfall the air became brittle, and we jumped up and down, slapping our sides, to keep warm. Our classmates were doing the Jerk in the Whitman gym, and we felt like the dance as we flapped in the dark. But it wasn't working, and I knew we couldn't do the Freddy all night. We needed to build a fire, as much as Jack London ever did.

If we didn't, we could perish, and we both knew it.

Then Ricky literally got a bright idea. The flashlight still worked, so why not unscrew the lens covering the bulb and put the remaining matches inside the glass, against the filament bulb, where they could dry from the heat of the light? We had five matches left, and inside they went. The flashlight remained on for twenty minutes as we continued our jumping jacks; then it started to fade. The flashlight was going dead. We unscrewed the top, took out the matches, and tried to light the first one. In my haste I tore off the head of the match. The second lit, but before I could touch it to the kindling it blew out in the cold wind. I cupped my hand around the third as I struck. It spat to life, and as I touched it to the shavings, the fire took. In minutes we had a bonfire. We curled our backs to a log and held up our clothes and sleeping bags to dry. All night we continued to feed the flickering scrap of fire and bathe in its warmth, and occasionally we looked down the hill at the Potomac meandering in the moonlight, in curves that somehow looked like Arlene's.

As with our classmates, that was a special night, one filled with danger and promise, with rites of passage, with friendship and warmth. The Potomac had dealt some blows since our first assignation, but she had given me some of the most exciting, some of the most exquisite moments of my existence. On that prom night, high on a limestone ridge, I realized how much I loved the river, deeply, wholly, and that I had found a consort for life. I discovered, as Tom Sawyer finally said to Huckleberry Finn, that all I really wanted to do was "have adventures plumb to the mouth of the river." On that prom night I lost and found a certain innocence and readied for the adventures of tomorrow, the great adventures cached just around the next bend, just out of sight, on the river.

CHAPTER 6

NAKED BUT
NOT AFRAID

John Quincy Adams was a first-rate swimmer. Once when he was skinny-dipping in the Potomac River, a women reporter snatched his clothes and sat on them until he gave her an interview.

—JUDITH ST. GEORGE

IT WAS EARLY MAY, AND I WAS FORWARDED A TYPED LETTER TO JOHN THOMSON, chairman of the Canoe Cruisers Association:

Dear Chairman Thomson:

I was appalled when two participants of the race from Great Falls to Sycamore Island held today crossed the finish line and landed on the island NUDE! I thought they should have had more consideration and respect for the many women and children watching the race, the reputation of the Canoe Cruisers Association, and most of all for themselves than to be a part of such actions.

I would like to recommend that these two gentlemen be restricted from participation in activities sponsored by the association for the next year.

Sincerely yours,
Mrs. Donald Callar

Yes, I was guilty, along with Ricky Vierbuchen, of streaking across the finish line.

We had practiced for weeks for the annual race down the Potomac and felt we had a good chance of winning. And as we pitched through Mather Gorge, a granite defile that was described at the turn of the century as "The Grand Canyon of the East," we negotiated through S-Turn Rapids, Rocky Island Rapids, and Wet Bottom Chute and past the ancient rocks that formed the exit gate to the canyon. We continued downstream on a wider, but no less magnificent, river, through Yellow Rapids

Richard, Ricky Vierbuchen, and John Kramer at Great Falls on the Potomac River.
RICHARD BANGS

and Stubblefield Falls, underneath the Cabin John Bridge carrying the Capital Belt-way past the Carderock Picnic Area, where climbers crawled like flies on impossible faces. In the final stretch we found ourselves in front of the pack, and we pumped the air with our paddles when suddenly we smacked into a barely submerged rock, turned sideways, and flipped. As we went about righting, several other boats passed, so thoughts of placing sank away. Chastened, mortified, we turned the boat upright, climbed back in, bailed out the excess water, and sunk our paddles back in. Yet our wet clothes slowed our movements and sent us shivering. Streaking, running nude through a public place, or even an awards show, was a rage. A naked man, Robert Opal, ran behind David Niven at the Academy Awards in front of sixty-four million viewers. We thought nothing of tossing our wet clothes in the bilge and streaking across the finish line.

So, ecdysiastly, we made for the finish line. A *Washington Post* photographer was there, and we ended up in the paper the next morning, paddles discretely covering our naked ambition.

What I didn't know in the summer of 1968 was that just as I was charting the river road for my life, another man on the other side of the world, a young man named Ian Macleod, was about to lose his life to the Blue Nile of Ethiopia. The loss would be one among many on the rivers of Ethiopia, including ones that would jolt my life.

CHAPTER 7

FALLING INTO THE GRAND CANYON

Well, once you've been in the Canyon and once you've sort of fallen in love with it, it never ends . . . it's always been a fascinating place to me, in fact I've often said that if I ever had a mistress, it would be the Grand Canyon.
—BARRY GOLDWATER

DESPITE THE ATTEMPT TO HAVE ME BANNED FROM THE CANOE CRUISERS ASSO-
ciation, the chairman allowed me to attend a chapter meeting in the fall. The main event was a Super-8 movie of members who had canoed the Colorado River through the Grand Canyon that summer. As the screen flickered, a spell was cast. I was mes-merized: The waves seemed oceanic, ten times the size of anything I had encountered on Eastern Seaboard rivers, even in spring spate; the scale of everything was over-whelming—the canyon walls, the crests, the troughs, the eddies, the wet grins. Some invisible, powerful hand reached from the screen and pulled me in. I drove home with a monumental craving: I had to run the Colorado River or die.

With no guiding background whatsoever, I composed a letter to Ted Hatch, the outfitter for the Canoe Cruisers' trip down the Colorado, asking for a job, lying through my teeth, listing all my river credentials that didn't exist. I had never rowed the Green; I had never traveled west of the Blue Ridge Mountains. Ted wrote back: *Report to Lees Ferry, April 28, for trip departing April 29. Welcome aboard.*

The flight into Page, Arizona, six months later over the southern rim of the Colorado Plateau, across magnificently cross-bedded deposits of Navajo Sandstone that coat the escarpment, was stunning. I'd never seen such a vast expanse of unin-habited land, devoid of almost any sign of human presence. In the soft, coral blush of daybreak, I pressed my nose against the window and could hear my heart beating to the sound of awe. No landscape ever appeared so dramatic. Then, like a giant gash in the skin of the desert, the Grand Canyon of the Colorado appeared, a dark crooked rip tearing across the landscape to the horizon.

We circled over the Glen Canyon Dam, the 710-foot-high plug that creates the 186-mile-long Lake Powell, before we began our descent into Page, Arizona, a town erected in the red dust of nothingness to accommodate dam workers. Within minutes I was standing in the parking lot of the Page Boy Motel, where I met Ted Hatch, scion to rafting royalty (his father, Bus, had pioneered many rafting runs in Utah and Colorado in the 1930s and 1940s). Ted extended a puffy, freckled hand in greeting, but he couldn't mask his disappointment as my skinny hand met his. Here he had hired a gangly, pale Atlantic seaboarder who appeared as guide-like as Ichabod Crane. But he rolled with it.

A float down the Colorado through the Grand Canyon is a stark descent through light and density and time. From the soft sandstones and flamingo limestones of the Kaibab Plateau, exposed at river level at Lees Ferry, the Colorado cuts through rock that progressively ages, hardens, and darkens. It plunges through the eons and the strata, through shales, conglomerates, and basalts, residuum of primordial seas and cataclysmic eruptions and upheavals. Until, at last, in the Inner Gorge, in the deepest corridor of the canyon, the river washes against the oldest, blackest, and hardest rock of all: Vishnu Schist. Dark as Dante's Inferno, almost two billion years old, the rock is a relic of a time when the earth's molten center disturbed its surface, imposing unfathomable heat and pressure that recrystallized sediments into new minerals. So dark it swallows light, Vishnu Schist is named for the Hindu deity worshiped as the protector, a syncretic personality composed of many lesser cult figures and associated with the sun. The rock, like depictions of the god, is dark-skinned and noble. From sandstone to schist, the voyage down the Colorado is one of dramatic change, a metamorphic journey. And like the peels of stone that compose the walls, the people who pass through the Grand Canyon change with each mile. They grow darker, harder, older. And some make the apotheosis to Vishnu himself.

John Wesley Powell, a one-armed brevet colonel, made his water-breaking trip down the Colorado River through the Grand Canyon in 1869. Fifty years later, on February 26, 1919, the sublime ditch became a national park, the fifteenth in the system. But while thousands flocked to view the deep cut in the casing of the continent from the rims, few had dared float the river below. In 1934, Bus Hatch, a carpenter by trade, captained the first paying participants down the Colorado River through the Grand Canyon in a wooden boat he had handcrafted, but that trip did not initially lead to a booming tourism business.

In 1968 the rafting business was barely that. Bobby Kennedy had floated the Colorado with Hatch River Expeditions, the company to which I was now attached, and through the wizardry of Press Secretary Pierre Salinger, the story was a worldwide pickup.

John Yost, Perry Owens, Richard (in striped shorts), and Breck
O'Neill in the Grand Canyon, 1971. PATTI GALES

Up until 1949, a grand total of 100 people had floated through the Grand
Canyon. By 1965 some 547 people had rafted the Colorado; in the summer of 1972,
the numbers had swelled to 16,432, and the Park Service stepped in and froze the
use at that level. But in the late 1960s and early 1970s, the wave of popularity was
becoming tidal, and the few concessionaires servicing the budding industry had to
find guides to meet the growing demand. My timing couldn't have been better, and
Ted Hatch, the largest outfitter on the Colorado, hired me for the following season
the day he received my missive. It was Halloween 1968. I encouraged John Yost, who
had become my best friend, to apply as well, but he had an even sexier opportunity.
His father was a Foreign Service officer at the State Department and was just posted
to Ethiopia as DCM (Deputy Chief of Mission, or vice-ambassador). So, while I was
to go rafting, John was going to visit his parents in Africa, at the US government's
expense, and explore exotic landscapes. I knew nothing whatsoever about Ethiopia
but asked John to look around and see if there might be any rivers worth rafting.

"You're swamping tomorrow's trip. We have the Four Corners Geological Society, 110 people, ten rafts. Drive the winch-truck down to the ferry as soon as you
change out of that blazer and try and help the boatmen rig. Welcome aboard, kid.
You'll be a good swamper."

"Ahhh, one question, Mr. Hatch."

"Call me Ted. Now, what's your question?"

"What's a swamper?"

Ted reared his Cabbage Patch Doll head in a cannonade of laughter before explaining, "You dig the toilet hole at camp, help the boatmen cook, wash the dishes, bail the rafts. And assist the guides in every way. Now, get on it."

He handed me the keys and pointed to the truck. When I sidled into the cab, I knew I was in trouble—it was a stick shift. I'd grown up in an automatic suburb. I'd never even been in a manual. I studied the diagram on the knob.

Holding my breath, I turned the key. It hummed. Fine. Toeing the clutch, I maneuvered the stick to first position and the truck eased forward. Beautiful. I finessed across the parking lot and then headed down the motel driveway, a wave of pride washing over me. I slipped into second. No problem. Then, a thunderclap and plastic shrapnel sprayed the windshield as the truck jerked to a halt and stalled. Leaping from the cab, I ran for cover, finally looking back to survey the scene. I had driven the winch, which stood a good five feet above the truck roof, smack into the middle of the Page Boy Motel sign hanging above the driveway. The motel owner, with Hatch in tow, bolted to my side, issuing obscenities at floodgate rate.

"Can you take it out of my pay?" I meekly asked my new boss.

"Forget it, kid. I'll cover it. But do not screw up again."

That was the beginning of a metamorphosis from sandstone to schist, boy to boatman, river ingenue to river god. And it took its toll.

Eighteen-year-old Richard (kneeling), river guide on the Colorado through the Grand Canyon. Back row: Tom Cromer, Pete Reznick, John Yost, Steve Bledsoe, and Perry Owens. PATTI GALES

Somehow, I managed to negotiate the truck down the fifty-mile route to Lees Ferry. One of the only access sites for the length of the canyon, it was named for John Doyle Lee, a Mormon fugitive who had ferried passersby across the river after being implicated in the Mountain Meadow Massacre of 1857, in which 123 non-Mormon pioneers were mysteriously murdered in southwest Utah. Lee was one of the first known non-Indians to find a new identity here, far from the persecution of Salt Lake City and civilization. Or so he thought. He was tracked down and arrested in 1874, apparently a scapegoat for the massacre, and executed in 1877. Perhaps progenitor to the waves of river guides who would come a century later, Lee was a man who had found his place in the sun on the river and was finally eclipsed because of it. He was also the Anglo embodiment of the fate of hundreds of Native Americans over the centuries—Havasupai, Hopi, Hualapai, Navajo, and Paiute—who had sought sanctuary and new lives in the rarified environs of the Grand Canyon, far from rival tribes, conquistadors, marauding white settlers, and Col. Kit Carson.

Lees Ferry is now designated Mile Zero of the 277-mile Grand Canyon experience, launching pad for all river trips. It was here, in April of 1969, I took my assigned spot on the pontoon raft and held on tight as we pushed into the Kool-Aid green that passes for the Colorado, so colored since the silt settles out in the reservoir 15.5 miles upstream and the remaining microplankton refract their dominant hue. In the first mile I spun my head around frantically, taking in a view as otherworldly as a landscape out of a Frank Herbert novel.

As we passed into the buff-colored, cross-bedded cliffs of the Coconino Sandstone and into the gates of Marble Canyon (not yet officially part of the Grand Canyon; that would come in 1975), propelled by a twenty-horsepower Mercury outboard attached to the orange transom of our baloney boat, I desperately gripped a line, fearful that if I let go, I'd be flung back to reality. We slipped into the soft red-and-maroon walls known as Hermit Shale, clifftops soaring two thousand feet on either side. The din of a rapid, like thunder over rain, sonorous and deep in timbre, thickened as we eased toward Badger Creek, named for the mammal shot by Mormon explorer Jacob Hamblin.

This was thrilling. After six months of anticipation, of poring over picture books, I was on the lip of a major rapid of the Colorado. Glancing to the stern, where Dave Bledsoe controlled the tiller, I saw nonchalance unrivaled, a face fairly dancing with the aplomb of a centurion. As we slid down the coconut-butter tongue into the yaw of Badger Rapid, the crisp forty-seven-degree water slapped me, and the pontoon pranced like a dolphin in flight. It was over in ten seconds, and we pulled to shore to set up camp.

CHAPTER 8

PAPER PLATE TECTONICS

You can't be unhappy in the middle of a big, beautiful river.
—JIM HARRISON

As WE WENT ABOUT OUR TASKS, ERECTING TABLES, FILLING BUCKETS, CLEARING THE beach of tamarisk (a loathsome weedlike tree encroaching on the beaches since the dam closed its gates in 1964, gates that denied the annual spring floods that once washed away such nonsense), Dave Bledsoe made a discovery—there were no paper plates. His veneer of pluck seemed to crack ever so slightly as he rifled the commissary boxes for a second look. "This is terrible," his words floated up the walls. "How can we serve 110 geologists without plates. We need plates."

Seeing we were camped at the mouth of a tributary canyon (Jackass Creek), I asked Dave if it exited to a road, and if so, then perhaps I could hike out and fetch some plates. He thought the canyon emerged somewhere near Highway 89A, connecting Flagstaff and the North Rim. He figured I could hike out, hitch to the Hatch warehouse near Lees Ferry, hire a jetboat capable of traveling down to the lip of Badger and back to the ferry, and get the plates to camp by dinner. So, with canteen filled, I took off up the twisting side canyon.

After an hour's hiking, the mazelike canyon divided into passages of equal size. Flipping a mental coin, I took heads, the left route, and continued. It divided again and again and again several more times. By the time I pulled myself up onto the flat plateau, I was completely disoriented, utterly lost. I could only guess the direction the highway passed. Kicking the red dust, passing a few Engelmann prickly pear cacti, I started east, away from the sun. But after half a mile I came to a sheer defile a hundred feet deep. Turning north, I came to another steep cut in the tableland. West, the same. It was Sartre-esque; a desert lobster trap; no exit.

Finally, toward the south, a spit of level ground streaked between two gorges and led to the shimmering asphalt of 89A.

On the climb out I had ripped my shorts, leaving a slightly obscene appearance, which didn't help the hitchhiking cause. It also didn't help that even in rush hour this highway served less than a car every quarter hour. Despite my frantic waves, the first four autos, all crammed with vacationing families, passed me by. Salvation came in the fifth, a Navajo in a pickup who delivered me to the warehouse, where I found several cartons of paper plates. I tracked down Fred Burke, who operated the Park Service jetboat, and in the waning light, we surged downstream.

As we approached Badger, I caught a queer sight on the right bank. On the spit of a sandbar, backed by a vertical limestone wall, a solitary man was hysterically waving his underwear at us. Fred spun the boat around and picked up the marooned man, who was on a few inches of dry land that was disappearing as the river rose. This Daniel Defoe character was part of the Four Corners expedition. Several hours earlier, when the group had stopped for lunch on what was then a broad beach, this Canyon Crusoe had decided to take a quick snooze behind a rock. He awoke hours later to find the cold Colorado nipping at his toes and the rest of the party gone. As one of the consequences of progress, the Colorado would rise and fall many vertical feet each day in an artificial tide created by the diurnal differences in electrical demands, flushing the four turbines that spin in the belly of one of the world's highest dams, Glen Canyon. In another hour, Crusoe would have had no place to stand, no place to go, save downstream, without a life jacket.

Reunited, just after soup, we passed out the plates in time for the salad and steak. I was treated like a hero for my derring-do hike, and for the first time I had a sense of how it felt to be a river guide. The marooned client settled into the group little worse for wear, and I took my first repast in the canyon.

I remember little of the next few days. As is not uncommon to first timers on the river, I picked up a bug and spent much of my time heaving over the gunwales or in delirium, collapsed on the duffel as we caromed through rapids and swept past unconformities, synclines, and other geological anarchy. At trip's end, I expected to be fired. I thought I had been a lousy swamper—sick for most of the passage, sluggish in my chores, not used to the harsh sun and physically demanding days.

But Hatch, in a moment of leniency, kept me on. He assigned me to the boat-patching detail at Marble Canyon Lodge, a ramshackle motel near Navajo Bridge. For a month I lived the life of a desert rat, filling my days with Barge cement and neoprene patching material and reading old adventure magazines like *Argosy* and *Saga*. Every few days another trip went out, and I stood aching at the Lees Ferry ramp, waving as the rafts dipped into the Paria Riffle just downstream. I grew so bored as to feel myself covered by a light film of ash about to turn into sneezing powder. Out of desperation one afternoon, after uncovering a supply box filled with cartons of rotten eggs left from a previous trip, I drove down the Lees Ferry Road and plastered each road sign with a battery of omelets. Waiting at road's end was John Chapman, the ranger, who promptly sent me retracing my yellow trail with wire brush and soap and water. It took me two days to clean the baked-on eggs off the metal signs.

Finally, miraculously, a trip was departing that was short on help, and Dave Bledsoe requested me. This was my big chance and I hustled at every turn. I clocked Dave's every move; I hung on his every word. He was fatherly to me, in a way my own had never been. Where my dad was cerebral and couldn't fix a broken widget, Dave was a doer and could take apart a Mercury outboard while floating through a rapid; while my dad was governed by a keen morality, Dave was expedient and bent the rules to get things done. While my father was a quiet soul, Dave was an artful storyteller. His lecture hall filled with stories of eremites such as Louis Boucher, who operated a copper mine from 1891 to 1912, and of prevaricators such as "Captain" John Hance, who claimed to have crossed the dense clouds from the South Rim to the North on snowshoes. But the lesson that sunk in deepest was the history in the making, the story of river guides.

My ascension up the Hatch hierarchy was not mercurial. I swamped seven trips the summer of 1969—a record, I believe, before being made river guide. Some newcomers—Perry Owens, Jim Ernst—were piloting by their third trip. I wasn't disappointed, though. I loved the river. I lived for each trip and socked away my $20-per-day earnings while on the river.

At last, on my eighth descent, I was given my badge and my own boat to steer. I felt joyfully robbed of any conventional grip on time; human history seemed a momentary blink against the immense scroll of eternity embedded in the rock. When we ran the enormous rapids, I felt a seam open onto a void whose terrible content was the inevitability of finality, and it raced the blood and evoked feelings of being more alive. It was an experience of enthusiastic terror, of shivering pleasure, of a thrilling, delightful horror, and the axis of my identity spun to a new North. I was a River Guide.

Now, peculiar things happened to me. My tan deepened, my chest filled out, my hair grew lighter and more lustrous. But beyond that, a heretofore unplumbed confidence surfaced, and I found people reacting to me in an entirely different manner. At Northwestern, where I was attending undergraduate studies during winters, I was undistinguished academically, athletically, socially. I was painfully shy with women and had never dared venture alone into a bar. But on the river, everything changed. I brandished the rudder through the rapids, affecting the stern purposeful look I'd picked up from Bledsoe. I uncorked lectures on the likes of John Wesley Powell and other explorers, and about the deltaic sedimentary Hermit Shale. I stirred Dutch ovens over the campfire like an outdoor Julia Child. People looked to me for guidance, wisdom, direction, political opinions, even sex.

My second year I guided the president of MGM, a celebrated political journalist, the editor of the *Chicago Sun-Times*, writers from *Newsweek* and the *New York Times*, Broadway actors, television stars, successful professionals of every sort. I was

Rafting Lava Falls, Colorado River, Grand Canyon. BART HENDERSON

in awe of these folks. I would never be able to speak with these people in the winter months, let alone eat, laugh, and play with them. But here they doxologized me, kowtowing, following my every direction, hanging on my every word. It was sobering, unbelievable. When the president of MGM sheepishly asked me to help him set up his tent (he couldn't figure it out), I felt like the roaring lion in the famous logo.

And this was happening to every other guide on the river, every country-rough-neck-cowboy-Vietnam vet-farmhand who somehow backeddied into this *nouveau* elite club. At night, women—single, coupled, married—sneaked over to guides' sleeping bags under the cover of darkness. River romances were as common and flighty and full of trills as canyon wrens. Back at Northwestern, I couldn't get a date to save my life. But on the river, I couldn't find an evening alone. Klutzy romantics in December transformed to lusty Don Juans in June, and egos soared.

Most boatmen were quick to capitalize on this center stage and let loose bottled histrionics, and I was no exception. We sang off-key before appreciative audiences, told bad jokes that sent laughter reverberating between the Supai Sandstone, played rudimentary recorder as passengers swayed. Every guide took advantage of the rapids, all 161 of them. Those pieces of effervescence in the long, emerald band of the river were chances to shine, to showcase mettle and stuff, to enhance the legend of dauntless river guide. Of course, we boatmen would never admit to the rapids' tendency toward impunity to visitors. We could flip, wrap, broach, jackknife, catch a crab, lose an oar, tube stand, endo, and swim the rapids and be relatively assured of emerging intact in the calm water below. But that was classified information.

As a critic said of Wagner's music (it has beautiful moments, but awful quarter hours), the Colorado had long sweeps of still water between the blood-thumping rapids. In these stretches we tried out routines and told apocryphal stories. All the theater was heightened in 1970 with the motor-driven pontoon raft. Nobody had yet figured out how to get through Lava Falls—the Colorado's biggest rapid and one of the last on the trip—with the engine running. The few attempts ended in broken shear pins, bent shafts, or outright loss of outboards, as the propeller invariably hit a rock soon after entry. So, two sets of twelve-foot oars, desuetude on a typical trip, were lifted from their straps on the sides of the raft and mounted on the thole pins marking the orange frame that gridded the pontoon's center. Then the outboard was lifted and tied flat, like a roped calf, to the stern floorboard.

All the passengers then walked around the rapid (Ted Hatch deemed the run too dangerous in those days) and watched and photographed in horror as two boatmen, one seated behind the other, entered the rapid, madly pumping the huge oars while being pitched and folded like laundry in the spin cycle. Then, as the last rooster tail was broached on the back side of the crest, the rear captain had to leap to the stern and, in a genuinely risky maneuver, pull out a knife, cut the ropes binding the outboard, pull the eighty-pound motor up, slide it onto the transom mount, clamp it down, and pull the starter cord.

Time allowed just three or four chances to kick the engine to life (and it was sometimes too swamped to catch) to power the raft to a wisp of an eddy at the mouth of Prospect Canyon, where the passengers could reboard. If the engine didn't start in those few seconds, the raft would dive into the next rapid, Lower Lava, which was walled by a seventy-five-foot cliff that fired up the south bank and prevented passengers from hiking farther downstream. They would have to wait for the next raft and crowd onto it as it taxied them down to their own carrier, waiting in a large eddy a mile downstream on the north bank. If the last raft in the party didn't make the critical landing or if all the boats on a trip were swept into Lower Lava—and this happened occasionally—the passengers would have to hike a half mile upstream, swim across the cold river, knowing that if they cramped, they could be sucked into Lava, and then hike a primitive path down the north bank to the waiting rafts. Or they could wait for the next rafting company to come by.

Richard and Breck O'Neill filming the miniseries *Dream West* on the Colorado River in winter. BART HENDERSON

All this action made a great spectacle for those on shore. What I soon learned was that rowing through Lava was really nothing more than a show. No matter what you did with the oars, be it snapping hard strokes throughout or freezing the blades in place, the results would most often be the same. It was, more than anything else, a piece of theater, and I learned to play it with Kabuki-like stagecraft.

This dashing, somewhat pretentious, rowing ritual was also employed, at some water levels, at the two other rapids rated 9–10 (the Grand Canyon has its own 1–10 classification scale for rapids): Hance and Crystal. A new addition to the fold, Crystal was created in December 1966 when a massive flood bulldozed a boulder-debris fan into the river at Mile 98. But at the cusp of the 1970s, motor routes were being pioneered, many by Hatch honcho Dennis Massey, regarded by some as King of the River, the man who could make his raft dance in any wave, hole, or eddy on the Colorado.

Whether Massey, or guides named Brick, Snake, Whale, or Bear, once below The Rapid, the boatmen would be feted as heroes, hailed as Galahads, Lindberghs, champions charged with extraordinary backbone and bravery. Prior to my guiding, my only work experience was as a bellboy and carhop, and that didn't quite prepare me for idolatry. The river guides, me included, were exalted. The problem was some began to believe it, creating a duality in personality and self-perception, an almost schizophrenic state that was not easy to cope with or resolve. We were walking, rowing oxymorons. All of us relished those moments of canyon adulation, but reality always returned at summer's end. Some turned to the slopes, some to carpentry or other crafts or service jobs. I went back to school. Still others dipped into the black books of summer clients, those, who tugged from the beach after lingering embraces, said through tear-stained smiles, "Whenever you're in town, you must look me up. Come stay with me." Following those words, many boatmen roamed from client home to client home, reliving the summer through slides, scrapbooks, and Super-8 movies, and wearing out welcomes. But wherever we wandered, whatever we did, it seemed mundane by comparison to our summer work and identities.

The Colorado changed me, as it does everyone. It fanned a false ego, then doused the fire. The boatman subculture was a strong one, a brotherhood bond formed in the summer months, and we kept in touch in the off-season, compared notes. Everyone seemed to suffer the same fate and searched in vain for a winter's equivalent of the astral light that caressed us in the canyon. But few found it. One bleak winter Dennis Massey, King of the River, was driving a pizza delivery truck, and he shot himself in the head. Years later, Whale, a ski-lift operator, did the same, on the eve of a boatmen reunion party. These were the extremes. Sometimes, though, the spool rolled the other way. Some people who were undistinguished in their normal lives, perhaps shy or living with untapped potential, found an unplumbed confidence while guiding, and that allowed them to stretch, assert and experiment, and sometimes become extraordinary in ways they otherwise might never have been. A few guides went on to become celebrated photographers, film directors, businesspeople, politicians, and one, perhaps the most envied, became the road manager for The Grateful Dead. And there was one who went on a half-century global quest to find the perfect river, and the endless summer, and the sweet cup of sublimity.

CHAPTER 9

HIDDEN EMPIRE

Fortune brings in some boats that are not steered.
—WILLIAM SHAKESPEARE

FOR THE 1971 RAFTING SEASON I CONVINCED HIGH SCHOOL RAFT CLUB FRIEND John Kramer to come out to the Colorado and be my swamper, with intent to graduate to guide under my tutelage. He proved a quick study, becoming a lead guide in near-record time. I had also tried to recruit John Yost, but he was heading back to Africa, with his own ambitions of setting up an import business. I also met a kindred spirit in Bart Henderson, from Vernal, Utah, where Ted Hatch lived. Bart came from river-running royalty (his Christian name was Royal) and was finally breaking into the Colorado. His uncle was with Bus Hatch in 1938 on the famous first descent of the Green River, a trip sometimes cited as the birth of modern river running. His father bought a pile of surplus ten-man rafts in the early 1950s and starting river running, often taking his young son on the water. Bart was guiding by the time he was thirteen years old. An artful athlete blessed with chiseled good looks and a lion's mane of blond hair, Bart was a great guy, and the first boatman I had met who would consistently beat me in chess. I taught Bart the ropes, but within a month he surpassed his teacher with sheer native ability and smarts and ended the season as one of the finest guides on the river.

By the end of the summer, my third as a river coxswain, I came to realize a common current ran through all those who drifted into the life of a guide on the Colorado River . . . it was the knowledge that the cosmos could be reduced to a cool, wrapping white wave, to the pull of an oar or the twist of a tiller, to the crest of a wave . . . and at that moment, the top of the world was reached, all magic was white, and all was good and great.

Once that gnosis soaked within, every guide, no matter how far pursuits carried him, came back to the river.

That winter, back at Northwestern, the longueurs made the season almost unbearable. But then I came across an old copy of *Argosy* magazine, one of those pulp rags that depicted brawny men bare-handedly fighting off large predators, often a grizzly or mountain lion, while scantily clad nymphs swooned in the background.

The issue reported on a 1968 expedition down the Blue Nile by a British Army team, a military-style enterprise distinguished for its lack of river-running experience and fatal blunders.

The article told of super-financing and over-the-top publicity, of an expedition that compared in pomp and stature to the British naval campaigns of two hundred years ago. With seventy men, a budget in the hundreds of thousands of pounds, and no whitewater experience per se, the army, seemingly out of fear of atrophy, marched forth to accomplish what it self-named "The Last Great First."

Though the righteous zeal seemed a bit impertinent, the photographs in the piece sold me. Looking at those pictures was like peeking through a window into the bedroom of a sleeping demon, peering into the pure soul of a river, glimpsing a divine afflatus. The Blue Nile somehow seemed special, untainted by commercial guiding, but naughty, all at once. It coiled through a mile-deep gorge, and by a member's own description it was a seething cauldron of giant boils, whirlpools, and hydraulic jumps.

Despite meticulous planning of the industrious operation (they practiced capsizing on land with color-coordinated paddles and helmets), things went awry. There were capsizes, missed airdrops, lost boats, injuries, and fatalities. It still called itself a success, and indeed members did accrete a glut of scientific data and specimens. However, there was a section they had not rafted as they deemed it too difficult . . . and that missing piece on their map inspired me. I showed the article to John Yost, who had just returned from a visit to Ethiopia, and he was charged with the possibilities. He said Ethiopia was the Tibet of Africa, a high plateau boiling with big, fast rivers, ripe for running, and that he was up for an expedition, if I could ever organize such a thing. This was a challenge I was ready to take.

I spent spare time that winter researching the Blue Nile. I found it had intrigued inquiring minds for centuries. Napoleon hoped to conquer it; Egypt feared it, for if it ever dried up, or were dammed, the Nile proper would lose most of the precious silt that has annually fertilized the land since time immemorial.

Rising from Lake Tana in the Ethiopian Highlands, the river plummets off the Afro-alpine plateau and snakes its way through a mile-deep gorge. Its waters travel nearly three thousand miles before reaching the Mediterranean. The biography of the river held scores of dauntless attempts to navigate its wild waters. There was the wealthy American big-game hunter W. N. McMillian, who in 1903 sailed less than five miles before his metal boats were destroyed in the rapids; Herbert Rittlinger and party, who in 1954 made thirty-five miles in kayaks before being attacked three times by giant crocodiles; Kuno Steuben, who in 1959 tried to make it alone down the river on a makeshift raft of logs and empty oil drums but was wounded in a skirmish with

Tom Cromer, Richard, and John Kramer rigging for first descent of the Awash River, on the US embassy lawn, Addis Ababa, 1973. LIZ SULLIVAN

local people and hiked out; Arne Rubin, who in 1965 canoed an upper section and then climbed out after a capsize lost his camera and maps; and the two Germans who in 1970 tried to float it in an oversized plastic bathtub (they actually made it ten miles before losing the craft in a cataract). And there was a dozen other daring, if not eccentric, explorers who answered the call to conquer the "Mount Everest of Rivers," the Blue Nile.

The British called the Blue Nile gorge "The Grand Canyon of Africa," and that image resonated with me. The America Grand Canyon, where I had guided now for three seasons, was such a powerful place, it had become the pivot of my identity, around which everything else spun and was measured. As I read the account of the British attempt, I became appalled at their inexperience and bungles, and their insensitivity to the land. Two men died on their expedition. One was from a car accident. The other, a man named Ian Macleod, tried to cross a swollen tributary of the Blue Nile while attached to a rope around his waist secured to a tree on shore. As he was swept downstream, the rope went taut, and he was pulled under and drowned. It was a stupid mistake. A violation of a simple rule of water mechanics. As I read about their blunderings and misadventures, I couldn't help but think I should be there. I understood whitewater; I knew the Grand Canyon; and for some twisted reason, I loved the notion of running rapids on a river with crocodiles.

Now sucked in, I couldn't read enough about Ethiopia. It was like a drug. I became obsessed not just with the Blue Nile, but also with all the rivers of the

Hidden Empire, and with the country itself. Locked away in remote mountains, Ethiopia, which means "burnt face" in Greek, had a three-thousand-year history. The Semites of present-day Ethiopia arrived from Arabia. They intermarried with local Cushites and later organized themselves into the kingdom of Axum. The Axum empire was converted to Christianity in the fourth century, and the new religion was institutionalized as the Ethiopian Orthodox Church. For thousands of years the rich land, watered by the Blue Nile basin and the watershed of a sister river farther north called the Tekeze, was tilled for self-sustenance. But as Ethiopia began to reach out beyond its borders in the 1960s, agronomists looked at its abundant rivers and predicted the country would transform itself into the breadbasket of Africa. Yet, at the time of my research, the early 1970s, it was one of the world's poorest and hungriest countries.

Once known as Abyssinia, Ethiopia was the land of Prester John, the nation of Cush, the last resting place of the Ark of the Covenant, the vault for King Solomon's Mines, the repository for the true cross of Christ, the site of the Garden of Eden, the tomb of Adam, and other legends and medieval myths. The bulk of the country occupied a vast, fissured plateau that for half the year soaked up tremendous rains that fell during two rainy seasons, creating massive serpents of water that spilled off the "roof of Africa" to the cardinal points, into thirsty deserts and lowlands. The biggest rivers were the Blue Nile, the Omo, the Baro, the Awash, and the Tekeze. I wanted to run them all.

CHAPTER 10

RIVER TRIP OF THE CENTURY

Leave paths that common sense, custom, or the average mountain sheep would point out . . . and go in some other direction where the chances appear to be in favor of breaking your neck.

—ALBERT FREDERICK MUMMERY

WHEN THE SUMMER OF 1972 ARRIVED, JOHN YOST WAS FREE AND JOINED ME FOR a few trips through the Grand Canyon as my swamper, as John Kramer had the year before. Throughout the season I made many new friends, guides and clients both, but none who bonded as tightly as a man I met on the final tour . . . a young man, just a few years older than I, who reminded me a bit of my father in the rigidness of his ethical compass, and in the awkwardness of his wilderness ways. But he also seemed a mirror of my being, with an enthusiastic willingness to try new things, a waking thirst for adventure, and a needle of curiosity pulled by the magnet of primeval places.

The man was Lew Greenwald, who with his wife, Karen, joined my raft on a ten-day run. Lew had a B.A. in psychology from the University of Connecticut and was working as a sociologist along with his wife. He was overweight, prematurely bald at age twenty-six, and pasty and pale from too much time indoors. On the first day of the trip, he tried to set up a tent, but it collapsed with a *whoosh* as we were all eating dinner by the river. But as the trip progressed, Lew loosened, a dry humor emerged, as well as a wild whoop as we rolled through the rapids. At one point, I taught him how to skip polished stones into the river, and the simple act gave him great joy. By the second week of the trip Lew was jumping off the raft into the bigger rapids and floating through with reckless abandon as other clients looked on jealously. By trip's end we were good friends and talked of getting together in Los Angeles in a couple weeks before he had to head back to Connecticut and his job.

When the season ended, things were different. I had graduated college, and though graduate or law school was in the plan, I wanted a temporary inoculation against adult sanity. Africa was still a similitude of a dream, seemingly inaccessible, at least for now.

So I did what so many boatmen had done before me . . . I opened my black book of clients and picked the most delicious: Patti Gales, a girl I met earlier in the season when her family vacationed on one of my trips. It was a potent river romance, and I was keen to follow up. John Yost and I hitched to San Diego and spent a week at Patti's house, waterskiing, hiking, and body surfing. One day while we were walking on the beach, Patti pulled out a brochure she had received in the mail from another river guide. It was entitled "River Trip of the Century," and it was advertising a National Geographic–sponsored expedition down Ethiopia's Omo River. It was to be led by Ron Smith, owner of Grand Canyon Expeditions, the company that had outfitted a National Geographic team down the Colorado in 1968 for a feature that ran in the magazine in 1969. Adventurers were invited to join the first descent of this great river for $3,000, more than three times my annual income as a river guide. And that didn't include airfare. But I suspected they needed guides for an expedition of this magnitude, and I fancied I was one of the best around. John Yost had more energy than a pot of cowboy coffee, so I thought we might propose ourselves as staff. Why not take a year off for a last yahoo before getting serious about life?

Richard piloting in the stern. GEORGE WENDT

I called Ron Smith and asked if we might get together and talk over prospects. He said sure, come on by after his next trip, which would get him back to headquarters in a couple weeks. It was an easier invitation to extend than to fulfill, as Ron lived in Kanab, Utah, a tiny town two days' drive away, and we had no car. But there were drive-away companies in Los Angeles, so we decided to hitchhike to the big city and find transportation north. Again I pulled out my address book of past passengers. Stuart Bruce, a past client who was a descendant of the great eighteenth-century Ethiopian explorer James Bruce, lived in San Marino, fashionably northeast of Los Angeles, and he accepted my request to come stay for a while. I also knew that Lew Greenwald would be in town and called the number he had left me.

CHAPTER 11

DELIVERANCE

What gives value to travel is fear.
—Albert Camus

John and I got together with Lew one afternoon in Los Angeles and shared a beer, and some of our Ethiopian plans. Lew's eyes lit up. He wanted to know everything. But neither John nor I took it too seriously. Lew had a real job, a wife, a car, responsibilities. That evening we all decided to see the film *Deliverance*, which had just opened. James Dickey's tour de force of violent adventure and inner discovery on a Southeastern river had become an instant classic with its publishing in 1970, and for river runners it was the Talmud. Now, John Boorman had brought the tale to the big screen, and the world premiere was at the Cinerama Dome on Sunset Boulevard in Hollywood.

The entrance to the theater was decked out with ravaged river gear, splintered paddles, and ripped life jackets. From the ceiling hung aluminum Grummans, severely bashed and dented. As we surrendered to the darkness of the theater, the story was so real, so powerful that the images singed my mind. I identified with Ed, played by Jon Voight, the WASPish city boy-man, who was one of life's sliders until he found a concealed inner strength through his confrontation with the river. I saw my new friend Lew as the Lewis of the film, who plows into the experience with abandon, believing he is immortal, and is nearly fatally injured in the process. When we emerged from the theater, we turned to one another, and John and I simultaneously asked the same question "Where was that river?" It was the Chattooga, Lew volunteered, having read some background on the making of the film. "We gotta run it!" I proposed. Lew and John agreed, and we shook hands on it. A few years later, John and I would make good on the promise to run the Chattooga, but Lew never had the chance.

Lew flew back to Connecticut the next day. He could afford a flight. He had a regular job. John and I cast about for a drive-away company that wanted a car driven east and that would risk the required bond on us, as we didn't exactly have established credit. We found one, AAA Drive-Away, which needed a Gremlin delivered to Annapolis. So we took it, and three days later we were at Ron Smith's warehouse looking at slides he had taken on a reconnoiter of the Omo several months previous. They looked so exotic I almost fell into the photos. Ron said they planned on making the first descent of the Omo in August of 1973, eleven months away, and that he hadn't yet selected the crew. I listened to Ron, swallowing his words like water. Why, we would be good candidates, I volunteered, and he looked us up and down and suggested I start a workout program and call him in a couple months. I took that as a good sign, and as we bowled across country John and I plotted and shared dream-streak talk of running the Omo and other great rivers of Africa.

As soon as we landed in Bethesda, I signed up at the local gym for a buff-up program and spent two hours a day lifting weights and running in place. The rest of the day I usually spent at the Library of Congress, drinking down information about the rivers of Africa.

Then, in late October, chest and thighs expanded in a way never before, I called Ron and said we were ready to go. He hemmed and hawed, then explained he had decided to hire his younger brother and some of his friends for the crew, so sorry, there wouldn't be a place for us. Unless we wanted to pay . . .

This was a blow. But I called John Yost and threw out a blunt idea. Why don't we do this ourselves? Why didn't we just go over the first of the year and head down some river? I knew as much as anyone about whitewater rafting, and he had embassy connections. John was intrigued, but he had committed the winter to opening an import store in Long Island with his college roommate, David Bohn, so he suggested I go over and get things started and he could join me later. That sounded fine with me, except that I had less than $500 in life savings, so my first order was to see if we could find sponsors. I wrote to all the rafting manufacturers in the country, all two; Rubber Fabricators of West Virginia, who was making boats for Ron Smith and didn't reply; and Holcombe Industries of Redwood, California, who had just started building a vinyl version of a rubber raft and was eager to promote it. The rafts would sell for $1,000 each, but the owner of the company, intrigued with my proposal, offered to sell me two for a total of $400. This was good news, except it was beyond my budget. It was clear I needed another partner. So I started calling my river-running friends.

First was John Kramer. Kramer lived a short way away in Bethesda, and when I approached him about running rivers in Ethiopia he threw in his hat, but not his money. He would love to join the expedition, but he had plans for graduate school in geology the following fall and didn't want to invest in a raft. The next call was to Tom Cromer, another Hatch guide, who hailed from Los Alamos, New Mexico. Tom's older brother, Roy, had started rafting the Colorado in the late 1960s, and he brought Tom into the fold. In our three seasons guiding together, we became close friends and shared a love of books, rare at that time among the river community. We even talked of going into partnership, opening a bookstore together in the mountains, as a career, when not plunging down rivers. Tom was also slated to go

Richard rowing in Costa Rica. PAMELA ROBERSON

to graduate school the following fall, in mathematics, and was saving his money, so he didn't want to invest in the concept, but he wanted to join up. Bart was very enthused with the concept but had family obligations for the winter months and asked that I call again if I made it to a second season in Africa. The subsequent call was to Lew Greenwald. When I asked, he admitted things were pretty boring. When I said I finally had a proposition for him about river running in Africa, he invited me up to present it in person.

I took a long weekend and drove my father's Oldsmobile to Connecticut. Lew said he didn't recognize me at the door, I was so buffed up. He still looked like an indoorsman, and he was even a bit balder, paunchier, and paler than when I last saw him in Los Angeles—but his wild eyes radiated a puckish sense of fun. Once inside his small den, Lew turned up his tape deck and put on his favorite artist, Van Morrison, and we sat back with a few beers to talk about music, about the film *Deliverance*, about how special the time we shared on the Colorado was, and about how little time there is to pursue dreams. When I made my proposition, asking for the money to buy a raft to become part of this scheme, he stuck out his hand to shake. He was my partner. Outside, the tips of a hazy yellow crescent moon pointed east to Africa.

CHAPTER 12

SOBEK, THE PERFECT KILLING MACHINE

It is a hideous blot upon the creation: the crocodile.
—Reginald Maugham, *Wild Game in Zambezia*

Lew and I spent the next several weeks seeking sponsors and doing more research. One weekend I met Lew in New York City, and we went to the Museum of Natural History, where we saw the skull of Phobosuchus, the Fearsome Crocodile, an ancient relative to the Nile crocs that had been 45 feet long, weighing 15 tons. The skull was 6 feet long by 3.5 feet across. Some of the teeth were 6 inches long and 2 inches deep. The crocs we would encounter would be at best a third that size. Nonetheless, the display gave us pause.

I knew there would be a lot of bugs where we were going, and that some perhaps were unclassified, so that gave me an idea. I called the Smithsonian Institution's Department of Entomology and asked if they might be interested in sponsorship in exchange for collecting bugs. They thought it an interesting idea and suggested I come in for a meet.

This put pressure on for a name. I felt we couldn't present ourselves to potential sponsors without a proper name, and after some deliberation I came up with one I thought quite clever. I had recently seen the Thor Heyerdahl documentary, *The Ra Expeditions*, on his attempt to cross the Atlantic from Africa on a papyrus reed boat (Ra was the ancient Egyptian sun god). So I figured we would be the R.A.W. Expedition. It would be an acronym: Reconnaissance of African Waterways; it would be a play on Heyerdahl's high-profile expedition; it was a celebration of the times (streaking was a rage, as was nude rafting); and it evoked the state of our enterprise, lean, crude, raw.

But when I wound my way through the inner corridors of the Smithsonian, found myself facing a line of white lab coats, and announced I was with the R.A.W.

Expedition, I was met with blank stares. The most senior of the researchers, Dr. Spangler, put his arm across my shoulder and walked me to a corner. There he gave me some advice: Lose the name. If we wanted the Smithsonian, or any prestigious organization, to be involved, we needed a more earnest name.

I spent the next several days at the Library of Congress, poring over books describing the many ways we could die while rafting in Ethiopia and thinking about a name. I learned there was a raft of nasty obstacles that might do damage. The rapids were certainly a given . . . they were likely big, and dangerous. But then there were hippos, second-largest land mammals after elephants and infamous for turning over boats and snapping occupants in two. The wild buffalo in the region had a reputation for charging unprovoked. I read about puff adders, black mambas, and spitting cobras, and about legendary twenty-foot pythons that capsized canoes. And there was a score of documented exotic tropical diseases, from onchocerciasis (river blindness) to elephantiasis; from trypanosomiasis (sleeping sickness) to trichuriasis (whipworm); typhoid, meningitis, hookworm, amoebic dysentery, leprosy, giardiasis, kala-azar; from yaws to several fatal forms of malaria. There were the local peoples, some with fierce reputations. The Blue Nile, the only river previously run in Ethiopia, had taken a toll of victims who fell prey to the ruthless *shiftas*, the roaming bands of bandits who ruled the outback. In 1962 a Swiss-French canoeing expedition was attacked in the middle of the night. Four of the party fled in a single canoe under a hail of gunfire, while the rest lay dead in the campsite. And during the 1968 British Blue Nile expedition there was a similar *shifta* attack, but the expedition escaped without serious injury.

But the one danger repeated over and over, in print and voice, underlined and accented, was the risk of death by crocodile attack. The ancient Greeks called it *kroko-drilo*, "pebble-worm"—a scaly thing that shuffled and lurked in low places. The deadliest existing reptile, the man-eating Nile crocodile has always been on the "man's worst enemies" list. It evolved 170 million years ago from the primordial soup as an efficient killing machine. More people are killed and eaten by crocodiles each year in Africa than by all other animals combined. Their instinct is predation, to kill any meat that floats their way, be it fish, hippo, antelope, or human. To crocs, we were just part of the food chain. Crocodile hunters, upon cutting open stomachs of their prey, often discovered bracelets and bits of jewelry and human remains. Huge, ravening predators, armed with massive, teeth-studded jaws, strong, unrestrainable, indestructible and destructive, crocodiles, if given the chance, eat people. It's their nature. The river is their turf, and we would be trespassing. I found myself in cold-sweat nightmares imagining the yellow chisel-sharp teeth of a giant croc ripping my skin apart. This would be the most awful way to die. But I thought about the alternative . . . law or graduate school leading to a real job . . . and facing crocodiles seemed the delightful evil of two lessors.

I read as much as I could find about crocodiles that month, though I quickly discovered not many people had ever navigated whitewater in Africa, and of the few who

Our rafts were repeatedly bitten by the aggressive one-ton hippos in the rivers of Africa. BART HENDERSON

had, and survived, less than a handful left reliable accounts of their experiences with crocs. I discovered there were two major schools of thought about how to cope while floating a crocodile-infested river: (1) Be as noisy as possible when passing through a crocodile pool to scare them off. (2) Be as silent as possible when passing through a croc-infested area so as not to attract attention. The rationale for the latter method was that since crocodiles have fixed-focused eyesight—meaning they can see things clearly only at one specific distance—a noiseless boat floating past at the proper distance could probably go unnoticed. One expert at the National Zoo even warned not to laugh in a certain manner, as it resembled the sound of an infant croc in trouble, and the noise would alert all larger crocs within hearing distance to rush to rescue. He demonstrated the laugh, and it sounded eerily like John Yost's high-pitched nervous laugh, so I silently vowed to keep topics serious if sharing a raft with John.

Another account was graphically presented in the book *Eyelids of Morning: The Mingled Destinies of Crocodiles and Men* by Alistair Graham and photographed by Peter Beard. It told of a Peace Corps volunteer, Bill Olsen, age twenty-five, a recent graduate of Cornell, who decided to take a swim on Ethiopia's Baro River, one of my targets, against the advice of locals. He swam to a sandbar on the far side of the muddy river and sat there with his feet on a submerged rock. He was leaning into the current to keep his balance, a rippled vee of water trailing behind him, his arms folded across his chest as he stared ahead lost in thought. Minutes later his friends noticed Bill had vanished without trace or sound. A few more minutes later a big croc surfaced with a large, white, partially submerged object in its jaws, whose identity was in no doubt. The next morning a hunter on safari, Colonel Dow, sneaked up on the croc, shot it, and then dragged the carcass to the beach. He cut it open, and inside found Bill Olsen's legs, intact from the knees down, still joined together at the pelvis. His head, crushed into small chunks, was a barely recognizable mass of hair and flesh. A black-and-white photo of Bill's twisted, bloody legs dumped in a torn cardboard box drilled into my paraconsciousness, and for days I would shut my eyes and shiver at the image.

In the end, I was not comforted by what I learned in my research—if anything, I was a good deal more afraid.

It was while casting about for a name that a thin book in the Library of Congress on the gods and goddesses of ancient Egypt wrought inspiration. There was Ra, the sun god, but that had been taken. There was Hesamut, the hippo goddess depicted in the act of demolishing a crocodile. But Hesamut Expeditions didn't resonate. One chapter spoke of the crocodile god Sobek, worshipped along the middle Nile.

The crocodile, in a fashion, was responsible for the pyramids and the great tombs of Egypt.

The ancient Egyptians watched helpless each summer as the life-giving Nile receded and left their fields barren. Then come September, under clear blue skies, the river would run in spate, bringing swarms of crocodiles and the rich soil and nutrients that would replenish the black and dead soil. It was a mystery from where the crocodiles and the new soil came, and why, but the Egyptians looked on as lifeless land was reborn and crocodile eggs were laid with the season.

Just as the sun died and was reborn each day, so the soil was resurrected along the Nile each year as the crocodiles came. Crocodile eggs hatched and created life out of nothing. These annuities, it might be conjectured, gave the Egyptians the idea that the crocodile was the agent for this rebirth, giving them reason to believe they, too, could restart life after death.

So Sobek became a god of fertility and rebirth, and Egyptians inferred that if Sobek could give the land a new life, then he could do the same for humans. Accordingly, the pharaohs endorsed the concept of an afterlife and believed they could bring possessions with them. They built enormous tombs, filled them with their effects, and had themselves mummified in preparation for the journey. As guides to the afterlife, crocodiles were also embalmed in sarcophagi in these tombs, placed alongside canopic jars filled with vital organs necessary for the thereafter.

If this theory is true, everyone who has ever admired the pyramids, or the tombs of the Valley of the Kings, monumental aesthetic gifts that have endured for millennia, owes a debt to Sobek.

Of no surprise, the library carried the Egyptian *Book of the Dead*, the cheat sheet to the afterlife for dynastic Egyptians, rich with references to Sobek. In one passage the crocodile god speaks:

"I am the owner of seed who takes women from their husbands whenever he wishes, according to his desire. I am Sobek, who carries off by violence."

A key description in chapter 125 of the *Book of the Dead* is that of the weighing of the heart, a precursor to the Christian concept of the Last Judgment. The heart of the newly dead was placed on one side of a scale. On the other side was a feather from the Goddess Maat, who represented order and justice. Looming nearby was the hell mouth of a crocodile-headed monster.

If the scale balanced, the god of the underworld, Osiris, would lead the deceased to reanimation in the next world. If unbalanced, the heart was tossed to the crocodile-headed monster and devoured.

Sobek as a spirited demiurge was associated with death, but also sex. In the Pyramid Text (Spell 510), Sobek's lusty stealth and sexual potency are described, wherein the king changes into a crocodile before robbing husbands of their wives. Another passage speaks to Sobek's contravening powers: Women would use the dung of crocodiles as contraceptives.

Still other texts suggest it is a stroke of good fortune to be gobbled by a crocodile. And so it is that the relationship with the Nile crocodile is a conflicted one; the croc was feared and worshipped, seen as an instrument of death, fertility, regeneration, and channel to the next world.

The brilliance of the ancient imaginings of Sobek was that its current of moral energy ran both ways, just as the Nile for navigation. Creator, destroyer; good, evil; a god, the devil. Like its amphibious nature, between land and air, it evoked ambiguity, a place between and of, a duality in motion, a spiritual device that covered all bases.

Excavations at ancient Tebtunis unearthed thousands of mummified crocs, many with papyri manuscripts entombed inside, including works by Homer, Virgil, Euripides, and even a lost play by Sophocles. A temple was built to the deity on the island of Kom Ombo between Aswan and Luxor, where mothers of children eaten by crocodiles felt privileged to have provided something for Sobek's delectation. And there were sacrificial pools on another island called Crocodilopolis. The story went that once upon a time Menes, first king of all the Egyptians, was set upon by his own dogs while out hunting. In his flight he came to the Nile, where lay a large croc baking in the sun. The croc, rapidly sizing up the situation, offered to ferry the desperate king across the river. With all saurian ceremony, Menes was sculled over to found the city of Crocodilopolis, about 3000 BCE. Hencefore, it was believed that if Sobek were appeased, he would allow the fragile papyrus boats used to ply the Nile to remain unharmed. About 300 BCE, when the army of Perdiccas was crossing the Nile at Memphis, it forgot to pay Sobek homage, and one thousand soldiers were killed and eaten. Naming our enterprise after a deity that would protect boats from sharp-toothed reptiles seemed like a good idea to me, so Sobek we became.

And with my return visit to the Smithsonian, I announced our name, and it seemed fine to the insect men. Dr. Spangler said they would officially sponsor our little expedition. This was quite exciting news, and I asked exactly what that meant, dollarwise.

"Nothing," was the reply. It meant the institute would supply us with a load of bulky and delicate insect-collecting gear, for which we would be responsible. It meant if I found some new genus of bug, they might name it after me. And it meant we could use the good Smithsonian name in soliciting from more commercial concerns. But it didn't mean money. Nonetheless, Sobek it would be.

With this start Lew, John Kramer, and I set out on a letter-writing campaign, and we ended up with a respectable list of sponsors, though none with cash. *Saga* magazine supplied us with film; Peter Storm, a British life jacket company, supplied floatation; and my mother threw in a poncho, a mess kit, a flashlight, and a harmonica. But we were stuck with our cash at hand.

Shipping could have been a problem; certainly, duty and customs. But here contacts made all the difference. Even though John Yost would not be joining our first expeditions, as the son of a diplomat, he arranged for us to use the diplomatic pouch, and several hundred pounds of rafts and gear went flying to Addis Ababa on US military transport. Getting ourselves there was another thing altogether. The commercial air ticket price was more than $1,000, way beyond my budget. So I went to a bucket shop.

These were the days before airline deregulation, and pretty much all carriers charged the same high prices to fly internationally. The one exception was for affinity groups, which were allowed to charter planes and charge whatever seemed fair. This spawned a whole underground airline industry, in which bogus affinity groups were created. Anyone could join for a small fee and receive a backdated membership card (you had to be an affinity member for six months to qualify for these special fares). I sought out a bucket shop in downtown Washington, D.C., paid my $25, and became a right guard on a rugby team. Tom Cromer became a goalie, and together we would fly February 10, 1973, to Nairobi for a sporting match, for $150 round trip. John Kramer and Lew Greenwald would take a later flight and meet us in Addis Ababa, where together we would put the pieces together to run some African whitewater.

Before getting on the plane, however, we had to undergo the indignity of pre-African travel: inoculations. In the days before departure, I was perforated with immunization serums for poliomyelitis, cholera, tetanus, smallpox, yellow fever, diphtheria, typhus, and infective hepatitis, both A and B. It was an exquisitely uncomfortable flight.

Our charter flight first landed in London for an overnight, and so Tom and I took a train to the Royal Military Academy, Sandhurst, to meet Richard Snailham, chronicler of the official account of the British Blue Nile expedition. He was proper and preppy, smoked a Holmesian pipe, and warned us of *shiftas* and crocodiles. Then we caught the next leg of our flight and landed in Nairobi.

Nairobi was thick with new smells, jacarandas and flame trees, grilled corn, and meats. We checked into the local YMCA and went off to explore. We visited the snake farm, where we learned of another dozen types of snakes who might do us in. We rented a taxi and headed out towards the Tana River, which I had heard from Geoffrey Kent, a young safari outfitter, might be runnable. The one other attempt, I was told, was in a single rowboat, but it only made a short passage before spooking a grazing hippo high up on shore, which then stampeded straight over a ten-foot mud embankment and belly-flopped, all five thousand pounds of it, onto the small boat, crushing it and its passengers. The story only fueled our curiosity, so we pooled resources and gave the driver a fixed amount to take us as far as he could and back. When the meter was halfway there, so were we, so back we came.

That evening, craving a touchstone of familiarity, I wandered over to the Hilton while Tom stayed behind in a bath. I went to the coffee shop, where I ordered a cheeseburger and coffee. While chomping into the watery ground meat, I looked up and saw a familiar face, a very glamorous face, with an aquiline nose, framed with hair like cascading heat, a camera draped around her neck. She asked if she might sit with me, as I was the only Westerner in sight. Of course, and then I recognized her as Candice Bergen. She proceeded to tell me she was hoping to switch careers and become a professional photographer, and that she was on assignment for a woman's magazine to shoot Jane Goodall and her chimps. She rambled on about how unfulfilling acting was, that her last couple films had taken a toll, and finally ended by asking me if she was making the right decision. Of course, I counseled . . . she probably would never make it as an actress, and her prospects as a photographer were much brighter. "Thanks," she said, flashed her great white smile, and left to pursue her destiny.

My destiny was north, and I spent a restless night rolling around my small bed in orthogonal thoughts: the excitement that courses on the eve of a great adventure intersecting with the anxiety about all the things that could go wrong.

CHAPTER 13

RUNNING OFF THE CLIFF

Travelers, like poets, are mostly an angry race.
—RICHARD BURTON

WITH MATINAL EXCITEMENT TOM CROMER AND I CAUGHT THE FLIGHT TO ADDIS
Ababa, on the western ridge of the Great Rift Valley, at eight thousand feet the
third-highest capital city in the world. Addis Ababa means "New Flower" in
Amharic, and coming in for a landing I imagined the tin-roofed shanties were its
petals, the tall buildings it stalks, and the eucalyptus groves its leaves. It was founded
by Emperor Menelik II in 1896, both for its central location and its therapeutic
hot mineral waters. It was a city of hills and spinneys of eucalyptus planted in the
1920s for fuel wood and construction material. And construction was everywhere.
Skyscrapers and modern buildings were being erected at every turn, yet at their feet
were the shacks of the poor. Still, it seemed a city of hope, a city on the march, a city
of new sights and sounds, and of pure exotica for me.

With arrival we sought out the local YMCA again, and while wandering about
like lost puppies, an attractive Western woman with dark hair motioned us across
the street, leashed us in. Without preamble, she introduced herself as Diane Fuller, a
public health nurse, and said we looked disoriented and asked where we were headed.
When we told our tale, she offered to guide us to the Y. Along the way we described
our reason for being in Ethiopia . . . wild rivers, and she suggested we meet her husband, Dr. George Fuller, an anthropologist, artist, and medical doctor with a special
degree in tropical medicine, who was also a hobby rafter. Having just read a historical
account of the nineteenth-century quest to find the source of the Nile, I also knew
that one George Fuller was the cousin to John Hanning Speke and was with Speke
when he fatally shot himself in the chest on the eve of his great debate with Richard
Burton as to who had discovered the true source.

At this point, we still weren't sure which river to attempt first. The Blue Nile
was the most celebrated and was the original seductress. The Omo was the river

The National Geographic had identified as the "River Trip of the Century," and we were in Ethiopia with gear and crew a good six months before the officially scheduled attempt. And the Tekeze, the most mysterious, myth-shrouded, and erotically appealing, beckoned from the north. But I realized a more modest and accessible flow might be the place to start, and that looked to me to be a river called the Awash, draining Addis Ababa and emptying into the sinkhole of the sun, the Danakil Depression, lowest point in Africa, where it sank into the sands at the border of the French Territory of Afars and Issas (it would emerge as the independent Republic of Djibouti in 1977). If we survived, we would try the bigger flows.

A couple days later Tom and I took the local bus down to the Awash River, a dusty, bumpy 140-mile, seven-hour journey with a radio blaring forth an unceasing stream of local music at earsplitting pitch. We scraped down the edge of the escarpment into the Great Rift, the giant geological fault that runs from Galilee, down the River Jordan and the Dead Sea to the Gulf of Akaba, across the Red Sea, then down a furrow of Ethiopia, into Kenya, Tanzania, Zambia, and Rhodesia (now Zimbabwe).

We got out at a small *buna beit* (coffeehouse) alone at the door of the desert. We pushed aside a curtain of bottle tops on strings. Inside a portrait of Haile Selassie hung on a wall of mud and chopped grass, blackened with candle smoke. The proprietor stood behind a wooden counter, fanning away flies with a horsehair whisk. We ordered hot tea, and asked where was the river? The owner pointed over a small rise, and off we went in search of moving water. As we approached what looked to be a crack in the earth, an animal snorted and shot out from behind a rock, galloping towards us. It had huge, curved tusks, a flat-iron face, and was charging at top speed, with a tail upright as a radio antenna. Turning on our heels, we ran pants-on-fire towards the canyon rim. When we got to the edge, we stopped, as it was four hundred feet straight down the canyon wall. And the animal, which we now saw was a warthog, kept jinking towards us . . . but twenty feet in front of our path, it veered sharply to the right, and in a crash-and-burn peripeteia, ran right off the cliff . . . we heard an awful thump a few seconds later, a noise like a mallet driving in a tent peg. We then peered over the edge to see what looked like a crumpled paper bag containing a broken bottle of red wine. The poor animal was flattened on a rock, encircled in a pool of blood. It was an eerie first contact with African wildlife. As we gazed down at the dead beast, a soft afternoon breeze, laden with the fragrance of the desert, blew up the canyon, circulated around our heads, and soared to the first battlements of the escarpment behind us.

We repaired to Addis Ababa and met up with John Kramer and Lew, who had just arrived. As a full-fledged guide, John Kramer was brimming with brio and leapt into the culture with both feet. Lew was more hesitant, reflective, cautious. I enjoyed showing Lew the ropes, how to get around, the rudiments of the language, where to get the best mango shakes. But one piece of advice he refused to take concerned the beggars. Over dinner one night before Lew arrived, George Fuller went into a rant about the acid qualities of begging. He postulated that naive, bleeding-heart tourists help perpetuate a system that demotivates street people to work . . . a causal quarter thrown to a panhandler is more than he would make in a few hours of hard labor. George steadfastly refused to give a beggar a break, and he brought me into his orbit, even if it was a bit of cognitive dissonance. When I explained this higher thinking to Lew, he rebuffed it. Wherever we walked about town he always had a few birr, the local currency, for a street urchin or codger, and a part of me always felt guilty when he did so.

The next couple weeks were spent in Addis Ababa, securing the necessary laissez-passers, buying food and supplies in the Mercato, wandering among the tumultuous color, the recherché fruits, spices, and narcotics (such as chat, the glistening green leaf of *Cattula aedulis* that provokes a caffeine-mixed-with-hemp buzz), and the rich stew of a foreign language. For recreation we played tennis at the US embassy compound (where they also served warm chocolate chip cookies and juicy cheeseburgers). Our funds were so lean, however, we made a pact as we moved about town . . . we would use only the local buses, which charged 7 cents a ride. The 25-cent fixed-price taxi fare was just too steep for our budget.

One day, as Lew and I were sharing a street-roasted ear of corn, about as cheap a meal as we could find, the usual city din was muffled by the sudden appearance of an entourage, headlights blinking, sirens wailing. First a jeep, then Land Rovers and trucks bristling like porcupines with solders' rifles, then, slowly, a long black Rolls-Royce. It was the great high forehead himself, Emperor Haile Selassie, the 225th direct-line descendant of Menelik I, son of the Queen of Sheba and King Solomon. He was handing out birr as he passed by. We needed every birr we could get to pull off our adventures, so I shouldered forward into the crowd to see if I might receive some royal beneficence . . . but Lew grabbed my shoulder and prised me back. "It's not fair money . . . they need it more than us. We can do without." The car passed, and the emperor's metallic eyes locked with mine. Then he was gone, and the pedestrians went about their business, or lack of, moving with the skittish walk of silent movies.

CHAPTER 14

WHAT MOST PEOPLE CALL MISERABLE, I LOVE

I want this adventure that is the context of my life to go on without end.
—Simon De Beauvoir

The night before departure for the Awash, Lew, John, Tom, and I went to the Three Tukuls disco just off Bole Road, a club equal parts African and expat. After a couple beers, Lew pulled from his jacket a 45-rpm record and took it to the DJ. It was Elton John's "Crocodile Rock," and it had us all hoppin' and boppin', and Lew was extending his hands as though the jaws of a snapping crocodile in a kind of handshake-dance. Lew's spontaneous dance floor contrivance would become the official Sobek handshake. When we sank back in our chairs after the sweaty jig, a woman, glassy and gorgeous, slid down next to me. Ethiopian women are legendary for their beauty, with coffee-and-cream skin, Levantine lips, fine bones, distinctive high cheekbones, and thin noses, but this woman, who called herself Diamond, had a beauty beyond I had imagined. I couldn't believe it when she agreed to dance with me . . . I didn't deserve such company and had never been this close to Praxitelean perfection. We danced for hours, and with every song she writhed closer to me, combining glissé and a grinding pelvis She touched me in intimate ways and smiled white embers of desire. Somehow in the scrum of our wild dancing, I noticed it was midnight. I panicked and said I had to go, as we had a 5:00 a.m. lorry to catch and some packing yet to do. She tugged at my sleeve and flashed an imploring, smoldering look that knocked me back. I had an idea. "Why don't you join us on the expedition?" I asked. "We have extra gear, everything you need. All you need is a toilet kit, your personal effects. I'll take care of the rest." She nodded approval, and I wrote on a napkin directions as to where to meet us. She took the napkin, stuffed it in her breast, and said she would be there. She winked and blew a kiss.

I couldn't sleep at all that night, restless with the upcoming adventure, but perhaps more with the prospect of rafting with the most beautiful woman I had ever encountered. There was enough sublimation that night to power a motorboat. It was the ultimate wet dream.

We had hired a sugar-agro lorry from the Ethiopian Distribution Company to tote our gear and ourselves down to the Awash River. A young administrator, who was sympathetic to our wild scheme, arranged for a driver at a deep discount. I asked the driver to wait a few more minutes, then a few more. Diamond hadn't appeared. I had no contact for her, only her word she would be here. Finally, the driver said he couldn't hold back any longer, and he revved up the diesel engine and steered the old Mercedes out into the road. I sulked in the back, until George came back to comfort me. . . . "You realize, don't you, she was a hooker? It never would have worked." In the naivete of youth, I hadn't made that connection, but with recognition of George's truth, I grinned. "You're right . . . it wouldn't have worked . . . but it would have been fun trying."

———

I strained on my left oar as the boat spun down a narrow chute at speed towards Tom's raft. Ifru was gone, tossed from the raft into the maelstrom. The boats collided, and Tom's inched upwards towards a slow capsize. "High side," he yelled, and Lemma dove for the rising tube and pushed it down. The rafts separated and spun down into a spell of quiet water. Ifru was spinning around in an eddy, life jacket scrunched around his head, his hands splashing like a dog paddling. I edged next to him, grabbed the back of his life jacket, and pulled him in.

This was in the first thirty minutes on the Awash River.

When we arrived in Addis Ababa, we were introduced to the narcotizing tempo of the country's customs officials. But that was less daunting than securing the permits to travel through seven provinces and two districts, all of which we obtained with much time and a few enveloped enticements.

We all knew that the repeated warnings and pleas against our expedition were not without reason. Besides the rapids, waterfalls, crocs, hippos, and tropical diseases, one official warned of twenty-foot pythons that would turn over our boats. Although each of us had been perforated with nine vaccinations, and we were carrying several pounds of medical supplies, one of our greatest fears concerned the peoples living along the river. The Blue Nile, the only river previously run in Ethiopia, took a toll of victims who fell prey to the ruthless *shiftas*, roaming bands of bandits who ruled the banks.

In Addis Ababa we found Ifru Gabreyes, who spoke Amharic, the agglutinative national language, as well as Saho, the language of the Danakil, the people who lived along the middle and lower Awash. But he didn't speak English. So, to communicate with Ifru we brought Lemma Tessema, who spoke Amharic and English, our translator for our translator. Both were former Imperial bodyguards and qualified wildlife guides, but they had never been on a river and did not swim. Rounding out

Richard at launch of first descent of the Awash River, Ethiopia. GEORGE FULLER

our crew was Dr. George Fuller, an anthropologist, artist, and medical doctor with a special degree in tropical medicine and hygiene. Fresh from postgraduate studies at the London School of Tropical Medicine, George accepted an "ambulatory medicine" fellowship sponsored by the Smith, Kline, and French drug company in 1971. The program took him to Kenya for three months and then Nepal for six weeks. A former ranch-hand who had spent his youth herding cattle and mending fences in Nebraska, George was now hooked on foreign travel; he'd seen Paris and would never return to the farm. Immediately after his fellowship, he signed for a three-month stint in Ethiopia to conduct backcountry research on Kal Azar, a protozoan organism that transmits a disease related to malaria and sleeping sickness. He was in his second year.

George's boss, Aklelu Lemma, of Haile Selassie University, hated the uncomfortable conditions and bad air of lowland Ethiopia and was pleased to find in George an enthusiastic researcher willing to embrace the hardships of the field. "They pay me expenses to go to places nobody else will go, which is fine with me, because I love those places," George explained over spaghetti cooked by his wife, Diane. "I'm attracted to the hot and humid. What most people call miserable, I love." He sounded like my kind of guy, and when he told me he had lost his raft while running California's Stanislaus River during medical school, I asked if he wanted to join our expedition. By evening's end, the small, freckled man with the thick glasses of a schoolboy who tinkers with bugs was officially signed on as trip doctor.

Our vinyl rafts were crafted with a revolutionary design for the times: Both ends spooned up at a twenty-degree angle to cut the splash factor, and they were quite light, weighing in at 130 pounds, excellent for portaging. The rest of our gear was a mixture of army surplus and donated gear from sponsors.

Stepping into the raft there was that first sensation of water rushing beneath the bilge of the boat, a sound like compression brakes. We pushed off and first rowed upstream to the seven veils of the sixty-foot-high Awash Falls and there took an early morning shower in its cool, clear spray. Life jackets tightened, we turned the rafts downstream and were off into the African unknown.

Though I had secured a classified set of maps from the CIA, I quickly found they had little basis in reality. In fact, because the maps were created from satellite pictures of the Awash in August, when it was in flood, there was practically no cartographic information of any accuracy. We really did not know what to expect.

I had read of Wilfred Thesiger's explorations of the Awash, in which he walked to its mouth between October 1933 and May 1934. He was twenty-three years old, a year older than me, and had written words that beaded up and rolled into my soul: "I had felt the lure of the unknown, the urge to go where no white man had been before, and I was determined, as soon as I had taken my degree, to return to Abyssinia." He did not leave any usable maps, only strong words of warning about several expeditions ahead of him that had been wiped out by fierce Danakil tribesman, or Afar, as they call themselves, the Hamitic people, linked by legend to the Biblical sons of Ham. The Danakil occupied the blistering Awash valley and the surrounding moonscape deserts, wastelands with phantasmagoric rock outcroppings and treacherous craters filled with melted chloride. If ever a people matched the personality of a landscape, these were they. "If you went down into Danakil country, you'd be unlikely to come back, and if you come back, you would probably be missing some of your vital organs," Thesiger wrote.

We had talked to a few pilots who had flown over sections, but they had little to offer, except that much of the winding course was hidden from aerial view by thick vegetation that canopied the water. All we really knew was that we would start the trip right below Awash Falls in the national park. If we had the time, we hoped to make it to the end of the river, an inland waterway called Lake Abbe, where the saline waters stilled before evaporating into the desert, 121 feet below sea level. The only other point of accessibility to the river was a small agricultural school near the arid town of Gewani. This was one hundred miles farther from our starting point by road, certainly much more by river, perhaps double, or more. The Amasabury Vocational School (run by the Peace Corps) was our first possible takeout, and from there we could call our friend Bob Denton, a communications expert at the embassy, who said he could pick us up in his Land Rover. What lay between Awash Falls and Gewani and Lake Abbe was anybody's guess. We estimated six days traveling time, purchased food for eight, and told the embassy chargé d'affaires not to worry if he hadn't heard from us by then.

CHAPTER 15

THE FIRST
FIRST DESCENT

An adventure is only an inconvenience rightly considered.
—G. K. CHESTERTON

THE FIRST MORNING THE BOATS LEAPT, TURNED, AND TIPPED DOWN CATARACTS IN
rapid fire. It was a great beginning; spirits crackled with excitement.

Being first to travel this river, we tried to stop and scout each rapid. We would
tie up the rafts and make our way along the cliffs until we found a vantage point
where we could best determine how to make the run. Then we'd cross fingers, make
the Sobek handshake that Lew invented, and go for it.

After fifteen miles of white-jacketed water, we spun into a tranquil pool, and
I shipped my oars. Frowning basalt cliffs, some four hundred feet high, framed a
bright blue sky. Silently we drifted around a bend and caught sight of a small herd of
lesser kudus drinking at river's edge. The antelope spotted us, hesitated, then trotted
off to the protection of a vegetation-choked flat. On the other bank I spied a black-
and-white-masked beisa oryx, his back jeweled with a red-billed oxpecker, his head
adorned with distinctive straight horns, each like the horn of a unicorn.

Shortly downstream we saw a strange dull blue and white object bobbing
through the water. We fell into silence as I pulled closer. A few feet from the object,
Lew shattered the silence: "It's a dead fish!"

It was huge, the size of a small dog. I poked its hard skin, and over it slowly
rolled. The entire bottom section was missing . . . it had been bitten in half. For a
beat nobody spoke a word, but we could all hear the roaring thought . . . crocodiles.
Up at the falls where we launched, we had met a Danish tourist who told us that just
two years earlier a couple of Germans had constructed a makeshift raft and headed
downstream. They were forced to abandon their trip after two days when their paddles were bitten to pieces by hungry crocs.

Believing crocodiles would be a problem, I had smuggled in, through diplomatic pouch, a collapsible .30-06 rifle. I now pulled it from its case, assembled it, and positioned it next to my leg, within easy reaching distance. Minutes later we spotted the pebbled skin of our first crocodile. As we rounded a bend, it splashed into the water, the speed of a rat. We guessed its length at about five feet. Nervously we all bunched toward the center of the boat, though I couldn't help but feel it was like rearranging deck chairs on the *Titanic*. If the crocodile wanted to sink our craft, he could do so with a snap. But the crocodile never resurfaced, perhaps more scared of us than we of him. We wondered. I asked Lemma how we should deal with a crocodile about to clamp down on a body part. His useful reply was that I should stick a knife into the croc's mouth and cut its jaw's muscles. . . . "But you must be fast," he warned. I had also read that because the reptile's jaw muscles are basically one-directional, a quick-thinking person could hold the snappers closed with bare hands. A third method was explained in a book I was carrying in my ammo box, *Animal Kitabu*, by Jean-Pierre Hallet. He said that crocodiles cannot turn heads sideways because their cervical vertebrae bear bony ribs that stiffen and immobilize the neck. Crocodile jaws are forced to operate in a strictly horizontal plane, and thus if a man can remain in a vertical position, he is, theoretically, in no danger. Jean-Pierre said he tested this theory once on Lake Tanganyika when a misfired dynamite blast threw him out of his boat, taking off his hand and severely lacerating his face. Not one to panic, Jean-Pierre—when he saw seven giant crocodiles speeding towards him—assumed a vertical position and did a one-handed dog paddle one hundred feet to shore. All the thwarted crocodiles could do was snap in vain, and occasionally sample bits of Hallet's shirt.

As we continued down the Awash, we sighted about a hundred crocodiles, some measuring up to twelve feet long, but all reacting in the same swift, nervous manner, without attacking or even charging us. Perhaps naming our exercise Sobek worked.

Under the ruddy light of pre-evening, we strained oars to pull into an eddy halfway down a passage filled with pointy rocks radiating water like fans. At the bottom of the run stretched some small, shale ledges. The ancestral fear of wild animals had us seek a safeguarded place to camp. The rapid, we figured, would offer protection from crocodiles, and with boulders walling in much of the camp, we had only to defend one side. But once the gear was unloaded, Ifru pointed out we were adjacent to a game trail. With that information, Ifru and Lemma began building a witch-burner fire, but one strategically placed so as not to illumine any sleeping figures on whom a Danakil could draw a bead. "They are bad people," Lemma explained, "who shoot first and use their knives afterwards."

Because we were just nine degrees north of the equator, the night fell like a guillotine at six. The stars trembled in the black, clean sky, undimmed by clouds or city lights. There was a rattle of breezes in the thorn trees. The crackling howls of hyenas, the eerie yelps of jackals, and the grumbling of other animals came out of the surrounding forests at disturbing intervals. Lions and other cats have been known

First descent of the Awash River, Ethiopia, 1973. Lew Greenwald in bow; Richard rowing.
JOHN KRAMER

to attack campers at night, but hyenas are the only animals that attack regularly. At park headquarters we had been told of some recent tourists who slept out in the open without a fire, and they were found the following morning with their faces chewed off.

Just as we sheathed into our sleeping bags, we heard a rustling just beyond the camp perimeter. I turned on my flashlight, swept the beam around, and caught the reflection of a spotted hyena's eyes thirty feet away. His was a loping, ghostly form, and his insane, windblown laughter sounded like some demoniac convocation of witches and sent a shiver down my spine. His marble eyes, chuckling and cunning, were devoid of innocence—no innocent creature survives along this river. I suggested we alternate vigils, volunteered for the first watch, and stoked the fire. The smoke of doom seemed to drift like a deadly gas all night.

I awoke at the crack of noon. It was 6:00 a.m. on my watch, but Ethiopia uses a clock that is six hours later than our own, which makes sense because a new day begins at dawn, rather than when one goes to bed.

Faces intact, we made breakfast, and each popped our once-a-week-on-Sunday malaria pill, a two-hundred-milligram prophylaxis tablet that would keep the sporo-zoan parasites from the bites of anopheline mosquitoes inactive. Then we loaded the rafts and spun downstream. We were scarcely an hour out of camp when we spied on the bank a young man leading a camel. A thin strip of leather was tied across his fore-head and back into his bushy hair. On his narrow hips rested a curved, double-edged knife as broad as a hand and almost as long as a sword. Over his shoulders rested a long, ancient rifle, supporting both hands. He was a Danakil.

From all the varied information and misinformation we received in Addis Ababa, one fact emerged without dispute: We would be traveling through the cruel heart of Danakil country. Ethiopia is a land of many nations, some of which pay no more than token allegiance to the government. We were in one of those places. The Danakils are traditionally a warrior people and place a different value on human life than most—especially a stranger's. In fact, for centuries, to kill a man was a prerequisite for social status.

Particularly disturbing was the manhood rite we were told was still practiced. When a man reaches marriageable age, he must leave his village on a quest to prove his worthiness. He cannot return until he brings with him the testicles of a member of an enemy tribe or a *ferenji*. We, like all foreigners, were *ferenjis*.

Wilfred Thesiger wrote of the cult of murder among the Danakil: "A Danakil man's prowess is rated by the number of 'kills' of other men. Naturally, proof of these kills is required, so the hunter castrates his victims, sometimes while still alive."

Even more alarming was that we had been told this was the marrying season, and that those on the hunt wore headbands, such as the one sported by the man on shore. We had few options, as the current swung us closer to the fuzzy-haired nomad. We could posture aggression, position my rifle with its plastic stock, but his was a more powerful-looking weapon, and he looked more experienced. We could ignore him, looking the other way. Instead, we all pulled out our harmonicas and began playing a lively rendition of the Marlboro theme song, slapping thighs in rhythm, trying to look happy and carefree. With insolent eyes he watched our antics. Then, just as we slid past his perch, he broke into a smile white as bleached bone and raised his hand to wave.

For lunch we stopped at a grove of tamarind and sycamore fig trees crowded with silky-furred colobus, barking like frogs and making acrobatic leaps among the bearded branches. The smell of sulfur assaulted my nostrils, and back from the river there was a sharp-edged wall, broken by scooped-out cavities and curves, down which a small waterfall trickled. The rock around the falls was dull red, like burnt brick, splotched with sulfurous yellow and faded, weathered brown. The wall looked unfinished, like an interrupted explosion. We walked back into the woods above the cliff to investigate. There we found a small mineral hot springs. An acacia spread across its dark pool. It's rough foliage, structured in horizontal layers, was unlike any tree I'd seen in America. Its formation gave it a heroic air, like a full-rigged ship with sails clewed up.

The acacia seemed so ancient it would have been easy to believe it had stood there for hundreds, perhaps thousands, of years. Around the springs were various offerings—a jar of oil, a heap of millet, a white, plastic button, curls of wire, small piles of roasted coffee beans. In their own way these oblations contributed to the peculiar character of the place: eerie, but by no means menacing. I shivered, feeling goose bumps for the first time in Africa.

What multiplied this otherworldly effect, however, was the fact that every branch of the tree to a height of about six feet off the ground had been festooned with woven strips of varicolored cloth and string. Rustling in the wind, these waving pennants and ribbons seemed to whisper and murmur, as though seeking to impart a message. We touched the living wood, sensed its age, and then, even though it was more than one hundred degrees in the shade, we stripped and slipped into the hot springs for some sort of sanctification bath.

After lunch, the sun unleashed its full power. It felt like we were rowing wrapped in hot towels. The air burned our throats like a poultice of broken glass. It felt like Hell. The effect was heightened by the presence of rows of marabou storks, some hooked around dead branches that looked like gibbets. With their bald red heads, dandy gray feathers edged in white, fleshy pink necks, rattling bills, and wings folded to an oval, they looked like undertakers in morning coats. They evoked an air of irredeemable depravity as one group gravely pecked at an unidentifiable carcass. But our infernal passage was forgotten with the next attraction.

We heard the splashing and shouting long before we saw "Maytag" beach. The town of Awash Station was nearby, and this was the municipal watering and wash-ing hole. Awash Station was the contact point between the desert nomads, Afars and Issas, and the Amhara highlanders, between Muhammadism and Christianity. This was a border few crossed with impunity. When the desert dwellers ventured to higher ground, their camels would die, and they would soon lose heart in the fearful cold. When the Amhara came down into the desert, his mules collapsed in the appalling heat, and he was soon driven back into the hills for lack of water. It is a conflict point between two absolutely separate ways of life. Only the river bound these opposing worlds together. And only the raft bound our two guides, Lemma and Ifru. Lemma, thin, lively, good-looking with light coffee skin, was a Christian Amharic, and he exuded a certain hubris that came with his highland blood and a religious tradition that dated back well more than two thousand years. Ifru came from the desert, was a Muslim with skin so dark it absorbed my camera flash. Yet, while working together to get our boats downstream, their differences disappeared, and the common goal erased all borders.

We couldn't have guessed at the reception, or at the numbers of people, clothes, fishing lines, camels, goats, cows, and donkeys we would pass. At least three hundred people were working, milling, playing along the shore. Bare-breasted women were slapping brightly colored cotton clothes on the rocks; others were filling goatskin water bags and then carrying them on their heads with perfect posture back to the village. Swart, butter-groomed men with rifles slung across shoulders surveyed the scene like room proctors from the upper beach. Children were bathing, splashing, giggling. Teenage girls were dressing each other's hair in multitudinous tiny plaits.

The boys spotted us first and hit the water from every direction and began swimming our way, yelling "Carmella! Carmella! (candy)." I cranked my rowing into a higher gear as we watched the armada of thrashing, naked swimmers get closer. "This ain't no Disneyland," Lew observed with a crinkly smile.

Awash River: Richard on harmonica; Lew rowing. GEORGE FULLER

Fortunately, a Class III rapid intervened and kept the swimmers at bay as we rounded a bend and left the human chaos behind.

Now all we heard was the rush of the river. We turned another corner and surprised the stateliest of antelope, the greater kudu, with its long spiral horns and distinctive white body stripes. Another turn and we spilled into a curvy, narrow, steep-walled canyon, which we dubbed "The Labyrinth." The river branched and brachiated, boiled into dusty eddies and side currents. Right-angle turns in the tight main channel caused us to collide with walls, glance off, and gyre down the maze. It formed a plexus of waterways so confusing it could never be mapped. Like billiard balls on a ten-cushion shot, we bounced through.

After the mitotic expansion of The Labyrinth, the river began to flow easily for some time, which was fine with us, as we were approaching the Awash Station Bridge and hoped to slip beneath it as unobtrusively as possible. It was here the young Wilfred Thesiger in 1930 did some spying for the British government, and a letter to his mother let the cat from the bag, "I am rather busy at the minute finding out about possible landing grounds, food, etc. for the air force. I have got to be rather discreet as the Abyssinians are not to know." Five years later the Italians invaded Abyssinia and blew up the Awash Station Bridge.

So it was with some justification there was a certain paranoia that existed around this reconstructed bridge. The reign of Emperor Haile Selassie I, King of Kings, the Negus Negesti, Elect of God, Conquering Lion of the Tribe of Judah, had not been without incident. Rebel groups had formed, had attempted assassinations, and had tried to take strategic sectors of the empire, including bridges. Haile Selassie was a strong-armed ruler, though, and had successfully snuffed out all insurgent attempts to this point. One way he had done this was by stationing armed guards at all bridges, at all times. We did not want to incur the wrath, or even provoke the curiosity, of the guards on the Awash Station Bridge.

Our goal was to silently glide beneath the girders and slip around the bend unnoticed. Just above the bridge, however, Tom's oar caught a rock in a trifling rapid. The rope holding the oar to the lock snapped, and he struggled to negotiate the boat with the single oar. There was no time to stop to try to fix the oar; he had to keep going. But the single-oar maneuver put the raft into a spin, and it struck several rocks, sending noisy splashes into the air, and the commotion caught the attention of two armed guards on the bridge. They waved their rifles wildly at us and shouted abruptly, clearly wanting us to stop. Instead, we picked up the pace, spun beneath the bridge, and began a dash for the next turn of the canyon. The guards ran across the bridge and then along the canyon rim chasing us, making threatening gestures. The swift water and tight rocky channels were making it tough for Tom to maneuver, but he kept his head low and kept pulling his one oar, bouncing off the big rocks at just the right angles so the raft would miss the smaller ones that could catch and hold it, which would give our pursuers the extra minutes needed to overtake us.

Finally, we outdistanced them and rounded a bend that put them out of sight. The water was calmer now. We had entered what we would name Warthog Canyon. As we drifted along, Tom repairing the oarlock, we surprised a convocation of warthogs. They seemed to be sniffing something on the north shore, but when they saw us, they shot their fly-swatter tails straight into the air and scrabbled away in line with neat small steps. We pulled over to see what had brought them to the bank, and there we found the carcass of the warthog, dried to a veiled vellum, which had taken the fall off the canyon rim a week before during our scout. Its ten-inch tusks curled into the gravel, and bouquets of flies buzzed its rotting flesh, and maggots negotiated its sticky, dried blood. Were the other hogs grieving, scavenging, poking about in curiosity, or some unidentified behavior? Unlike the big-eyed primates that attract researchers and funding, the warthogs, so ugly by our standards, have never had a Jane Goodall or Dian Fossey to devote long-term study and analyze behavior, so what they do and how they act in the wild is still a mystery.

A few hours later the walls tapered back, the valley through which we sailed wrinkled into dry ridges, like a badly healed cicatrix, and we entered a zone we would call "The Doldrums." The landscape became monotonous: mud banks, hard red termite mounds, trees with finger-size thorns, a sun-fried furnace under a bleached sky. Dust devils whirled like great columns of smoke. The river accelerated from inertia to paralysis, and the boats seemed to hang motionless on the water like junks in a Chinese painting. We could shut our eyes for an hour and when opened see exactly what we saw before. Not only were there no signs of life or current, there was also the smell of death in the air. Spaced along regular intervals were the carcasses of dozens of wild and domesticated animals snared in the broken branches of countless logjams that clogged this section of the river. The hot sun scooped up the smell and spread it like a thin mist.

We were seeing the results of a drought that had been gripping parts of Ethiopia for years; one the outside world knew little about, as Haile Selassie had done his best to conceal it for fear of international repercussions. He was a wealthy emperor, with huge land ownings and Swiss bank accounts, and the world might not understand if he continued to wrap himself in opulence while thousands of his subjects were dying in drought.

For days we were never able to get our backs into the oars before we had to stop for a tree blocking the way. Most of these, we could see, had been chopped down, likely by local herders to bring the buds and green tree stems to their hungry livestock and camels to feed. This was one obstacle even our perfervid imaginations never anticipated.

While negotiating The Doldrums the chief excitement was listening to the soft threnody of the emerald-spotted wood dove and watching black kites float without moving their wings in the currents above. Even the crocodiles didn't oblige us with a scare. The river's dry banks jeered at us, grinning through mustaches of driftwood left from long-ago high water. We prayed for the long-overdue short rains. We couldn't go for a swim to cool off for two very good reasons: It took just one crocodile sneaking up from below, and there was the distinct possibility of schistosomiasis, or bilharzia, a fatal snail-borne disease found in slow-moving tropical waters. George Fuller, who in his capacity as a pathobiologist was studying schistosomiasis distribution for Haile Selassie I University, had brought collecting nets on the trip and had in fact scooped up some vector-carrying mollusks in this section, and he accordingly announced we should avoid even the briefest contact with the water (it takes only a few seconds of exposure to contract the disease).

For four days we strained bodies and oars through this snaking trench, the river surface flat as a griddle, hoping each bend would be the last, watching the right bank like hawks to be sure we wouldn't miss the little stone schoolhouse that meant we reached our first target destination—Gewani. Yet all we ever found was another bend, and more camel flies. Then the current died completely, petered out in a haze of heat, as though dammed or confined in some way farther down, and we were deprived the luxury of drift. Along the banks shards of dead branches stuck out in frantic directions like bones broken through skin. Dead leaves bobbed motionless on the water as oars clumped against the frames, rhythmic and dull. Something seemed wrong. Did the river just dead-end? I knew the river eventually emptied into the briny waters of endorheic Lake Abbe in the Danakil Depression, 380 feet below sea level. Lake Abbe was the ultimate goal. Even though our maps had lost their grip, they showed this lake to be two hundred miles away. Wherever we were, the river here certainly wasn't going anywhere . . . it had simply stopped running.

CHAPTER 16

THE TESTICULAR TROPHY HUNTERS OF ETHIOPIA

You only live twice. Once when you're born, once when you look death in the face.
—IAN FLEMING

WE ALL FELT THE CHARGED AND SUSPENDED AIR. SUDDENLY WE HEARD A SOFT roar and scanned the distant river line for the telltale signs of a cataract—smooth approach water, the occasional tossed spume, and the perceptible fall in the tree line on either side. The water beneath our boats began to agitate almost imperceptibly; delicate swirls appeared on the surface as if traced by a feather. Then they multiplied, and cut deeper, and the sound came on. This was more than a rapid. This was the deep-throated thunder of a waterfall. We moored at the top of the falls and ran ahead to see what we could hear. Starved for excitement over the past days of "Sargasso River," there was a flickering of hope in all our minds that we would be able to run it. The falls took a sheer fifteen-foot drop across the entire river, except for a rock-scattered ledge that descended diagonally down the escarpment on the right side. If we attempted it, it would be the biggest falls any of us had ever run, with a likely capsize outcome. But the botfly of boredom had been buzzing our boats, so we were ready to try anything.

We would have to enter dead-on, going as fast as possible, with all our weight in the back. We wanted to shoot the bow out into the air as far as possible to avoid an end-over-end flip. The approach, unfortunately, was narrow and rocky. We decided to ship the oars and use the paddles to get through, as a bad oar stroke could catch a crab and turn us sideways on the brink.

We lined up above the target channel when a precious moment was lost to indecision.

"To the left of that round one?" Kramer asked, pointing at a nubbin-rock near the lip.

"No, to the right," George answered.

"To the left," I screamed.

My paddle cracked against a rock; we started to pivot sideways. "Straighten us out!" I cried.

Too late. The raft hung sideways on the brink of the falls for a long instant. Time seeped like syrup as the boat started to tilt. We were capsizing, sideways. I looked below and tried to scout the rapids into which we were about to tumble. I thought of holding on in hopes my weight might right the boat. But it was futile. In a flash we were over the edge. George Fuller, on the other side of the boat, directly below me, was framed in the foam at the foot of the falls, his face the look of a puzzled sheep. We landed softly enough as the boat plowed underwater on one side and folded lengthwise to absorb the shock. I pushed myself off the raft while it was still falling, but it was directly above me now. I was suddenly underwater. A muffled explosion echoed above me.

"I've got to get clear," I thought to myself, recalling tales of drowned boatmen on the Colorado caught beneath rafts.

I felt the blow of tons of water thudding down on my head. I thrashed a few desperate strokes toward the direction I hoped was up and suddenly found myself gasping those first precious breaths of air. Looking back, I saw the slamming cascades of the falls not ten feet behind me. But I saw no sign of Kramer and George. Were they knocked out? Swept downstream? Caught beneath the raft? First George broke the surface, sucked in air, breathing like a bus. Then Kramer was vomited up in a whirl of whitewater. We each struggled to shore. The upside-down raft spun into an eddy, and there, with the entire crew, we righted it. Nothing lost; just a layer of grit, and pride.

There was no time to rehash the run over the falls. The sun was setting, and we had to find a campsite. As fast as we could, we carried the other raft around the falls and then relaunched. Below us were three smaller falls, which we maneuvered uneventfully, and then we pulled into a pleasant-looking spot for camp. We had just begun to unload the first of our gear when I glanced up. What I saw made me drop the bag I had just been handed. It was a graveyard silhouette of two men with rifles and long knives. They were unmistakably Danakils, wearing the telltale headbands, indicating they were out to prove their manhood by stealing someone else's. We quickly reloaded the boats and pushed back into the current. The tribesmen followed us along the shore, ululating and waving their weapons. After a couple miles we lost sight of them and came to a booming rapid we didn't want to run in the fading light. So we pulled over, with intent to camp, but first we scouted the long, steep rapid with flashlights, trying to memorize the run, just in case we might have to abandon the site in the middle of the night.

That night, we did our cooking on a Gaz stove, ignoring the multiform firewood on the shingle beach. While other nights we built huge fires to keep the wildlife at bay, here we figured it might act as a beacon to Danakil testicular trophy hunters. This time I volunteered for the last shift, so I quickly slipped into my bag after our dinner of fried tuna and cheese and tried to force sleep. But the étude of the African night was too loud. Insects, birds, and monkeys screeching in the most bloodcurdling manner kept me awake, or so I thought. Kramer shook me awake as the gibbous moon began to set. I wrapped my sleeping bag over my shoulders, sat cross-legged with the .30-06 across my lap, and hummed Beatles songs to keep me awake. I was aware of the faint effulgence shed by the clusters of stars and the moon, and I could just make out the silhouettes of wild animals at our perimeter. But I would blink, and see they were bushes and trees. The long, lonely hours with the barrel barely glinting in the bright starlight gave me time to reflect on what I would do if attacked. I had gone on a white-tailed deer hunt once but never saw one, just a pair of antlers on a trail, which I brought home as my trophy. Now I wondered if I could pull the trigger on a human.

The cool streaks of dawn nudged me awake. I had fallen asleep on the job, but we were no worse for my failing, and nobody seemed to hold it against me, if they even knew, and I didn't volunteer. We didn't dally, though, especially when Ifru noticed a deeply rutted camel track to the river adjacent to camp . . . he figured this was a watering hole, and drivers and guards would be here with the sun.

We didn't float far before encountering a small boy, perhaps ten years old, with a camel on the bank. He waved us over with a frantic gesture. "Don't go," George said sternly, "it could be a trap." But as we hied by it looked as though the boy was in pain, and he pointed at his eye. "Let's take a look," Lew suggested. . . . "He's just a boy." So I turned my raft in and beached at the feet of the boy. We all got out and the boy pointed to a suppurating right eye, which had the beginnings of a yellow film and gobs of mucus dripping down his cheek. George was our trip doctor, and we asked what we might do, and George looked at the eye and pronounced it beyond saving. "Can't we do anything?" I implored.

"No . . . and what's the use? If we give him something it will run out and he'll be back where he was. And the others who are sick in the village will give him an unfounded higher status if he gets medicine from *ferenjis* . . . it's akin to begging . . . it will encourage all of them. In Calcutta, some parents cut off the limbs of their children because they make better beggars. It's a slippery slope if we give out medicine randomly. I say we just keep going."

It all seemed well articulated to me, and I began to wrap up the bowline. But as I was readying to push off, Lew snapped open his ammo box, pulled out a small tube of infection medicine, and handed it to the boy, who bowed deeply several times in gratitude. "I don't care about George's rationalizations . . . if I see someone who needs help, I will help." With that George and Lew climbed on different rafts, and we pulled into the current.

By this time, the drudgery of slogging through the blazing "Sargasso" stretch was forgotten, and we welcomed the rest a short section of flat water afforded. We didn't relax long, though, before discovering the cause of the laggard water: immense strands of lava, twisted like cordage, wrapped around a tremendous blob of basalt, damming the river. A nearby volcano had erupted millions of years ago, and a molten hunk the size of a city block landed in this spot, causing the river to go mad and making our passage a bit of a dilemma. Here the water entered a dark warren of waterways, honeycombs of falls, secret passages, and channels that went in circles. Half the water escaped into hidden catacombs; we could get a boat into this mess without much problem, but we would never be able to get it back out again . . . a Hotel California: We could check out, but we could never leave.

We had reached the beginning of the most hated remit of all river runners: the long portage. This was to be a hot, joyless, backbreaking task. As we lugged our equipment the half mile around the grotesque formation, there was no smiling as we passed one another coming and going. We began by hauling the lighter stuff, the fifty-pound food bags and water-saturated clothing duffels, dragging them over unavoidable barriers and down the steep final drop that stepped to the river. Then we hoisted the boats onto our raw, sweat-soaked shoulders and stumbled through the scoriae, balancing precariously as we alternately dropped into dry sinkholes and stepped over crusty crags. There were moments when each of us stepped into a hollow, and the weight was momentarily carried by the others; worse was when one of us stepped up while everyone else went down, and the entire two hundred pounds was suddenly on a single neck. One slip would be a broken neck or leg, or a crushed skull. Six hours after we began, we had the boats back in the water, fully dressed. We had been lucky . . . our only casualties were one severe headache (Lemma's) and one badly wrenched neck (Kramer's).

We had traveled less than a mile on this, the eighth day, and wanted to take advantage of the smooth water ahead to make up lost time. Our friends in Addis were expecting us two days ago, and we had no idea how much longer it would take, not that we ever really did.

We had barely stoked the oars to cruising speed when we once again heard the liquid thunder. Just downstream the river went roaring over another fifteen-foot waterfall and landed in a pile of sharp rocks before falling twice more and coming to rest in a swirling pool. For a moment I thought there was a slim chance of making it, and I might have tried it, but for Lew, who in his unschooled wisdom looked at the maelstrom and said, "Jesus, a guy could get killed in there." The words were a reality check, and I backed down. I recognized that besides the objective dangers, after a day of grueling portaging in the desert heat, our reflexes were sluggish and there was a sort of woolliness in our minds. Judgment was probably not at peak levels.

My body felt like it had been used for batting practice, my mind numb, and my consuming desire was to finish our journey. So I called camp at the most dangerous spot yet—a watering hole right above the falls. There was no escaping downstream if visited in the night. We readied the rifle, axes, and knives, prepared a soul-strengthening dinner of lentils, chicken soup-cubes, canned fruit, and hot peppers with

Portage around the deadly waterfalls in the Awash Gorge.
GEORGE FULLER

at least 200,000 BTUs, and built a zareba of thorn bushes and hedges around the perimeter of the camp with various used food cans hanging from branches at intervals. Lemma and Ifru volunteered for an all-night vigil, despite Lemma's bad headache and what must have been exhaustion as severe as mine.

With the rifle neatly tucked into the bilge, I pillowed my head on my hands and tried to sleep in the boat, thinking I might protect our only means of transportation in a last-ditch effort. But just as I was drifting off, I heard the sound of crocodiles splashing and moved my feet closer to the middle of the raft. Knowing that just twenty-one inches of plastic tube was all that separated me from the water, I couldn't bring sleep, despite utter fatigue. In the middle of the night, I looked over to see Ifru and Lemma both fast asleep. I considered getting up, but exhaustion overcame anxiety, and I at last slipped into sleep. A hot snake of pain in my neck jolted me upright ... I had bent a muscle trying to use the raft tube as a pillow. I looked to shore. Lew was reheating the lentils; Lemma was stuffing a wetpack. The sky was purpling with the first thin cast of dawn.

"Lining" the boats, or lowering them down the falls on ropes, is easier than portaging. We decided we would line the boats at this juncture. The only question was how?

We considered a Tyrolean traverse that would extend diagonally from the island over the falls to the left bank. The British Army team had tried this on the 150-foot Tissisat Falls on the Blue Nile, only to have one of the boats get caught in the thrashing maelstrom for twenty-four hours. We considered belaying the boat from certain rock or tree anchor points. We finally decided that all plans had the same likelihood of failure as the simplest one of all: Kick the boats over the falls (with ropes tied to the bows) and pull them in below.

And that's what we did. We emptied the boats and carried the gear and provisions around the falls. We tied our goldline to one end of the first boat and uncoiled it out to Lew and Lemma waiting below the falls. Then Tom and I, with the bowline, positioned the boat atop the falls, anchored by a chrome-moly piton we had hammered into a crack. Then we pushed the first raft into the current. It hung up on a nubbin at the edge of the falls, a titled flange of rock with water sculpted over it in a long, forelocked curve that broke at us. This was a nasty spot we didn't particularly want to broach. While arguing options, a Danakil suddenly appeared, hair daubed with ghee, his snow-white teeth filed into points so they looked like fangs. He waded into the fast current to his waist and pushed our boat off the rock and over the falls. Lew and Lemma were able to pull the raft in like a big fish at just the right moment and paid the boat into a tiny chute free of rocks. The Danakil assisted with the second raft as well, then waded over to Lew, took his hand, and kissed the back of it. Lew bent over and returned the gesture. Then the lone Danakil stepped up the bank, strode across the hard-packed bank, and disappeared into a portable brushwood hut the size of an igloo. "He may be a murderer," Lew said and laughed, "but no one could call him inhospitable."

In the sweet liquid light of the African morning, we loaded the boats and set off to interrogate the river. The rapids were easy to run and consisted mostly of sharp fin waves with few rocks. These were the most pleasurable rapids run so far, and we were as giddy as the needle of a cheap compass. Lew suggested this would be a fitting end to the trip.

By midday, however, the sun had the weight of molten lead. The current quickened, and around one bend we were ripped into another pipeline. Dry wind in our faces, a buckle of noise in the air, mist kicking over the bow, down the Awash we sped. We dodged a small rock to the left, then a promontory on the right, and scraped a boulder in the center as the channel narrowed.

The river was now less than ten yards wide. The current roared down a funnel between two boulders. We were headed for something terrible, an arrow in flight. At the touch of the left bank, Lew leapt out into the air with bowline in hand. I pulled back on the oars as hard I could to try to slow us down. The only way we could stop before being hurled into the explorer's lacunae, that space between the known and

Takeout, Awash River, 1973. John Kramer, left with oar; George Fuller; Tom Cromer; Lew Greenwald; Lemma Tessema; Richard with oar; and Ifru Gabreyes. JOHN KRAMER

imagination, would be if Lew could arrest us from shore. But first Lew had to get past the slick and slimy moss coating the rocks at waterline. Lew slapped down one foot after another, running at full speed but losing ground to the frictionless surface beneath his feet. I could see him running even while his head disappeared into the muddy water. His dunking, though, didn't last but an instant. Propelled by fear, he lurched from the water, draped his whole body around a boulder, and used the added traction of pants and life jacket to embrace the shore. Lew established a beachhead and tied us in. The rope went taut. We stopped at the edge of oblivion: a thirty-foot waterfall that crashed into a rack of sharp rocks.

The portage around the falls took several hours, but we launched again in late afternoon. The rest of the day was spent charging down a river writ with lightning. Below one cataract, we spilled over to a rock patch, and I dipped my oar into a crack to hold the boat while I waited for Tom's raft to catch up. And while watching upstream, I felt the blade of my oar move in an unnatural way. I turned and jumped back at the sight . . . a rock python, maybe eight feet long, was slithering across the blade of my oar, up towards me like a train coming into a station. I grabbed the oar with both hands and shook it violently. The snake fell off, plopped into the water, and swam away.

As the hot red sunset burnt out the remnants of the day, we pulled the boats over to stop and bed down for a well-deserved night's sleep. As the rest of us were rolling out sleeping bags, George, ever energetic, donned a headlamp, slipped on his rubber collecting gloves, set out the castor oil plates, took out a mist net and aspirator, and began his nightly search for exotic insects and ectoparasites. Whenever he found something he liked, he would drop it into a tube filled with formalin solution or display it volant in a collection book. He alone was fulfilling our obligation to the Smithsonian, and it was his favorite part of the trip.

A pale dawn swallowed the ink of night. It was our tenth day on the river. Since we really expected to be out only six, we hadn't packed an excess of food and now were running short. However, there was no reason to fear going hungry. The fish in the Awash apparently had little experience with fishermen (who could ever get into these gorges?), and the only problem was that so many were breaking our 6-pound-test line as we hauled them up the cliff that we were losing most of our barbed hooks. One large fish I pulled in flopped about camp, whiskers spitting water, and I reached down to prevent it from flipping back in the river and was knocked back several feet, my hat flying off, as though I'd put my hand in an electric socket. It was an electric catfish. Nobody intervened as the fish wriggled to the edge of the cliff, plopped back into the river, and finned away. But the other fish, mostly Nile perch and tilapia (a bream-like fish), made for good eating.

We didn't have to go far before the next obstacle presented itself. Protruding rocks, like giant, black crooked shark teeth, shielded the entrance to a 500-foot gorge. By the simple expedient of standing still, these rocks dashed hopes of easy navigation. Beyond the rock jaws, we couldn't see a thing. Tying the boats to a crack in the wall, Tom, Kramer, and I scaled the cliff to a ledge from where we could see what needed to be done. The only way through was to turn the rafts on their sides and squeeze them through like toothpaste. With four of us standing on one entrance rock, three on the other, we tugged, nudged, yanked, dragged, crammed, and pinched the boats through.

Another mile and the canyon walls began to retreat. Lew ventured, "This looks like the end of the gorge." The last rapid was an easy pitch, and then the Awash took its foot off the accelerator, never to speed again.

The following afternoon we drifted to the Gewani Peace Corps School. Lew, in best Al Jolson imitation, broke into song: "Gewani, how I love ya; how I love ya, my dear old Gewani." We pulled in and were greeted by two men from the nearby Trapp Construction Company, who had flown over us that morning and calculated our arrival time. They took some photos and treated us to an ice-cooler full of beer, Fanta, and Ambo, Ethiopia's own sparkling mineral water.

As we posed for a final shot, holding an oar between us, Lew smiled expansively and said, "We made it! Two hundred and forty virgin river miles in eleven days. That's history, man!" It was a full hundred years after Stanley had found Livingstone, and I felt like a pioneer. I reached over and held the heels of my hands together, the fingertips yawed wide like the open rictus of a crocodile. Lew looked at my gesture and then winked and slipped his hands between mine to work the Sobek handshake. We each then went to the others and performed our ritual. We'd done it.

We were in the Danakil Depression, the lowest plug in Africa. But we did not make it all the way down the river, to the terminus lake with no outlet, Lake Abbe, which spreads its alkaline waters across the border into the French Territory of the Afars and Issas, which would become Djibouti a few years hence. Its landscape is so phantasmagoric it was featured in *Planet of the Apes*. We were just short of Lake Abbe, so our expedition left incomplete. Someday, I vowed, I would make it to Lake Abbe and finish what the first Sobek expedition set out to do.

CHAPTER 17

MONSTER BITES BOAT

An appeaser is one who feeds a crocodile, hoping it will eat him last.
—Winston Churchill

Back in Addis, we reveled in our success. I gave a slide show to a packed house at the USIA (United States Information Agency) center, and the embassy threw a party in our honor. I appeared on Ethiopian TV, my first time on camera, and I felt like Henry Morton Stanley as a guest on Johnny Carson. I traded in my torn cutoffs for a new pair of khaki shorts and strutted like an explorer. Four weeks later, still basking in the shine of our successful Awash expedition, it was time to get back on a river. As we went over the list of possibilities, we decided on the Omo, as we felt emboldened and a bit competitive. Why not beat National Geographic to the River Trip of the Century?

On April 24 we piled into the back of a long-bed truck with high, vertically slatted wood sides, the sort used for hauling animals to the abattoir. We bounced four hours down a rough gravel road south to the Jimma Bridge at the village of Abelti, the put-in for our Omo expedition. At noon we were unceremoniously deposited along with our two rafts and nine wet bags at the upstream side of the bridge. And without so much as a farewell honk, the truck drove off. Kramer was no longer with us; he had had enough of the company of men and was anxious to get back to his girlfriend. Ifru was no longer part of our party either, as nobody spoke his languages where we were going. That left Tom Cromer, Lew Greenwald, Lemma, George Fuller, and myself. To the group we added Diane Fuller and Tadessa Wolde Gossa, who had been on the British Blue Nile expedition and was much lauded as a team member.

Late April was just after the "little rains," and the water swirling between two steep hillsides was more creek than river. A couple of herders drove a dozen dusky lyre-horned cattle to the water's edge as we pumped our rafts. Late afternoon the rafts were rigged and loaded, and we shoved off into the swift current, three months ahead of the scheduled Ron Smith–National Geographic "First Descent." The river here, called the Gibe, caught and sped us along beneath the arching spans of the bridge, where a dozen spectators stared as though watching the condemned on the way to an execution. In a couple minutes we passed around a sharp bend marked by a molar-shaped volcanic plug, looking like a big "thumbs-up." The bridge and people disappeared . . . we were committed to a bigger, longer river than the Awash, one that truly flowed into a heart of darkness.

Three miles downriver the Gibe merged with the Omo, and the combined stream took on the latter name. The hills rose steeply on either side and soon became cliffs, the cliffs formed themselves into precipitous gorges of columnar basalt, and we were dropping deeper and deeper into the Omo canyon. In a few days we found ourselves at the bottom of a magnificent 4,000-foot gorge, and the river was littered with boulders, so much so we spent much of our time wrestling the rafts through rock gardens. Radiating out from the main canyon, though, were an increasing number of tributary streams, and each one added a little bit of water to the mother river and made floating easier. Much of our time was given to exploring these smaller canyons, hiking back through tangled undergrowth, along well-trodden hippo trails, up rushing streams that sang to themselves among the stones. There were waterfalls, some plunging more than a thousand feet, the crooked wind catching the flow and blowing great billows of mist over the forest below. At one such falls I climbed to its lip alone and gazed down on a landscape that might have been seen from an airplane. The river slipped illimitably between narrow cliffs. Some of the plains looked manicured, so meticulously had they been mowed by the mouths of munching hippos. And the green hills rolled like surf into a distance where they turned purple. I felt certain no human had ever gazed upon this scene. I couldn't resist the moment, and I sat down on the lip, legs dangling over a thousand-foot drop, and broke out into song: "I'm sittin' on top of the world . . ." The off-key performance echoed up the canyon, warbling back and forth across the boundary between fettered human and feral beast.

As we explored, we found emerald grottos dripping with velvet mosses and delicate ferns, still, deep pools, perfect for swimming, with rocky perches to one side for diving, and ideal chutes for watersliding like otters. Hours were spent in steamy hot springs, body-size basins carved from the rock, beveled and polished smooth as bathtubs. At one point I shared an unsuppressed feeling with Lew, one of superiority that comes from moving fast through a pristine wilderness. Because the river appeared so devoid of people, it was easy to imagine that whatever I saw belonged to me. Who else would want it? Simply by traveling so far, did I not have some special claim? Lew let out a great gout of laughter. . . . "You don't own the river; it owns us. It decides what we see and feel, whether we're in awe or dread, whether we live or die. For now, it likes us."

The first few days our most constant companions were the brown-haired Anubis baboons. Frequently, troops of thirty to fifty baboons would race ahead along the river's edge. Some were mothers with tiny babies clinging precariously to their backs. At a specific call, they would all dart into the security of the trees while their pack leader assumed an exposed position atop a rock, barking fearlessly at us as we glided by.

The goat-horned bushbucks, duikers, and dik-diks were all new notches in a burgeoning career of wildlife encounters. One day I swung the boat beneath some overhanging tamarinds, and a three-foot monitor lizard dropped into my bilge . . . at first, I thought it was a crocodile and made quick-time for the gunwale, ready to dive into the river, but the lizard beat me to it.

But the biggest kicks, literally, were the hippos. Our first encounter with the ponderous quadruped was innocuous: We spotted a pair of beady eyes and wiggling ears sticking out of the water. A few miles later we watched one stroll along the far shore. He walked with elevated deportment, shifting his weight as though he had weak ankles, a great pig with an enormous head and a long-upturned smile. Seeing our rafts, he slipped into the river, opening his mouth to an incredible forty-five degrees, the angle of his jaw starting just behind his eye. Then, on the fourth day, I was sawing my oars through a rocky rapid when my left blade struck a gray rounded boulder . . . and to my shock, it stood up, and with a crooked grin and pink tail spinning, it waddled downstream.

About five feet tall, weighing in at about five tons, about the same as two Land Rovers, hippos are proportionately the fattest animals on earth. And the hippopotamuses were by far the most abundant form of wildlife along the Omo. In the cooler hours of the day, we often surprised them ashore feeding on the greensward or simply sunning on the beach, and they would react to our sight by stampeding into the river, creating a small tidal wave that would rock the boats. During the heat of the day, they wallowed at the bottom of the river and would constantly bob up out of the water, catch a fast breath and snort at our passing fleet, and then dive back under the river's dark lid. Because the river was so silt-laden and murky, the hippos could not see well when submerged and never really knew where they would surface. More than once the clouds got closer, and my stomach sank deeper as an unsuspecting hippo surfaced under my boat and temporarily changed my altitude by several inches. Bolder ones would often stay above water and perform for us, aquatic prima donnas, bulky ballerinas, diving and leaping like the frilly pink-tutued dancers in Disney's *Fantasia*.

As we sank deeper into the Omo canyons, the hippo population increased to the point where crowds constituted a navigational hazard. Sometimes a score would pave the Omo like giant pink stones. One lardy lady rose from the waters about two feet from my gunwale, clacking jaws like an industrial steam shovel. I reacted by stabbing my oar down her throat, a giant tongue depressor, and she plopped back underwater, leaving a thundering silence. On the day of our greatest count . . . we dodged 375 hippos in a twenty-mile stretch and collided with four . . . it was like maneuvering through a sea of land mines. Cries of "Hippos right!" or "Hippo left!" rang out every few minutes all day long. From then on, we learned to run the gauntlet, carefully hugging first one bank, then the other, always keeping to the shallowest water, where best to see a submerged river horse.

On shore the hippos had a nasty habit of spinning their tails while scattering dung to stake out private territory. On a couple occasions we watched two hippos in disagreement dueling with each other, back-to-back, using the same far-flung technique. Often there was dung sowed around our campsites, and sometimes we would stake out our own territory as a disincentive to midnight contentions.

Afternoons on the river were hot affairs. Sunlight, reflecting off the water, skip-bombed our eyes. We all wore long pants and shirts, not because of fear of too much sun, but fear of the tsetse flies. Tsetse flies, with their sinister whizzing, dive-bombed into their human targets, hypodermic snouts boring through shirts, pants, even sneakers, sucking our blood with no regard for insect repellent. Though no humans lived in this part of the gorge, it was not because of sleeping sickness . . . it was that these flies carried disease fatal to cattle. "The tsetse fly," George proclaimed, "is the savior of the African wilderness." "But this is a rich valley. People are starving in the north. Wouldn't it make sense to eradicate the tsetse, and let people move here?" "No way," George countered, "there are too many people already and not enough wilderness," and he pulled his raft away.

Halfway down the river we came to a place where the hills jostled each other to the water's edge, and spanning the river was a Bailey bridge, a bizarre edifice as the road on the western side wound up to the village of Soddu, while there was nothing but a cul-de-sac on the eastern side. Here Tom, Tadessa, and Lemma decided to leave the trip. It was the last marked exit point on the river, and the hippos, the heat, the rapids, the portages had taken their toll. We gave them a compass, a Chinese flashlight, some first-aid goods and money, and made our adieux as they clattered across the wooden planks and headed up the hill. That left four of us: George and Diane Fuller in one raft; Lew Greenwald and me in the other. We were heading down the vein of darkness. We weren't even certain of the takeout. We had food for two more weeks and a map that showed the Mui Game Reserve off the eastern bank near the Kenyan border.

Below the Soddu Bridge the crocodile population increased to frightful numbers, but they generally proved elusive and difficult to photograph. Sometimes we would catch a blur as one scrambled down a bank, its long jaw slightly agape as it vanished into the water. Usually, we spotted them floating in the brown waters, pairs of turreted eyes and long nubbined noses, armored backs showing, looking like harmless waterlogged pieces of driftwood. Most were leery of our little flotilla, and as soon as they'd sense our presence they would dive underwater, where they could hold breaths for up to an hour. Some bolder ones would resurface for a second glimpse, checking out dinner possibilities, and of course these gourmands were the biggest, with the beadiest eyes and the yellowest teeth. Their diet consisted mainly of catfish and Nile perch, but they loved the occasional antelope or bird, and a human was a special treat. Since most of their catches occurred at the eddy line below rapids, they hung out there in big numbers, making the incentive to stay in the raft during a rapid all that much greater. Often when we spilled into the eddy below a rapid, a croc or two would charge the boat with motorboat speed. To deter the charging crocs, we used the modern method tried and tested by the British Army on the Blue Nile: We shouted obscenities and threw rocks at the approaching heads.

On day fifteen we were feeling seasoned, accustomed to sharing the river with the crocodiles. There was a subtlety in the predators that defied description and eluded cameras, a capacity to move without exciting attention, a wraithlike quality of unobtrusiveness. Most crocs dove as soon as we'd make a peep, and as we wanted to get some photo documentation of the crocs, we decided to withhold shouts and croc rocks until the last second so we could get some movie footage.

George was our cinematographer with his Super-8 camera, and he was grinding happily away as a fifteen-foot croc slipped off the bank and started steaming towards George's hippo-gray raft. Water skimmed off his snout like spray off the bow of a speedboat. George desperately tried to focus. Twenty feet. George steadied himself in the raft, tightened the grip on his camera. Ten feet. George could see the syrupy eyes and the acid-yellow teeth. Five feet.

George saw the fleshy yellow lining of a crocodile's throat filling the entire viewfinder. *Wham!* George came back to reality to find the thirty-six sharp teeth on each jaw wrapping around the deflating tube of his boat. Cursing, George jumped to the oars and started rowing downstream as fast as he could to prevent a half-ton of carnivorous vengeance from climbing on board.

Lew and I were upstream and turned when we heard George shouting. I started rowing as hard as I could to catch up, but George was practically hydroplaning, dragging the leviathan like a water-skier, and I couldn't make headway. Over my shoulder I watched as Diane leapt to the bow of the boat and started beating the bewildered croc on the head with a metal bailing bucket. Crocodiles have unidirectional jaws; they can slam their jaws shut like an iron trap, but almost any pressure can prevent their opening them. The croc's teeth were stuck in the fabric of the boat, so it couldn't release, and it began shaking the raft back and forth like a dog with a rag. George rowed faster, and even though he was dragging several hundred pounds of crocodile, he set a new world-rowing-speed record and left me in his wake. After a seeming eternity, perhaps ten long minutes, the dragon finally broke free and disappeared into the river's Cimmerian depths, still hungry, and perhaps shedding crocodile tears. The front section of George's boat was reduced to a shriveled blob. When Lew and I caught up, George was still cursing. Not because of the narrow escape, or the punctured raft. George was livid because he missed the shot.

Although baboons, hippos, and crocs were our most constant companions, they were not the only ones. We passed vervet and colobus monkeys, rock hyraxes, defessa waterbuck, wild dogs, hyenas, warthogs, and klipspringers. May was a good time for game viewing, dry in the highlands, and animals sought the water of the river. There are about 830 distinct species of birds in Ethiopia, a couple dozen unique to the country, and we identified a good number. We saw sacred and hadada ibises (with their hilarious mocking cries), snowy egrets, yellow-billed storks, herons, bee-eaters as vivid blue as sapphires, bateleur eagles, malachite and giant kingfishers, a covey of plump blue and gray guinea fowl, masked weavers, and the African fish eagles, with their regal white breasts, tails, and heads. Egyptian geese were everywhere, and at every alarm, imagined or real, they would take flight, hissing and honking about the rafts with a proprietary air. We caught catfish and Blue Nile perch, and when one unidentifiable silver fish jumped into Lew's raft as he was negotiating a ripple, we had the tastiest dinner of the trip.

On the eighteenth day of the expedition, we sighted tidy fields of corn and sorghum on the west bank, nodding in a breeze, and a large needlelike dugout canoe hollowed from a tree moored at the bank. Then we sighted a half dozen hemispherical huts, dotted aimlessly like molehills on the bank . . . our first village. Several women who were winnowing grain stopped mid-toss, dropped their huge wicker trays, grabbed their children, and ran into to their windowless beehives. The men cautiously stepped down to greet us. Regal in simple robes of beaten bark and ivory bracelets, they stood quietly, leaning on the butt-end of seven-foot spears, waiting. They were evidently Nilotic, with their tall, lithe bodies and features much finer than the Bantu tribes to the south. Each man had plucked out all the hairs on his head, save little weaved tufts on the frontal lobe of his head, braided and tied with colored beads and pointing upwards like antennae. All of them had their share of decorative scar tissue (keloids) on their shoulders, stomachs, arms, and faces. All were uncircumcised, and we envied them the size of their genitalia. A few had smeared their skins with ashes, a natural sunscreen. It was, perhaps, a first contact, as these people lived in the geographical and cultural formaldehyde of seclusion for centuries and had no connection with a country called Ethiopia, and as we later learned from anthropologist David Turton, there were no previous recorded encounters with outsiders. We smiled, made friendly hand gestures, and offered gifts of salt, soap, sugar, cigarettes, and fishhooks, and they warily accepted all. When I offered an Ethiopian coin with Haile Selassie's visage stamped on the front, the leader looked at for a long time, rubbed his thumb over the face, turned it over, and then gave it back to me . . . he had no idea what money was and could think of no use for it. Lew and George made attempts to try to record their unrecorded language by pointing to familiar things, such as rocks and trees, and eliciting words.

This was, indeed, a primitive place. The year before, a hundred and fifty miles downstream, near the Kenyan border, paleontologists discovered a group of hominid fossils about three million years old, almost double the earliest dated fossils to that point. It was easy to imagine here: the Garden of Eden, the Cradle of Man, the Font of Life . . .

Our crude maps showed only two ways to exit the Omo: floating all the way into Kenya, to the soda waters of Africa's second-largest lake, named for Prince Rudolf of Austria, where the river flows in and nothing flows out; or by hiking twenty-five

Richard and Lew departing the Omo River National Park, 1973. GEORGE FULLER

miles up a tributary called the Mui River until reaching an airstrip that served a C-47 that brought supplies in once a week to a primitive game park in development. The former option would require an extra two weeks, as the Omo gooosenecked for two hundred torpid miles, with upstream winds, before effluing into Lake Rudolf, and we were down to our last couple days of food. Even if we could make it to Rudolf, there was nothing there, save the biggest single population of Nile crocs in the world, some fourteen thousand by recent estimates. Eight years earlier a palm-log "hotel" was built one hundred miles down the lake from the Ethiopian border. But bandits attacked it one night, killing the manager and a Catholic priest, who was the sole guest. They captured a third man, an Italian driver named Tony, and forced him to drive the hotel Land Rover until it ran out of gas. Rumor had it that after killing Tony, they skinned him, and members of the gang were reputed to be wearing pieces of his skin to this day. The hotel never reopened.

So we had to find the Mui River. The canyon had opened to valley, and the river had taken a sharp turn to the south past the Maji Mountains and was littered with islands. Matching compass bearings with our map, we knew we were in the general area, across from a region cryptically marked as the "Plain of Death." At every tributary on the eastern bank, we would stop and hike up a ways to see if it might fit the tracings on the topos. But every tributary turned the wrong way or didn't seem to carry enough water to qualify as the Mui "River." Some came close, and we debated if we should commit to an extended survey, which would cost days when we were down to hours of food supply. But we always voted to continue. If we missed the Mui, we figured we could starve to death. The stakes were suddenly high.

On day twenty-three, Lew was rowing. I was crouched in the bow, lethargic from the heat, feeling as though my veins were filled with silt. My calluses burned, and I gave up swatting tsetse flies. I skimmed a glance over to the eastern bank and saw beneath the shiny dark leaves of a spreading fig tree a clear creek spilling into the Omo, but we were past it. "Lew . . . pull in!" I yelled. He turned the raft and bent his back to fight the current and get the boat to shore. George and Diane were upstream, saw our maneuver, and followed suit. Lew pulled in several yards down from the confluence. A missed glance, another few minutes, and we would have passed it.

This must be it, we all agreed, though none was certain. We agreed George and Diane would camp at the confluence and wait with the gear, while Lew and I would hike up the tributary and hopefully find the Mui River Camp and airstrip. We had two cans of tuna left and split them between our two parties, and Lew and I set out. For hours we splashed up the clear river, finding no sign of any human presence. Strawy elephant dung, electric with flies, littered the banks. At one point we turned at a bend in the river and found ourselves face-to-face with a Nilotic buffalo, a mean-spirited beast, heavy of hoof and horn, that usually charges first and never asks questions. He glowered with almost tangible menace, pawed the ground, and snorted short Hemingway sentences, resonant with ill will. We beat a quick retreat to the woods and wandered among the ficus and tamarinds. We wandered for hours. Still, no sign of a camp, trail, or strip. As the sun was ready to call it a day, we decided to climb trees, and each shimmied up as far as we could go on separate trunks. But we could see nothing . . . just the midnight green of endless primary forest. The ultimate in hopelessness is to be lost, and we were.

We set up our tiny $30 Sears A-frame tent in a tight clump of nettles and bamboo, thinking it would prevent buffaloes or other large wildlife from making unwanted visits. We crawled in and opened the last can of tuna. As we shared it, we reflected on the adventures we had shared since being in Ethiopia and wondered aloud if they might be our last. Then we talked about how if we made it out of the Omo, we would work hard to make our little enterprise, Sobek Expeditions, a viable one, one that would take us around the world exploring and adventuring. We admitted we would never get wealthy or well-known doing this, but we would have fun. "Wait a minute, Rich" Lew injected. "I have an idea . . . when we get back . . . I'll change my name to 'Famous' . . . then we can be 'Rich and Famous,' and have fun too." We laughed ourselves to sleep.

Next morning, I awoke to a rustling. I pulled back the tent flap. There, not ten feet away, was a white-buttocks waterbuck, noshing on breakfast leaves. The delicate animal turned and stared at me, twitching its pointed ears, but continuing chewing, showing no signs of fear. "Look, look, look!" I nudged Lew awake. The waterbuck saw Lew's face emerge and, softly as waves, he strode towards the tent. Somehow motion seemed frozen as he strolled towards us, pausing a few feet from our portal. Lew gently pulled back the mosquito netting and extended his hand. Instead of running away, as I expected, the waterbuck walked closer. Lew and the antelope exchanged looks and touched each other for a second, the black nose nuzzling Lew's big hand. Then the waterbuck quietly stepped back into a stand with leafy branches that hung like waterfalls and disappeared.

For a few thaumaturgic moments, I didn't harbor any regrets for being lost, didn't begrudge our predicament. I only thought about the unpredictability of nature and how accepting that can open the mind to surprise and wonder and the delight of serendipity in body Africana.

But my stomach snarled, and the moment broke. We needed to get going if we were to emerge alive from the Omo Valley. We decided to hike inland from the tributary, as we might be able to see farther from the savanna than from within the dense riparian vegetation. But as I took my first steps, arrows of pain shot up my legs. In high school I had been on the track team, and occasionally I would suffer from shin splints. Now, perhaps because I had spent so much time in a raft over the previous weeks, my shins were splinting. It was terribly painful to walk, and I could only do so with a slow limp. To make matters worse, we had to hike through a fence of sharp spicules that lacerated our legs. Lew offered to help me along and carry my pack, the tent, and my canteen. Still, it was tough going.

All day I limped across the savanna, one hand on Lew's shoulder, hunger and exhaustion welling. At one point I stepped on something, and it slithered out into the open . . . it was a giant rock python, we guessed about seventeen feet long. But I was in too much pain and too exhausted to react. It vanished in the undergrowth, and we continued. Late in the day Lew insisted we climb a small hill to see if we might see something. He practically dragged me to the top, and once there I scanned the horizon to all points, and I saw herds of Burchell's zebra, stotting gazelle, a couple of eland and hartebeest, even a running ostrich . . . but no airstrip . . . just endless wilderness and wildlife. I was ready to lie down and admit defeat, and I told Lew so. "No, we're gonna be rich and famous . . . hang in there," he soothed as he continued to look. Then he stopped and grabbed me. "Look . . . out there." I strained but saw nothing. "Look, beyond those trees." And yes, I saw it . . . a tiny metallic glint. The sun had lowered enough to send back a flash of reflecting light. It was something man-made. And a renewed energy charged through me.

We practically ran down the hill and made in the direction of the glint. An hour later we summited a small rise, and there in front of us was a thing of phantasmal beauty . . . a small mud shed with an aluminum roof. Next to it was a hand-painted sign: "Mui International Airport," and beyond, a rough airstrip cleared from the elephant grass. In the shade of the hut was a sleeping teenage boy, and when we woke him up, he stared as though in the midst of his worst nightmare. But he gathered his senses and led us down a path to a small-tented camp beside the Mui River. There we met the park ranger, Mesfin, an Amhara with a Land Rover, and he pulled us into his canvas tent and fed us mountains of millet. Our faces creased as we remembered how good it felt to scratch the elemental itch of hunger. Then, because my leg was still on fire, Mesfin tucked me into my sleeping bag and drove back with Lew to fetch George and Diane Fuller, who had given us up for lost and were preparing to relaunch to cast their fates to the river. For three days we lounged in relative luxury. Mesfin had an old copy of *Reader's Digest*, featuring a piece on 101 ways to make hamburgers, and Lew and I drooled over the pictures, vowing to make every recipe with our return to the United States. Two days later, the Ethiopian Airlines C-47 flew in, and we made the noisy three-hour flight back to Addis, back up over the magic medley of ravines and valleys that made up the Omo catchment, another exploratory under our belts. River water was now my plasma.

Back in Addis, the dynamics were changing. Up to this point, aside from my time on the Colorado, nobody had ever seriously asked my opinion, had ever entertained consulting with me. Now, people sought me out . . . especially the ethno-ists. A man named Leo Sarkesian, calling himself an ethnomusicologist, cornered me at the embassy and wanted my recommendations for Ethiopian instruments. . . . "Listen to the Krar tunes," I proffered, but he misinterpreted and thought I was talking about animation. A young Harvard Medical School graduate, Andrew Weil, found me in the Mercato and introduced himself as an ethnopharmacolgist. He asked if I could recommend any natural drugs found in Ethiopia. "Try chat," I said. "It can put you in an altered state." Lisa Conte, an ethnobotanist, asked if I knew any shaman native medicinal cures. If the tagline meant looking for something in the non-White world, I guessed I was an ethnoadventurer.

The Colorado River season had started, so it was time to get back home, to replenish my pockets, and to start developing our enterprise, which Lew and I now vowed to turn into a business. But just as I was leaving, we got caught up in the final scenes of a Hollywood film being made in Ethiopia: *Shaft in Africa*, with Richard Roundtree. Several of my friends in the embassy had walk-ons, and I stood in the wings starstruck as I watched the workings of a big-budget film. For hours Richard Roundtree as John Shaft did takes on an entrance into the Addis Hilton, past an uncooperative lion and a consular officer with whom I had shared several cheeseburgers at the embassy. It was a thrill to be this close to Hollywood, here in Africa, and I had never watched anyone in the process of making a film before. I had met Candice Bergen, but this was different . . . this was celebrity in action.

CHAPTER 18

CAPITOL PUNISHMENTS

Usually speaking, the worst-bred person in company is a young traveller just returned from abroad.
—Jonathan Swift

Lew and I flew back to Bethesda together in May 1973, where we planned to spend a few days before heading in different directions for a couple of months. I planned to head west and guide a few Colorado trips and look for clients and more guides so we could start a commercial Sobek season in September in Ethiopia. We wanted to make an exploratory descent of the Baro, a commercial Omo expedition, and then explorations on the Blue Nile and Tekeze. Lew was going to Connecticut to sell his car, close his practice, and then meet me in Ethiopia for our first real season as a company.

After a couple days of decompression, we picked up my film of the Omo from the drugstore and made our way to downtown Washington, D.C., to 17th and M Streets, where the venerable National Geographic building stood. We went inside and I asked the receptionist for Joseph Judge, assistant editor. She called and cited my name, and he said he had never heard of me and didn't have time to meet. I asked the receptionist to call back and say we had just returned from the Omo River and brought our slides. In minutes Joe Judge was escorting us into the inner chambers of National Geographic and sitting us down in a conference room. He called in Gilbert Grosvenor, the editor, as well as assistant editors Bill Garrett and Bill Graves, and he put my slides in a carousel and projected them to a screen at the head of the conference table. I knew well that in a few months' time, Ron Smith's team, heavily funded by National Geographic, was headed for what was proclaimed in his published brochure as "The River Trip of the Century" and that we would deflate sails that had been billowing for months. We had just successfully navigated the same stretch of river Ron Smith's literature was billing as "The First Descent of the Omo." But I still hoped that perhaps there was a way Lew and I might be involved, perhaps as guides on the historic trip. If nothing else, I hoped National Geographic might want to publish some of my pictures.

I carefully narrated the slides, and a funereal silence gripped the room. At the end, Joe Judge asked me how much our expedition cost. . . . I mentally broke it down, calculating shared costs for food and transport, as well as time in Addis. "About $1,400 for the whole of the expedition," I replied equably. "You mean $1,400 per person?" Joe asked. "No, for the whole thing. For the four of us who went the whole way it was about $300 per person. Tom Cromer, who left halfway, made up the difference." It was apparent the editors were upset. We had heard they had joined with Britain's Survival Anglia television and some wealthy clients, and in all committed upwards of $60,000 for the privilege of exclusive coverage of the great first descent. I asked if they might want to publish any of my slides. They declined, and Joe accompanied Lew and me downstairs and to the door. As we shook hands goodbye, I offered Joe some information I hoped might be of use: "You know, August is not the best time to run the Omo . . . it will be in flood." Without acknowledging my notice, he turned and stepped back into Explorers Hall.

In August 1973, the Ron Smith–National Geographic team, with famous wildlife photographer Alan Root, made the second descent of the Omo River. It was indeed in spate, and as such it was impossible to hike up the flooding tributaries to the spectacular waterfalls; the wildlife stayed in the highlands, and little was seen at river level. And, in a rapid that had become ferocious with the high water, one of their rafts flipped, losing Alan Root's cameras and exposed film. The Omo article never ran in *National Geographic* magazine.

I spent the summer trying to find an additional partner for Sobek Expeditions, as we needed more boats, gear, and boatmen if we were going to make a business. Lew and I were broke. John Yost promised to buy a raft with the monies he expected to make in his import business over the summer. But we needed more. I wrote to the largest Grand Canyon rowing outfitters, ARTA, Wilderness World, and OARS. ARTA never answered; Ron Hayes, the actor who played the father in the TV series *Lassie* and part owner of Wilderness World, called me and asked how much I would pay to have his company join as a partner. George Wendt, owner of OARS, called and said he thought it was a neat idea and arranged a meeting.

A week later I was on an old school bus at Lees Ferry meeting with George. I proposed he supply a brand-new raft, life jackets and other essential gear, and two guides for the upcoming season; that he use his mailing list to solicit clients; and that he advance a little money to take an ad out in the *New York Times*, for a quarter of Sobek Expeditions; the other shares would be divided equally between Lew, John, and myself. We shook hands, and George went out to fetch his first candidate for a guide: Sam Street. Sam was somewhat of a mystic character in the realm of macho Grand Canyon guides. He brought his own macrobiotic menu on trips, meditated whenever possible, wore loose-fitting long paisley pants in a culture of cutoffs, issued crunchy environmental wisdom, and spoke Zen bumper-stickerese. He often said he didn't use his muscles in rapids, that he would find the flow and go with it. When he came into the bus to interview to join me on African rivers in the fall, I told him about the crocodiles and how they had almost done us in. He listened respectfully, paused, and with a shake of his waist-long blond hair replied crocodiles were not a concern for him . . . that he would commune with the crocodiles, connect with their psychic center, and intone them to leave us alone. I thanked Sam and said I would get back to him.

When he left the bus, I told George the partnership was off to a shaky start . . . that we had to do better. Meat-eating crocodiles were not going to stand down for Sam Street, or anyone. George said he had a couple other candidates, Robbie Paul and Jim Slade, and as they were on the river, he would have them call me in a week. They did, and I liked their take on river running and signed them both on. Slade in particular seemed to have a formidable intelligence and was ready for the job. We talked for an ocean of time, and he gave me his background: a degree in economics from Williams College, a slew of athletic awards, an acceptance at Columbia Law School that was on hold while he explored adventure, including a recent climb up Orizaba, an 18,000-foot Mexican volcano, and a raft run down the Rio Grande de Santiago that was interrupted with bandit fire. The fact that Jim wanted to go to Africa after the experience of running rapids with bullets whizzing by his head impressed me . . . he was just crazy enough to fit in. I gave Slade the date to rendez-vous in Addis and a phone number to call on arrival and suggested he cut his hair before arriving. Our first trip would be the Baro in September.

I also spent time with Bart Henderson that summer (we competed for favor from a lovely Swedish girl named "Sunshine," and I lost), and I invited him to join me in Ethiopia. He said sure and promised to be there early so he could make the scout of the Baro with me.

With George Wendt's advance, I sent a check for my last $300 to the *New York Times*, and in the September 2, 1973, Sunday edition the following appeared:

THE ADVENTURE OF 10 LIFETIMES!

Be among the first to run the Omo, Blue Nile and Tekeze Rivers—through the high mountains of Ethiopia. More than 350 miles of just-discovered river . . . rapids as rousing as the Colorado's . . . through mountains, desert, and jungle. Many truly wild (but unhostile) tribes. Big game and birds for photography by the hundreds. All it takes is 2 to 4 weeks. Trips are scheduled between September and February—with prices ranging from $665 to $1500 plus airfare and a touch of the pioneer. Write right away!

To my amazement, the ad actually generated response . . . about a dozen inquiries. The only takers, though, were four Americans posted in Asmara (Clyde and Betsy Selner, Mary Ann Straton, and Rich Miller), who called and said they would go if I offered a 50 percent discount. I had no choice, but at least we had a trip.

Just before leaving for my second season in Africa, I stopped in Bethesda to visit my family. My mother, little sister, and brother met me at the airport. My father was at home, having just returned from a mental hospital . . . he had suffered a series of nervous breakdowns and was on medication and practicing meditation under the guidance of a psychiatrist. When I talked with my mother about the breakdowns, she said it was common among CIA employees . . . the secrets, the isolation, the bureaucracy got to a lot of people.

For the first twelve years of my life, I had no idea what my father did for a living . . . when required in school to fill in the blank, "Father's Occupation," he had instructed me to put "State Department," and it seemed sufficiently innocuous that I never questioned further. Things changed in October 1962. My father came home one day visibly distressed and had us haul cans of food and water to the basement. He put his hands on my arms and locked his eyes onto my eyes to explain something. He said he worked for a sector of the government that engaged in spying, and that something had gone very wrong. A terrible thing might happen, a big bomb might be dropped, and if the air-raid siren went off, I was to rush to the basement and wait for him to come home. A few days later, on October 22, he insisted the family sit in front of the television set as President Kennedy announced a naval blockade around Cuba and demanded the USSR dismantle and remove ballistic missiles and other weapons it had assembled on the island ninety miles south of Florida. I didn't really understand what was going on but sensed it was serious, and I could see the uninvited guest of fear in my father's eyes. He hugged me hard that night. Four days later Khrushchev blinked, agreeing to Kennedy's demands, and to keeping secret a US counter-agreement to remove its east-leaning missiles in Türkiye. I remember my father saying at dinner, "You'll never know how really close we came to a nuclear war."

My father's career was not satisfying to him. He sometimes talked of how he was recruited from college, "pale, male, and Yale," as were so many of the early recruits. Just short of his Ph.D. in psychology, he was persuaded to go to work for this young intelligence agency that suggested he might become a real-life James Bond. He admitted he was attracted to the adventurous career and the romantic notion of a globetrotting spy protecting freedom for the Free World. But the reality was nothing like that. Long before the CIA became a popular whipping post for all that was wrong with the Vietnam War, my father was troubled with his employer and with his own choices. Occasionally he lamented not having gone into theater, or broadcasting, or teaching. And then one day, July 3, 1967, he went berserk, crashing around the house, breaking things, toppling his piano. He was taken away in a straitjacket.

As my mother drove me to the drugstore to pick up some medication for my father, she blurted something I had never heard before . . . that he hadn't really ever been the same since he got back from Iran. "When was that?" I asked. "1953 . . . he made a movie there for the Company. And then again in 1956, where he went to train something called SAVAK." I tried to remember 1956. I was six years old.

But memory palters with truth . . . my only recollection was of a camping trip he took me on, when a tent he set up collapsed and I fell into the river and enjoyed the feeling of being swept downstream.

The day before departure I noticed in the paper that *Shaft in Africa* had premiered. I thought it a good idea to take my father, who was back home and in recovery, to see a movie that showcased the country I had fallen in love with, and that had scenes (less than seven seconds long) with people I actually knew. But the film wasn't playing anywhere in the suburbs . . . its only showcase was the Howard theater, in southeast Washington, D.C., a predominantly Black neighborhood with not the best of reputations. My dad was resistant . . . the neighborhood was just not the place for us suburbanites to visit, and, though a movie buff, he really didn't have much interest in films of this genre. Still, I exhorted and pleaded . . . I so wanted to share this piece of my life with him. At last he relented, and we agreed we would take in the early show, so as to be back to the Oldsmobile while still light.

So we trekked down to a part of town we didn't know and eased into the theater. We noticed immediately we were the only Whites in the crowd, and when the film came on, I found the theme a bit uncomfortable, that Whites were orchestrating an odalisque ring that Shaft was sent to bust up. Every time Shaft beat up or killed a white man, the crowd went wild, yelling "Kill the honkie," at the screen. And every time they yelled, I slouched deeper in my chair, trying to become invisible . . . and I watched my father do the same. With the movie's end, we hustled out to the street and made our way to the car. Once there I noticed I was missing my wallet, and so I asked if my father would go back in the theater with me to find it. He insisted he stay with the car, so I mustered the courage and walked back in. It was filling with a new crowd, and a large man who looked like Isaac Hayes with chains dripping from his sleeves was in my seat. I meekly asked if he would look underneath, and he obliged, found my wallet, passed it to me, and I bolted to the door.

Two days later I was back in Addis, preparing for the Baro River expedition with Jim Slade, John Yost, George and Diane Fuller, Bart Henderson, another Hatch guide I had recruited, Gary Mercado, and Lew Greenwald and his wife, Karen, who was here on a mission of marital therapy. Ever since Lew had thrown his hat into my ring, things had become strained with his wife. Lew now called his relationship "estranged" and talked of a life beyond Karen. Now, she was here to see if she might become a part of this new passion in Lew's life, exploratory rafting. In addition to our core few, we were joined by a couple of newcomers to river running. It would be a trip that would change us all, forever.

CHAPTER 19

SUNK BY HIPPO

There is an eagle in me that wants to soar, and there is a hippopotamus in me that wants to wallow in the mud.

—Carl Sandburg

After the disastrous Baro, we retreated to Addis to lick our wounds and contemplate next moves. Lew thought perhaps we should pack it in and head home . . . the death of Angus seemed to spook him the most. But the rest of the group wanted to move forward and make our planned commercial Omo expedition, and Lew agreed to come along. So, the second week of November we piled onto a local bus, caromed down the rough road, and camped under a full moon at the Jimma Bridge. There were sixteen this time, including the four Americans working in Asmara who had seen the ad in the *New York Times*; Jerry Shea, a filmmaker and ex-boyfriend of George Wendt's wife; Karen Greenwald; Jim Slade's girlfriend, Cherry Jensen; and one full-paying client, Anne Mulqueen, a single Pan Am stewardess whom I had met on the Colorado on the last trip of the season, and who ponied up $1,500 for the privilege of joining our expedition full of single guides.

Shortly after sunrise we were up and patching the rafts. As per agreement, John Yost had paid for a fourth boat for his quarter stake in Sobek, and it had arrived via diplomatic pouch two days before the Omo departure. But the other three rafts we had salvaged from the Baro, and they were riddled with holes and rips. One was still scarred and leaking from the crocodile bite on the Omo in May. Since the special vinyl glue required for our Holcombe Industries Havasu rafts had only arrived from the States with the new raft, this was our first chance to patch, and we weren't certain the rafts would ever float again. After two and a half days of mending, we had four well-nigh-usable rafts. Bart's raft had leaks bow and stern and needed new air every half hour, but my boat leaked the most, and the front section had to be pumped every fifteen minutes. Since we had lost several oars on the Baro, I had commissioned a woodworker in the Mercato to fashion a half dozen with a wood he called "*wonza*."

When we finally cast off, Bart was pulling on a pair of "wonza wonders," and a few strokes into the first rapid an oar snapped in two. Was it Bart or the oars, we all wondered. An hour later another wonza oar snapped, this time under my scripting, so we knew it was the wood, not strength, that was busting them. We had only sixteen oars for the three-week expedition, twelve made of wonza wood, and the future didn't look promising at that moment.

The water was much higher in November than on our May exploratory, and on the fourth day we entered a gateway where jets of water danced like tongues of white flame on the surface. We pulled over at the entrance to the black canyon to scout the quarter-mile-long rapid, full of holes, powerful eddies, and back-crashing waves. I was tempted to plot my course on paper, analyzing the hydraulics, factoring the weight distribution on my boat. But anatomizing rapids is like translating a poem . . . it risks missing the unanalyzable spirit of the thing.

Bart wanted to portage, but despite my failures on the Baro, I thought it runnable and jumped in the raft with Lew as my passenger and bounced safely through. Bart went next and got caught in a hydraulic for a churning five minutes, during which another wonza oar washed from the raft, floated a hundred feet downstream, and promptly sank. Next, Robbie Paul tried the route, with George on board. Halfway through, they washed up on a steep rock and Robbie flew out of the boat into the crocodiled waters. George turned around to find Robbie gone. Face frozen in panic, he grabbed the oars and managed to maneuver through the rest of the rapid and into the eddy. Robbie, though, still hadn't surfaced. Seconds dragged by . . . he could have drowned, been pinned underwater by a rock or snag, or grabbed by a croc . . . then, finally, he popped up from under the boat, where he'd been snared. He had come within a few breaths of drowning.

Early on John Yost took the title of chief cook, as it was clear he had a talent and passion for creative outdoor cooking. One day, after a filling breakfast of Yost toast (bread dipped in egg batter and then fried to a crisp over the campfire), we were lounging naked in the cool spray of a large falls, enjoying a respite from the aggressive tsetse flies that turned entire days on the river into long swatting sessions. The spot was an Eden of butterflies, some big as pie tins and colored like Shanghai silk, others yellow as buttercup petals. There were rainbows, and waterslides, but our attention turned to the unexplored canyon above the falls. Unable to resist the allure, Jim Slade, Cherry Jensen, and I set off up the steep gorge. We forged through vegetable matter that resembled barbwire, sometimes swinging across gullies on creeper vines like Tarzans. Our bodies glistened with sweat, hair netted with cobwebs, as upwards we scrambled. Finally, the canyon walls began to echo with a growing roar, until we turned a corner and faced the most spectacular waterfall any of us had ever witnessed. As is the privilege, and burden, of explorers we needed to name the natural wonder, and in the long tradition of naming discoveries after the discoverers, we agreed to name the high cascade "Slade-Bangs-Jensen" Falls, and it was true.

One afternoon I started to hiccup incessantly, something my father occasionally did. It went on for hours, all through the night, into the following day, each time feeling like I'd been kicked in the stomach. I tried all the tricks—swallowing water upside down, thinking of ten bald men—but nothing would stop the hiccupping. I asked George Fuller for help, but he just said, "You'll be fine." That was George's prescription for practically everything. George refused to attend to the normal cuts and bruises that were the daily doses of an expedition. "You'll be fine," he'd scoff whenever someone complained of an abrasion or a loose stool. And, more often than not, whenever an expedition member sought George out for medical advice, or a fresh Band-Aid, the doctor was out—nowhere to be found. In fact, he was usually off photographing or collecting bugs.

When, at last, on the afternoon of my second day of hiccupping, a hippo, with the biggest open mouth I'd ever seen, clamped its jaws down on Bart's boat in a short-but-damaging display, my hiccupping went away. It took a day to repair Bart's boat and used up the last of our glue. And we were getting low on spare fabric to use as patching material. When a coffee smuggler from Kaffa Province crossed the river while balancing on a tightly inflated goatskin, we eyed his craft with envy and impure thoughts.

Dinner was often after dark, as the sun set so early, and instead of candlelight, there were hundreds of blinking fireflies creating that special ambience. In the distance, on the upper slopes of the canyon, we would sometimes see the eerie spectacle of wildfires, looking like a faraway city in the desert at midnight. They were fires set by Galla tribesmen, burning the forest to enhance the soil with nutrients to fertilize their crop seedlings. Under the necklace of these lights, John would do his best to metamorphose another macaroni and cheese dinner into a gourmand's delight, and, with a deft ladle turn and a pinch of spice here and there, he often succeeded. Afterwards, Bart would sometimes cook up a batch of Jiffy Pop, a snack he carried over from the States for my benefit, as he knew I was addicted to the stuff. Then, we would retire to the tents, lie in our bags, and listen to the symphony: tympanis played by an assortment of cicadas, the tenor band saw of flapping bats, the soft clarinet of the Cape turtle dove, the soprano whine of mosquitoes, and the basso profundo of hippos bellowing in protest that we were in their seats. Hippos exit the river when the last smudges of light blot away to wander the grasslands and graze, cropping a couple hundred pounds of grass a night. In most cases when we chose a wide beach to pitch our tiny town of tents, it was also a hippo passageway. One evening I crawled into the pup tent I was sharing with John Yost on a beach pockmarked with hoofprints across from a bloat of hippos blowing their tubas. In the morning, we awoke to an earthquake. We looked at each other and simultaneously yelled, "Hippos!!" . . . We knew they were rampaging through camp on the way back to the river before sunrise. The zipper was jammed, so we ripped the fly apart and jumped out to see several tons of river horses thundering through camp, tripping over guy lines, and diving into the Omo.

A few days later John Yost was rowing my boat while I lounged in the bow. We saw a pair of baby hippos and rowed over to admire the cute, pink creatures. With a *whoosh* of thick air, the mother popped up three feet from my face, grabbed the inflatable in her jaws, and shook so hard I almost fell out. John's high voice shot

People of the Omo Valley. BART HENDERSON

an octave, like a tire ripped open. A hiss, like a punctured lung, discharged from
the raft, and the cow submerged. A pause. The whole canyon inhaled and held its
breath. Overhead, a black cormorant silently rode an updraft, for a second blotting
the sun. Then with a snort, mother torpedoed to the surface, a great, gray hulk, water
washing from her head as though off a whale's back. I looked directly into a pair of
angry, flashing eyes and an awesome mouth stretched to its limits. They were huge,
old jaws, pitted and scored like corroded chunks of cast iron, studded with short,
sharp carrot-sized teeth, wielded by bulging neck muscles, displaying enough ivory
to cover the keys of a Steinway. I could feel my vagus nerve thrumming. John pulled
his oars with everything he had, but the mad mother porpoised to keep up, and then
the fleshy, saliva-rimmed cavern closed. The raft exploded. I scrambled to the frame
as the fabric beneath my feet sank into the river. Her points made, oral reprimand
delivered, she swam off triumphant, leaving us sinking in her wake. Other hippos
in the river seemed to blow a uniform Bronx cheer. When John got the boat to
shore, we surveyed the damage . . . three sections and a seam were badly torn. The
raft was Yost Toast. We folded it up, stashed it in the stern of Bart's boat, and then
fitted Bart's raft with the extra 2×6 frame and extra people for the rest of the trip.
We called the raft that then carried all the extra gear and people "The African Pig."

At the Soddu Bridge, Karen Greenwald left the expedition . . . she just wasn't getting along with Lew . . . and a primate researcher who had worked at Gombe with Jane Goodall, Anne Pierce, joined, bringing a fresh supply of food and drinks. It was a good thing, too, as the following day was Thanksgiving. Thursday night John pulled out all the stops, and even though we were in the wild heart of Africa, we sat down to a feast of baked ham, sweet potatoes, haricot beans in creamed mushroom sauce, sautéed zucchinis, coleslaw, fruit salad, rum cake, and spiced tea . . . and Lew led us in grace, thanking God for allowing us to share friendship and bounty in such a special place.

In the months between the two Omo expeditions, I contacted David Turton, an anthropologist at the London School of Economics, who was studying the tribes of the lower Omo. He told me the two main tribes above the Mui River were the Bodi and Mursi. Though he had never met them, he was planning to hike in early next year and spend time there researching for his doctorate. He couldn't offer more than rumors he'd heard of their existence and was keenly interested in our observations.

So it was with a more appreciative eye that we rounded a bend on the lower Omo and saw a group of naked hunters gathered around a freshly speared hippo. They were tall and thin, as if half their bodies were in their legs. They were just starting to skin the mammoth ham as we pulled to shore to watch. At first, they were aloof and distrustful, but once they realized we wouldn't steal their meat, they became friendly and curious. We laughed and talked in sign language and showed them our boats, and they proudly showed us their dugouts. They cocked heads like birds at the black boxes we held to our eyes, and they giggled as we let them look through the viewfinders. They got a bigger kick wearing our sunglasses. After a while, the headman had one of the younger men build a fire and roast strips of meat, which they then offered graciously to us. Though little more than chunks of pig fat, this was the first fresh meat in weeks, and we shnorked it down, even as it made my tongue curl like a millipede. Jean-Pierre Hallet had written that "the smoked flank of a hippo is the most delicious treat that Africa can offer," further eroding his credibility in my young mind. However, when the bladder and stomach of the dead hippo were cut open and spread along the beach, a nauseating stench rose and hung like a fog about the carcass. It was time to leave. While boarding my raft, and holding my nose, I asked if the people were "Bodi," and the chief nodded as if to say yes. We then waved goodbye so vigorously our armpits threatened to crack and hurried to fresher winds.

A bit farther downstream we came to a Mursi village, and this time, with Cherry leading the way, we were able to meet the women. Several were in front of their huts grinding guinea corn and sorghum with stones, and they stood up excitedly to greet Cherry. They tugged in disbelief at her golden hair, rubbed her breasts, and touched her pale skin. They'd never seen such a specimen before and couldn't seem to land a feeling, a response—aloof or astonished or amused. An elder man approached me and gestured to several of the village women, then to Cherry, over and over . . . he seemed to be offering a trade. I was tempted, but Cherry wouldn't hear of it, despite the royal possibilities of fulfilling an H. Rider Haggard role.

Mursi tribesman. BART HENDERSON

Unlike the men, the women weren't naked, but wore crude tan bark cloth skirts from their narrow hips to knees. No hair at all anointed their heads, and the ear lobes had big loops for earplugs. About half the women wore lip plates, a holdover from slave-trading days, when the desirable East African women made themselves and their children as ugly as possible to discourage slavers from dragging them off. The lower lip was pierced and stretched out slowly until it fit around a clay disk several inches in diameter. While the women looked bizarre wearing the plates, when they removed them, the loop of the lower lip hung down around their chins and dangled like a rubber band that had lost its snap. It seemed unlikely they did much kissing.

Several in our group wanted to trade for their tightly woven baskets, the three-legged stools the men carried as pillows on hunting treks, and some of the women's bone and feather finery. T-shirts and shorts were pulled from wet bags to start the bargaining. George spoke up and said, sotto voce, he thought trading was a bad idea ... that it would accelerate an inevitable process that one day would have the Mursi looking like second-class Western citizens instead of the regal tribesmen they were born to be. Lew argued that we should let the Mursi decide their fate. He called George's benign-neglect proposal specious and elitist, imperialist and anti-evolutionist. We were all aware of Lew's real career as a sociologist, and his liberal leanings for the betterment of the common man, but we weren't prepared for such a loaded reaction. He cited sentiments from those who live in the rain forests of the Amazon reacting to khaki-wearing Americans and Europeans who showed up proclaiming they were there to save the planet. "Who are we to think we have a right to impose strictures on these people? Look around you, George ... these people are in a better space than we are. We've already cut down most of our trees, killed our greatest herds, polluted our cities, dammed our rivers. These people should decide their future; not us. I say if they want to trade with us, let them."

After the lively debate, the group sided with George and agreed to forgo trading this passage. But a few days later, as we pulled out into the current at the final village, I looked back upstream at a waving Mursi, and he was grinning beneath a pair of sunglasses. Simultaneously, one of the clients from Asmara proudly held up a stool he had traded for the glasses.

Just five months previous, on the first Omo expedition, we met the Bodi and Mursi peoples and spent hours exploring one another's effects and sharing food and drink, but we didn't take anything from them, nor leave behind anything that wouldn't be gone in a short while, such as soap and spices. Then we disappeared around the bend, leaving them in the Stone Age.

Streaked with guilt, thinking we may have introduced something to a culture that would upset its value and more systems (à la the Coke bottle in *The Gods Must Be Crazy*), perhaps alter its cosmology (the cross in *The Mission*), even elevate the status of the man who randomly received the glasses (like winning the lottery), Lew and I decided to seek out the right thing to do. So, upon returning to the States, we wrote up an account of the incident and concluded by stating we hoped to return again and again to the Omo with more clients, but we hoped for some guidance as to how to handle this intercultural exchange. We then sent the query to the head of every college anthropology department in the United States, and some overseas. Within a couple weeks replies began to fill my mailbox. A month later I received a call from my little sister, Cindy, an undergraduate at the University of Wisconsin, who said my query had ended up as the final in her anthropology class and wondered if I had insights as to how to write the essay. I didn't, but I had a pile of wildly differing opinions from the experts.

Maybe a third of the respondents chastised our fledgling business for venturing into a pure environment, a rare field laboratory circumstance, in which an untainted culture could be examined by trained social scientists. With nary a Ph.D. among us, we were contaminating a petri dish, and we were advised to cease and desist.

Another third wrote back and commented that progress was inevitable, that freeways would soon be passing through these villages, and we need not concern ourselves with adversely affecting a culture doomed to dilution anyway, so raft and enjoy.

Then there was a middle ground. Several professors advised that change is destined, and the wise course is the one that attempts a sensitive, responsible, softly stepping approach. They suggested we trade with the people we met on the river, but in a judicious way, trading simple things they could use (fishhooks) and biodegradable items (soap; spices), rather than Hawaiian shirts and yo-yos, or icons that could radically revise a system. And that became our policy.

A lot had changed since that first descent of the Omo. Anthropologists from around the world dropped in on the Mursi and Bodi and came out with Ph.D. theses. There is now a money economy, and tourism is a major part of it. Not far away there is a clinic to which the Omo peoples take their ill, and a few have left the valley for schooling.

At least one Bodi still has a pair of sunglasses. Change has occurred, as it always does and always will, and is the desire of the locals. There are downsides to change, to cultural evolution, but from the point of view of those in the midst, it is better than being dammed as a museum piece to serve the romantic or academic confections of tourists.

CHAPTER 20

BLUE NILE *SHIFTA* ATTACKS

Between flattery and admiration there often flows a river of contempt.
—Minna Antrim

Back in Addis Ababa after the second Omo trip, I was wandering through the recesses of the spice market when a vendor I knew approached me. "Mr. Richard. Did you hear about Mr. Angus? They say he is alive. He was found by villagers on the river, and he is living with them now. It is the talk everywhere. I do not know from where the story comes."

I went to the British and US embassies. People there, too, had heard the rumor. One consul said he'd heard a fanciful embellishment to the story—that Angus was living fine and well as king of a tribe of Amazon-like women. As the story went, Angus had been visited by outside villagers and invited to leave with them, but he declined. He was in Paradise.

Hearing the rumors was hard. I wanted to squelch the sensationalistic gossip, to finish business left undone, to determine beyond all doubt what really happened to Angus. And to cleanse my conscience. So, in January of 1974, I made another trip to the upper reaches of the Baro. This time the river was ten vertical feet lower than on our last trip: It was dry season in a drought year. What was before a swollen rampage was now a slow, thin trickle, the bones of the river poking through what had once been the flesh of great rapids. This time there were four of us in a single raft: Lew Greenwald, Gary Mercado, Professor Conrad Hirsh of Haile Selassie I University, and me. John Yost left to float the Congo and collect art for his store, the clients had gone back to work, Jerry Shea returned to Los Angeles to edit his film, the Fullers didn't want to have anything to do with another Baro attempt, and Jim Slade and Cherry Jensen decided to take some time to climb the mountains of Kenya but hoped to return for another river descent in a couple months.

As with the initial Baro attempt, we reached the first rapid within minutes. This time, though, it was a jumble of bus-size basalt boulders, the bedrock that fashioned the falls during times of flooding. It was unnavigable, so we stood in chest-deep water and wrenched the inflatable boat over and down the rocks, turning it on its side to push it through the tighter passages. A similar configuration constituted the next rapid, and the next, and the next. The routine was quickly established. It was a constant battle against rocks, water, heat, fatigue, and insects. We had naively hoped to run the raft some 150 miles to Gambella, near the Sudanese border, where the river flows wide and flat. We had rations for a week. With all the portaging, we were making less than five miles a day.

Scattered along our course, sometimes in branches high above us where the water once swirled, we found vestiges of the first expedition: five oars, Jim Slade's sleeping bag, a torn poncho, a pack of the insect-collecting equipment donated by the Smithsonian, crushed pots and pans, and a ripped sweater that had belonged to Angus, one he had packed in his duffel. But no sign of Angus.

After six days we had made only thirty miles; our bodies were pocked with insect bites, and we had exhausted our food and strength. A trail up the steep slope put an end to our ordeal. We returned to Addis Ababa with no new answers.

At this point I had achieved a small measure of infamy among the expat community in Addis. Some thought my explorations were worthwhile endeavors; others thought them stupid and dangerous and cited the death of Angus Macleod as proof. Kathy Chang, the exotic-looking owner of the China Bar and Restaurant, rumored spy, and part-time journalist, did a profile on my adventures for the *Ethiopian Herald*, the government-owned English-language newspaper. She made the classic mistake of new journalists, though, and allowed me to look at the story before it was published. I read it, thought it was lacking, and called Kathy to ask if I could noodle with the piece. She said sure, and I ended up completely rewriting the story. It ran the following Sunday, to much praise, under Kathy's byline. A week later she came to me with a story on hippos and asked if I would help her, as I knew the subject. Again, I rewrote the piece, this time so that every word was my own. It ran under her byline, and again it was lauded. This happened a few more times before Kathy came to me with a proposition: Would I like to move in with her, free room and board, in exchange for writing her weekly features? I accepted, more out of lust than economics, and began a period of blissful indentured servantry.

Kathy was well connected, and I found myself attending fashion shows at the Hilton, sipping G&Ts under Cinzano umbrellas, schmoozing at embassy parties. Through her contacts I was even asked to photograph the crown jewels at the Jubilee Palace.

Kathy drove me through the palace gates, past some of the forty black-maned lions kept as pets, as well as several long-necked swans and peacocks. In a bedroom full of brilliant chandeliers, an attendant laid out the jewels on a shiny, inlaid desk and stood back to watch as I set up my flimsy tripod and began to click away. Then there was a phone call, and the attendant gathered up the jewels and told me to stay put . . . he'd be back. I was left alone in this regal bedroom, and as I looked around it dawned on me that this was where the emperor slept. An opened closet showed off dozens of crisp uniforms, and photographs around the room showed the emperor with various heads of state and celebrities. The canopied bed was old and short, and a thought struck. I turned the camera towards the bed, put it on self-timer, and raced to the perfectly made bed and lay upon it. A click, and I was immortalized on Haile Selassie's bed.

After a few weeks of living with and writing for Kathy, I had to change. I felt guilty. Lew was staying at the Itege Hotel, the country's first government hotel, founded by Empress Taytu in 1907, and seemingly untouched since. And I had written a story I was particularly proud of about crocodiles. I had asked Kathy for a byline, or even a co-byline, but she refused. So I moved back with Lew, and we spent our time running one- and two-day Awash trips for the expat community, and we were pretty happy.

With the river season approaching in North America, we decided we had time for one more Ethiopian River expedition before heading back. Of the Grand Slam river expeditions we had originally targeted (Omo, Awash, Baro, Blue Nile, and Tekeze), two remained on our list: the Blue Nile and the Tekeze. But it was March, and with the continued drought we figured the Tekeze too low and would have to wait. The last unrun-section of the Blue Nile, from below Tissisat Falls to the Second Portuguese Bridge, was also too low, so we would postpone that as well. Instead, we would close out the season in Ethiopia running the 140-mile stretch of the Northern Gorge of the Blue Nile, the section the British had hailed as the Grand Canyon of Africa when they passed through in 1968. Jim Slade and Cherry Jensen had successfully climbed Mounts Kenya and Kilimanjaro and telegraphed they wanted to join the Blue Nile expedition, so we awaited their return before heading to the northern tablelands. While waiting, I met a young American, Scott Johnson, who had been inspired by Colin Fletcher's book *The Man Who Walked Through Time*, an account of the author's traverse by foot of the entire Grand Canyon. He decided he wanted to make a similar traverse through the Grand Canyon of Africa, the Blue Nile gorge, and author a book and become famous. He asked if he might set up an arrangement wherein we would bring him a resupply of food about halfway down the Northern Gorge. We rolled out a map and agreed to tributaries where he would leave notes about his progress tied around the closest tree. He would leave a week before us, and we would catch up about seventy miles downstream. I agreed to the plan, shook his hand, and wished him luck.

When Jim and Cherry arrived, we took the once-a-week flight to Mota on the edge of the Blue Nile gorge, hired donkeys, strapped our rafts and oars and gear to the wooden saddles, and whacked their hindquarters to begin the twelve-and-a-half-mile trek into the canyon. It was a path that curled and scrambled like a lizard, and it kept the Blue Nile hidden from us until we reached the lip of the last gorge. There, suddenly, was the river and, spanning it, this unlikely structure—Sabera Dildi, or the Second Portuguese Bridge. A stone structure built originally by the Portuguese in the seventeenth century, it had two arches over the river and three increasingly smaller ones on each side. There were two quite impressive approach ramps, with low walls. But the setting of the bridge was bizarre, for both the Gojjam and Begemdir banks rose almost sheer above the bridge, and there was nowhere for the approach ramps to go; they ended abruptly at the foot of a daunting rock scramble some three hundred feet to the cliff top.

The bridge had collapsed at some earlier stage, and Emperor Menelik II in 1908 ordered its reconstruction. Menelik added an imposing gateway on the Gojjam side, on which there was a cement panel commemorative of this work. At low water, as it was when we arrived, the bridge loomed high over a deep cleft like some Victorian railway viaduct. But we could see the high-water marks when the river swirled at the tops of the ancient legs.

More recently it suffered another grave blow. In the late 1930s the Ethiopian Resistance was trying to stop Italians in Begemdir from joining up with those in Gojjam. A local squireen with a band of forty men dug up the central arch. Unfortunately, while digging, it collapsed into the river, and all forty drowned. The Italians shot a further six men in Mota as a reprisal.

Since then, the bridge had never been permanently repaired. It was made usable by a rickety balk of logs, saplings, and gravel, across which herdsmen unconcernedly drove their tan and white goats. Rather than cross this precipitous arch, we turned down a tortuous trail and emerged at river's edge, where we supped on a freshly slaughtered goat purchased from a passerby. That night I sat by the river and marveled at its hoary currents, a bewildering skein of contradictory forces. So much water rippling along at different speeds, displaying a glittering richness of surface texture, gave the Blue Nile a dangerous, vibrant look. I couldn't sleep, as the stringy goat meat hung all night in my belly like a stone.

The next morning we inflated our two rafts, rigged and loaded, and then set off down East Africa's most famous waterway. The stream pulled at our oars as it churned down between rocky banks. The rapids were modest by our standards, Class II and III, and the gorge was nowhere near as stunning as that of the Grand Canyon of the Colorado. And we saw no wildlife or village life. After a couple days of rafting, we began to wonder if the river had been oversold. At least we found the notes left by Scott Johnson at the appointed tributaries, and that added a dimension to the adventure.

On the third day we turned into a region of natural grandeur. Across the line of the river from the Gojjam bank a great vertical slab of basalt reared up. It was fifty feet high and relatively smooth, with here and there trees sprouting the spherical nests of busy, black-headed, yellow-bodied weaverbirds.

The cliff went on for miles, increasing in height as we passed along it, first to 60 feet, then 80, and finally after some miles to a cathedral-like scale of about 120 feet.

At water level the amygdaloidal basaltic lava was constantly washed, so that it shone like a black sculpture.

Around one long corner we encountered two huge, isolated pillars, slices of cliff cut off by the river. They soared, narrow and sheer, to about 120 feet, beautifully shaped and crowned with mossy trees and shrubs. Beyond was another cliff, this one lined with a restless nation of black vervet monkeys, all with their long tails hanging down.

In all this wildness it was a shock suddenly to see in the cliff face a man-made wall and doorways to two caves, one triangular the other semicircular. There were no signs of steps from the river to the grottos, twenty-five feet up, or from the top of the cliff downwards. How did people get there? We had a climbing rope and some pitons and were able to make our way to the caves, which were filled with pottery and old basketwork. My eyes had to scavenge light to see the depths of the first cave. It seemed to be a natural excavation by river erosion. The only human modification was a platform of dressed stone at the mouth. There was no sign of any permanent or even temporary arrangements for getting in and out of the cave. Yet its umber floor, liberally heaped with pungent bat dung, showed traces of human use: broken shards, arrowheads, strips of rattan, fragments of old wickerwork, and in the furthermost corner on a constructed stone platform, the bases and lower parts of two terra-cotta storage jars. It was possible to move around and up to the semicircular entrance of the other cave, which was shallower in depth, but which was divided between two levels. On the upper one we found a complete black canopic pot and more fragments, some of which clearly fit together. We had no idea how old these finds were but felt they looked ancient. I decided to take the black jar to the Institute of Ethiopian Studies in Addis Ababa, so experts there could determine if we had stumbled onto anything of significance.

Back on the river, we floated a few miles when, from the top of the cliffs, we heard a number of whooping cries, the sort often heard exchanged between travelers in the quiet of the Ethiopian countryside—but here, they were excited and in concert. We were all slow to appreciate the significance of the whoops echoing back and forth across the gorge. Suddenly, our reverie was disturbed by a fusillade of rocks. We looked up and about seventy-five yards away, along the rim of the cliff, among the fringe of gnarled trees and scrub, appeared a motley crowd of about a dozen men shouting angrily and gesticulating. As the ragtag warlord of the group gave a signal, a rock was fired down into the river, then another and another. Spurts of water danced up in the stream about us.

We were dumbfounded. We knew the British Army had been attacked by *shifta* gunfire in this section of the Blue Nile, but up to this point all our encounters with Ethiopians had been friendly, even among the famously fierce Danakil. However, it didn't take long to react. I leaned into my oars and started rowing as hard I could, and Jim Slade piloting the other raft did the same. Still, angry men were picking up jagged pieces of basalt and flinging them down at us. At the next bend we were

Blue Nile, from left: Richard, Kim Nichols, Cherry Jensen, Diane Fuller, Gary Mercado, George Fuller, and Tadessa Wolde Gossa. GEORGE FULLER

pulled into the magnetic field of a rapid and whipped out of sight of the *shiftas*. For whatever reasons, they didn't use their rifles (bullets are expensive and hard to replace), and we suffered no scars for the attack.

We camped by a tributary where Scott Johnson was supposed to leave another note, but we could find none. We checked every side canyon for the remainder of the trip, and we never saw another note.

Beyond here the gorge opened out and the cliffs were replaced by sloping hillsides. These were dotted here and there with plantations of maize, guarded by ramshackle watchtowers on which small boys were set to protect the corncobs from baboons. There were some uniquely beautiful hikes up tributary side canyons, and occasionally a natural arch or basalt monolith would wow us . . . but it didn't make up for the extreme heat that left us breathless and weak . . . even the flies were torpid, unable to muster enough energy to bite. On the final days of the trip, we were showered with a heat so terrifying and unbearable, we decided to alter our routine. Before the dawn was whole, we would get up and float in the relative cool until midmorning. Then we would find shade beneath an acacia or cliff and rest until around four-thirty, playing endless games of Botticelli. Then we'd float until dark. It was the only way to beat the truly brutal midday heat.

We took turns standing guard at night, knowing *shifta* were around. It was downstream that the Franco-Swiss Expedition of 1962 met grim disaster. The six expedition members were sound asleep on an islet when, at about 1:30 a.m., under a full moon, the *shifta* opened fire. Two men were killed instantly; another was wounded as he and the survivors took to their boats and launched downstream in the darkness. Another hail and the boat was holed and a paddle smashed. But the remaining four survived.

With the relief of relief, after nine days and 140 miles, we reached the steel supports of the Shafartak Bridge, the only modern span that arches over the length of the Blue Nile in Ethiopia. Moving slowly in the breathless heat, we exchanged the Sobek handshake, took the obligatory takeout photograph, and headed up the hill to flag a passing bus. We asked all who passed if they had seen another *ferenji* walking solo down the river, a man called Scott Johnson, and nobody responded. Scott Johnson was never heard from again. For the first time, I wondered if I wanted to return to a river to run its undone section.

It was time to head home and reevaluate. But I had one more obstacle to clear. When we entered the country with our last set of rafts, the customs authorities wanted me to pay an outrageous duty (150 percent of the cost of the rafts) or prove we exported them after our trips.

So they stamped my passport with a notice that conveyed such, and unless I had my passport stamped again with proof of export, I would be assessed and fined, maybe even jailed.

But at this point we had lost two rafts to the jaws of river beasts and another to the capsize on the Baro. We needed a plan. It was too expensive to ship shredded rafts back to the United States. But Jim Slade had an ingenious idea. For just a few dollars, we could put the damaged rafts on the train to Djibouti and have our passports duly stamped as having exported the goods. We didn't know anyone in what was then the French Territory of the Afars and Issas, so we made up a recipient, Pierre DuPont, and off the torn boats went up the Horn of Africa, never to be heard of again, or so I thought.

CHAPTER 21

FIRED

Africa, amongst the continents, will teach it to you: that God and the Devil are one.

—KAREN BLIXEN

THE OIL CRISIS ALSO AFFECTED ME. AS WE PACKED OUR GEAR FOR STORAGE AFTER our Blue Nile expedition, I was looking forward to heading back to another season guiding the Grand Canyon. I now had five seasons under my belt guiding for Hatch River Expeditions and loved it. But as I got back to our rented house near Arat Kilo, I saw an envelope with the familiar Hatch logo of a boat with long oars rafting the globe. I ripped open the letter, and it was a short message from Ted Hatch himself: "Due to the oil crisis, we find we have to cut back on our personnel this season. As such, we won't be needing your services. I hope you have a good summer. Regards, Ted Hatch." I was crushed. I was fired. Defenestrated. And the oil crisis was such a bad absolution. I had heard rumors that Ted wasn't pleased with my founding of Sobek and that he considered my enterprise competition. But I couldn't help but wonder if there was more to it. If I had somehow not done the best I could; if I had fallen below the mark.

But good things come out of bad situations. Instead, I called George Wendt at OARS and asked if Lew and I might come to Angels Camp, California, and work there for the summer. George said fine, and Lew and I flew back to the United States in April after having spent eight months in Africa. Before heading to the Gold Country, though, Lew and I drove to Los Angeles to help edit and write the Omo film that had been shot by Jerry Shea. We moved into the tiny Hermosa Beach apartment of Anne Mulqueen, who had been on the expedition, and for the following month we dutifully drove over to Jerry's house on Centinela Avenue every morning and edited and wrote all day long. Finally, in late May the film was completed, and we somehow recruited Marshall Thompson, the B-movie star of such film classics as *Clarence, the Cross-eyed Lion* (1965) and *East of Kilimanjaro* (1957), and the lead in the 1960s television series *Daktari*, to narrate the film. It was a high-light of my life at that point to go into a real Hollywood sound studio and direct a real actor in how to read our script.

In late May Lew and I hitched up to Angels Camp and settled in an old bunkhouse for a fabulous summer. During the weekdays we would trek over to George Wendt's basement, where with a single manual typewriter and a single bare lightbulb hanging from the ceiling, we would tap out letters of invitation to join us in rafting the Omo. We would divide up and personally call every lead. On the weekends we went rafting, down the Stanislaus, the South Fork of the American, the Tuolumne and the Merced. Lew became a full-fledged rafting guide and was loved by all who rowed with him.

One summer weekend Jim Slade, who was out between Grand Canyon trips for a few California runs, fell suddenly sick. He had a steep fever, then wild chills, and a croupy cough. Lew and I piled Jim into his light blue 1966 Ford Econoline Supervan and drove him to the Mark Twain Hospital in San Andreas. We checked Jim in and waited in the emergency room for an answer. An hour later the doctor walked in and threw up his hands. He said it was vivax malaria, not a typically fatal variety, but a nasty one nonetheless. And while there had been, he said, the occasional bout of malaria in the San Joaquin Valley, the San Andreas hospital didn't carry any quinine, at least not any that could be accessed on a weekend when the pharmacy was

In Aspen: Lew Greenwald, Candy Uenyo, and Richard. RICHARD BANGS

closed. "You might try Stockton," the doctor suggested. So Lew drove the Supervan the ninety minutes to Stockton while I stayed with Jim and was back late afternoon with the medicine. The doctor gave Jim strong doses of quinine and warned a relapse could come at any time. Jim took it all in stride and left for the Grand Canyon again, promising he would see us in the fall back in Ethiopia. A similar bout of tropical malady hit Robbie Paul that summer, and as he rolled around in pain he begged out loud for the doctor to put him out of his misery. When finally released, he vowed he would never do another overseas raft trip, and he disappeared from the scene.

By summer's end Lew was as trim and tan as any nineteen-year-old guide, and happier than a puppy. And with summer's end we had some decisions to make.

Our little company was making a little money, but its future wasn't something anyone would bet on. The writing bug had bitten me, having published several pieces now about our adventures in Africa, and I had dreams of becoming an author. After so much time on water, in the social vertex of rafting, I liked the notion of the desert of lonely creation. As such, I had applied to graduate school at USC in journalism, and I was accepted for the fall term, beginning late September 1974. We had managed to sell an October commercial Omo trip, and we had talked all summer of attempting the last two major exploratories: the unrun section of the Blue Nile and the grand prize of African river exploratories, the Tekeze.

After much soul-searching, and not a small amount of angst, I decided to forgo the commercial Omo expedition, as well as the Blue Nile exploratory, in favor of graduate school and a job as a waiter at a Bob's Big Boy outlet. My experience with the Blue Nile, despite its great name and history, had not been overwhelming. And I was still haunted by the drowning of Angus. Missing the next Blue Nile exploratory was an act of self-abnegation I immediately regretted. But I reminded myself and all who would listen, I would be there for the Tekeze, which we were now scheduling for the fall of 1975. But with all the trouble in Ethiopia of late, most of it in the north, we would need permits for both the Blue Nile and the Tekeze. We agreed that I would go over to Ethiopia in early September, before starting journalism school, and work to get the necessary permits, and then Lew, John Yost, and Jim Slade would head over to Ethiopia in October to run the Omo. In January they would attempt the unrun upper section of the Blue Nile.

I had fallen in love with OARS guide Candy Uenyo over the summer, and she moved into my apartment in Playa del Rey, just underneath a jet-landing path at LAX. She offered to oversee the place while I made a quick trip to Addis Ababa to see if I could nail down the permits.

CHAPTER 22

CAUGHT IN THE COUP D'ÉTAT

There are decades where nothing happens; and there are weeks where decades happen.

—Vladimir Ilyich Lenin

I arrived in Addis Ababa the second week of September, just after the rains. The day was cool, washed in a flat, white light. As I drove down the Bole road, I looked through a spiderweb of cracks running from a bullet hole in the taxi's windshield to the sight of buses overturned, charred, and cannibalized. Anger soaked the air. I checked into the YMCA for my short stay, and all night long I heard the crack of rifle shot and the howling of dogs. The next day, after a soak at the Filowa baths, I visited geologist John Kalb, who was exploring the Awash for fossils of the "missing link," and who was storing our rafts in exchange for occasional use. When I approached, he was rubbing his hands up and down between his knees, like a man separating wheat. He had unwelcome news. The government had nationalized our rafts and confiscated them. We'd have to bring over another set. In the afternoon I visited my friends at the embassy, who expressed great concern over the deteriorating situation and who had heightened security around the compound. They talked of the US ambassador who was assassinated in Khartoum and didn't end their sentences, but the train was clear. Trouble was brewing. I missed curfew, so an embassy van took me back through the near-deserted streets, peopled only with whores who scissored their legs and kissed the air at my passing.

The following day I awoke to the prayer call of a muezzin, something I hadn't remembered from earlier visits. I got up and walked to the offices of ETO, the Ethiopian Tourist Organization, run by a smart, fast-talking Columbia University–educated Ethiopian named Hapte Selassie (no relation to the emperor). Director-General H. E. Hapte Selassie had helped me in the past and was intrigued with my introduction of adventure travel to Ethiopia. I had given him many slides from our previous expeditions, and he had already made some into posters and postcards and was planning a government brochure on the rafting and adventure opportunities in the country.

Dark-suited, with pointed shoes and an Italian cigarette, he greeted me graciously. With the distant manner of an aristocrat, he gestured for me to sit in an oak chair in front of his ornately carved desk beneath an Italian oleograph. Everything about Hapte Selassie spoke breeding and money and a lifetime of privilege. Yet, he was drawn to the rough and raw adventure I represented. I had written him well in advance of the meeting requesting the permits. As I laid out my plans, he reminded me things were not so stable in the north. I said I knew that, but that my team was willing to assume the risks if we could secure the permits. After a pause of consideration, he clasped his hands together in front of him and then rested them, like a completed sentence. He said he would issue the permits, and he pulled from his desk two pre-typed letters of authorization for us to make our rafting exploratories on the Blue Nile and Tekeze. He placed them neatly on his desk and proceeded with a flourish to sign the first one, the one for the Blue Nile. He then pulled out a government seal, stamped the paper with a thud and handed it to me.

Then, as he looked at the second paper, the permit for the Tekeze, the door burst open with a crash. A file of army soldiers in combat fatigues, olive-drab garrison belts, and spit-shined jump boots stormed into the room and surrounded us. There was the harsh metallic clunk of rifles being cocked. One man yelled in Amharic, and guns were raised and leveled at Hapte Selassie. More commands were issued, and Hapte defiantly sat in his chair, his hand tightened angrily around the stamp. Again, the same words were yelled, but this time four soldiers went to the back of Hapte's chair and lifted him to a standing position. Then the officer in charge marched over to Hapte Selassie and undid his tie. He pulled it off in a burst, picked up the papers on the desk, and then barked more orders, at which the soldiers shuffled His Excellency out the door, slamming it behind them. I was left alone with the single permit. It was September 12, 1974.

Little did I know that at that same moment around the city, various ministers were being rounded up by a cabal of junior army officers leading the coup d'état. As each was arrested, his tie, a symbol to the revolutionaries of neocolonistic hierocracy, was ripped off, and he was taken to jail, or to a wall and shot dead. Just a few blocks away another set of soldiers burst into the Imperial Palace and arrested its eighty-two-year-old occupant. He was ordered to take off his regal robes and change into commoners' clothes. And he was told he could not bring his beloved Chihuahua, Lulu, with him as he was escorted out the door, his last African walk. Three thousand years of Solomonic rule ended with His Imperial Majesty Haile Selassie I being driven unceremoniously from his palace in a Volkswagen Beetle.

After Hapte Selassie's arrest, I walked out to the street, and Addis Ababa felt ugly, out-of-joint, in a way that was entirely new to me. I wanted out and headed home.

On the way home I routed through Washington, D.C., and stopped by the Ethiopian embassy to assess the situation. The new government, a socialist-inspired military coordinating committee, known as the Dergue ("committee" in Amharic), assured me we would be allowed to run the Omo, and they would honor the permit for the Blue Nile, but certainly there was no way to run the Tekeze. Back in California I consulted with Lew, Jim, John, and our eight clients, and they all agreed to go forward. Even Candy was willing to make the trip and seemed thrilled with the added edge of rafting a river in the midst of a revolution.

I drove Candy to the airport, kissed her goodbye, and went back to bury myself in my studies. I wondered endlessly if I had made the right decision. And then a month later she returned, tan and happy, with tales of how wonderful Lew had been . . . a bit of my own spirit sailed with her through him. Over Christmas I got a call from Ethiopia. It was Lew, who asked if I might change my mind and jump on the upcoming Blue Nile exploratory. I hesitated, but then said no . . . I had to follow this course for a while. "Then promise me we'll do the next one," he said through the scratchy phone connection. I did. I promised I would be back. Of that I was certain.

CHAPTER 23

A DEATH TOO SOON

Even at the height of the dry season it tears and boils along too fast for any boat to live upon its surface.

—ALAN MOOREHEAD

THINGS WERE GOING FINE. I WAS ENJOYING MY STUDIES, WORKING TOWARDS A MASters in journalism. After school and on weekends I attended to the business of Sobek, answering the letters and phone calls, mailing out our flyers. But it didn't take a lot of time, as we didn't have much product to offer, and we didn't have many customers. Ethiopia wasn't suffering from an overabundance of good press, and we had yet to explore a river beyond its boundaries. So the job of president of Sobek Expeditions was not a taxing one, and I even had time to start an adventure travel magazine, *Bush League*, which promptly went bankrupt after publishing its one and only issue.

January 1975 rolled around, and I wondered how my pards were doing on the Blue Nile without me. When neighbors came over, Candy often showed slides from her recent Omo trip, and I felt a tinge of regret well up.

The morning of January 21 I got a call. I recognized the sonar voice of an overseas operator. She had me hold for a long minute, and then I heard the voice of John Yost, phoning from Addis Ababa. It was a scratchy connection. "Lew drowned," John said matter-of-factly. "Can you repeat that?" I spoke back into the receiver, my lip quivering, hoping I heard it wrong. "Lew is dead. He drowned on the Blue Nile," John said in slow measured tones. He continued to speak, but the whole world seemed to crash around my head. I hung up the phone. My temples began to throb. I buckled to the floor and cried.

They had launched just below the First Portuguese Bridge, Agam Dildi, the entrance to the Northern Gorge, and immediately found themselves in a concatenation of tight, twisting black basalt gorges, packed with Class V and VI rapids. Much of the trip they spent portaging or lining. The second day, January 17, Jim Slade awoke and wrote in his diary: "Dreamed my brother had died, and that Lew was my

brother. Hope it was not an ill-omen or presentiment of things to come on this trip."
It was the first time Jim had ever dreamed about death. Downstream later that day
they came to a rapid not as bad as what they had battled. The river split and then
reunited. They took the right channel. Then it split again, and the boat got caught
in a small recirculating eddy on the right side where the water piled up against a
blue-black wall. It didn't seem too dangerous, and they were tired of portaging. It was
January, the water was low, and they felt the current was forgiving enough they could
push the boat down the side of the wall and back into the main current.

Nobody was rowing. The oars were shipped. John Yost, Conrad Hirsh, Lew, and
Jim Slade were standing on the tube and pushing the boat, working the boat, along
the wall. They were making satisfactory progress. But a section of the wall stuck out
a few inches, and the boat got lodged at the strongest intersection of the main river
current and the back current of the eddy. With the powerful main current pushing
against the outer tube, the boat slowly started to rise up the wall. The four tried to
push the raft back down, but the current was far too strong, and it continued to rise.
It became clear the boat was going to capsize. John was closest to shore, and he made
a flying curvet and landed on solid ground. The boat continued to rise to a near tube
stand. Conrad was next, and he jumped as far as he could and landed waist-deep in
water. The raft was now starting its roll over, and Lew jumped next into water over
his head right where the stern line was trailing. He went under and surfaced with a
frightened look, and then in an agonal effort screamed that his life jacket had clipped
to the stern line. Slade jumped last, but by then the raft was over. Jim and the boat
sailed out into the main current and over a steep drop-off rapid. Jim was out front,
and a couple hundred yards downstream he managed to make his way to the left
shore. He then saw the raft charging towards him, and he swam back out, grabbed a
D-ring, and with all his remaining strength he dragged it to a gravel bar.

John was on the opposite shore, and as Jim was catching his breath, he watched
John jump into the raging current and swim the entire width of the Blue Nile. He
splashed to the boat and between gulps told Jim that Lew was missing and before
disappearing had yelled he was caught on the stern line. They immediately checked
the stern and bowlines and found a nick in the former where it looked like something snagged. They checked under the boat, where people often get caught in a
capsize. And then they searched the banks, howling Lew's name, sweeping the river,
fearing the worst. At nightfall they collapsed in exhaustion.

With daybreak they could think of nothing to do but head downstream. A few
turns downriver they found Lew, floating in an eddy, his orange Mae West life jacket
pulled halfway up his head. Like Shorty Burton on the Colorado, who died when his
life jacket clipped to a gas can during a capsize, it seemed Lew had jumped into the
water and his jacket had clipped to the stern line . . . he was then dragged over the
next falls and downstream until he drowned, and then somehow let loose.

The surviving crew pulled Lew to shore and weighed options. They had an
unknown distance yet to run and, in all likelihood, many dangerous rapids yet to

A last picture of my friend and partner Lew Greenwald, who drowned on the Blue Nile. RICHARD BANGS

face before reaching the Second Portuguese Bridge. And from there it was a full day's hike to the village of Mota, where they could catch the once-a-week plane to Addis Ababa. Lew had loved rivers, and they had changed him for the better. So they decided to lay him to rest by the Blue Nile. The ground was too hard to bury him, so they found a small hollow and covered him with stones. Then they built a small fire, a funeral pyre, on top and performed a simple ceremony. They had no idea they were being watched, but a year later Karen Greenwald hiked into the gorge and met villagers who said they witnessed the funeral, and they took her to the spot. She removed Lew's remains and took them to a Jewish cemetery in Addis Ababa, where he was laid to rest in consecrated ground.

The news of Lew's death sent me into a tailspin. Up to that point, I saw river rafting as the finest expression of freedom and self-validation that existed, and the death fifteen months earlier of Angus Macleod a rare aberration. I believed that the American idea of freedom was Huck rafting the Mississippi, or Thoreau going up the Merrimac. I had seen firsthand the transformational power of river journeys, and Lew was living testimony: He had trimmed down, found a confidence and a lightness that had been hidden, and let it be known that his life was full of joy. But with his drowning, I saw the dark side of adventure. How could anything be celebrated that snatched away lives so full of promise, charity, and happiness? What sort of Faustian bargain had I struck? I had spent six years challenging wild rivers around the country and two in East Africa and had amassed more than my share of thrills and spills. Now, not only did the guilt of Angus's fate resurface, but also the shock that my close friend was dead numbed my world. Shame ran through me like a sword. The life jacket in my closet hung like an accusation beside my winter coat. Suddenly the thought of rafting down a river seemed evil, a frivolous exercise that had such an insidious downside that I couldn't imagine why people would risk it. I saw it all as a photographic negative of the way I had seen it before; everything white was black. The thought of laughing while paddling through the raised fist of a wave, a slap of whitewater that could knock a person unconscious and suck the life from a precious body, was abhorrent, pornographic, insane. I wanted to call all my past passengers and tell them the truth about river running and urge them to stay away from rafts and rivers.

My attitude about rivers bent like a gooseneck. Rivers didn't assert life; they took it away. They weren't innocent; they were dissolute. Wormwood embittering the tree of adventure. Rivers were acid baths. I didn't ever want to go near one again, didn't want one to come within my compass. I hung up my paddle.

I was in such a sulfurous funk, I was a monster to live with. I carved out my own little meat department of metaphysical angst, and it stunk. I cooked food and didn't eat it. I put on music and didn't listen to it. Candy moved out; moved to Montana and not long after married a doctor. I never saw her again. I buried myself in studies and tried to forget the pain. My life became bland and vapid, a world behind glass. But as the months wore, I began to soften. Friends would stop by my apartment on their way to run a river, and when I tried to explain my hostility for what they were doing, their eyes looked over my shoulder. And, at social functions, I couldn't ignore the palpable excitement across the room when talk finally steered to rivers run and yet to be. That spring my most exciting endeavor was watching the tomatoes grow.

CHAPTER 24

THE MIDDLE FORK WAY

In the midst of winter, I finally learned that there was in me an invincible summer.

—ALBERT CAMUS

WORD SPREAD LIKE WILDFIRE. TOM BROKAW, THE NBC NEWSMAN, HAD TAKEN A trip down the Middle Fork of the Salmon with some friends. It was the end of June, and the water was unusually high. Two of the three boats flipped in Weber Rapids, one of the last rapids. Brokaw made it to shore safely after a short swim in the minus-four-degree water. Two others were not so lucky—Ellis Harmon, a twenty-nine-year-old Century City lawyer and militant Sierra Club member, and Gene Teague, age fifty-eight, a longtime professional river guide who had been rowing at the moment of capsize. Four other people drowned that week on the Main and Middle Forks of the Salmon.

All this sad news reinforced my sentiments about the dark side of river running. But, curiously, a piece of me was piqued. I still felt I was fluent in water dynamics, and I might have made it through where Brokaw's raft had not.

So when fellow river guide Breck O'Neill called and suggested we take a stab at rafting the Middle Fork of the Salmon, resistance melted like butter. It did sound like fun, a break from the flat pitch my life had become.

I screwed up my courage and asked my dad for the car for our little adventure, but he said no without explanation. My dad's bitterness towards his work and employer had intensified, his nervous breakdowns had continued, and with each he seemed to retreat deeper into an inner space. He had been several times hospitalized, had attempted suicide, had undergone more violent episodes. He was still in therapy, trying different meditations and new medications, and seemed increasingly disconnected from his family. He really had no idea how rivers had affected my life and never asked, never probed. He was exploring another current.

So we hitched to Breck's mom's house in San Jose, where we convinced her to loan us her station wagon. We also picked up Breck's high school friends Dave Plapp and Mary Pollino, who, while not river runners, wanted to share in the adventure. Together we headed for central Idaho, the long way—in that we first went to Vernal, Utah (five hundred miles out of our way), and the warehouse of my former employer, Hatch River Expeditions.

I cornered co-owner Don Hatch and asked if we could borrow a raft for our journey. Everyone knew that the Middle Fork was Don's favorite; besides, his father, who had recently died, had made a pioneering run down the river in 1936. I thought we would be tugging at his heartstrings with our cri de coeur. Nonetheless, Don was not enthusiastic about loaning out one of the tools of his trade, especially to a young buck who the season before had ripped the bottom out of a company raft on the Colorado. I persisted, likening our quest to a holy mission, and at last he consented, warning that we had to return the raft in exactly the same condition, or we would have to pay for full replacement. He then pulled a black blob from the back of the warehouse, dusted off a layer of talcum powder, and presented us with our means of conveyance.

"She's one of my best boats. Take real good care of her." Don curled his lips.

I recognized that smile. It was on the face of the dealer who sold me a 1963 VW bug that blew up a week after I bought it. It was the smile on the face of the Mercedes owner as he passed me in a whispering blur. Still, we graciously accepted Don's offer, strapped the frame and oars on top of the station wagon, pushed the blob in the back, and waved goodbye.

The drive north into the massive western edge of the Rocky Mountains was humbling. To an Easterner accustomed to the long, rounded ridges of the Appalachians, these mountains seemed desolate and impenetrable. No wonder the Middle Fork had been spared dams, highways, and other developments, though not for lack of trying.

In 1805 William Clark, of the Lewis and Clark Expedition, attempted to explore the Salmon as a possible water route to the Columbia River, but he turned back when it became clear the rapids were impassable by boat and the canyon walls too steep for horses and men. A century later, with the advent of specialized boats, access by water became a reality, but the rugged terrain kept all but the most determined, and intrepid, at bay.

The following twilight we rolled into Stanley, Idaho, where a cloud rose in a last ferment, remaking the day before it died. We quickly found the hot spot in town—the thermal springs—and immediately slipped in for a soak. The night was so crisp the stars seemed to crackle, and in the torpid curls of steam I could see the eddies and waves of the river we were about to encounter.

Designated by Congress in 1968 as part of the National Wild and Scenic River system, the Middle Fork of the Salmon is the last great American river remaining, throughout its course, unfettered by dams or hydro projects of any kind. It begins life at the confluence of Bear Valley and Marsh Creeks twenty miles northwest of the hot springs we were enjoying. The source was discovered in 1863 by a mining party led by Capt. John Stanley, for whom the closest town is named. Running in the shadows of the 2-mile-high peaks of the Sawtooth Range, the river plunges 1,600 feet in its 104-mile race to a union with the Main Salmon. En route, it cascades through the Frank Church River of No Return Wilderness, named in 1984 after the late Idaho senator cited as one of America's "premiere wilderness champions."

The dawn broke hard and fast, with cascades of supersaturated sunlight gushing over the canyon walls like a broken dam. We bounced down to the Dagger Falls put-in and, for the first time, unrolled our borrowed boat—a thin-skinned cotton neoprene survival raft shaped like an Easter basket. The raft was designed to carry a dozen survivors on the open sea with the sinking of the mother ship; it was not meant for sharp rocks or downriver negotiation. Yet, in a pinch, penny-pinching outfitters often used these boats, which could be purchased as government surplus, to carry clients on lenient runs. Our version looked as it if had already run the Styx—it was covered with patches and caramel streaks of hardened Barge glue.

"If this boat doesn't make it, we're all responsible for paying for a replacement," I reminded our little group as we all stared at the wad of rubber at our feet, a wad that looked more like a dead seal than a raft.

Breck and Mary nodded in agreement. They were anxious to get on the river, whatever the costs or consequences. Dave took a couple minutes before replying; he'd never been rafting and was questioning the wisdom of this little excursion.

But then he hesitantly said, "Okay, I'm in," and we prepared to cast our fates to the river.

After repatching a half dozen pinhole leaks, tying down the orange wooden frame, and attaching the nine-foot white ash oars, we shoved off into the fast, cold currents of the Middle Fork and held on for a ride down a bolt of liquid lightning.

Almost immediately, before I had managed more than a dozen strokes, we whizzed by the first tributary on the left, Sulphur Creek. We launched at an elevation of 5,700 feet and were dropping fast, some forty-two feet per mile, on a waterslide with eddies, down a bowling alley with no gutters. I was at the oars, pulling frantically against the current to slow us down, but we were in the river's grip and were being pulled toward our first test: the coarse fabric of Velvet Falls.

The face of the ranger at the Challis National Forest stations had creased to a dolphin smile when he told us of Velvet Falls, five miles below the put-in, the first Class IV rapids on the run. He said the run on the wrong side—the right—dropped sheer and spun a web of whitewater chaos. The trick to running Velvet was to spot the large marker rock on the left while approaching and then position for a left-side plunge.

The advice seemed easy to heed, only now amid the millrace, I couldn't tell how fast we were going or how far we'd traveled.

"Think we've gone three miles yet?" I called out.

"I don't think so," Dave answered as we barreled down the right bank.

Seconds later, Breck screamed, "There's the marker rock. Pull over!"

No way could I make the left shore, so I strained my back, pumped the oars like pistons, and managed to scrape the eastern bank. Mary jumped out with the stern line and tried to hold us. But the boat wouldn't brake, and she was dragged along the lichen-covered rocks, desperately grasping the end of the rope.

"It's burning," Mary called, face wrenched in pain.

"Don't let go," Dave shouted back, but it was a useless call.

The rope yanked like a snapping winch cable from her raw hands, and the raft shot back into the current, heading for the hairy lip of the terrible right-hand side of Velvet Falls.

The three of us braced for the drop, and down we fell. The raft struck the bottom and started to twist sideways, as though crouching for a capsize. I took one concentrated, correcting stroke with the left oar, and tang, the oarlock snapped, sending the oar into orbit, and me into the duffel pile. The raft kissed the edge of capsizing and then plopped back down and spun toward the right shore, where Breck was able to secure the boat to a tree.

The damage was minimal; the loop of the oarlock was gone, probably two dollars' worth of metal. But it was a critical piece, and we had no replacement. So we found a sturdy piece of Engelmann spruce branch. I whittled it down to the thole pin size with my Swiss army knife and then lashed the oar to the makeshift pin. The process took an hour, about the time it took Mary to thrash through the overgrowth to reach us. The jury-rigged oarpin setup didn't inspire confidence, especially since we had thirty-four rated rapids to go, but it was all we had. So, with equanimity punctured, we reloaded and headed downstream.

The going was easier now, although rowing with an oarlock on one side and a crude thole pin lashed to the oar on the other made for less-than-smooth navigation. It was like running on crutches.

The next day we shot through Artillery and Cannon Creek rapids on target, not even a powder burn. We also passed tributaries named Mortar, Springfield, Winchester, Remington, Colt, and Popgun. The hot sun broke along the black raft, but the water was refreshingly cold when it splashed my skin, and it was clearer than any gin I had encountered. In the calm stretches I could lean over the raft and watch the colored, cobbled riverbed glide beneath me as though we were riding on glass. Sometimes the river was utterly still, and the only movement was the lazy turning of my own thoughts.

As though detonated, we blasted through the barrel-tight S-turn of Pistol Creek and then purled into Indian Creek, a level strip of bank where small planes bring in clients and gear during the later weeks of summer when the water is too low to launch upstream at Dagger Falls.

Though the river was fattening with each feeder stream, it didn't slow down, and for the next thirty miles we were treated to a full course of Class II and Class III rapids, all in a setting that would rate VII on the I–VI scale. Icy, printless peaks surrounded us on all sides, the Salmon River Mountains to the west, the Bighorn Crags to the east; some craggy with bald rock faces, others blanketed with quilts of conifers and golden grasses. The canyon we were traversing was carved from the Idaho Batholith, a 100- by 200-mile mass of granite that once lay under volcanos long since eroded away and dated at more than one hundred million years old.

On the third day, we came to Tappan Falls. A series of four closely spaced drops, Tappan is rocky even in high water. The lashing holding the makeshift oarlock had loosened so that the blade of the oar bounced though the water as though rubber. I managed to steer the raft down the roiling right side of the river, but in the second drop the boat grated over a kernel of exposed granite, and the sound of the raft ripping drowned the rapids. In a flash, Dave and Mary and the duffel pile were sucked out of sight, as though dropped through a trapdoor. I looked down between my legs and saw the river. The raft's bottom was gone, torn into two segments that flapped in the water like the wings of a stingray.

Frantically we wrestled the remains of our raft to shore, finally connecting at a small eddy below the last of the Tappan drops. Dave and Mary splashed to shore a couple of hundred yards downstream and made their way back up to our anchorage as Breck and I pulled the blob up onto a level spit of shore that was overrun with sharp grass, thorn bushes, and ninebark. A bow-to-stern rip bisected the floor, a rip that would take at least half a day to repair. So we gathered what had been retrieved of our gear and spread it out like pieces of a jigsaw puzzle to dry, and I set to work sewing the floor with a huge, hooked needle and a spool of 30-pound-test nylon fishing line.

Clouds of mosquitoes rolled around our heads, and I spent more time scratching and slapping than patching. With the last rays of sunlight, I finished, pleased with my handiwork. I stepped onto one of the raft's tubes to raise my hand in triumph, and an explosion threw me to the ground. My weight had burst the tube. Half the boat was suddenly deflated, looking like a collapsed lung. While most inflatable whitewater rafts have at least four independent chambers, and some have six, our little craft had just two. I looked closely; the fabric of the tube was rotten. The whole boat was cursed. Our expedition was coming apart at the seams. And we were halfway down the river, with the biggest rapids yet to come.

I suffered through a miserable night in my wet goose down sleeping bag, listening to the river making obscene swallowing noises by our bivouac. With the first frosty light, I was up and patching. The repairs were finished by breakfast, but it took another half day for the glue to set. Dave, looking wan and feeble, had spent much of the night bent behind a tree. He was afflicted with giardiasis, picked up, we suspected, from the untreated Middle Fork water we'd all shared.

By noon we were on the water again. We had only inflated the raft 80 percent to ease the pressure of its flimsy skin. We made it through Aparejo and then Haystack, where another boater had drowned the year before. At the confluence of Big Creek, we entered Impassable Canyon, where the worst of the Middle Fork rapids had torn holes in the river. The gorge was named by US First Cavalry captain Reuben S. Bernard in 1879 when he led an ill-conceived expedition to capture the Sheepeater Indians in the area and was turned back by the terrain. Our expedition seemed equally ill-conceived. The river was now huge, the size of the Colorado, and a chilly wind blew upstream as though from a tomb. We ran Porcupine Rapids with no new difficulties, and then we careened through the center of Redside, a major rapid named for its colorful cutthroat trout.

Suddenly the floor I had so meticulously mended split open again, and once more the river yawned beneath me. I was out of control. My strokes meant nothing. And we were now in the angled waves of Weber Falls.

I struggled with the oars, threw my weight to the high side as we plunged through wave after giant wave, and saw three companions doing the same, faces white as the water. We dropped into a horologic hole sideways, the frame cracked, and my tube patch blew out. Somehow, we managed to hobble into the calm water below right-side-up, with everyone miraculously still in what was left of the boat.

Again, we pulled over for repairs, but I had used all the Barge cement glue last round. Dave was slapping his sides and his speech was slurred—the beginnings of hypothermia. We talked of hiking out, but the 4,000-foot-high walls were too steep. The gorge was named Impassable for a reason. With no interrupting edge of riverbank, the sheer flat rock face of dark gray granite formed a cryptlike chamber that revealed no end or exit. The map showed just ten river miles to go, and about as many rapids. We decided to go for it.

First, we re-laid the patch that had popped off. Without new glue, it barely stuck, so Mary agreed to sit on the patch, which reduced the situation to a slow leak. Then we fastened the nozzle of the foot pump to the valve of the leaking tube with duct tape. Breck sat on the thwart with the foot pump in his lap and continued to pump with his hands as I rowed.

We limped through Cliffside, then with five miles left we rolled into Rubber. The waves were huge, with trenches of sudden air, and we rode them as though surfers on the North Shore. In the last wave, the raft pitched up a crest, stalled at the top, and bent both the bow and the stern on opposite sides of the wave, and again we heard a horrifying pop.

The other tube had split a seam, and half the raft immediately deflated. We all scrambled to a perch on the tube with the patch, and Breck continued to pump.

The frame hung limply, half in the water, completely useless. There was no way to row to shore. Dave threw me a terrified glance. All we could do was hang on. The blob with four passengers drooped through Hancock, Devil's Tooth, House Rocks, and Jump Off Rapids, and then we were finished. Like shipwreck survivors hanging onto flotsam, we drifted into the confluence, the clear water of the Middle Fork disappearing into the gray water of the Main.

When I returned the shredded blob of a boat to Don Hatch, I complained it wasn't all it was cracked up to be. Don insisted it had been in perfect condition before we trashed it and held us to our end of the bargain—we had to pay for a replacement. I swallowed and asked how much, thinking he'd want a couple thousand or more.

"Fifty dollars, and we'll call it even." He grinned that grin.

I peeled the bills and grinned back. The moment was incalculable, the trip priceless.

In the end, I refused to be dissuaded by the thought of my own demise. I joined the little expedition and was once again washed in the rapture of moving water. I vowed to make a go of Sobek.

It was August 25, 1975. As I emerged from the river reborn, on the other side of the world Mengistu Haile Mariam was smothering to death with an ether-soaked pillow his prisoner of almost a year, the 225th consecutive monarch in a royal line tracing to Solomon the First, the son of David: Emperor Haile Selassie. The remains would be secretly buried under a latrine.

CHAPTER 25

LAST SEARCH DOWN THE BARO

We shall not cease from exploration. And at the end of all our exploring will be to arrive where we started and know the place for the first time.
—T. S. ELIOT, "LITTLE GIDDING," 1942

THAT FALL I RETURNED TO GRADUATE SCHOOL AND BECAME RE-ENGAGED IN SOBEK, designing a new brochure, plotting new expeditions in New Guinea and Türkiye, running a few western rivers over the weekends. I wasn't sure, though, whether I would ever go back to Ethiopia. The deaths still haunted me.

In November of that year, 1975, I got a call from a friend, a tour operator. A trek he'd organized to the Sahara had been cancelled by the Algerian government, and his clients wanted an alternative. Would I be interested in taking the clients to Ethiopia for a trek? Two weeks later I arrived in Addis Ababa, where I met up with John Yost, Jim Slade, and a trainee-guide, Gary Bolton, fresh from a Sobek raft tour of the Omo River. They were surprised to see me, here where nobody expected I would return.

By late December, after escorting a commercial trek through the Bale Mountains of southern Ethiopia, John, Jim, and I were wondering what to do next, and the subject of the unfinished Baro came up. The mystery of Angus still gnawed at all of us. I confessed that over the months, sometimes in the middle of a mundane chore— taking out the trash, doing the laundry—I'd stop and see Angus's frozen features as I cut him loose. In weak moments I would wonder if there just might be a chance that he was still alive. And I'd be pressed with a feeling of guilt, that I hadn't done enough, that I had waded in waist deep, then turned back. And I wondered how Angus had felt in those last few minutes—about himself, about me. Jim and John admitted to similar feelings, and we collectively decided to try the Baro once again. We needed a fourth, and Gary Bolton agreed to join as well.

This time we put in where I had taken out almost two years before, at the terminus of a long jungle path. Again, we had a single raft, with the minimum of gear to make portaging easier. The river pummeled us, as it had before, stochastically tossing portages and major rapids in our path. But during the next few days, the trip gradually, almost imperceptibly, became easier. With Christmas morning the early sunlight made a jewel of every leaf. I decorated the helmet of a bush with my socks and passed out presents of party favors and sweets. Under an ebony sapling I placed a package of confections for Angus. It was a curiously satisfying holiday, being surrounded by primeval beauty and accompanied by three other men with a common quest. No one expected to find Angus alive, but I thought that the journey—at least for me—might expunge all doubt, exorcise guilt. I wanted to think that I had done all that was humanly possible to explore a death for which I was partly responsible. And somehow, I wanted him to know this.

As we tumbled off the Abyssinian Massif into the Great Rift Valley of Africa, taking on tributaries every few miles, the river and its rapids grew. At times we even allowed ourselves to enjoy the experience, to shriek with delight, to throw heads back in laughter as we bounced through Colorado-style whitewater and soaked in the scenery. Again, we found remnants of the first trip—a broken oar here, a smashed pan there. Never, though, a hint of Angus.

After one long day of portaging, I went to gather my wetpack, holding my clothes, sleeping bag, and toilet kit, and it was nowhere to be found. Apparently, it had been tossed out during one of the grueling portages. I trekked back upstream for a couple miles but could find nothing, and it was getting dark, so I picked my way back to the raft and the plain pasta dinner John was cooking. At that moment, I had no worldly possessions save the torn shorts I was wearing, my socks and tennis shoes, and the Buck knife that hung from my pants. I slept in a small cave that night, rolled up like a hedgehog, with no sleeping bag, no pad, but I slept well. With the morning, I awoke fresh and energized, ready for the day, and though I had practically nothing to call my own, I felt a richness for the moment . . . I was with friends, on a mission, and was touching something primal. In an odd way, this all seemed liberating . . . no accoutrements to weigh down the soul . . . just a clear, present reason for going forward, for being. And I allowed something that would be called joy to wash over me.

On New Year's Eve we camped at the confluence of the Baro and the Bir-Bir Rivers, pulling in as the copper light of dusk was thickening to darkness. A lorry track crossed the Baro opposite our camp. It was there that Conrad Hirsh, the professor from the second Baro attempt, had said he would try to meet us with supplies. We couldn't see him, but Jim thought there might be a message waiting for us across the river. "I think I'll go check it out," he said.

"Don't be a fool," John warned. "We're in croc country now. You do not want to swim across this river." We weren't far from where Bill Olsen, the Peace Corps volunteer, was chomped in half while swimming.

The first Sobek brochure, which offered the first raft trips to Africa.
UPPER PICTURES: GEORGE FULLER; BOTTOM: JOHN KRAMER

An hour later, just after dark, Jim had not returned. We shouted his name, first individually, then as a chorus. No answer. Jim had become a close friend in the two years since we shared a tent on the upper Baro; he had been a partner in ordeal and elation, in failure and success. Now John and I swept our weak flashlight beams along the dark river. We gave up. We were tired, and we sat around the low licks of our campfire, ready to accept another loss, mapping out the ramifications in our minds. Suddenly, like a whisper, Jim walked in from the shadows and thrust a note at us.

"Conrad arrived three days ago, waited two, and left this morning," he said, his body still dripping from the swim.

"You fool! I knew you couldn't disappear now—you owe me $3.30 in backgammon debts." I clucked with all the disciplinary tone I could muster.

The following day we spun from the vortex of the last rapid into the wide, Mississippi-like reaches of the lower Baro. Where rocks and whirlpools were once the enemy, now there were crocodiles and hippos. We hurled rocks, made threatening gestures, and yelled banshee shrieks to keep them away. Late in the day on January 3, 1976, we glided into the outpost town of Gambella. The villagers there had neither seen nor heard of Angus Macleod.

I never told Angus's relatives of our last search; we didn't find what might have given them solace. What I found I kept to myself, hidden like buried treasure in my soul. It was the knowledge of the precious and innate value of endeavor.

I wanted to believe that when Angus boarded my tiny boat and committed himself, he was sparked with life and light, that his blood raced with the passion of existence—perhaps more than ever before. On that first Friday in October of 1973, ten of us thought we knew what we were doing: another expedition, another raft trip, another river. Only Angus was exploring beyond his being. Maybe his was a senseless death, moments after launching, in the very first rapid. I would never forget the look of horror in his eyes as he struggled there in the water. But there were other ways to think about it. He took the dare and contacted the outermost boundaries. He lost, but so do we all, eventually. The difference—and it is an enormous one—is that he reached for it, wholly.

CHAPTER 26

ADVENTURES GONE WRONG

However great a man may be, there are always some subjects which "ought" to throw him off his balance; some, by which his poor human capacity of thought should be conquered, and brought into the inaccurate and vague state of perception, so that the language of the highest inspiration becomes broken, obscure, and wild in metaphor.

—John Ruskin

After the last Baro expedition I returned to graduate school and completed my masters in journalism, a program that provided me with a skill I found useful in promoting Sobek by writing articles about our adventures. I then enrolled in a doctoral program in cinema, thinking the craft of filmmaking might also aid in advancing Sobek. But the academics of cinematography bored me, and I hungered to get my hands dirty again with real expeditions. So, a year into the program I quit and moved back to Angels Camp, where George Wendt offered me a bedroom, rent-free, as I plotted new exploratories and tried to turn Sobek into a real concern.

During this time, my father continued to be in and out of hospitals and sanitariums, and I would tramp home over the holidays to attempt a connection or understanding. But he seemed impenetrable, inscrutable. Once I asked about the film he made in Iran back in the 1950s, and he perked up a bit. He said that the finished work was in a vault at CIA headquarters in Langley, and that someday he wanted to show it to me.

"What's in the film?"

"I can't tell you, but I can say we recruited a famous Hollywood director for the job. I was very proud of that."

In June 1978 John Yost, Jim Slade, and I were at the airport in Istanbul, having just completed the first descent of the upper Euphrates River in Türkiye. We were about to board the Pan Am flight to Frankfurt, which would connect us back to San Francisco, but we were on standby tickets, school was just out, and the flight was full. I studied the OAG (Official Airline Guide) info and saw that we could catch a flight to Tehran that would require an overnight, but then the following day it connected via Bombay and Hong Kong across the Pacific back to San Francisco. It didn't take much convincing for Yost and Slade to join the plan, and a few hours later we were at the airport in Tehran. It was middle afternoon, and the continuing flight was scheduled for 6:00 a.m. the morning following, so Jim and John elected to stay in the airport and read, play backgammon, and sleep on the plastic chairs rather than venture to town. I had private reasons, though, so I grabbed the bus and made my way to the city center, and the public library. Though the capital was renowned for being the closest thing to a Western city in the Middle East, it was choked with cars and smog and angry faces. As I walked down the streets, I stood out as a foreigner with my blond hair and backpack, and passersby stooped to pick up stones and toss them at me, or spat at me. Outside of our brief encounter on the Blue Nile, it was the most hostile place I'd ever been. Little known to me, a cycle of protest and violence was under way, and I was walking through a time bomb. I passed an English newspaper, and its headlines quoted the Shah: "Nobody can overthrow me. I have the support of 7,000,000 troops, all of the workers, and most of the people. I have the power."

In the library, I found the bound copies of the English-language newspaper going back to the early 1950s. There I read about how Mohammad Reza Pahlavi, an imperial leader in much the same mode as Haile Selassie, was forced into a brief exile by domestic opponents in 1953. This I knew from readings Stateside, as well as the fact that the CIA had engineered and stage-managed the return of the Shah to the Peacock Throne in a covert operation headed by Kermit Roosevelt. Those were the salad days of the CIA, when clandestine operations were conducted against the North Koreans, in support of Japan's Liberal Democratic Party, by orchestrating a coup in Guatemala, and by assisting the Tibetan uprising against China. The year I was looking for was 1956, when my father was in Tehran. I found nothing, except two unrelated items . . . a mention that an American documentary film crew was returning to the city for several weeks and that a new secret police force had been formed by the Shah, called SAVAK, to combat the pro-Moscow Tudeh (Communist) Party, which had been declared illegal.

The next morning, we couldn't get on the Pan Am flight to Bombay, it too being overbooked. Instead we caught a flight back to Istanbul, and there we were upgraded to First Class to take the last remaining seats on a flight to New York. It was a thrill to be in the front of the plane, but also an embarrassment when I took off the hiking boots I'd been wearing for weeks and a smelly cloud billowed through the cabin. I sunk into my seat to avoid the stares and coughs.

Seven months later, on January 16, 1979, the Shah was forced to flee the gathering storm of revolution in Iran, fueled by the corrupt way he used his country's oil wealth, and perhaps more because of the brutalities of SAVAK, his secret police, which was blamed for thousands of deaths and unspeakable acts of human savagery.

The Shah moved from country to country in search of secure asylum: first to Egypt, then Morocco, the Bahamas, and Mexico. On October 22, 1979, just as John Yost, Jim Slade, and I were making the first descent of Pakistan's Indus River, the Shah came to the United States for a gall bladder operation and treatment of cancer. Thirteen days later, militant Iranian Moslems invaded the US embassy in Tehran and took Americans there hostage to demand the Shah's extradition and a confession of his "crimes" in Iran, especially those concerning SAVAK. Secret documents were discovered in the US embassy after its seizure, including ones describing the CIA coming to Iran in 1956 with a clandestine operation to set up and train SAVAK, the secret police who terrorized the country during the Shah's reign.

That same month my father, after twenty-five years of service, took an early retirement from the CIA and moved as far away from Washington, D.C., as one can and still be in the continental United States: San Diego. After finishing his doctorate there he became a family counselor, specializing in sex therapy.

Seven years later, by chance I saw an item from the Associated Press. Former president Jimmy Carter admitted that a small documentary film company, financed by the CIA, helped six Americans escape from Iran during the hostage crisis early in 1980. After Iranians stormed the US embassy in 1979, six embassy employees hid at the Canadian embassy, and the film company was able to perform its cloak-and-dagger rescue under Ayatollah Khomeini's nose, as the leader wanted as much publicity as possible about his revolution and gave the filmmakers wide berth.

I then called my father and asked once more if he could tell me about his documentary film in Iran, and he said he could not. His voice cracked a bit. He sounded angry and sad at once. He said, if it hadn't been for Iran, his life would have been different, the world might have been different, his life with me would have been different . . . we would have spent more time . . . and his voice trailed away as he handed the phone to my mother. He wouldn't, couldn't talk about it. I sensed that my father, like me, had been involved in an adventure gone wrong, one that spilled blood and left families bereft . . . only there was a difference of scale, perhaps an enormous differential, and I understood at that moment that he had not recovered, and never really would.

CHAPTER 27

PAPUA NEW GUINEA FIRSTS

It is the wisdom of crocodiles, that shed tears when they would devour.
—Francis Bacon

The redbrick, Tudor-style town house on East 70th Street in New York is undistinguished from the outside, but once one passes through its arched portal, another era is entered. It has a solid, masculine atmosphere: Leather trim is everywhere; and mementos of Africa from when Burton and Speke tramped its interior, of the North and South Poles, of the Andes, of the Himalayas lend its rooms historical resonance. The musty smell of rare and wonderful books wafts down the stairwell, and members' books are signed by the Roosevelts, the Hemingways, the Hillarys of exploration. The dramatist and essayist John Baillie, in his 1747 treatise, "An Essay on the Sublime," suggests that a building can achieve, through architectural features such as columns, arches, and space, a kind of code that works like language to evoke a feeling of The Sublime.

I first entered the Explorers Club in the summer of 1973, having just returned from our first major expedition under the Sobek imprimatur, the Omo River in Ethiopia.

The tall man who greeted me in the dark, leather-trimmed hall was Lowell Thomas, the man for whom the building is now named. He listened carefully as I recounted tales of high adventure on Ethiopia's great river. His attention was rapt, perhaps because he himself had organized a similar rafting expedition down the Indus River in Pakistan a few years earlier, an expedition that ended in tragedy: One of his close friends had drowned.

When I concluded my stories of the Omo, I asked the man who for decades had broadcast reports from the far ends of the earth what he would recommend for a next river expedition.

"New Guinea," he said, his gravelly baritone cutting through the mannered atmosphere of the club. "New Guinea's got what you're looking for. Steep mountains, plenty of rainfall, and original cultures up every ravine."

He rose to leave early, shook hands firmly, and then stood for a moment in the doorway, his tall, solid frame silhouetted by New York's dusty afternoon. "Go to New Guinea. That's the place," he repeated. Then he waved goodbye. "And so long until tomorrow."

So I started looking into the possibilities of river running in Papua New Guinea. At the outset I was warned by a friend at the Smithsonian that the highlanders of the island "have a long history of head-hunting and cannibalism and are not by any means completely pacified." Some weeks later, while flipping through a copy of *Oui* magazine, I stopped at a full-page photo of a painted South Pacific islander. "Is this the man who ate Michael Rockefeller?" asked the headline. An anthropologist who had been poking around New Guinea claimed he met and lived with the tribe that had eaten the son of New York governor Nelson Rockefeller after he washed ashore in a storm in 1961. It is a theory long debated and debunked by many familiar with the region over the years. But in 2012 I found myself at a birthday bowling bash for Pulitzer Prize–winning author Jared Diamond, who had just published a book, *The World Until Yesterday*, for which he spent months studying the peoples of New Guinea to decipher what Westerners might learn from traditional societies. We were teamed as bowling partners, and we were losing when I asked his opinion of Michael Rockefeller's disappearance. "He was eaten," he declared.

But back in 1978 I was not sure what to believe, and the prospect of sailing into the remote regions of the second-largest island in the world gave me pause. But I committed, nonetheless.

One day before departure to New Guinea, I picked up the *San Francisco Chronicle* and read an article about a clash in Enga Province of Papua New Guinea in which ten thousand local villagers fought and two died. Our target river was in Enga Province.

The *Chronicle* story lent some details about this jungle-mountain fastness that was the subject of several early Margaret Mead treatises. The people (the name Papua comes from a Malay word, Papuwah, meaning "frizzy haired"), who received independence from Australia in 1975, still practice a ritual warfare called "Pay Back," in which arrows and spears are tossed at rivals until somebody draws blood. Then everyone retires until another day.

The villagers in the highlands of New Guinea have most everything the human animal needs within easy grasp, a condition economists call "Primitive Affluence." Fruit trees pullulate like weeds in the fertile soil. Good food is abundant. Housing materials can be plucked from the trees. The weather is temperate. They've got at their fingertips much of what Westerners slave lifetimes to get.

From the plane, the steaming jungle below looked like Kong's habitat. From pre-trip research, I gathered some factoids that made the intended visit all the more alluring.

The island has the highest proportion of mountainous country, the wildest rivers, and the most luxuriant vegetation of all like-size areas on the globe. It holds great garamut trees with flange-buttressed trunks; strangler figs send down their writhing trunk-like roots, beclouded with jungle flowers. The mountain chains of New Guinea, four degrees from the equator, are by far the most impressive in the oceanic world. The razorbacks and gorges of the island's unbroken massive cordillera seem to rise and fall like the dark green billows of a frozen sea. Thwarted climbers have claimed that ascending a simple hill in New Guinea is more difficult than climbing a steep peak in the Alps.

I was coming to this land of 700 languages for the multitude of rivers that dissect New Guinea's terrain into islands of isolation. Many rivers are muddy, hanging like greasy tresses down the mountains; other are feather-white, torn by rapids. In these rivers, and along the coast, are 1,400 distinct species of fish and 2 varieties of crocodile. There are tortoises and lizards, including the giant monitor lizard. Overhead wing some 650 species of tropical birds, including the birds-of-paradise, among the most imaginatively colored in the world. The birds have a particularity, an inexpressibility, so high-pitched they attract myths. The island also hosts the indigenous cassowary, which looks like a cross between an ostrich and a peacock. Animal life is sparse, but that which exists is quirky—tree kangaroos, wallabies, cuscus, red bandicoot, and others about which I have no familiarity.

The people of the island are a varied lot. There are brown-skinned pygmies, bearded highlanders who look like ancient Assyrians, hook-nosed lowlanders with the faces of Pharisees, mountaineers with abnormally strong legs, and swamp dwellers who have difficulty walking on solid land. Their stock is primarily Melanesian, and their history may extend from 50,000 BCE. Europeans first landed in 1526, but not for another 350 years were attempts made to penetrate its forbidding interior, and the highland plateau wasn't reached until 1933. The physical ferocity of the island made exploration difficult, as did the fierce reputation of the locals. Many reacted strongly to foreign religion being rammed down their throats. Christian missionaries began proselytizing in the early 1800s, but by 1864 the number of missionaries killed and likely eaten exceeded the number of villagers baptized. Today, though Christianity has permeated the island, many villagers still believe in and practice magic, mysticism, and spiritualism. When a helicopter pilot I met landed in a remote patch of forest, villagers crawled underneath the flying machine to check its sex.

I got off the Air Niugini plane in Port Moresby, the capital city, and was met by Jim Slade and Randy Simpson, both experienced rafters. Jim had kissed goodbye to Cornell Law School for the life of a wilderness guide. Randy, only age nineteen, had worked as a commercial guide on the Colorado River through the Grand Canyon for two years. It was a good feeling having traveled 14,000 miles across the Pacific to be met by familiar faces. The three of us cleared our 650 pounds of boats and expedition equipment through customs.

We all congregated at a small house in the city outskirts, belonging to Geoff Sadler, a lusty Australian on contract in Papua New Guinea with the Department of Agriculture. He was one of the members of our team and had run the Colorado with me two years earlier. Rounding out the crew were John Yost and Tom Cromer, who had been on our first descent of the Awash River in 1973. The one guest on the trip was David Dworsky, a Hollywood screenwriter who was gathering material for a script about the subculture of boatmen.

With a couple days to kill before we headed to the highlands, I took to the streets. The crocodile, I noticed immediately, was the most common motif in the country. The currency featured crocodiles on the coins, crocodile-shaped popsicles were sold on the streets, and crocodile tail was a delicacy served in the finer restaurants. "I'll try the crocodile," I ordered in one of the better eateries, "and make it snappy."

A favorite pastime was chewing betel nut, the mildly narcotic fruit of the areca palm. To counter its laxative effect and neutralize the excess acid it produces in the stomach, the locals carried gourds of lime, and using a spatula of wood or bone they dipped lime into their mouths as they chewed. After prolonged use, their gums turned dark red and their teeth went black, almost disappearing in the layers of tartar. Women sometimes tattooed their faces and breasts in unsymmetrical patterns with blue ink.

In the afternoon we visited the city's crocodile farm and watched as the keepers threw huge chunks of raw beef and fish to the crocs. The saltwater crocodiles, which grow to twenty feet or more, gave good shows as they swallowed whole whatever was tossed in their direction. Saltwater crocodiles can be found several hundred miles up New Guinea's larger rivers and are not shy about their taste for mammals' flesh, including humans. The river we planned to attempt was the country's fourth largest and was known for its crocodiles in its lower sections.

The day next, we flew to Mount Hagen, near our put-in. I got off the plane and a man with a kina-shell smile in a grass skirt stepped up, reached out, and squeezed my balls. I was lost for the proper reaction until Geoff explained it was a greeting meant to ensure a stranger was not carrying a concealed weapon. It was known as the Chimbu handshake, named for the highlands province into which we had landed. I chose not to reciprocate his gesture.

Our target river was the Yuat. In 1966 Jon Hamilton, a New Zealand jetboater, and several geologists tried to make an ascent of the Yuat. Hamilton was famous in river-running circles for his spectacular first ascents of rivers. He made it up the Colorado River through the Grand Canyon in 1960, the first and last attempt. Subsequently he forged up the Indus, the Ganges, the Congo, the Sun Kosi in Nepal, and others. In all his history-making runs, only one river thwarted his efforts: the Yuat.

The rapids were just too big. The only other attempt to sail the Yuat was made in August 1970 by Ross Allen, an Australian patrol officer stationed in New Guinea. He tried to kayak the river with several friends. Two men hiked out midway. The others spent most of their time portaging and patching battered boats. At one point they had to haul their boats up a steep cliff, burn away the topside grass, and dodge three death adders and a python that scudded out of the blaze. But they made it.

The Yuat is the main tributary of the Sepik, which is the country's largest river. It is known for both its crocodiles and its intricate native wood carvings. The river begins as a small stream, gurgling through a cloud-cloaked canyon, feather-white and torn by crystal cataracts. When it merges with the Jimi, the flow looks like weak coffee and bile, now one hundred feet wide. Several dozen tributaries later it is a rampaging, roaring, gamboge torrent charging through scalloped limestone bursting over geological faults and spitting into the glossy rain forest that rims the winding course. The Yuat exhausts itself when it merges with the Sepik, which from that point purls through palms, wild figs, and lowland jungle to the Pacific. We hoped to follow Ross Allen's route, but without portaging. We had the technical expertise and equipment, we felt, to run the rapids that had stopped both Allen and Hamilton. We hoped to make the first full navigation of the Yuat.

The day before departure we made the obligatory aerial reconnaissance, which was more frightening than fascinating. Small planes have a high mortality rate in the country. As we raced down the runway, our pilot turned to us and nonchalantly muttered that his service, MAF (Mission Aviation Fellowship), had lost four planes that month.

The Yuat was beautiful from the air, a rich, rushing chocolate stream swathing through rills of lush jungle. With its many tributaries the river system seemed etched as finely as circuitry. A hundred miles down the twisted path we came to the Yuat Gorge, where Allen and Hamilton had their troubles. It was wedge-shaped, limestone, coated with primeval growth, almost a half mile deep. In it we saw three very large, long rapids, and at the end of every eddy fell the shadows of monsters. After the gorge, the river slowed, passed some villages, and finally merged with the meandering Sepik. The run looked possible.

On the flight back we spotted a couple of crashed planes, C-47s left from World War II. General MacArthur was headquartered in Port Moresby. The Japanese occupied the islands off the New Guinea coast. The remnants of some of the fiercest fighting in the Pacific are scattered throughout New Guinea.

Our last night in town we spent shooting pool and drinking piss (beer) with the local Aussies. They treated us like condemned men. I couldn't sleep.

Early the next morning we started for the headwaters. We spent the day getting stuck in a mud hole, dangling two wheels over the edge of a cliff, making a wrong turn towards the wrong river, converting our four-wheel drive to a two-wheel drive on the rocks, but finally getting to the put-in. In 1956 an Australian patrol had been attacked here by two hundred bowmen. Our reception was more well-disposed. A group of malaria researchers appeared from a bamboo hut and offered us fresh papaya and avocado. Then we swam in the target river, which was hyaline clear and spanned by a vine bridge.

Launching day was sunny and scintillating. Tom caught a fish for breakfast; we loaded up and shoved off. A mile downstream, the Jimi River joined us and turned the gin-clear water to a turbid malt. The current was fast, about five miles per hour, and the jungle thick and black. The mountains in the middle distance were magically verdant and cloud-swirled. We passed beneath hornbills, pelicans, lorikeets, herons, kingfishers, and rainbows of flying colors.

While maneuvering around one sweeping curve, we were washed against a group of overhanging bushes and a crocodile spilled from a high branch into the bilge, right at my feet. This was déjà vu all over again, as the same drop-in happened 7,500 miles away and a few years earlier on the Omo River in Ethiopia. Our visitor was not a croc but a giant monitor lizard, common along these rivers. The monitor is the source of rumors in the 1700s that New Guinea harbored the world's only tree-climbing crocodiles.

We swirled downstream, passing under a number of vine bridges, supported by bamboo poles and woven in complex lattice designs. Masterful crafts, but no signs of their builders or users. It was here that Ross Allen claimed to have seen pygmies. No doubt, as bushwalkers claimed, we were seen without seeing for a good portion of the journey.

At one point while we cruised along a quick but easy stretch, Dworsky, a white-water rookie, asked if the eddies and whirlpools in the river ran counterclockwise in the Southern Hemisphere. "Only when you flush," retorted Slade.

We pitched camp on a long, butterfly-covered beach. Tom and I set up our tent closest to the river, about twenty-five feet away. Throughout the night I awoke

Helicopter portage in New Guinea. GEORGE FULLER

thinking I heard the river close to our tent, but I dismissed it as imagination each time. With the first brushstrokes of dawn, though, we stepped outside to find the river had risen to within two feet of our tent and was rushing along at a much greater speed than the day before. Palls of steam rose from the surface. There had been an angry rainstorm upstream. Our two food bags, which had been left below our tent, were missing. There was a rising panic until Geoff confessed he left his tent in the middle of the night to take a leak and moved the bags above camp, saving us from a diet of betel nuts.

The morning was filled with seesaws in the quickened current, roller-coaster wave trains that whirled us up giant crests and rolled us down the far side into deep troughs. The romp continued into the afternoon, until we came to the Yuat Gorge. Suddenly the walls closed in; the pace of the river kicked into fourth, and just ahead, the racing water disappeared—it just fell off the earth. We edged closer and banked. It was the first rapid. The water went crazy. It dropped over a series of furious waterfalls, crashed into house-size boulders, and kicked and spit an angry path to a pool a half mile downstream and several hundred feet below. Impossible. No way in the world could anyone run this "rapid" and survive. Niagara offered better odds. We scouted this ugly mess along the eastern bank, at the same time plotting our portage route.

The fact that we couldn't run this crazy cataract was a terrific blow to our egos, but worse was the prospect of what faced us downstream and around the next bend. Ross Allen had indicated the second rapid in the gorge was worse than the first and that there was not an easy portage route. It was there that he hauled his kayaks up a steep cliff with ropes and mechanical ascenders, a grueling job even with light kayaks, and a Herculean labor with two large inflatable rafts and several thousand pounds of gear.

We decided to sleep on it. We also decided to feast on it. We opened as much of the canned food as we could stomach, to lighten the load. I dozed off wondering if Ross Allen was getting a chuckle over our predicament. He had told us he thought we could run these rapids easily in high water, and the water was as high as it gets.

I awoke at first light and packed up to start the portage. My first load was two duffel bags of food and gear. The path groped like an enormous sentence over slippery sheets of shale, through briar bushes, around and over mammoth boulders. It took ninety minutes to walk the half mile carrying a load and forty-five minutes to get back empty-handed. On my second trip, about three-quarters of the way down, my shirt soaked with sweat and my glasses covered with a thick film, I stepped on a loose boulder at the lip of a small cliff. It gave way and sent me down a landslide tumbling down the face. Thinking I might get crushed, I leaped for clearance, executing a somersault with a pack on my back. Somehow, I emerged unscathed save a sprained finger and a broken shoelace.

With all the dunnage portaged, we turned to the boats. These we carefully lined, whenever the current allowed, and when it didn't, we pulled them on shore and pushed and shoved them over and through the rocks. Twice a lined boat wrenched its way into strong currents and the rope I held ripped through the flesh on my callused hands, but I managed to keep hold at the end of the line. As the sun was setting, we finished the portage. We had to find a campsite, but we were still in the gorge and level ground was at a premium. Groping around in the rocks, John found a spit of sand big enough for two tents. We squeezed four in, plus a firepit. My head ended up in Tom's tent, my feet in Jim's.

With the next morning we tied down the gear tightly, drew cards to see who got to captain (I won a spot), pushed off, and swirled into the main current. We careened through two hundred yards of fifteen-foot convergence waves and then sloshed through another three hundred yards of calm water. Then, boom! The second rapid. Ross Allen was right. It was worse than the first.

A tumultuous half mile that dropped more than two hundred feet. It was so supernaturally screwballed that the light seemed to bend when passing over its mantle. Ross was wrong on one count, though, thank Pukpuk (New Guinea's crocodile god). There was a portage route at water level. That was about our only blessing. While carrying the first load, Randy slipped and broke his ankle. Randy was the strongest member of the team. Then, while trying to heave the boat overland without Randy, we made a united, comedic shove that threw the raft against a sharp, pointed rock. With sonic timbre the front left tube exploded, sending me flying into a nearby pandanus tree and leaving a five-foot jagged rip in the boat.

We tried to continue portaging with the limp section, but it was too awkward. It would have taken a day to repair. So we rolled it up around two oars and tried to carry the load slung on shoulders, Kanaka style. Again, too awkward. We fell every three steps. Exhausted and hot, we abandoned the idea of moving the boat by land. We decided to portage the other boat to where the injured one lay like an old cigar. Then we set the good boat in the river and wrestled the rolled-up dead one to the deck and tied it down. Then we lined the two boats together for the remainder of the rapid.

We successfully roped the boats past several tricky spots, sometimes with considerable finesse. Finally, with the late afternoon, we made it down to the last seventy-five feet for the final lining around a granite jetty that stuck out into the current just above a rock shaped like a peacock tail, where a current hosed into it and then plumed out like a parachute.

We were spent, our senses less than keen. John got in the raft to assist our ropings by pushing the boat off the rocks. We wanted to sneak the boat around the projecting rock and pull it and John back to shore and safety, just above the falls. But our ropes were set wrong. Mine ripped from my hands, then it jerked from Jim's, who was backup. That left Tom holding the last rope. He tried, his face blue and hands red with blood, but he couldn't hold the boat back. It swept out into the main current and started for the falls. We were helpless on shore. The falls were a death trap. John's first reaction was to leap for the oars, with hopes of powering back to shore. But with one stroke he saw this was hopeless. He was powerless against the overwhelming current. So he jumped to the bow, made a flying head dive into the water just above the lip of the falls, and with superhuman strength thrashed his way to shore. He clutched a rock right at the edge and pulled himself out.

But the boats weren't so lucky. The good boat pitched over the edge and miraculously stayed upright, though it was caught in a churning hydraulic where it canted and heaved for forty seconds. On one violent shake the ropes securing the injured rolled boat snapped, and it bounced off the deck into the churning swill and sank. The now lighter good boat spat out of the hydraulic and spun downstream. Jim and I bulleted down the rocky shoreline with desperate abandon. We were bounding over wet, slippery terrain we would ordinarily inch across, but we weren't gaining. The current was sprinting at eight miles per hour, twice our land speed. Like running dogs, we continued downstream hoping the boat might get caught in an eddy or against a snag. I considered swimming, but I had torn my life jacket off at the falls so I could run less hindered. Then, seeming out of nowhere, John appeared next to us in the water, floating the main current. He'd recovered from his swim and made the most sensible move by diving in the fast water below the falls. He overtook us and was soon around the corner, out of sight. But the boat was a half mile ahead at this point. When Jim and I made it around the corner and saw nothing, we assumed the worst. The nearest village, Ruti, was a good two-day hike through dense, knotted jungle and across a raging river. And then there was Randy with a broken ankle. Should we try to help Randy hobble there or leave him behind until we could organize a rescue?

We continued at a slower pace now, distraught and exhausted. After another mile it seemed we were defeated. But John was yet to be seen, so we forged onward. At last, around a bend, we saw the boat—upside down but moored to a cliff, with John prostate on an overhanging ledge . . . all above a long, large rapid.

We raced down to John, who was passed out next to a pool of puke. He came around and told his story. He had seen the boat heading for the rapid and swum madly to catch it. Then he had to pull it to shore, so he grabbed the bowline in his teeth and pumped his arms and legs. Fifty yards later he was clawing at a cliff. He found a nubbin and managed to pull the boat in and tie it down before he collapsed.

When John recovered, we righted the boat, tied it securely to a thick tree, and dragged our broken, tired bodies back to the falls. Randy had dinner going, and when he heard we had recovered a boat he was thrilled he wouldn't have to limp out of the choking jungle overland. There were no beaches nearby, so Tom and I hacked out some tent sites with machetes, and after a spaghetti dinner we sat back to a few hands of bridge, a therapeutic diversion after a long, tough day.

The river rose eight vertical feet overnight, turning a bad dream into a nightmare. It was a two-mile hike from the falls to where the boat was moored, and we had to portage all our gear that distance. I had my daily fright when stepping across a crevice. Two leek-green critters whizzed past my feet and plopped into the river, eliciting thoughts of death adders or other venomous snakes. Of the most venomous snakes in the world, six are found in New Guinea. But as they swam away I saw they were giant frogs. A few steps later I scared two wild pigs out of the forest. Or vice versa. We finished carrying everything around by 2:00 p.m. We had spent, at that point, three full days portaging and only one floating on the river.

We jettisoned the frame and deck to the lost boat and a broken oar. We then loaded the surviving boat with seven large packs, fifteen small ones, nine metal camera boxes, and seven people. Then we shoved off. With the added weight on the boat, and with the added volume and speed of the river, it was impossible to control the raft with just a set of oars and one oarsman. So we distributed our supply of paddles and practiced turns and stops. We shot downstream and stitched some big rapids like needlemen, though I was too scared to enjoy them. Towards the end of the day, we found a long creamy beach where we made camp and went straight to bed, dead tired and worn.

We saw our first crocodile the next morning. We eased around a corner and there he was, about four feet long, sleeping with mouth agape. We all squeezed to the center of the boat, and he slid into the water and disappeared.

Around noon we came to another formidable rapid, about 150 yards long and bigger than Lava Falls, the largest rapid on the Colorado in the Grand Canyon. As we had just the one remaining boat, containing all our food and supplies, we decided to portage once more.

Experienced portagers at this point, it took less than an hour to carry everything around, and then we were off again. The next several miles were some of the best we'd ever navigated. About every hundred yards there was a major but runnable rapid, which we sported through without difficulty. The walls of the canyon began to taper, and the river turned drowsy.

The next day we were gliding through a tropical aviary. We watched golden herons, sulphur-crested cockatoos, multihued parrots, darters, and sea eagles. Above one spirited rapid the sky suddenly blackened as a flock of hundreds of flying foxes, members of the bat family, crossed the canyon. We stopped at an empty village and groped through abandoned treasures: spotted cuscus pelts, birds-of-paradise feathers, dried corncobs, and animal skulls. But no sign of people. What happened here? Another New Guinea mystery.

The river began to braid and sweep through logjams. Feeling slothful and wasted after an afternoon in the equatorial sun, we didn't take notice when we yawed into a side channel that took us past a debris pile with a curious, gray mass draped over it. We were well past when someone yelled, "Hey, that's our other Avon raft!" We pulled over and blazed up the bank to the spot where the boat was trapped. John, assuming again the hero cape, volunteered to go after it. He dove in with a rope between his teeth, wrestled the boat free, tied it to the rescue rope, and we pulled it in. The five-foot rip notwithstanding, it was in decent shape. It wouldn't be worthwhile to patch it on the river . . . it would take too long . . . so we rolled it up tight, put it in the bilge of the good boat, and used it for a bridge table.

Late in the afternoon we encountered the first people of the trip, a family tending their garden of mango and coconut trees. We greeted them, and the father asked with gestures if we would like some coconuts. When we produced fifty-five toea, the local currency, he expertly plucked six ripe coconuts from a tall tree using a thirty-foot bamboo pole. He cracked the tough shells with several whacks of his machete, and we relished the sweet meat and the clear, tasty milk. That night we camped on an island and encountered our first mosquitoes. Hamilton had commented about the "plagues of mosquitoes" on his 1966 trip. There were cyclones of them, and I was in a tent with a broken mosquito net. At dusk, a group of villagers in dugouts, decorated with expressively carved crocodile prows, paddled across the river, silhouetted against the silvery twilight, dipping their spear-shaped paddles in perfect unison. They brought us bananas and conversation we couldn't understand. But we enjoyed both. We retired early in a rainstorm that collapsed the back of my tent.

With bruised backs and egos, we made our way to Bewat, a village with a Catholic mission and an airstrip. But it was just the beginning of our appointments with New Guinea.

CHAPTER 28

LEAPING FROM THE CHOPPER

Knowledge is only a rumor until it lives in the muscle.
—Saying from the Asaro tribe of Papua New Guinea

The crown of Mount Wilhelm is Papua New Guinea's watershed divide, the cap on the vertebrae of an arched back that spines across the country. Rainfall north of Wilhelm drains into the Sepik; the south, the Waghi, nicknamed "Eater of Men," as so many who have fallen into its raging waters have been swallowed.

The Waghi Valley, first penetrated by Australian gold miners Mick Leahy and his two brothers in 1933, was the last major population center to be revealed to an unsuspecting outside world, as featured in the remarkable documentary *First Contact*. Over a million highlanders had lived locked in mountain fastness since an unknown time, never a notion that white-skinned people existed or that there were civilizations at all beyond their fertile hanging valley. Maps of the day rendered the cloud-cloaked interior of New Guinea blank.

Today the Waghi Valley, stretching from Mount Hagen to Kundiawa, is no secret. The river meanders past groomed tea and coffee plantations, several tourist lodges and bars, and a paved highway. But at Kundiawa it turns sharply south, and there it enters *aqua incognita*, plunging off the plateau into steep gorges and over nightmarish rapids. It twice changes names—to the Tua, then the Purari—and finally empties its massive load into the Coral Sea at a seventeen-mile-wide delta.

The BBC was in the midst of filming a series called *Great River Journeys* and wanted to include a true exploratory, so they called me. I recommended the Eater of Men. A few weeks later we were on the river.

At first the Waghi was kind. Waterfalls weaved down bright limestone cliffs; klinky pines clung to ridges; glossy fronds and succulents lined the banks. A Raggiana bird-of-paradise, the national symbol of Papua New Guinea, wheeled between the walls. But the rapids quickly fired up, and we endured capsizes and portages, one with the help of the BBC Bell Jet Ranger helicopter. We were nine Sobek guides, plus our regular expedition doctor George Fuller, photographer Nick Nichols, and my friend and author David Roberts, on assignment for *Geo* magazine. We all relished the full exploratory experience, especially camping on the broad beaches beneath the canopy of stars. But the BBC were not into the hardships of camping, so each night, along with celebrity host Christina Dodwell, they took the helicopter out of the canyon and back to the hotel for a restaurant meal, a shower, and ironed sheets.

On the tenth night we camped, as usual, some thirty feet up the sloping beach at the edge of the jungle where the trees smacked down to the stones. In my REM sleep I heard the river lapping, sucking, teasing as it advanced in an effort to swallow me. When its wet tongue licked my foot, I sprung awake and realized this was no cycloramic dream. The river was in the tent and rising. A rainstorm upstream had put the Waghi in flood. Flashlights, in furious strokes, painted the night as we scrambled to higher ground. With machetes we cut into the thick tangle and transported our village of tents out of the Waghi's reach and spent the last murky hours of morning in fitful vigil.

Dried out midmorning we cautiously moved as the river pulled us into a narrow limestone gorge. Powder-white cliffs arched a half mile upwards. Clouds wrapped the pointed peaks. If a pterodactyl suddenly screamed up the canyon, it would have seemed natural.

It was here, as the river plummeted southwards through New Guinea's greatest gorge, that we met the largest, angriest rapid yet. Standing on a boulder above the torrent, a couple of the Sobek guides traced a possible route with outstretched hands. I didn't see it. It was August 24, my birthday, and I did not cherish the thought of drowning on my birthday. I elected to walk around and set up safety throw lines at its base.

Skip Horner, a Class VI oarsman, and the only man to have successfully guided the Seven Summits, entered first. His boat was tossed like a cork in a tempest, but it emerged upright, intact. Then Mike Boyle, a legend as a raft guide, made his entry, five feet to the left of Skip's course—and he capsized, spectacularly, end-over-end. Mike swam like a speedboat to shore, but his two passengers, Dr. Fuller and young Sobek guide Renee Goddard, got sucked into the worst of the maelstrom. It was eerily quiet as they disappeared underwater. Even the wind seemed to sleep. I waited, and waited, my hand hard against the throw line. At last, their faces burst the surface, gasping for air. Fuller swam safely to the bank. Renee climbed on the bilge of the upside-down raft, which was racing towards me. At the perihelion point I threw the line at Renee, but the toss fell short. I grabbed the second line and hurled again . . . and missed again. We knew from our morning helicopter scout there was a lethal waterfall not far downstream. "Jump," I screamed as the raft careened towards an exposed rock at the lip of the next rapid. She didn't move, frozen in fear. "*Jump, damn it!*" She leapt and clutched the slippery rock as the unmanned, upside-down raft disappeared in a dark wave.

The runaway raft was carrying critical food, equipment, and cameras, heading towards the waterfall. John Kramer, watching the unfolding drama in his boat above the predatory rapid, flew to the rowing seat and made a choppy but successful run through and then started pumping the oars in an attempt to catch the lost boat.

A George Fuller painting of Richard jumping from a helicopter to save a runaway boat in New Guinea. PAINTING BY GEORGE FULLER

The helicopter had been filming this money shot, and it was now hovering just above me. I leapt onto the runners and pulled myself into the back of the chopper, which then zoomed downstream. Two miles later we saw the flipped boat sprinting through the gorge towards the deadly waterfall. The pilot lowered his machine until it hovered over the twisting inflatable. The pilot nodded, and I jumped, landing on the slick black bottom of the raft.

I reached under the bow, found the painter, then dove into the water. I tried to tow the boat ashore but was making little progress against the headlong center current. I could feel my strength sapping. I knew the waterfall was close. I began to doubt I would make it. Then, the cavalry arrived. John Kramer, still pumping his oars, appeared from upstream and quickly caught up with me. Together we wrestled the raft to shore. We turned it over, and miraculously, nothing was missing. Plausibility sat cowed in a corner and said, "Don't look at me. I have nothing to do with this."

By twilight we were all reunited on a broad beach above another major rapid, and collectively we decided to exit the expedition at that point. We were spent, and the worst of the river was yet to come. The remaining 391 miles to the Gulf of Papua were left unrun, a prize for future expeditioners.

The BBC crew departed on the first flight out, while the rest of us retired to Geoff Sadler's home twenty miles outside of Port Moresby. It was a quiet place; no phone, no radio or record player, a perfect place to recover.

CHAPTER 29

RAPE IN THE RAIN FOREST

I find it easier to claim that I am friends with a monkey rather than with a man.
—SHAHLA KHAN

IT WAS A STICKY FRIDAY, PAYDAY IN PORT MORESBY, AND A NIGHT WHEN MANY IN town turn to drink and too often violence. But it was quiet in this small retreat, and we all took to bed early, Geoff in the upstairs master, and the rest of us in two separate rooms, with John, Randy, and I sharing one floor on mattresses in our sleeping bags. It took some tossing and mental games to force sleep. Then, somewhere at the margins of sleep or madness, I heard it:

"Help me . . . Aww. No. Stop . . . Ahhhhhh. You're hurting me!"

I turned over and punched the portable pillow I carried on trips. The screams did not seem to fit the dream.

"Pleease. Somebody help me. . . . Arrrggh."

I sat up spring-loaded. The screams hammered my head. I yelled across the room to Randy and John. "Wake up. I think someone's being raped outside."

John gave a hollow stare then turned over in dismissal and resumed snoring. John knew I had a history of sleep antics. Once in Ethiopia, I saw a burglar creeping across the room in the half-light. When he was in range I lunged. I tackled him and grappled with flailing feet amidst a freshet of obscenities: "What the fuck?"

The lights shot on, and there I was, arms wrapped around the beating legs of Lew Greenwald, who had been faultlessly sleeping across the room when I attacked.

Then, one night in Alaska, sharing a tent with another Sobek crew member, I awoke when a grizzly stuck its head through the front flap. I roared and attacked the intruder, punching his hairy face. A flashlight went on and I found I was grappling with my bewildered tentmate's head.

I could hardly blame John for ignoring me, and I kicked my bed to check if he might be right—that this was another nocturnal imagining. The bed shook with my kick, and I felt pain. I pulled on my pants and slipped into my sandals, bolted out the door. Randy, still recovering from his broken ankle on the river, also got out of bed but did not bother getting dressed. He limped out into the night stark naked.

We could hear the screams . . . deathlike squeals . . . but couldn't tell where they were coming from.

"Please don't. Noooo." Her cries were shrill and desperate. At first, I thought she might be a local girl, but as we moved through the darkness her words became clearer. *"Help me. Somebody please help me. He's hurting me."* Her voice had an Australian inflection. Rape and violence are major issues in Papua New Guinea, and I became fearful as we swiped the ten-foot-high kunai grass wondering if we might encounter a gang rape. But we thrashed forward, trying to decode the direction of the cries. The sounds were farther away than we initially thought, emitted at infrequent and irregular intervals in the middle distance. After foraging for twenty minutes, I realized we were downwind. But zeroing in on the right direction was difficult, as the victim's calls and bleats were fewer and fewer, punctuated by minutes of silence. We bellowed back offerings of rescue but got no response. She never answered.

After half an hour of flailing and flattening the grass, during which we advanced about a thousand yards, dawn began to break, the last stars fading in the pale sky. Randy and I exchanged glances, and he looked down at his scratched and naked groin. He said his state was not the right way to interrupt a rape. Rather than risk trying to explain his circumstance, Randy elected to turn back and clothe.

I paused for a second wondering the wisdom of one white guy entering a gang scene of drunken aggression. Then, *"You're hurting me. You're hurting."* A chill raced down my body. They are killing her, I thought. Her words were retched in spasms. I picked up my pace and headed for the sounds.

In places the mud was knee-deep, and the grass sliced my skin. One of my sandals disappeared in the sludge. I started to crawl; it was easier. Then another guttural scream. It seemed close. I came to a barbed-wire fence, wobbled my way to the top wire, and lost balance. Toppling over the other side I curled up and tumbled through the grass into a clearing. Eight inches away were two naked, writhing white bodies.

It took a few seconds to assimilate the scene. For a quick instant, the thought flashed I was intruding; that this was role-playing, consensual. A snapped ceremonial spear lay adjacent to the two sweat-gleaned bodies. The man, middle-aged and beefy, looked up to me in a glazed, uncomprehending stare. The girl, a blonde-tressed teenager, took a second longer to register my presence. Then she let loose a cracked scream, her neck cords taut like a ship's rigging. With his grip loosened, she beat his face and struggled with renewed strength. I tried to yell a command to stop, but my throat seized. In a frantic, adrenaline-driven frenzy she wrenched herself free, vaulted up and wrapped herself around me. She buried her face in my shoulder, inhaling me in long deep draughts. "Help me. Please take me to my home," she whimpered.

The hulk collected himself. "Hey, man, it's alright. Leave us alone . . . she's my girlfriend," he slurred. Was he telling the truth? He looked twenty years her senior.

"He's not my boyfriend," she shrieked. "He's married."

That injected a moment's courage, and I tried to look threatening as I glowered down to the much larger man. "You better get the hell out of here." It didn't faze him, so I added a clincher. "I just called the police. They'll be here in about ten minutes. Split while you can, asshole." It was a brazen bluff, and if he looked closely, he would have seen my body shaking. But he reacted. He telescoped to a standing position and wrestled his pants to his waist. I swallowed. He stood a good head taller than me, so thickly slabbed with muscle I could imagine him being herded to high pastures for the summer months. His eyes looked like a crocodile's before the kill. I closed my eyes and braced for a blow. I heard a crunch but felt nothing. Opening my eyes, I saw a folded body at my feet. He had collapsed. He was trembling on the ground. I could smell the stench of alcohol on his clothes.

"Patsy, come with me. Let's leave," he half-coherently babbled as he pried her away from me.

"No. Leave me alone." Then, turning to me, "Please . . ." in the most imploring voice. I tried to pull her back, and for a second she broke his grasp, but he grappled her back. We tug-of-warred for long seconds as he moved us down a dirt road towards a solitary car. I kept insisting the cops were on the way and the best course of action would be to simply leave alone. He ignored me. Instead, he cajoled Patsy in quasi-comprehensible sentences to leave with him. As we approached the car, she seemed to be losing her resistance. The lie of impending police did not seem to faze the man, so I tried a new one. "My buddies are right behind me," I muttered with all the menace I could muster. Then I turned and bellowed into the swamp, "Hey John, Jim, Randy—hurry up. We're right here." No answer, of course. He sensed I was bullshitting and got bolder.

"Listen," he snarled. "Stay out of this." He gave Patsy a resolute tug and spun her around to face him. "Patsy, come with me now. If you don't we'll get involved with the police, your parents will find out, you might go to court, everyone will be shamed and embarrassed. Come with me and I'll take you straight home. Honest."

We reached the car at this point, and he pulled open the door. I expected she might kick him in the groin with his spread stance. But she eased her grip, shook my hands free, and blubbered to him: "Promise?" He nodded yes and she crumpled into the car. He slammed it shut. My head spun. How could she?

The window was down, and she pleaded with me, "Please don't tell the police."

Then she turned to her assailant and said, "What about my spear?"

"We'll come back and get it later," I heard him say.

I didn't know what to do. I'd come to help a victim, and she was leaving voluntarily with her attacker. I stepped back and saw the beginning letters of the license plate: TT. The car was sleek, peacock blue, but I didn't recognize the make. I didn't see any identifying logo. It looked new and not inexpensive.

The engine jarred to life, revved, and lunged into first. As the car roared off and around a bend, I thought I saw, through the dancing dust, Patsy peering through the rear window with wide, wet, pleading eyes.

My stomach squalled. I sat down on a chunk of limestone and tried to sort out the last hour. The sun broke the horizon, a cockatoo cawed, and the wind worried my matted hair. I was in shock, and it wasn't until Randy reappeared, still limping but clothed, and gave me a good shake that I gathered my senses.

Back at the house I shared the story with the rest of the team. When I gave the license letters I saw, Geoff, our Australian host, made an audible wince.

"What's wrong?" I asked.

"TT plates are trade tags that can't be traced," explained Geoff. "Sounds like this wanker planned his evening."

"Let's go to the police then."

"That's a waste. Rape is part of the culture here. They will likely shake you down, and maybe lock you up."

"Let's take this to media then. The local paper at least."

"Rapes happen nightly here. They won't report it. Let it go. Shit happens."

This seemed the end of the episode. I was scheduled to fly north for another expedition in three days, and then two days after returning to Moresby I was to fly back to San Francisco. Port Moresby had more than twenty thousand Caucasians, so the odds against running into two particular people in that time seemed long.

The next three days were a whirl as we ran around town preparing for the next expedition into the interior, an attempt to make the first descent of the Watut River in Morobe Province, a tributary of the Markham River that runs into the coastal city of Lae, the last place from which Amelia Earhart took off before disappearing into the clouds.

I kept an eye out, though, in case I might run into Patsy or her aggressor. A few times I thought I saw one of them from behind or in silhouette, but I was always wrong.

I'd given up when we arrived at the airport Monday. Randy was off buying orange juice and I was purchasing our air tickets when I turned, and she bracketed into focus. Seated on a vinyl chair between what looked to be her parents and a little sister, she looked down hard at her shoes. She was wearing a white cotton bombazine dress.

I walked past her chair to see if she might look up. She did. She turned, pulled her father's sleeve, and said, "Dad, this is the guy who helped me."

Father stood up, stuck out his hand, and thanked me. "We really appreciate what you did."

"Did you report this to the police?" I asked.

"No." He shook his head. "That doesn't work here."

He invited me to sit. But before the cushion was compressed, the mother rose, face red in anger. She grabbed Patsy and spun her around to face me, pulling up sleeves to show a series of purple bruises. "She's flying back to Australia to school," the mother spat. "She will never come back."

She continued, saying she wanted to file charges in Australia and asked if I would be a witness. The father butted in, saying she could not arrange to extradite someone out of the country where the crime was committed. "Sara, we have to drop it," he said with finality. "It's over. Let's forget, just forget the incident. He's a well-respected businessman."

I was shocked and confused. Patsy turned to me and filled in some backstory. She was eighteen years old and had lived in Port Moresby for two years. Her attacker was her former employer, a German who, at age thirty-eight, was among the wealthiest expats in Papua New Guinea. She was a waitress in one of his swanky restaurants. His car, the one I didn't recognize as it roared away, was a Lamborghini. There had been a going-away party for Patsy at the restaurant, and her former employer was there.

Sometime in the waning hours her ex-employer, thoroughly soused on champagne, offered to drive her home. She accepted, never expecting a four-hour detour that might have cost her life.

Patsy continued with more details. He drove to the isolated edge of town, turned up a dark dirt road, dragged her from the car, and proceeded to tear at her clothes. She tried to stab him with a ceremonial spear given to her that night as a going-away gift, but he snapped it in half. She explained how she played the cat . . . at intervals she would relax, and he'd ease his grip; then with a burst of energy she'd scream and strike. But he was too powerful to escape.

The PA announced my flight departure, gate three. . . . The father thanked me again, and I slipped him my business card and volunteered to do anything I could to help, though I could not imagine what I could do. The father did not return the gesture, so I never got any last names.

Two weeks later I was back in Port Moresby after our successful descent of the Watut River.

I had one night left in Papua New Guinea, then back home to the States. I had an idea for a send-off dinner. Our ragged team put on our best T-shirts and stepped out to the restaurant Patsy had cited was owned by her attacker. We took a corner table and studied the menu. The prices were high. We ordered anyway.

In the back of the restaurant, through the kitchen portal, I saw the owner pass by a couple times. He looked larger sober than he had that night.

After our meal, I called the waitress over and asked for the check and a pen. On the reverse I wrote: "To the owner: We made a timely acquaintance two weeks ago on a dirt road at five a.m. I saw Patsy just before she left for Sydney, and she gave me your name and that of this restaurant. Now you know that we know, and we will inform everyone we meet in Port Moresby of what you did. You should turn yourself in and pay your debt. We will be watching."

I squeezed the note into the waitress's hand and instructed her to give it to the owner. We chose not to linger and witness the reaction. We dropped a healthy tip on the table and scrambled for the door. We piled in the car and sped away.

We made our flights back to the United States the next morning, but the restaurant owner had no idea we had departed. I never heard anything from Patsy or her parents and had no way to contact them. Years later when I returned to Port Moresby, the restaurant was gone.

CHAPTER 30

FIRST INTO CHINA

The further one goes the less one knows.
—Lao Tzu

By the late 1970s Sobek was making some noise in the travel community as an explorer of wild rivers in wild places, from the Bio-Bio in Chile to the Toa in Cuba, the Tatshenshini in Alaska to the Euphrates in Türkiye, and a dozen more.

But I was becoming increasing interested in the world beyond the banks.

Then, out of the blue, I received an invitation that would allow a new exploratory pursuit.

Before rapprochement, but after ping-pong diplomacy, through a series of sublime accidents in 1977 I ended up with a permit to escort the first American travel delegation to Mainland China. At the time China had no external air link, no internal tourism infrastructure, but in the wake of Mao Zedong's death the year before, and the Gang of Four under house arrest, Vice Premier Teng had decided to dip toes into tourism as a possible new source of state income. Through our little adventure company, Sobek, we had been conducting raft tours down the rivers of Ethiopia since 1973, through the coup of 1974 that ousted Emperor Haile Selassie, and throughout the communist-styled revolution that followed. The Chinese were assisting Mengistu Haile Mariam, the leader who was, in a fashion, modeling himself after Mao, and so they turned to Ethiopia for suggestions of a US tour company that might want to organize a first tour to the Hidden Kingdom. When I got a call from Ethiopian Airlines inviting Sobek to take up the mantle, I was beside myself. We were granted a permit for twenty-five tourists, and I immediately crafted a letter to past clients and inserted it in an envelope with "Red Alert" bannered across the side. Within a week the tour was filled, and a month later we were on a flight to Addis Ababa, where we waited until evening before making the connecting EAL flight to Beijing. The Chinese wanted to make sure we passed over China at night so we could not take any aerial photos. We arrived as the sky squeezed the lemons

Richard leading the first American tour into China, 1977. PAMELA ROBERSON

of dawn. On the forty-minute bus ride to the city center we passed hundreds of Chinese running, all uniformed in Mao jackets (baggy, in proletarian dark gray or revolutionary blue), "liberation" shoes (khaki rubber-soled sneakers), white gloves, and white gauze masks. Scores more were practicing Tai Chi, some with real swords, sending stretched arms and legs through the half-light at underwater speeds.

Beijing in December, stung by winds from Mongolia, had the look and feel of cold, gray steel. Barren poplars lined broad boulevards, devoid of advertising, signs, or color. Nothing had been spared to ensure that each brutally architectured building was indistinguishable from the others. And the pollution was ghastly, thick as soup, created not by motor vehicles, since there were none privately owned and only a relative handful maintained by the State, but by black coal, used by virtually every one of the millions of families in Peking for heating.

We checked into the Friendship Hotel in the far northwest corner of the city, a former Russian compound before relations between the countries turned icy. After check-in, eager to stretch after the twelve-hour flight, my friend Micki McEwen and I slipped on our Nikes and headed out for a quick run down the street (there were no sidewalks). More like *Rollerball* than running, there were rivers of bikes sweeping in great crosscurrents and eddies down the streets. It was difficult enough to cross a street, let alone run along it. So we abandoned the pavement for the packed dirt of the compound, and even then, we couldn't go far for the sandpaper air quality. Then we were shuttled onto our bus to begin the official tour. We were told not to shake hands, touch, or engage with any people we met along the way and not to look them in the eyes. In tight formation we were escorted to visit pandas, pagodas, and temples, and our handlers made sure we never strayed. Every day began with a lengthy propaganda lecture, proclaiming the superiority of Chinese socialism, which enjoyed, they said repeatedly, no crime, cancer, or poverty. We paid visits to cooperative farms, clinics, and factories. It was an interface with a slice of a culture now lost to time. Each day ended with a fifteen-course meal in an overlit hall where we were the only diners.

During our stay I convinced our hosts to take me to the Tiananmen Square headquarters of the newly formed CITS, China International Travel Service. There I slapped down a stack of rafting brochures on the desk of the highest official I was allowed to see, Mrs. Hu Muying, properly dressed in gray chinoiserie. I took a deep breath and asked a big question. "Do you think we could come and raft the Yangtze?"

Her nod was vacant, like a cow watching a train go by. There is rarely a no in China. Instead, they serve tea. Looking at Mrs. Hu Muying was like looking at the Chinese emperor in the Marguerite Yourcenar story: "beautiful, but blank, like a looking glass placed too high, reflecting nothing except the stars and the immutable heavens." It was clear rafting was something entirely new to my host, and her thick eyebrows nearly went through her head staring at the photographs of rubber boats pitching through huge ricks of whitewater. After much consideration she suggested I put my request in the form of a written proposal and send it along after my return to the United States. And so I left her offices to rejoin the group, and compose in my head an appeal that would go on for years.

Just seven miles north of Beijing the Summer Palace was picturesque and comparatively pristine. It was a retreat for royal families as far back as 1000 CE. During the Opium Wars of the mid-nineteenth century, the British burned most of the palace, but it was rebuilt by an empress in the Manchu dynasty by using funds meant to modernize the navy. Her misappropriations were now appreciated by Chinese and visitors alike, who strolled the groomed park and the arched bridges, past pedestals of naturally sculptured limestone, up Longevity Hill, and around the glinted Kun Ming Ho Lake.

Bordering Tiananmen (Gate of Heavenly Peace) Square, the vast paved area where Mao first raised the flag of the People's Republic of China, was the colossal entry gate to the Forbidden City. Forbidden because for five hundred years only emperors and their concubines and attendants were allowed within. Protected by high walls and a moat (which was frozen, supporting a few daring, deft skaters), the grounds were some 250 acres in area, all smooth with marble and stone. Backdropped with pavilions, red overhanging pipe-eaved museums and pagodas, extravagant halls and simple concubine quarters, the ambience was all ancient China of brocade-silked emperors and gold palaces. We seemed to be the only guests, and we never came close to any Chinese save our guides.

A chartered plane took us to Shanghai the next morning. "Before Liberation," the party line went, "Shanghai was a pit of imperialistic decadence and debauchery." Now, the guides insisted, it had been deloused, swept up, and rolled out again in scrubbed socialist form. But much of the flavor of the colonial days, when foreign powers shamelessly exploited the city at the mouth of the Yangtze and its port, remained in the mock-Gothic mansions, gray-stone consulates, bow-windowed banks, and trading firms and hotels constructed in representative motifs from a range of hegemonic countries. The most evocative walkway in the city was the tree-lined Bund (from *bundong*, or "riverbank"), which followed the waterfront of the Whangpoo River. On one side, with one sweep, I could watch a thousand years of water transportation, from sloppy junks and sampans to sleepy supertankers. On the other side was an incongruous skyline of steel and glass high-rises. At one end, in the former French Concession Territory, was a waterfront park and several small, sweet shops selling pastries, tea, ice cream, and the ever-popular carbonated orange soft drink. Where prostitutes, opium, and all sorts of colonial shenanigans once thrived, proletariats chastely paraded, keeping their good distance from us.

That evening we were treated to the acrobatics of the circus. But somewhere mid-show my stomach began to rumble. I excused myself and went looking for a toilet. My hosts watched me intently but did not leave their seats. I found some relief but did not feel well enough to return for the rest of the show, so I decided to make my way back to the hotel. I was fairly sure I knew the way.

But once outside in the swarming streets, I quickly lost my way. This was life under a different sky. There were no signs in English, and no building or site recognizable. I moved about in ever-increasing radiuses, but I seemed to fall deeper into disorientation. I tried to approach passersby, but each time I got close, they bowed heads and moved quickly away. I found a policeman, but as I approached, he blew his whistle and put his hand up for me to stop. I felt forfeited, invisible, and began to wonder how I might spend the night. Then, out of the crowd an old man stepped. A river of people parted around him. He stood bent and rigid. His eyebrows flared upwards like feathers, and he looked at me with the cold focus of a raptor. "You lost?" he asked, his voice bearing the lingual mists of British English. "Yes," I said.

"Do you have hotel?" I fumbled about and pulled out my hotel key, which was emboldened with Chinese letters, but nothing in English. I had forgotten its name. He inspected the key and shared "Before the Revolution I worked at the Astor House Hotel. I know your hotel. Follow me."

We turned and turned again down several crowded streets and stopped in front of the Gothic facade that was my hotel. I thanked my Samaritan over and over and offered him money or whatever might please him. But he shrugged, shook his head no, stretched a smile that reached into his cheekbones, and said, "You would do the same." I scribbled my name and address on a piece of notebook paper and handed it over, asking if he would do the same. He again shook his head no, looked around to see if anyone was watching our interactions, and then turned and walked away.

I was scolded the next morning for abandoning the group and told I would be summarily sent home if I broke the rules again. I promised I would not, but inside I was thankful for the serendipitous prohibited encounter.

We next flew 115 miles south to the soft-hilled city of Hangchow, the silk capital of China. It looked lifted from a watercolor, with looming, steep, deep green mountains hugged by low-hanging, wispy clouds, all above a dappled lake, rippled by little rowboats and rimmed with willows. The scene looked so delicate that if I sneezed, it seemed it would crack and crumble.

This was a place for runners. We shared the isthmus each morning with several hundred Chinese joggers, from teens to geriatrics, whisking down the Soo Causeway over six vaulted bridges and back.

Marco Polo visited Hangchow at the end of the thirteenth century, and the parks and landmarks he passed were little changed, and the names the same: "Watching Goldfish in a Flowery Pond," "Listening to Orioles among Willows," "Autumn Moon on the Calm Lake," and "Three Pools Reflecting the Moon." We were "Two Occidentals emitting much perspiration" by the time we crossed the sixth bridge each morning.

The final day of the tour we were escorted to the last man-made object visible to astronauts as they shot to the moon: the Great Wall. Started more than 2,500 years ago, during the Chou dynasty, and more than 3,500 miles long, its chief purpose was to keep out barbarians. It also protected the Chinese from themselves, as various states were forever warring with one another. And it aided farming, breaking up the razor winds sweeping off the Mongolian Plains.

Much of the Great Wall had crumbled into the soil, but a mile-long section at Chu Yung Pass was resurfaced and restored, and it was here that visitors came to gawk and take pictures. Every news photo of famous personages, from Nixon to Shirley MacLaine, posing on top of a wonder of the world, was taken here. And we did as well. Micki and I double-tied our shoes and took off towards Mongolia, once more without permissions from our hosts. It was not easy running. First, the wall snaked up and down sharp hills, ignoring the natural contours whenever possible. And once we got past the restored area, the top was a rubble pile of loose stones, weeds, and potholes. Nevertheless, there was something magical about striding across the ancient architecture in the cutting-cold wastelands of northern China. We ran for an hour and returned to find our hosts seething with our errant run. But there was no reprimand. Instead, they took us to an acupuncture clinic, where I was subjected to a set of painfully large needles. It was less punishment than the idea of *chi ku*, a Cultural Revolution expression that translated to "eat bitter," or endure hardship. We were to depart the next day, and our hosts would make a report describing the behavior of this alien untamed class of people called tourists.

Launching for first descent at the Great Bend of the Yangtze. RICHARD BANGS

CHAPTER 31

THE ADVENTURE WARS

There Is No Happiness for Him Who Does Not Travel.
—Aitareya Brahmana, 1500 BCE

As Sobek found some traction, we evolved our little brochures from black and white to color and mined more potential travelers with small, classified ads in a new magazine called *Outside*. Our volume of mail increased to the point the Angels Camp post office said no PO box was large enough to handle, so staff suggested we just drop by each afternoon and pick up a bag or two. "What should we use as the address?" I asked. "Anything you want, as long as you include the zip code." So I changed our official mailing address to "One Sobek Tower, Angels Camp, CA 95222," although our office was merely a rambling wood single-story former brothel and chicken coop. More than once a visiting guest, including ministers of tourism, would poke their head inside the door and ask, "Where is the Sobek Tower? I can't seem to find it."

It was evident early on that we were not the only shop offering adventure. While we were operating in our tower in the Sierra foothills, a company in Albany across the bay from San Francisco was offering treks and climbs to remote mountain regions of the world: Mountain Travel. In a way we were competing for the same travelers, those who shunned the passive horizonal vacations of beaches and cruise ships and instead sought active, engaged experiences that challenged mind and body and connected with faraway cultures and environments. The Venn diagram of activities had not overlapped until I picked up the latest Mountain Travel brochure and it listed a raft trip down the Omo. How was that possible? That was the Sobek signature trip. We had pioneered the run; we owned it, or so I assumed. I knew then I wanted to raise our competitive metabolism. This was war. What were their most popular trips, I asked Jim Slade, who had done some guiding for Mountain Travel. "Nepal and Kilimanjaro, I think," he replied. That was it. We had to offer Kilimanjaro in our next brochure. I sent a note to past clients asking if anyone would like to join me in a climb, a first for Sobek. And I booked a flight to Arusha, Tanzania.

Richard in the best office in the world. DAVE SHORE

Sobek expanded to offer every adventure from rafting to climbing to sailing to skiing.
LAURA HUBBER

CHAPTER 32

CLIMBING THE ROOF OF AFRICA

The Sublime dilates and elevates the Soul, Fear sinks and contracts it; yet both are felt upon viewing what is great and awful.

—JOHN BAILLIE, 1747

THE WAKE-UP CALL CAME JUST AFTER MIDNIGHT. DANIEL, OUR GUIDE, STOOD OVER me with a cup of tea that sent tendrils of steam snaking up around his yellow-toothed smile. Rolling out of the bunk, I clutched at my toilet bag. Dr. Nelson repeatedly ordered me to take my daily dosage of Zestril, a ten-milligram tablet for high blood pressure. I'd been remiss in keeping to the regimen, but here, on the mountain, he said it was critical. This was summit day.

I opened the toilet bag and pulled out the bottle of Zestril. But the cap was off, the bottle empty. I groped in the bag, retrieved another bottle, and saw the label was for codeine. It too was empty, the top off. And in the bottom of the bag there was a pile of pills, all indistinguishable in the half-light of the hut. I needed to take the Zestril to get up the mountain, so I picked a pill and popped it in. It would either propel me upward with dilated arteries or put me to sleep.

Up to that point the highest I had ever been, outside of a plane, was the 14,495 feet at the summit of Mount Whitney, the tallest mountain in the contiguous United States. It had been a tough effort. I had a headache, felt nauseated, and struggled with every step. My epiphany at the top: Mountain climbing was not for me. That would be my ceiling.

Yet, here I was, off into the high chill with five layers of clothing, heading up the final pitch of the highest mountain in Africa, Kilimanjaro, at 19,340 glaciated feet above the sea.

I thought about my toe. The big toe on my left foot. As we plodded higher in the icy, burning blackness, I wiggled my toe, sheathed in three layers of socks and

Climbing the highest peak in Africa. PAMELA ROBERSON

my guaranteed waterproof boots. It moved, felt fine, except for a tingle inspired by Diamox, the diuretic that helps prevent altitude sickness by draining fluid from the lungs. Nobody said a word. Though we began as a dozen first timers, we splintered into smaller groups. Pamela Roberson, my photographer wife, stricken by altitude sickness, retched through the night. With the aid of four Tanzanian guides, she had stumbled toward the Horombo complex of huts, back at 12,336 feet, to recover. Mike had bloody sputum; Rhea had diarrhea. Patrick was constipated. Carl and Susan were attorneys. Dana, a forty-one-year-old California river guide who had come to work on the mountain, was wondering if he was too old for this profession. We were all trespassing here. Yet five of us marched out in a knot: Dr. Steve, Bob, Lee, Gary, and me. The headlamps atop our hunched figures cut into the raw, inky air as we followed the trail's zigs and zags up the vertical gravel pit. It felt good to walk, though I was feeling drowsy. I realized a distinction between descending a river and climbing a mountain was the social currents. The raft is a communal *zendos*. When rafting a river, the deeper you travel the warmer it generally gets, the more clothes come off, and the interactions between fellow paddlers increase. Yet when climbing high mountains, the higher you go, the more insulated you become. The cold whittles wits down to awareness. The layers increase, and talk between companions dwindles and falls. But interior dialogues accrete.

Now, in my mind I heard: *"There is the possibility you may never walk again."*

Eight months previous I was in Hawaii, recuperating after a cross-country lecture tour. I was renegade diving in Maui. Renegade because I had never certified as a scuba diver, had never completed a course, though I had tooled around with a tank and regulator in Bali, the Caribbean, the Galapagos, the Andaman Sea, and the Tuamotus without ill effects. Yet this time something seemed different. I didn't feel quite right as I swam among the coral-colored fish in Ahihi Bay, and I was oddly pleased when the fifty-five-minute dive was over.

The next morning at 3:00 a.m., we left our hotel to drive to the top of Haleakala, the two-mile-high volcano that looms over Maui. We arrived in time for sunrise and then saddled up on bikes for a six-hour ride down among the steepest roads on earth. But halfway down, a sharp pain bayoneted my left leg. It spread as we continued and became unbearable. I aborted the bike ride and grabbed a van to the airport. I visited the airport nurse and described my pain, and she recommended I drink as much alcohol as possible while flying, since she could not prescribe any painkillers.

I thought about that pain as I continued climbing up Kilimanjaro. The air was thin and dry. It didn't crowd, it didn't weigh. We were moving like astronauts, bodies bent into the mountain.

Kilimanjaro is only two degrees south of the equator, but as we ascended its flanks, we passed through five climatic zones roughly parallel to the vegetation belts one would encounter traveling from the equator north or south to the poles. And we seemed to be tracing nature's evolution in reverse, from the big animals at the base to the first stirrings of bacterial life on the high reaches of this ancient cone. I liked the skein of change that unwound with every footfall.

Once back in Oakland I saw my doctor, who guessed my muscles had locked up and sent me home to a heating pad and bed. Yet even with a pharmacy of pills—Flexeril, Vicodin, and Naprosy—the pain sharpened and spread to my other leg. Then my left toes turned cold and began to go numb. This could mean nerve damage, so I made my way to the emergency room. I had a spinal tap, a CT scan, and MRIs. The diagnosis: I had something called a spinal dural arteriovenous fistula, or a hole between an artery and a vein. The blood was shunting the wrong way, creating ischemic pressure against my spine, and I could become paralyzed.

After two and a half hours switchbacking through the atramentous night, we clambered into Meyer's Cave at 17,000 feet. Only 2,340 feet to go, I calculated with much difficulty. It seemed unsporting that a shallow cave was named after Dr. Hans Meyer, the German geologist who first breathed the rarefied atmosphere of Kilimanjaro's white roof in 1889. Yet it was a cave of mythic architecture. For a long time, the Chagga people who lived at the underpinnings of Kilimanjaro refused to pass beyond this grotto, believing it to be the entrance to the "House of the Dead." Now Daniel spat into the cave, which he said was for good luck.

I took a maintenance break, slapped my swollen face, and choked down some water. The primary thief at altitude is dehydration, yet at the same time it is tough to carry much water. I carried three quarts, about half of what is recommended for a day at altitude. I also noted my internal sphygmomanometer. I was groggy. Did I swallow the wrong pill? Two days earlier we had taken an acclimation day at Horombo Hut, where I wandered among the giant heather, pulling on the mosslike lichen known as Old Man's Beard. I began taking Diamox, the drug of choice on this contour line. On the second evening I was feeling quite chipper and told Carl, one of my roommates in the hut, that Diamox was truly a miracle drug and that it was working wonderfully, except perhaps for the diarrhea.

Appetite was nonexistent at this level, but I forced down a boiled sweet and a bite of wild berry PowerBar. Then off again on the pre-dawn slog.

> Just before putting me under, the anesthesiologist held a clipboard in front of me with a release I had to sign. He explained there was a chance I might not wake up, that I could die. I didn't have time to think about silence as an ecumenical state before the nitrous oxide swam through the mask and the sodium pentothal penetrated my blood. Counting backwards I made it to ninety-seven before oblivion.

It was getting harder to concentrate as we crunched up the deeply pleated cinder cone, the lava scree shifting like shards of glass. The slope angled about fifty-five degrees, and the loose gravel swallowed a good portion of every step. I needed assistance, so I turned on my Walkman. Earlier in the trip I tried listening to a series of tapes as we trudged the seven and a half spongy miles through dark moorland between the Mandara and Horombo huts. I sampled the Brandenburg Concertos, Sade, Bonnie Raitt, Marvin Gaye, Ladysmith Black Mambazo, James Taylor, and Cream. Nothing seemed to have the right energy to move my feet along. This time I punched in Aretha Franklin, and when she began to wail "Natural Woman," I couldn't control my face. Euphoria brought a vale of tears. I felt great, and my body moved to some ancestral beat.

After two rounds of Aretha, it was time to change tunes. We stopped for a water break, and I went through the complex task of changing tapes. It seemed like calculus. Finally, I slipped in Bobby Brown and found myself jack-swinging upwards. My head seemed unclouded, my anatomic checklist showed no red lights. I even had CCU (clear, copious urine), a good sign. Just the night before, as we tucked in after watery soup and a game of Hearts, my head pounded, my stomach protested, and I felt on the verge of vomiting. I took a Diamox, two aspirin, and a Halcion. Better climbing through chemistry. Dr. Steve, a gastroenterologist and oldest member of our team at age fifty-four, was the most vocally obsessed with making it to the top, and he had been taking dexamethasone (a steroid) prophylactically. His demon was altitude. He said he got headaches flying into Denver. Doctors have the lowest summit rate of any profession, attributed to a resistance to take the advice of guides and seeking medical solutions to every challenge.

We all had demons here. Bob, the ex-marine, suffered from bad knees. Lee agonized about his weight. Gary, who had the cautious temperament of a chemist, which he was, was in a troubled marriage. I rolled around my sleeping bag considering if I was going to be sick, wondering if I had the stuff to make the summit. Was I stupid to attempt this after my diving accident? I felt like a spy in my own soul. I could not fox myself.

The sky was beginning to lighten, and as the silhouette of a wall appeared above me, I turned off my headlamp. For a moment, the mountain looked like it was receding, and I stopped to calibrate myself. I'd been third in our alpine chain gang, but Lee passed me now. *"Pole, pole"* was the Swahili mantra I breathed to myself. It rhymed with its translation, "Slowly, slowly."

We started this twenty-five-mile trek five days ago at the park entrance gate, at six thousand feet, in air cool as a clean sheet. We had thirty porters for our dirty dozen, each deftly balancing approximately forty pounds of gear and food atop his head, while we suffered along with headaches, day packs, and cameras. In the evenings they would cook up a storm, using camphor and podo wood collected around the brown, geometric A-frame huts built by the Norwegians in the early 1970s. For the last hut, the cement-block Kibo, at 15,520 feet, well above any flowing streams, the porters also toted up a supply of fresh water.

As we made our way up the interminable hill, we examined, in some continuing ritual, the faces of those loping down. Some were cadaver-like, some contorted, some an unadorned elegy of war and memory, and a few were blissful, eyes urging us to ask if they made it to the summit. A hearty woman from Tasmania we met at the first hut was barely recognizable as she passed us two days later, eyes suppurating, lips cracked, being braced down the mountain by two porters. Then, as we approached the Saddle, the long, red windswept shoulder connecting the fraternal peaks of Kilimanjaro, Mawenzi, and Kibo, two porters rounded the bend rolling a wheelbarrow-like stretcher with a dull-eyed European tucked inside. I pictured myself in the same stretcher, violently ill with pulmonary edema. Daniel, our guide, asked the porters what happened to their patient. Daniel translated the answer: The young German fell out of his bunk in the Kibo Hut and broke his ankle.

I stopped to look back down and saw the first pink flush of the African landscape spread beneath me. Unencumbered and flat, shiny as fresh paint, it was the floor of the Great Rift Valley. Just a week ago we were rambling along those steppes among the megafauna. The mountain creates water, and the water seeps to the fertile volcanic plains, which in turn supports a menagerie of wildlife, and the nomadic Masai. For five days we roamed the base in a *bourrée* of foreplay for the ascent. Ever present, even when obscured by clouds, was the reason for our long journey to Africa: the isolated dome of Kilimanjaro.

I was higher than Mawenzi, the old, grim 17,564-foot peak seven miles away from the high cone of Kibo. It was messy and worn, as though composed of scrap dumped from some celestial chariot. Between the drifting clouds, hundreds of feet below, I could see the curve of the Earth. The sun appeared, balanced on the central spire of Mawenzi, as if the volcano had spewed it whole from its belly. A long-hanging halo of clouds reflected the rays down onto the snow-mansarded western face and over to Kibo. As the sun climbed, it looked like a hot-air balloon approaching the mountain.

I was on my third tranquilizing play of the Bobby Brown tape. Then abruptly, at 6:33 a.m., we crested a ridge, and we were at Gilman's Point, 18,650 feet, the lowest spot along the almost perfectly circular, 1.2-mile-diameter crater. At least a dozen others were on this aerie, fellow soi-disant climbers and guides who started out before us. And suddenly all the Tanzanian guides broke out into a jazzy, multi-harmony song in Swahili, with a chorus of "Kili-man-jaro" ringing over the howling, icy air. This was the point where most climbers turn around; around 20 percent of those who attempt the climb continue around the crater rim to Uhuru Peak, the true and final summit.

> I awoke in a white room, my body one massive ache. A doctor came in and said they had not been able to find the fistula with the angiogram, and so after I rested, they wanted to go in again. I asked what had caused this sudden condition, and he said nobody knew. It seemed to be a spontaneous incident. And if not plugged, paralysis was the likely outcome. Already, he said, there had likely been some permanent nerve damage, but they wanted to go in again and find this hole and cork it. He asked if I could feel anything in my left toe as he poked it. I couldn't. He scheduled the next operation for the following morning, so I had a day to think about what life would be like without legs. This time I couldn't paper over my emotions. When my friend Russ Daggatt came to visit, I broke down and cried uncontrollably.

There was nothing fake or stupid about this mountain. I couldn't fool it or myself. I couldn't stop at Gilman's and say I did the mountain, as so many do. Neither could my four companions. We were trapped by an inner honesty that didn't exist at lower climes. So, off we went along a rib of broken rock, into a wind that cut like a lie.

Things changed for me at that point. I could no longer keep up with the team. Though we were told to breathe through our noses, retaining more precious moisture in our bodies, I simply could not do that. I sucked air through my mouth, into constricted lungs. And I heard the racket of my breath, something I was told was a bad sign. The wind whispered "*pole, pole.*" I had to downshift, and I remembered advice Bill Broyles gave me the week before departure. He had climbed the 23,036-foot-high Aconcagua, the tallest mountain in the Western Hemisphere, at age forty-two, a critical crossroads in his life between being editor in chief of *Newsweek* and executive producer of *China Beach*. He discovered the way to continue walking upward at altitude was to take a step and pause with the foot midair for a breather. I tried the technique, but it didn't seem to work. Instead, I found if I took two steps and then stopped for several seconds of deep-dish breathing, I could then proceed, slowly, slowly, but surely.

The clouds were beginning to part, unveiling spires of blue ice and terraces of glaciers surrounding us, huge glaciers, bigger than hospital bills. I was thankful Gary was right behind me, especially when he broke the silence with an inspirational poster caption, "We're gonna make it now. Nothing can stop us." But then he coughed the dry cough of edema. Though Gary, too, had never been above 14,500 feet, he was an avid runner, hiker, weight-trainer, and cyclist. At age fifty he was in the best shape of our team. Yet perspiration gleamed on his forehead like Mylar, and every time I stopped for a breath, he stopped as well, a commiserative shadow.

I reminded myself I was traveling with a round-trip ticket; that this was not Hemingway's awe-inspiring place of the dead, that we were beyond myth and above illusion.

Again, I awoke in the hospital room. Across from me was another patient, an old man in extreme pain who rolled around and screamed. When a nurse arrived, he thought she was his daughter and blabbered incoherently about family memories. I checked my body, and though there was some soreness from the operation, I felt okay. The pain in my legs was gone; I could move my feet, even wiggle my big toe. Yet there was no strength in my legs; they were like rubber when I swung around and planted them on the floor. A physical therapist helped me to the bathroom using a walker, and I thought of what life would be like if this were my permanent condition.

My image of myself as an adventurer broke up on the rocks of this ward. But the doctor finally paid a visit and reported they still did not find the fistula, but he believed it clogged itself, which sometimes, though not often, happens. He thought I would be able to walk in a few days, and that likely the paralysis would not return. There was some permanent nerve damage, which would mean a loss of some feeling in my big toe, but it would probably not impair me. Why, in a few months, I could probably climb a mountain, he suggested. "Though be aware of any recurring symptoms," he said, "and get to a hospital if the pain or numbness spreads again beyond your toe."

Later, my family doctor dissented. "I'm not sure I agree," he said. "I think the sickness was related to you going to altitude so soon after diving, something like the bends. I'm not sure if going up a mountain is a wise thing to do."

Gary and I were alone on this mountain, animals in a space capsule. I was prowling in an uncomfortable place conjured by Hemingway in "The Snows of Kilimanjaro." What is *that* leopard doing at *this* altitude? Twice we saw the summit and mustered the strength to make the last triumphant steps, only to see it roll away as though on wheels. Every false crest revealed white scapes beyond that were higher still. So we continued trudging along, trying to react to the extraordinary scenery.

It was so close, but I was wondering if I could make it. My home was near the sea, where oxygen density is more than twice that at this altitude. I was attempting this slope with the equivalent of one lung. I was breathing like a chain-smoker chasing a bus. I was in the wrong skin for climbing. What could I do to keep going? The only reality was the mountain in my face. I could not cheat this one.

I kept on trekking the thread of razor wire between horror and triumph.

Then we were there: top of the touchstone, the peak called Uhuru—-Swahili for "freedom." The tiara of an extinct volcano, it was higher than any ground east of the Andes and west of the Himalayas. We stepped up to a shelf and became part of the sky. Daniel, our guide, squatted by the sign that declared this the highest point in Africa. He puffed on a cigarette. A torn Tanzanian flag wrapped tightly around a pole. "Congratulations. You made it," I wheezed to Dr. Steve, whose face looked like a gym bag. But then, nobody looked good here. "Yes, I did it!" he coughed.

I pulled my camera from inside my jacket and prepared to take a group shot, but the batteries were frozen. It was truly cold, the wind violent in a strobe-like way. The day before, knowing that my mind would be cloudy on top, I wrote a list of photos I wanted to take of gear I used—my knife, watch, jacket, pack. But it was too cold to go through the exercise. Even Bob, the retired marine, who brought an American flag to unfurl on top, couldn't dig it out.

Still, I had to have one shot. With the wobbly movements of an old man, I pulled out my laptop, set it up, and asked Bob and Gary to take a few pictures with their cameras. I blinked my eyes to stay in focus. Computing on top of Kilimanjaro. That would be my First.

Then I stood up and looked around for a last time, faintly aware I was gazing at something terribly beautiful, something wonderfully awful, something genuinely sublime.

I was so tired. I was sleepy. But I wiggled my toe. It wiggled fine.

CHAPTER 33

KRAK OF DOOM

The smell of sulfur is strong. But not unpleasant for a sinner.
—MARK TWAIN, 1866

As so happens with resolutions made on a mountain, I returned and tossed out my reservations about climbing. Now that Sobek was offering treks and climbs, in direct competition to Mountain Travel, I thought we should explore and offer experiences on tropical challenges. One volcano off the coast of Java was especially enticing.

"You've got a 20 percent chance of making it out and back in a small boat; 80 percent in a large boat." Dr. Ridder's warning echoed in my sleep-resistant mind as the boat shuddered with another wave. We had hired a "large boat," the *Ernarosa*, a thirty-foot traditional Pinisi diesel-powered fishing trawler, to navigate the twenty-five miles across the Sunda Strait from West Java. But I had twice put my hand through the dry-rotted sideboards of the *Ernarosa* while being bounced about below deck. We were attempting this crossing in January, the stormiest month of the monsoon season.

The boat's rhythmic pitching slapped an untethered hatch door to time, and I felt myself drifting to sleep.

A wild list of the boat punched the dusty moment of unconsciousness, tossing me off the hard butt-worn bench I was using as a bed and onto the keel floor. The boat lurched again, and, with a crack like a cannon report, a wave burst through the compartment and washed over me.

"I think we're sinking," I yelled to George Fuller, who was clinging to a narrow bench.

Above, our Indonesian crew scrambled about and screamed at one another over the sounds of cracking wood. Then another wave crashed into the hold. Robert, the one crew member who spoke a bit of English, poked his head into the hold. "We go island," his voice wavered. The boat pitched again, and this time it seemed to stay at its cant, a forty-five-degree angle. We grabbed our kits. George and I climbed up the ladder through another rolling wave to a tilted mid-deck. The only exit to the island side of the boat was through the privy, but a plywood wall blocked passage. Robert crashed it down with a clumsy martial arts dropkick. I jumped first into the inky water and was surprised to find it was just waist deep. George threw our packs to me and then leapt in. The rest of the crew followed. We waded to shore, George holding his camera high above his head. Once on dry ground we turned our flashlights back to the *Ernarosa*. It lay collapsed on its side and moved in small breaths with the waves, like a dying sea mammal.

As a means of conveyance, the *Ernarosa* was washed up. It was 4:00 a.m. We were shipwrecked on Krakatau, one of the most destructive volcanoes of all time.

On August 26, 1883, Krakatau roared and belched a pillar of steam that took the shape of a gigantic pine tree that reached upward to a height more than double that of Mount Everest. To one witness, a Dutch telegraph master on the Java coast, it appeared as if thousands of white balloons had been suddenly released, rolling, twisting, turning, expanding, and bursting—a lyrical image, in the poetry of grand concussion. Captain Sampson, of a British ship anchored off the Sumatran shore, was more reverent when he wrote in his log, "So violent are the explosions that the ear drums of over half my crew have been shattered. . . . I am convinced that the Day of Judgment has come."

The next day, at 9:58 a.m., the cone of Krakatau ripped itself apart with the biggest bang ever recorded on our planet, clocking in at 310 decibels. The volcanic gunshot was heard over one-thirteenth of the Earth's surface, from Sri Lanka (then Ceylon) east to the Philippines and south to southern Australia, almost 2,500 miles away, where sheep were startled into a stampede. If Krakatau had been in New York City, the big bang could have been heard in both London and San Francisco.

An artist's rendition of the explosion of Krakatau.

With the explosion Krakatau sent up a record fifty-mile-high column of ash, rock, and pumice. The energy released from the blast was equivalent to one million times that of a hydrogen bomb. The airborne pressure waves spread out in all directions, meeting on the opposite side of the world, near Bogota, Colombia, and bouncing back to their origin, where they rebounded outward again so that some barographs recorded the same wave seven times. Dust clouds traveling at seventy-five miles an hour plunged the Earth within a 300-mile radius into darkness for three days. In Poughkeepsie and New Haven, fire departments were called out when the intense reds of the sunsets created by volcanic aerosol in the atmosphere looked like conflagrations in the distance. For three years dust circled the Earth, creating strange tangerine sunsets. The fine particles filtered out enough sunshine to lower global temperatures by nearly a degree Fahrenheit for several years.

Within seconds of the blast, a landmass the size of Manhattan was obliterated. Hundreds, perhaps thousands, of people were burned to death by the rain of red-hot ash and rock that had been molten until it exploded upward and solidified on contact with the air. Far more destructive were the tidal waves that were triggered by the collapse of Krakatau's cones into its empty belly. Giant tsunamis, more than 130 feet high, swept over the nearby shores of Java and Sumatra, hurling one steamship two miles inland. One survivor was lifted by a wave and deposited on a hill while still lying in his bed. Another found himself being swept inland next to a crocodile. He couldn't swim, so he climbed on the reptile's back, hanging on by pressing his fingers deep into its eye sockets. Another man found his saving angel in the corpse of a cow. He climbed on and floated to safety. One woman gave birth to her child while racing up a hill. Tens of thousands of others weren't so fortunate. A mosque filled with people was dragged into the sea, as were offices, homes, lighthouses, forts, and some 165 villages.

The resulting waves were recorded as far as Hawaii, the Bay of Biscay, and Cape Horn. Even the level of the River Thames was affected. More than 36,000 people were killed in southern Sumatra and along coastal Java, a record at the time.

George Fuller, the carmine-haired epidemiologist and physician I met in Addis in 1973, became a lifelong friend. Together we authored first descents of rivers in Ethiopia, Sumatra, New Guinea, and Alaska. We trekked across the Amazon and sailed the coast of Antarctica. But on the eve of departure for this exercise, George called to say he was bowing out. He had many good reasons: He crushed his foot in a recent car accident and couldn't walk any distance; he could make some good money staying in California and working his shift at the emergency room; he could tend his garden.

But one reason chilled me. George said he had a bad premonition about this expedition. He also revealed he had had similar premonitions before the Baro expedition, where Angus Macleod disappeared, and again before the Blue Nile, the river that will forever in my mind evoke the death of a friend, and of a part of me.

After hours of phone calls, George relented and promised to join the trip. I was relieved he recanted, but my own qualms were swarming. I had given George every argument I could muster as to why his atavistic fears were unfounded, yet as I spun them out, my own doubts crawled in. Was it crazy to explore an active volcano as a possible Sobek offering?

Smack in the middle of the Ring of Fire, Java was the most populous and most volcanically active island in the world. Though 121 volcanoes (about 35 of which are active) dot the island, our plan was to climb the most infamous cinder west of Java.

To get to Krakatau we first traveled four hours and 110 miles southwest of Jakarta, Indonesia's streaming, teeming capital, to the Carita Krakatau Beach

Richard climbing Krakatau. GEORGE FULLER

Hotel, an unpretentious ramble of bungalows set amid tangled pandanus and coconut palms. In this set piece worthy of Joseph Conrad, we found Dr. Axel Ridder, a Berlin-born refugee from civilization who had become something of a student of the volcano he could see from his wicker breakfast table. Ridder arrived in Indonesia in 1970 to teach economic management in Jakarta. When his contract expired three years later, he decided to drop out and carve out his own little piece of paradise. He now ruled over Carita Beach like a *dalang* (puppet master) of his own Wayang shadow show, the only Westerner for miles.

"It's far more dangerous to live in San Francisco with its earthquakes or Germany with its Pershing missiles than here, twenty-five miles from Krakatau. It would be near impossible for effluviant to hit us. And it's more likely Manhattan will be leveled by a tsunami than Carita Beach." The locals don't agree. For weeks after the August 1883 explosion, bodies washed up on the beach where Ridder has a seventy-five-year lease to operate his hotel.

Hawaiians believe volcanic activity is the work of Pele, an orgiastic goddess. The Romans acknowledged the existence of a god of fire, Vulcan, and the Sudanese of West Java know that the smoke and fire of the Sunda Strait flares from the nostrils of Orang Alijeh. Tales of terrible destruction caused by the awesome anger of Orang Alijeh circulated the region after the big blow. And the bay facing Krakatau became known as the "Beach of Stories" (Pantai Carita). Survivors of the eruption and succeeding generations feared the area, and even today only small, isolated settlements and one small town, Labuan, exist in this fertile stretch of shoreline on the planet's most crowded island. For most Indonesians here, Krakatau and its environs are still a danger zone, and Orang Alijeh could vent his anger at any time.

Krakatau was a lifesaver for our little crew, the only solid ground for miles. We toted our gear above the high-tide mark and crawled under a plastic tarp to await dawn. Since we were just six degrees south of the equator, first light came at six, as it does every morning throughout the year. The first order was to inspect the *Ernarosa*, which had been left high and dry on its side by the receding tide. The hull was damaged beyond repair. We guessed the accident occurred because the captain had not secured a strong anchorage after we arrived in early evening following a choppy four-hour trip from Carita. We had dropped anchor a hundred yards off the island and decided to sleep on board, where it would be cooler with fewer insects. When the storm came up early in the morning, it pulled the anchor loose and beached the *Ernarosa* like a piece of flotsam.

We were castaways. There was nothing we could do to get off the island except wait for a rescue party. The boat had no radio. We had no communication with the mainland.

Technically we were not on Krakatau but Anak Krakatau, which means "Child of Krakatau" in Bahasa Indonesia. Thousands of years ago the cone-shaped mountain of Krakatau, over a mile in height, was destroyed in an unrecorded but no doubt devastating eruption. Legend had that the islands of Sumatra and Java were once connected by an isthmus. The wrath of Orang Alijeh changed all that. A mention in the Javanese royal annals, *Paraton* (Book of Kings), said that in the year 338 Saka (or 416 CE), "The world was shaken with violent thunderings that were accompanied by heavy rains of stone. . . . Kapi (probably an ancient name for Krakatau) burst into pieces and sank into the depths of the earth. The sea rose . . . inhabitants were drowned and swept away with all their property . . . and Java and Sumatra were divided into two parts."

In the summer of 1883, Krakatau was a group of islands, the tips of a huge underwater caldera, the main one of which was also called Krakatau. For the previous couple hundred years it had been considered a dead volcano. When the collection of cones blew itself out in 1883, the Earth's crust collapsed, forming a monstrous submarine caldera a thousand feet deep with a bubbling sea where once a luxuriant rain forest had covered the islands.

In 1927 fishermen saw reddish glows at night where the mountain had once loomed. Deep beneath the surface, volcanic vents were vomiting magma, and by late January 1928 a small island had emerged. Anak Krakatau, or Krakatau Junior, a baby volcano, was now seven hundred feet high and growing, a phoenix rising from the ashes of its own destruction. Or, rather, it was rising like a Garuda, the mythical Indonesian sunbird that reincarnated from the cinders of its own pyre. This current incarnation was our sanctuary and our prison—our own Devil's Island.

George and I decided to hike to Junior's rim. We first had to whack through a wall of rank vegetation about sixty feet thick. Then we emerged on the base of the basaltic cone. We stepped along fine pumice sand and then obsidian gravel, pitchstone, and pieces of glass-rich augite andesite as we began the steep ascent. Above we could see little puffs of white smoke, a good sign, as gray was supposedly a portent of trouble.

We puffed ourselves as we scrambled up the detritus slope, and after twenty minutes we stood on the rim—of the wrong caldera. This was a false summit, a newer, currently inactive vent. A few hundred yards to the west and a few yards above was the true caldera, the bowl-like depression that characteristically caps a volcano. We trudged along the ridges, reached the thin lip, and looked down into the hissing fire and brimstone of Hell itself, nature's crucible of death. It was terribly thrilling, and delightfully frightening at once, on the edge of one of the most powerful and destructive of all Earth's forces, knowing that it could, and would, explode again. If experiencing The Sublime is when thought trembles on the edge of extinction, yet without crossing that line, then this moment qualified.

The air was thick with the smell of sulfur dioxide, and fumaroles by the score were spitting steam. Deep in the ash-gray guts of the volcano, a pool of boiling mud plopped, hissed, and sputtered in a scalding dance. Beyond, we could see a shimmering, pearl-colored, calm sea and the holms of the prehistoric caldera rim that survived the 1883 blast and have grown, by layers of pumice and ashfall. Now completely cloaked in vegetation, the remnants surrounded Anak Krakatau like giant sentries. To the east we could barely make out the hazy shore of Java; to the north, Sumatra was tracery on the skyline. We drank it all in for a couple hours and tiptoed around the knife-edge ridge for different perspectives.

At one point I stepped on a yellow-brown layer of crust that crumbled like old cake, sending my leg into a fumarole, microwaving the bottom of my foot amidst belching sulfur fumes that caught the back of my nose and throat. This seemed a good excuse to head back down to base camp and reevaluate our situation.

In our absence the crew had constructed a series of shelters out of tarps and rain gear. I checked our food and water supply: a jar of peanut butter, a loaf of moldy bread, a bag of hard candy, two packages of raw peanuts, a tube of Crest toothpaste, and seven bottles of water for the nine of us. Maybe we could last a week?

I stripped down to my shorts and started some barefooted beachcombing to see if I might find some additional sustenance. The tide was low, so I wandered along a black-sand beach that curved around a short horizon. The shoreline was piled high with debris of all sorts: rubber balls, shampoo bottles, Japanese lightbulbs, American aerosol cans, a brassiere, bottles without messages, and flip-flops—hundreds and hundreds of those cheap rubber sandals. It looked like a flip-flop barge had capsized off the coast of Krakatau.

I continued my tramp and surprised two yard-long monitor lizards, who scampered into the sea. Their flight disturbed a dozen ghost crabs, which burst pale green and rectangular out of burrows in the sand and, bodies raised high on absolute tiptoe, skittered around from one piece of jetsam to the next. Nine months after the 1883 eruption, only one microscopic spider could be found on the remaining ancient rim wall. Today there are more than six hundred species of animals (though none that I could catch) and some two hundred species of plants binding the island into a dense, matted tangle.

After about a mile the beach ended where a paw of basalt clawed its way into the sea. I thought I could scramble over and continue my walk along the beach. But the hardened lava was too sharp for my feet. My foot was bleeding after a single step, with pieces of glass-like basalt embedded in my sole. Not to be defeated, I simply stepped back down the beach until I found a couple of flotsam flip-flops that were my size and favorite color and then headed back into the basalt. Two hours later I was still picking my way across this sharp, hot jumble of black razor rocks, with no end in sight. The beach was the exception for Anak Krakatau's shoreline; lava was the rule, and about 70 percent of the island has basalt cutting its way down the cone and spilling directly into the water.

Then it happened. My right flip-flop blew out. The front strap that pokes between the toes popped from its hole through the sole. On the beach or in the backyard, this is no big thing. But several miles deep into a pile of rock razor blades, it seemed disastrous. I forced the strap back into its socket, but after a step it ripped out again. I repeated the exercise a half dozen times with the same sad results.

The landscape was so jagged I could barely balance myself on one foot as I kept trying to repair the blowout. I tried to place my bare foot on the jagged rock, but it was too painful. I couldn't even sit down to think about it. I was in a vast garden of hot, burnished broken glass, truly marooned. With panic welling, I tried to think creatively.

I took off my expedition shorts and fed the sandal strap through the broken sole hole and then through the buttonhole of my shorts. The reinforced cotton canvas shorts acted as a buffer between the glass-like basalt and my foot. I could walk again, though I was naked from the ankles up. I flopped my way across the jumbled lunar-scape, finally reaching the black sand two hours later. I limped into camp, completing perhaps the first shoreline circumnavigation of Anak Krakatau, an achievement no sane soul would want to repeat.

That night a storm ripped through our camp, knocking down our tarp tent, but filling our water bottles.

After a breakfast of peanut butter on wet bread, I rousted our Indonesian crew for an impromptu game of stickball, using a driftwood bat and a plastic jetsam ball. Then, while George retreated to a book, I decided to head back up the flank of the volcano for another look.

Halfway up the cone I passed an uneven row of lenticular locomotive-size chunks of basalt, somber as tombs, looking as though they'd been planted in black cement eons ago. They were recent ejecta, spewed like spitballs as the volcano cleared its throat. As I looked over the horizon, I could not imagine a scene more serene:

a mirror-smooth sea, a brilliantly clear day, and a hint of a breeze that stirred like a petal brushing. It felt like I was on terra firma, but of course I wasn't.

A volcano is little more than a hole in the ground through which hot gas, molten material, and rocks erupt like the sudden opening of soda pop, with superheated steam rather than carbonation bubbles.

Indonesia, in the strike zone of two of the earth's most restless and relentless tectonic plates, is the most volcanic region in the world, the Andesite Line, a rattling string of giant worry beads. The high number of eruptions, combined with the high population density, claims 33 percent of the world's total of volcanic-related fatalities. Despite this toll, population density remains strongly correlated with volcanic activity, because in regions where the nutrients in new ash are swiftly leached by heavy rainfall, the enriched soil can support more people. The Javanese volcanoes are instruments of destruction and vessels of replenishment.

The original elements of matter in Javanese cosmology were water, air, earth, and fire. As in the case of Krakatau, all four would periodically collaborate to impress their awesome powers of life and death by rousing from slumber one of the majestic edifices of the great Sunda mountain system, which extends from Burma to Bali, the same length as the Cordilleras del los Andes of South America.

Stumbling back to camp I passed tree trunks carbonized from a recent eruption and a freshwater spring percolating from a lava spit. This could be a saving grace for our stranded crew, as we could survive without food for weeks, but likely only three days without water. Dehydration happens quickly, causing extreme thirst, fatigue, and, ultimately, organ failure and death.

The crew of the British naval ship *Discovery* landed on Krakatau in February 1780 on their voyage home after Cook's death in Hawaii and reported finding a freshwater spring. It was a different mountain back then. Every step I took was forged on ground sparked from nature's forge in the last thirty-five years.

To share the freshwater news, I scurried back to our makeshift camp, which was as animated as the rock backdrop. It was steamy hot, and there were few diversions, so all took to lounging. At noon, after a feast of peanut butter smeared over sourballs, I drifted off to sleep under the scant shade of a fig tree. Thirty minutes later I awoke to a buzz of activity beachside and the hot scent of brine: A rescue boat had appeared. The arriving crew surveyed the *Ernarosa* to see if there might be a way to pull it back into deep water and make repairs. But that notion was quickly dismissed. Within an hour we were hoisting a lateen sail over the new boat and heading back to Carita. The boat was a poor man's version of the *Ernarosa*—narrower, shorter, older, and nameless, but it was headed in the right direction. The captain sat high on a box at the stern and used his bare feet to work an ironwood rudder hanging in a plaited sisal sling, while a couple of prepubescent boys stoked a fire on the bow for tea and fish. I looked back over my shoulder, across a sea the color of a slug's tail, and watched as the pyramid of Krakatau faded.

Back at the Carita Krakatau Beach Hotel, Dr. Ridder served up cold Bintangs, rubbed his Coke-bottle-bottom spectacles, and fired questions about our brief maroon. In turn, I asked if he had figured the odds of our getting into trouble at the outset.

"I've done some field research," he volunteered. "About twelve years ago I thought I'd be clever, and bought a sleek, inboard speedboat that could zip tourists out to Krakatau in just two hours. On my first trip I filled the boat with VIP travel agents and the general manager of a major hotel in Jakarta, who had the clout to send a lot of business my way. About halfway across the straits the engine died. We drifted all night in the open boat and luckily washed up on a beach not far from here the next day. Needless to say, I didn't recruit any new business from my passengers, and barely escaped a lawsuit. Ever since I've been somewhat of a follower of the fates of those who attempt to meet Krakatau. I know the stats. I know the odds. I know the crap games Krakatau likes to play."

Voltaire said that while men argue, nature acts. Krakatau is a spokesman for nature, speaking now in whispers and moving in mild ways, but who will someday rear his head and roar again.

And it did. On December 31, 2018, Krakatau erupted again, triggering a tsunami that killed more than 420 people—making it the deadliest volcanic eruption of the twenty-first century, with more than 14,000 injured. If George and I and our stranded crew had been on the island, we would all have been snuffed away.

CHAPTER 34

NAKED DOGSLEDDING

There are two kinds of Arctic problems, the imaginary and the real. Of the two, the imaginary are the most real.

—VILHJALMUR STEFANSSON

NOW THAT WE WERE ROUNDING OUT OUR ADVENTURE REPERTOIRE WITH RIVERS and mountains, I thought we should continue the expansion. I had met Will Steiger, who made the first successful dogsled trek to the North Pole, and was inspired by his focus, his passion, and his North Star. I decided to check out dogsledding as an opportunity for Sobek.

"To me / High mountains are a feeling," declared the protagonist in Lord Byron's narrative poem "Childe Harold's Pilgrimage."

Cliff felt it first. He had left the tent to answer nature's call, and from beyond the canvas flap we could hear his shouts. We threw coats over our long underwear, tugged on our vapor-barrier boots, and rushed into the cold darkness.

Looking up, a faint, green glow appeared in the northeast, upriver, in the direction of the North Pole. Then, very quickly, shafts of aquamarine stabbed the sky. Howls and hurrahs rose from Ken, Carol, Steve, and then the dogs as the streaks split into bands and danced and fanned across the firmament. We were standing in front-row seats for nature's greatest show: the aurora borealis.

The lights waxed to a pulsating green and then grew into an electric fury of ten or more assorted colors flashing across the horizon in seemingly syncopated rhythm. Each change in intensity, each new display, brought hoots and hollers from us, and the lights seemed to answer in some sort of visual chorus. The whole sky gradually filled with hues and harmonies of the Northern Lights. I had to sit down on a sled to avoid vertigo.

For almost an hour the show simmered, exploding in purples and reds, transforming greens to yellows, while we watched open-mouthed. Even with my red-green colorblindness, the chromatics popped and painted my eyes.

At around 10:00 p.m. Ken and Carol drifted back to bed, despite little decrease in the show's intensity, and I fetched my tripod and camera. I kept a faithful vigil, waiting for the grand finale. It did not disappoint. The sky darkened, making the silhouettes of the twin mountain masses of the Gates of Arctic, named by Arctic explorer Robert Marshall in 1929, separate substance from ethereal. I had the feeling of being inside some great fishbowl, a captive on the inside, peering out to a larger universe. A thin, nebulous cloud of green appeared directly overhead and hovered, changing every few seconds. Suddenly, the fishbowl was alive as flickering tongues of green licked at the "glass" of the bowl, and dancing flames encircled us, spreading up toward some unknown height.

When the sky faded enough to permit us to wearily consider returning to the tents, I took off my glove and grabbed my tripod. My skin instantly stuck to the metal leg, and for the first time that evening I recognized how cold it was . . . forty degrees below zero.

Dogsledding, once the preserve of Eskimos and far north country trappers and hunters, had become a bucket-list activity for adventure seekers. I organized this little exploratory and invited fashion designers Ken and Carol Jarkow from New York, neurosurgeon Cliff Roberson from Seattle, and talent agent Steve Marks from Hollywood. We converged at the river village of Bettles, north of the Alaska Range, north of the Yukon, north of the Arctic Circle, north of almost everything on the planet. From Bettles, Dave Ketscher, owner of Sourdough Outfitters, flew us in his baby blue M-6 Maule Stole single-engine ski plane even farther north to the frozen North Fork of the Koyukuk River, about a hundred miles north of the Arctic Circle, over the icy halls of cold sublimity. Here we met our guide, Bill Mackey, who came from a royal lineage of dogsledders. Both his father and brother won the world series of dogsledding, the annual Anchorage-to-Nome race, the Iditarod. Bill owned the sixty-five-dog Kobuk Kennels, the supplier of our Alaska-bred Huskies, and had spent his three decades living in the North among sled dogs. Bill had yet to visit a real city in his thirty years.

Our first night was spent in a 15- by 18-foot white spruce cabin on a tributary called the Tinyaguk. It had no electricity, but a lantern gave off a lambent glow, and a stove turned the space into a toasty haven, even though the "Mackey" meter (as Steve called the thermometer) said it was fifteen degrees below zero, a three-dog night.

The next day, when the soft light of the sun finally peeked over the southern flank, we suited up and fed the dogs clumps of frozen whitefish for breakfast. Then we stepped on the back compartment of the sleds and began to mush in earnest. Bill harnessed up a team of dogs for each sled, giving Carol a team of all female dogs, and off we skirred into the vast whiteness. My team included Creamo, Spooky, Zipper, and Gus, all Iditarod veterans.

John Baillie in his 1747 essay described sublimity as a "contradictory" sensation of pleasure and pain: "The Sublime dilates and elevates the Soul, Fear sinks and contracts it; yet both are felt upon viewing what is great and awful."

Dogsledding Gates of the Arctic, Alaska. STEVE MARKS

The key word here was "viewing." For Baillie there was a difference between being in the actual battle and contemplating it from afar. Where the former involves a real possibility of death, the latter is just the thought of it. And as I glided over the dry, powdery snow at frightening speeds, at the edge of capsizing on the sharp curves, feeling the torque and rattle in my bones, my heart feathering through my breast, it occurred that this was a modern example of Baillie's sublime. It was pleasurable because I was reasonably certain that the dog team would contain me from catastrophe. Racing up and then plummeting down slopes mimicked a suicidal descent into the abyss, providing me with a glimpse of what a free fall down the mountain might really be like. Hurtling down this unmarked trail, banking through the sharp turns and shooting through the landscape like a bullet, I felt energized, vibrantly alive.

Robert Marshall, founder of the Wilderness Society, called this region as beautiful as "a thousand Yosemites." The valley was ringed with silent, snow-shrouded peaks rising from the scraggly timberline, meshing with the white-on-white winter sky. The wind snapped at my face. Silence hung over the land like a cold smoke; there was the rhythmic jingle of the harnesses, the squeaking of snow beneath the runners, the panting of the dogs, and Cliff singing Motown songs from the 1960s. We passed the tracks of moose, lynx, the star pattern of snowshoe hare, and caribou. We slid past ghostly stands of cottonwood, willow, and spruce and sailed towards the famous granite spires known as Boreal Mountain and Frigid Crags, the guardians of the 600-mile-long Brooks Range, the Gates of the Arctic. The ice on the Koyukuk River, which splits the Gates, had become thin and watery with the relatively warm weather, so we had to turn back just shy of the twin peaks, not far from the north-ernmost tree line. We paused for photos, and Steve Marks stripped to his birthday suit for a Christmas card shot of him mushing with the reins strategically covering his assets. Ken, the garmento, said he shared his building in Manhattan with five thousand people, and there were five thousand other buildings within the distance we had traveled by dogsled that day. Thomas Jefferson wrote in 1787 that "when we get piled upon one another in large cities, as in Europe, we shall become as corrupt as in Europe." There is no corruption here.

Despite the sub-zero temperatures, it seemed agreeably temperate to me, after the exertions of tugging on the lead lines and alternately stepping on the brakes. I could think of no place I would rather be. We were the only people in the entire 7.2-million-acre Gates of the Arctic National Park, second largest in the United States, hardest to get to, the least visited, but the most threatened.

That night, camped in a heated Quonset hut tent, we dined on moose stew, moose ball spaghetti, and spicy reindeer sausage, washed down with swigs of Yukon Jack. We didn't worry about calories or cholesterol. I recalled Will Steiger saying that while dogsledding in the Arctic he would eat a stick of butter a day to balance his burn.

The next day we continued on Bill's excellent adventure, this time heading south, over the frozen back of the river, towards Bill's home in the turn-of-the-nineteenth-century mining outpost of Wiseman. But before heading out we divided the neces-sary chores: Cliff fed the dogs; Steve melted water for the canteens; and I chopped wood, which we would leave behind in the tent, a courtesy extended by backcountry

Polar bear. DIDRIK JOHNCK

travelers here so a tired pilgrim stumbling in during a snowstorm could start a fire without having to chop new wood.

About midafternoon our southbound slide ran into trouble: overflow. This was a section of river in which water had squeezed to the surface through cracks in the ice as the heavy top snow and ice settled. Sometimes this overflow water was deep. Bill claimed he once sledded through overflow up to his chest. We splashed through water that reached our knees and poured into our boots, soaking socks and feet. It made me shiver for the first time. But we had little choice but to continue in the riverbed . . . the snow above the banks was too deep for sledding. Not a single maintained road or trail exists within the park, which is three times the size of Yellowstone. So we cautiously, gingerly plowed over the ice and through the river-wide puddles. When the water got deeper, I climbed on the sled frame, but that sacrificed control of the dogs, and I came dangerously close to capsizing. But we managed to make it to refuge and warmth at Peggy's Cabin, named for Bill's sister-in-law. It was a tiny sanctuary, with a door so small we had to crawl through (designed that way to keep bears out and for heat retention). Nearby was a bubbling spring in the ice. I dipped my Sierra Club cup and put my lips to the cleanest, clearest water in North America. No Rocky Mountain water; no bubbly from the south of France, could match this spring, as pristine and clean as any on the planet.

The final day was a twenty-mile trek through a southern spur of the Brooks Range, the Blue Cloud Mountains. As we whizzed along, I could not help but think of the mountains as exotic dancers, teasing with their veils, sometimes revealing their faces, their necks strung with glaciers like shards of extravagant jewelry. They seemed foreign, far away, alluring, and dangerous.

The last few miles were like the downside of a roller coaster, plunging into the Wiseman Valley. It was a heady, gasping ride, the wind against my face like the beating of leather wings. We bounced through the drifts, careened around corners, and hung on tightly as the dogs, knowing they were close to home, turned up the speed, horses to the last stretch to the barn.

At 5:30 p.m. we arrived at the real-life rendition of Dogpatch—Wiseman, the dogsledding capital of the world, with a ratio of thirty dogs for every human. We received a howling reception and then hotfooted it for nearby Coldfoot, on the Dalton Highway, for a hot shower and a dinner at the world's northernmost truck stop, featuring the famous Coldfoot burger. Behind us, out of sight now, a pair of peaks reached into the Alaskan sky like giant hands folding for prayer.

CHAPTER 35

BALLOONING OVER AFRICA

Wonder is the first of all the passions.
—Descartes

ADVENTURE TRAVEL WAS OPENING MY MIND TO ALL SORTS OF STRAY THOUGHTS and possibilities. The affair was to lean into the world with appetite to know it, to move, preferably through a wild place, and to seek wonder. Wonder is an offensive against the repetition of what we know, and so I continued to explore new ways to experience things I did not know; things we might tie up in a ribbon and offer the world of travelers.

For a moment I imagined we did not need butane. There was enough ego on the ground to lift the gondola. Still, the flame burned cold, and the twelve-story-high envelope of the balloon gasped, panted, exclaimed like a giant lung over the Tanzanian clay. With the blast from the burner, a lick of light into the *Double Eagle II* replica, the wicker gondola would rise a few feet then drop like ballast to the hard ground. Sally Field bear-hugged Ben Abruzzo's waist, squeezing so hard his face went red. Kilimanjaro, flat-topped, cloud-cloaked, surveyed the antics with indifference.

"It won't lift. Butane is no good. We must lose some weight," said the man who crossed the Atlantic and Pacific Oceans in the *Double Eagle II* and *Double Eagle V*. What to jettison? The 5'2", 100-pound, former flying nun, multi-Oscar and Emmy-winning actress, or the fabulous gold necklace hung around the record-setting balloon pilot. "Jump out, Sally," Ben commanded. And up, up and away the balloon sailed for another flight over the wildebeests, Sally left on the savanna, washed in relief.

We were gathered here, knee-deep in Napier grass, by John Wilcox, executive producer of ABC's long-running series *The American Sportsman*, to film another episode. I had been in New York a couple of months earlier and pitched the idea to

John, saying I had flown a hot-air balloon in Ethiopia, but never over vast herds of wildlife. He loved the idea and ran with it.

A few weeks later we were perched on the floor of Ngorongoro Crater, the twelve-mile-wide volcanic caldera on the edge of the Serengeti, harboring within its 2,000-foot-high rim walls, the largest permanent population of wildlife in the world: 14,000 wildebeest, 4,000 zebra, and 2,000 gazelle. The plan: to balloon across Ngorongoro, above the herds and flocks and bloats, and to videotape the event for an ABC special.

I flew into Dar es Salaam, where the air is thick and hot as blood, only to find all connecting flights to Arusha, where we planned to begin production, were cancelled. I sought refuge at the US embassy, where the deputy chief of mission, Lew MacFarlane, fretted: "You picked a great week to fly Sally Field in a balloon. There is no aviation fuel, no diesel, no petrol, no butane . . . and no hard currency to buy the goods."

But the wheels were in motion. The production crew were boarding a charter flight from Nairobi and would arrive at Arusha in a few hours; Sally would arrive by private jet tomorrow.

Lew was right. I tramped around Dar, whose streets were littered with dry-tank vehicles, a scene from *The Road Warrior*. Nobody had gas, nobody had the butane needed to fuel the burners and lift the balloon. I decided to ask the CIA station chief for a drink to share our sad state of affairs, a million-dollar shoot with no lift. The spook grinned: "I can help you. But's it's gonna cost."

Filming the Maasai for an ABC special with Sally Field. RICHARD BANGS

I didn't ask where the fuel came from, but $3,000 and twenty-four hours later I was trundling north in a seven-ton truck, gas tanks full, its bed stacked with canisters of compressed gold, butane.

With time to kill before Sally's arrival, Ben decided to attempt a crossing of the 19,340-foot-high Kilimanjaro, which straddled two countries not on speaking terms, Kenya and Tanzania. The butane, it turned out, was no bargain. It was low grade, with water in the tanks. "We'll never get above five thousand feet," Ben grumbled. He hit the trigger on the burner, tickling the throat of the balloon with long feathers of flame. The black-and-white nylon envelop filled, billowed, swelled like a pustule, and rose—a huge lightbulb, appearing as though the crater had just had a bright idea. It hooked a thermal and was suddenly sucked upwards into the clouds above Kilimanjaro. It kept rising, to twenty-two thousand feet, nearly out of control. Ben and his sole passenger, David Breashears, the cameraman who six months earlier lugged the first professional video camera to the top of Everest for ABC, giddy and half-conscious with the altitude, worked the balloon down, down. They wrestled the wind to avoid landing in Kenya, where they would not be welcome. They crashed near a Masai village, a mile from the border.

"You could have been shot," a villager elder scolded. "If you had landed over there," a long finger pointed north, "you might be dead." Ben Abruzzo glowed, a sappy smile consuming his round face, as he retold the story at the hotel, adding to his already considerable legend.

Meanwhile, John Wilcox escorted Sally Field through Customs and Immigration for her first trip to Africa. As they exited the terminal, they ducked quickly into a waiting Land Rover amid cries of "Sally Field! Look! There she is! Get her autograph." Here in a country with few televisions and fewer movie theaters, and no announcements of her arrival, she still caused a stir. Sally was on vacation, of a sort, with Peter and Elijah, her two children by a former husband. She wasn't being paid for lending her plucky persona to the ABC show . . . instead, she and the kids were hosted for an all-expense-paid safari and balloon rides.

All was good, until Wilcox learned that one of the cameras had been badly damaged in the hard landing at Kilimanjaro. "Get another camera here, and fast!" he commanded.

"How?"

"Hire a plane."

"No planes for hire."

"Call Nairobi; call New York."

"The phones are down. Welcome to Tanzania."

The country, a self-proclaimed experiment in an idealistic brand of socialism, conceived by founder and then-President Julius Nyerere, did not lend itself to solving celebrity problems. Only Tanzanians, tempered from years of privations, seemed to survive unfazed by the system. It was about as far from the controlled environment of a Hollywood sound stage as one could get. Wilcox, who had produced shows of expeditions up the peaks of the Himalayas and in the jungles of New Guinea, was about to face one of his biggest challenges: making a phone call in Tanzania.

Resigned to filming with the two remaining cameras, the show went on. With a blast from a rare canister of near-pure butane, the balloon eased upwards, with Sally and Ben in the basket and David Breashears in a special camera-sling hung off the side. It worked beautifully, the balloon gliding over buffalo, elephants, flamingos, and the fleet-hoofed gazelle. It was a flight of fancy, of a former flying nun merging with trace elements over a canvas of wildlife and wilderness.

In an effort to gain government support for our scheme, I had written Julius Nyerere two months previous inviting him to attend a balloon-launching ceremony, replete with champagne and toasts to Tanzania. Not unexpectedly, there was no reply from the State House, so we dropped the ceremony from the schedule and proceeded. Then, the second morning of the shoot, the prime minister, second in power after Nyerere, rolled in with his retinue to the Crater Hotel. A high-ranking minion sat me down. "The prime minister is here for the launching. Where will the ceremony be held?"

"Ah, well . . . we did not invite the prime minister. We invited Julius Nyerere, and as we received no reply, we cancelled the ceremony," I waxed less-than-diplomatically.

"*You* must have a launching ceremony." His message and menace were clear. So we scheduled a champagne launch for 10:00 a.m. the following day.

Political clout notwithstanding, the weather was not impressed. It was gusty and fat with fog, the crater a bowl of cream soup come midmorning. We couldn't fly, so we waited and sipped coffee. By 11:00 a.m. conditions were better, so we drove to the launch site. There sat a seething prime minister, a man unaccepting of the vagaries of wind and clime.

"I must go," he proclaimed in royal tones, shaking hands with Sally from within his Land Rover, then speeding off. Behind he left a three-piece-suited, bespectacled delegate to preside over the ceremony. In front of the gondola, in measured rhetoric, he thanked Sally and Ben for coming to Tanzania and promoting its natural wonders through film and wished them success in a venture he didn't understand.

By late afternoon conditions were finally right for flying. Ben led a contingent of Masai women who carried the balloon, Chinese-dragon-style, to the site. With two portable fans we inflated the balloon, and at the correct instant a nervous Sally climbed in; the tether was released, and off they went into a sky of unnatural depth, African aeronauts above Ngorongoro. The shrieks and clamor from the villagers at the site equaled NASA's mission control when a rocket made a successful launch. For the Masai this was beyond tourist technologies . . . this was outer space.

Along the western rim of the crater the balloon swam the invisible currents, a silhouette adrift in the air, receding into the Serengeti. Over several baobabs (looking like "upturned carrots," in David Livingstone's phrase), around a knoll, then the balloon dropped from sight. We piled in the chase vehicle and roared through the tufted grass, necks cocked to the clouds.

Two hours later we found the balloon collapsed like an overcooked yellow cake, and a hobbling Sally Field. One of the butane canisters had slammed her knee on impact, cracking her patella. Her right leg was swollen to pig-in-a-python size. She could barely walk and would end up with a full leg cast once home. She took it gamely, but it was clear this was the end of her ballooning career in Africa. Word spread fast, and a bottle of champagne from Burt Reynolds was delivered to her hotel room. The next day I drove Sally and her kids to the airport to take a jet home. As she was departing, I asked if she might leave behind her pink hat. I promised to return it once home.

Sally's premature departure notwithstanding, the show had to go on. It lacked action and enough animals. But more than that it lacked enough shots of the star in flight. I drove into town and went shopping, returning with a wig the color of Sally's hair. David Breashears had dark features, similar to Sally's, although considerably taller. I fitted the wig on David and tied on Sally's hat, and he climbed into the gondola. We inflated the balloon in an erratic wind with the gondola anchored with two three-quarter-inch manila ropes to a five-ton Bedford truck. As the envelope filled, Ben squatted in the gondola, working the burners like a rodeo rider. Then, with an explosion of wind, the balloon and basket stretched horizontally, like a flag in a gale. In the storm or confusion, a sound ripped our ears . . . the anchor ropes snapped like bullwhips, and the balloon was off, speeding towards a small lake bloated with hippos.

"Grab the rip cord," someone screamed. A red nylon strap trailed behind the basket, the cord which when pulled split the envelope for instant deflation. Three of us raced for the trailing cord, which was kicking towards the lake at leopard speeds. Ten feet from the water I lunged. My body tore across the ground, arms stretched, fingers extended . . . I missed. And the runaway balloon continued, scudding over the water. From the basket came a garbled "Help!" Long seconds after the envelope collapsed, the basket settled upright in the middle of the lake in eight inches of water. Silence screamed at us from the lake. "Where's Ben?" Breashears yelled. The worst was feared.

The lake was dead calm, just the baritone harrumphs of hippos on three sides. Then, up popped a mud-cloaked Ben Abruzzo from inside the basket, white smile shining through the ooze. "That's the first time I've ever yelled 'Help.' I really thought I was going to drown or be eaten by crocs."

We shot for two more days, mostly long shots featuring a kneeling David Breashears as Sally Field. Most of the shots were taken of his backside, looking down at the wildlife. When we had enough imagery of Sally's double, Wilcox called it a wrap.

The show aired a few months later and won no awards. But it logged one victory: Nobody seemed to notice that the aerialist in the pink hat flying over Africa was not Sally.

Two years later Ben Abruzzo died when the Cessna 421 he was piloting crashed near Albuquerque, New Mexico.

CHAPTER 36

THE PAKISTAN OSAMA BIN LADEN NEVER KNEW

You cannot swim for new horizons until you have courage to lose sight of the shore.
—WILLIAM FAULKNER

THE PLACE WHERE OSAMA BIN LADEN LAST WALKED, THE HILL STATION OF Abbottabad, is also the gateway to the Silk Route, the ancient trade path to China through the Karakorum Mountains, the deadliest chain of peaks in the world. Due north of Abbottabad roars the deadliest river in the world, running through a cave-pocked canyon, the Indus River.

The Indus rises from a holy peak called Kailas, a symmetrical mountain of quartz and ice in the high plateau of western Tibet. It is cited as the source of wisdom, and as it spills from the jaws of its glacier, it is called the Lion River.

As it leaves Tibet and the rarefied realm where belief overpowers fact, the Indus slices like the blade of a sickle between the Himalayas and the Karakoram, passing into India in the region known as Little Tibet, Ladakh. There it is joined by tributaries from the top of the world, gathering force as it drops twelve thousand feet in 350 miles, crossing the northern provinces of India into Pakistan and joining with the Gilgit from the north. The redoubled flow twists through deep canyons to the base of Nanga Parbat, the world's eighth-highest peak; then the Lion finally breaks free of its mountain domain and winds and wanders across the plains of Pakistan, across the Sindh desert, finally depositing its load of silt and glacial dust into the Arabian Sea from its broad delta near Karachi.

Cutting through Tibet, India, and Pakistan, slaking the thirst of three major religions—Buddhism, Hinduism, and Islam—the Lion River has also tempted the explorer's hunger with its promised feast of firsts. Several score have died on the slopes of Nanga Parbat, the 26,660-foot peak that marks the Indus's midpoint. The peak is draped like a coffin with the sobriquet "The Killer Mountain." And the narcoleptic currents of the Indus itself have carried many to the farthest shore.

Early in July 1956 a strange crew converged on the banks of the Indus some thirty miles north of Skardu in the contested Baltistan region, claimed by both India and Pakistan since partition in 1947. One was Lowell Thomas, the journalist and broadcaster; he was with several of his skiing buddies—two actors and television director Otto Lang. Their reason for being there was a new film technology called Cinerama, which they hoped to boost with a full-length drama, showcasing its best qualities. A short Cinerama production, a roller-coaster ride, had already created quite a stir among audiences who viewed its huge, wraparound screen and lifelike resolution made possible by its three-lens camera system. Thomas's planned film, *Search for Paradise*, was to be about two newly retired air force pilots who search the top of the world for a personal Shangri-la, only to return to the States when they discover at last "there's no place like home." The thin plot was an excuse to film some of the most extraordinary scenery on the planet, including a rousing finish with the first-ever raft trip down the Indus.

To run the two inflatable boats for the film, Thomas enlisted the father-son team of Bus and Don Hatch, dab hands in the whitewater rivers of the western United States. Bus, at age fifty-six, was something of a pioneer in river running, having taken commercial passengers floating as far back as 1929, and having made a number of historic first descents in Utah, Colorado, and Idaho. His twenty-seven-year-old son was brought up in the family tradition, and it was said he could row before he could walk. They were probably the best river rats around; even so, nothing had prepared them for the power and the treachery of the Indus.

They brought with them two rafts: a twenty-seven-foot pontoon bridge of the type used on the Colorado, controlled by two Johnson outboard motors mounted on a rear transom, complemented by three sets of oars; and a small assault raft, sixteen feet long, manned by a single oarsman. Their first run was a trial, without cameras. Otto Lang, the Hatches, and a crew of four put on the Indus some thirty miles above Skardu and immediately were swept away by the overwhelming current. The Indus was running close to its peak, nearly 100,000 cubic feet per second (by comparison, the Colorado through the Grand Canyon runs about 10,000 cubic feet per second). Haystack waves towered as high as the pontoon raft was long. After covering thirty miles in four hours, including an enormous rapid squeezed deep between the walls of the gorge where a portage was impossible, the crew drifted into Skardu, the first to raft any portion of the Lion River.

The thrills notwithstanding, Lang and his crew decided that this stretch was too violent to risk the project's expensive cameras for extended shooting. The operation was moved to the Gilgit River, a major tributary from the north, about a hundred miles downstream of Skardu. A comparatively gentle run, with just a fraction of the volume of the Indus, the Gilgit also afforded views of Nanga Parbat wheeling in the background of river shots.

For several days, the crew negotiated the Gilgit without mishap, encountering heavy but runnable (and filmable) rapids. The only problems were from the monsoon's clouds, squalls, sandstorms, and flash floods. The Gilgit met with the Indus, and the filming drew to a close on July 20. On the final run, before wrapping the production, Jimmy Parker—one of Lowell Thomas's friends, playing a pilot in the picture—decided to try the raft for the first time. There were only seven life jackets on the expedition; Jimmy was the eighth person on the water that day.

They pushed off and almost at once came to the first rapid. Don Hatch led the way in the small assault boat, sliding down the tongue and riding into the standing waves of the turbulence below. As the pontoon followed, one of its outboard motors died. Bus couldn't get it started again and lost control as the huge raft slid sideways into a hole. The craft was tossed up and over, capsizing ninety seconds after leaving shore.

Six swimmers struggled to shore through the mad glacial waters. Don Hatch rowed to an outcrop in the smaller raft, having barely taken in any water. The eighth man was missing. The soaked crew ran along the edge of the surging river yelling, searching, looking. A reward of a thousand rupees was posted for any trace of the lost rafter. It was never collected. Jimmy Parker's body was lost forever in a region some have called paradise.

At the foot of Nanga Parbat, the Rakhiot Bridge crosses the Indus. Carved into one of its stone columns are names of climbers who lost their lives trying to conquer The Killer Mountain. Now the traveler crossing the bridge finds not only the names of climbers but also that of Jimmy Parker, first rafting victim of the Indus.

I was eighteen years old when I began working for Hatch River Expeditions as a river guide on the Colorado. Bus Hatch had died a couple years earlier, and now Don and Ted, his two sons, ran the business. Sometimes late at night, with campfire shadows dancing on the canyon wall, talk would turn to Don's Indus expedition. None of the guides knew the full story, just tidbits dropped by Don at the office, the bar, or the put-in. He didn't talk much about it, but enough for the stuff of a legend. "I'd give my right oar to row the Indus," a guide once told me. And whenever I'd screw up a rapid, break a frame, wash a passenger overboard, or simply scare myself with a close call, I'd think of the Indus. This is nothing, I'd say to myself. Don ran the Indus—ten times the size of the Colorado, three times the speed, and cold as winter.

Such it was I found myself in Pakistan with nine companions, under the banner of Sobek, ready to retrace Lowell Thomas's expedition and do what he had not done: connect the line between Skardu and the Gilgit confluence by rafting the Indus.

It was the first week of October, and besides my friends we were joined by Captain Sohail Iqbal of the Pakistan Army, on assignment as chaperone in this politically delicate region. The Indians held that their border extended north to the Hindu Kush range; the Pakistanis felt the northwest frontier was theirs. The liminal place was a tinderbox, with both sides possessing nuclear weapons and unafraid to wave them as threats. Knowing we were headed into this flashpoint, the CIA asked me to take careful notes of what we saw and experienced and to send in a report with our return.

We took off from Rawalpindi, flying over Abbottabad towards Skardu. Looking up I saw the underbelly of great gray frigate clouds, and higher still a sky nearly black, pulling into nothingness. Moving out over the plateau, the land spread in shelves, in straggling eaves, in ripples like the hide of a monster. The road looked like an infected scratch across the weathered skin of the plateau, curvilinear in some places, sharply angled in others.

Upon landing we were met by a landscape wild beyond the ken. A great oval basin, 7,500 feet above sea level, some twenty miles long and eight miles wide, the Indus Valley here was enclosed by mountain ridges and peaks that soared up to 17,000 feet. The air was thin and crisp, and the details of shapes and colors, even at long distances, showed dazzlingly clear. The valley was carpeted in fine, pale sand, gray as tarnished silver, patched occasionally with ochre, lemon, and purple. In the middle distance, across the broad valley, the Indus snaked lazily between wind-ribbed dunes. Over millions of years the river had progressively cut its way into the rock, and the cliffs that now walled the valley were ledged and terraced at different heights by the old beds of the river. Farther back, the dry and bony mountains rose to their saw-toothed crests, intricately folded and overlapping. At the two ends of the basin, where they converged, it seemed impossible that even a great and ancient river could force a passage through.

It was a landscape that could have been created only by earth forces at their most influential, and the entire welt of mountains that defines the north of Pakistan—the Karakorams—is indeed the product of a phenomenal series of events. It dates from Gondwanaland, the semi-mythical "first continent," whose outlines were long discernable only to the imaginative who perceived in Africa's west coast and South American's east a near fit. Imagination gave rise to investigation, and investigation showed odd parallels between the rock, the history of the land, even the life-forms on these opposite shores.

With the recent science of plate tectonics, this impossible supposition had been confirmed: Most of the landmasses on Earth were once joined in a solid hunk of matter, floating on a primordial soup. Over the eons Gondwanaland split, and bits and pieces were borne away along the convection currents of the molten mantle, separating into today's continents. The Karakorams were created—are still being created—by the collision of the Central Asian Plate with the Indian Plate, which was once tucked against the east coast of Africa. Along the front of collision, the crust uplifted and folded and thrust and folded again into a mountain range more than fifteen hundred miles long and, at its roof, five miles high.

An ancient camel trail ran from Skardu to Gol, where the Hatch party began its first descent. A police jeep escorted us up the winding road to the put-in. Precipitous cliffs of somber rock, ancient metamorphic seabeds, and long-frozen lava towered over the milky flow of the river, and over the eight men and two women who had come to challenge it.

In the shadows we unloaded the two Avon rafts that would be home, hospital, diner, and means of conveyance for the next three weeks. I slipped down to the river's edge and dipped my hand in the dark water, as Don Hatch had done on his arrival. It stung with the cold, though the air temperature was in the eighties. Captain Sohail Iqbal recounted that local lore tells of a bare-headed man who once stretched his legs into the water after a long overland trek and fell asleep in the sun. When he awoke, he found he was suffering from heatstroke and frostbite simultaneously.

Since it was after the summer monsoons, the water was at a medium-low level and dropping, whereas Hatch and crew arrived at the river's peak flow in July. We estimated the flow to be about twenty thousand cubic feet per second. Beneath a wall of pictographs, depicting ibex and Buddhist temples, we made camp. I drifted into sleep with the Indus softly calling at my feet.

The day dawned diamond clear. The high, clear sunshine seemed to light up an infinite landscape. The boats were rigged, loaded, and launched with little fanfare beneath the curious, silent gaze of a score of Islamic villagers—all men and boys. Almost at once the judgment of Don Hatch that Indus was a river of deception rang true. Veteran Sobek oarsman Jim Slade steered the lead raft into what appeared to be a moderate rapid, but the raft and crew were grabbed by a hidden hole and shaken like ice in a martini shaker. The Lion River growled its warning.

Slowly rolling through the big waves and hydraulics, our party made its way down the gorge toward the huge cataract above Skardu, the point at which the Hatch party had been persuaded to move filming to a less dangerous tributary. With the lower water it didn't look like the monster Hatch had described, so I slid in with some semblance of confidence, sneaking down the left side, stepping down toward a funnel that disappeared between two boulders that turned the air between them white. Slade's run was also clean, and so, reassured by success, we set up camp just downstream.

Evening brought a villager floating down the river, on a craft more easily portaged around the big drops of the canyon. His was fashioned from six inflated goatskins, tied together with legs upright and supported by a framework of sticks. Using a pole rather than oars, he carried a cargo of fruits and vegetables downstream to the market at Skardu. The goatskins leaked, but to reinflate a sagging portion of the vessel, he merely blew down the upright legs. After we traded rides on the two far-distant generations of inflatables, he floated off into the sunset towards Skardu.

In the cool light of the Pakistani morning, we pushed off and entered the natural amphitheater of Skardu, passing the first major tributary along the route, the Shigar River, which drained the Chogo Lungma and Biafo Gyang glaciers to the north. The Shigar increased the flow of the Indus by a third, and the current sped past Skardu to the second night's camp at the Askandria Fort. Its origins were lost in the crucible

The Indus first descent team, from left to right: Joy Ungritch, John Yost, Helen Clyatt, John Kramer, Mitchell Fields, David Slade, Richard, Captain Sohail Iqbal, Nick Nichols, and Jim Slade. RICHARD BANGS

of history, but it was at least four centuries old; some said even older, dating from the time of Alexander the Great, whose easternmost thrust brought him to this region in the fourth century BCE. Standing on a narrow mesa a thousand feet above the Indus, the fort overlooked the entire Skardu basin and afforded an enviable security for its occupants—whether rajas, Sikhs, or Muslims—during the conflicts between India and Pakistan in just the past few decades.

Jagged peaks filtered the morning light as though in a cathedral. We departed the sanctuary of Skardu's valley and rode the current downstream into the gorge. At first, the rapids were runnable, though enormous in power and complex in design. At the start of the second day the peaks unraveled themselves from the morning fog, and the rapids were littered with huge boulders, which the water twisted off, over, and around to create enormous hydraulics and holes, some deadly. Portaging was the only course for some passages, an exercise anathema to river runners, a depressing tug on the leash by reality's grim hand. The portages increased in frequency and difficulty as we lurched downstream. Two crew members broke toes in the carry-rounds.

By the fourth day the river was dropping one hundred feet per mile (by comparison, the Colorado through the Grand Canyon drops seven feet per mile). There was more ground time than water time. Morale was dropping fast as the river, and there was talk of mutiny and abandonment. Meanwhile, the residents of the isolated gorge, who would sometimes gather by the hundreds, watched passively the labors of portaging. They rarely made a sound or displayed a hint of emotion or judgment. Most simply stared at the foreign navigators on an incomprehensible quest.

Finally, a labyrinthine rapid broke the river's course . . . it was a mess, defined by a series of rock columns and right-angle turns; but somehow it looked feasible, and everyone wanted to avoid another portage. So, with half the team crouched in the bow, the first raft made the entrance.

We dropped down the tongue as planned, but at the tip two recirculating cross-currents bounced the boat like a ping-pong ball in a pot of boiling water. We threw our weight from side to side and dug into the aerated water with paddles, desperately trying to force the boat out of the hydraulic, to no avail. The raft filled with water, which soon swirled around our chests. Finally, the current washed the raft up against a mid-river boulder, and we leapt to the slippery top of the rock. On shore, Jim Slade slung a hundred-foot rescue line out to us, and we attached it to the bow, wherein the shore crew was able to pull it out of the washing machine, and as it passed our rock, we all leapt into the bilge, out of the frying pan, into the fire.

Still brimming with water, the raft barreled out of control and pitched down-stream at a frightening speed. Grabbing buckets, we bailed like madmen. I used my own hat and tried to kick out water at the same time. Another rapid was quickly approaching, hurling spray high into the sky, thundering its invitation. Oar strokes were having negligible effect on the swamped, ton-heavy raft, and two hundred yards above the approaching rapid, John Yost acted.

Leaping from the raft with bowline in hand, John swam for the crew on the left bank. His dive, however, had the effect of pushing the raft toward the opposite shore, orthogonal to the line John was frantically swimming. Hearing warning screams behind, Yost looked over his shoulder, saw the boat moving the wrong way, dropped the bowline, and stroked for his life.

Both Yost and the raft made it to shore—on opposite sides—at the lip of the falls. Slade and the crew of the second raft decided to portage.

For the next several days, the pattern was of long spells of grueling, body-beating portages punctuated by moments of electrifying thrills running the huge standing waves. Then, one afternoon a six-acre voice of rumblings rolled out of the distance at dusk. Avalanches? Glaciers groaning? Drones? A renewal of the Pakistan-India border conflicts over the region?

At daybreak we moved about our morning tasks silently, like ghosts cleaning house. After packing the boats, we floated into the source of the ructions: a Paki-stani army road crew was blasting cliffs four hundred feet above the northern bank of the Indus to repair the all-weather highway connecting Skardu and Gilgit to Rawalpindi. Some ten thousand troops participated in the task, motivated by Paki-stan's claim to the region. The road's route was along a sheer rock cliff plagued with landslides, and one officer said that two men were lost for every mile of progress. He agreed to hold up blasting for four days, to allow us to pass beneath, but warned he would start up again on schedule, regardless of any Western presence.

For four frenzied days we unloaded the rafts, enlisted jeeps to trundle personal equipment to a downstream campsite, portaged as few rapids as possible, and ran others we would only attempt with a light boat. On the fifth day, as the expedition was fully loaded and on the river again, a peal of thunder split the air, an ax to a melon. An entire cliffside was blown across the river just upstream; dust billowed hundreds of feet into the sky, and rock shrapnel sprayed the river like langrel, missing us by a few boat-lengths.

Day followed day in the dark confines of the gorge. After almost two weeks on the river, the configuration of two portages for every rapid run set in. On the fifteenth day another tortuous stretch confronted: a maze of boulders ringing the river like ramparts, followed by a twenty-foot falls, with razor-backed rocks at its base. After the portage of the first raft—a misadventure during which the bag containing the spare paddles was washed overboard and lost—we all took a much-needed break and lunched on mutton and goat cheese. John Kramer didn't join in, however. He spent the repast staring at the rapid. When it came time to portage the second boat, Kramer made an announcement. "I don't want to jeopardize the expedition, but I'd like to try running this rapid. I think I can do it . . . alone. No extra weight."

Looks of surprise were exchanged, but no one protested. Nobody wanted to portage again if not necessary. . . .

George Fuller, the trip doctor, then spoke up. "I'm worried about you."

"Hey, none of us is going to die of old age," Kramer squelched.

We then went about setting up safety lines at the rapids' finish. Kramer prepared himself out of sight upstream; the winds keened across the river and emphasized the silence that settled over the moment.

Then, from around the bend, the raft came flying in mid-current, Kramer whooping as he executed pivots and pirouettes between the waves and holes, moving every bit like the dancer he was in college. As he arabesqued toward the rapids' end, jaws dropped along the shore: John Kramer was wearing no clothes, save his life jacket. Normal attire for the expedition had been a full wet suit or baggy wool overclothing to guard against hypothermia in the frigid, glacial-melt waters of the Indus. But Kramer decided all the outerwear was too cumbersome for his dance, and too dangerous should he need his strength and agility in a swim. He slid between the sharp rocks at the end of the run and pulled in with a worthy swagger and grin.

After a few more bends in the river, another curious sight appeared: a sign held high by a Pakistani in Western attire: "Pakistani TV welcomes the Americans." Khalid Zaida, a television producer from Rawalpindi, heard about our little expeditions and, eager to capture on video the inside story, wanted to ride along down the river. After his inspired welcoming, it was hard to deny his wishes, and we received him onboard to shoot the rapids with his brand-new camera.

Late in the afternoon of his second day on the river, Khalid sat with me in the bow as John Yost rowed. This was a rascal of the river, and a slight miscalculation put the boat in the wrong place at the wrong time. It dropped into a huge hole and flipped. For a second the world seemed to balance on a point of silence, broken by the hollow hiss of the currents above us.

It was dark and cold and typhoon-like underwater, but Yost and I had capsized on six of the seven continents, so the feeling was not of panic, but rather purpose. We popped back into the light, gulped for air, then grabbed the overturned raft and pulled it to shore. But looking about, Khalid Zaida was missing. We raced down the stony bank, and with relief we found Khalid floundering in an eddy below the next rapid.

But as we pulled him in, he said he was blind. He confessed that he couldn't swim, but figured that since we were Americans, we were infallible in our navigations. He described the experience, saying he was sucked to the river's bottom and spun violently; he lost consciousness, lack of oxygen he thought. When he surfaced, he was awake, but he couldn't see. After a few tense minutes, his sight faded back in. On inspection it seemed he burst an eardrum, but for him the worst loss was his $1,800 camera, for which he had saved three years.

The continued savagery of the Lion River was wearing us down. Then we heard rumors from soldiers along the shore of a monster rapid downstream called Malupah. We decided to park, claw up to the road, and flag a jeep to scout this myth.

It turned out the river was very much navigable to the entrance of Malupah, and so quiet was the gateway, an unwitting boater, or swimmer, could easily be swept in. But once in, it was a circle of Hell Dante didn't know about, a liquid inferno without escape. A granite wall, the size of El Capitan, blocked the direct flow of the river, so twisting and turning to find a way out, the Indus had cut a fissure barely a boat's width and hurled an angry, fuming torrent twenty-five feet to a trough below. No living thing carried into this abyss could survive Malupah.

And it was a portage that could take days. So we decided to employ the jeep to scout farther downstream, as far as the Gilgit confluence, passing all too frequently small stone monuments to victims who had plummeted off these cliffs. I become nauseated, not so much for the roughness of the ride, but from the constant reminder of how near death is along this seam of Pakistan. As we lumbered downriver it was apparent the rapids were getting worse, not better. The gorge became narrower. In some stretches there was no level shoreline at all, so it was impossible to portage. There were more and more waterfalls. The Indus here was unrunnable; impossible.

It was time to concede. The two rafts floated down to just above Malupah, where we hired a transport truck painted like the walls of a cheap disco. We loaded up and left behind Malupah and the maw of the Lion River.

It was thirty miles to the confluence of the Gilgit, where we once again launched the rafts on the waters that hosted the Hatches back in 1956. Both Bus and his son Don had passed, but we raised a cup of Indus water to them. It was clearly a terrific location for a wide-screen movie. High above the blue foothills, almost floating in the sky, Nanga Parbat looked too beautiful, too detached, too innocent to deserve its Western nickname, The Killer Mountain. It seemed an emblem of dignity, repose,

One of many portages around killer falls on the Indus River, Pakistan. RICHARD BANGS

a white vision in a gauzelike haze of blue. To the mountaineers who have grappled with it, however, it deserved its handle. It claimed more deaths per attempt than any other major mountain in the world.

As the river swerved closer to the mountain, Nanga Parbat revealed its structure more clearly; rather than a single peak, it was an enormous mass of rock ascending in successive ridges and cliffs to culminate in an icy crest, which pushed through the high mist like a Hershey's Kiss. No other peak within a radius of fifty miles reaches to within 10,000 feet of its 26,660-foot summit.

At the last camp on the Indus, within a few miles of the Rakhiot Bridge takeout, a local villager stepped out of a cave in twilight. Dressed in the ragged clothes of the mountain native, he quietly told tales of the mountain looming over us. It was protected by spirits of uncertain temper; fairies inhabited its snowy peaks, and when the sun shone hotly, the smoke at the mountain's crest was that of djinns cooking their bread. He spoke of demons, of giant frogs whose croaking shook the snows, of snakes a hundred feet long hidden in the glaciers. He then took his leave and disappeared into the darkness of his cave.

Just shy of the Rakhiot Bridge, where Jimmy Parker's name was inscribed with those of the climbers lost on Nanga Parbat, the canyon squeezed together and presented a series of three rapids, all of jaw-breaking difficulty. Neither Hatch nor any of his party left a detailed description of where the fatal accident occurred, but we agreed it was likely here. After more than three weeks on the Indus, with superstition in the air, a quick vote ended the expedition at this spot, at the head of the final gorge. Pakistan's Lion River proved its purpose was to take waters from the roof of the world to the sea, and men of reason were not necessarily invited along for the ride.

CHAPTER 37

LOST ON A BIKE

Get a bicycle. You will not regret it, if you live.
—Mark Twain

Not far down the road from our growing shop there was another niche travel company finding traction, Backroads. Founded in 1979 by Tom Hale, it specialized in guided bicycle tours. By the late 1980s it was competing for our pool of clients, and it seemed to be gaining ground. A friend and client, Jim Zukin, an investment banker, thought Sobek should move into the popular adventure biking space and suggested it better to buy than build. Together we made a pilgrimage to meet Tom and talk about an acquisition. He was gracious, listened to our proposal intently, and seemed flattered with our visit. But then he said no . . . this was his company, his vision, and he was not going to let it go, no matter the terms.

I decided I had to find out why the popularity of biking was surging, so I signed up for a bike trip in France with several friends.

We were lost. We were doubly lost. And I love being lost. This was supposed to be a tour on paved secondary roads winding down the *route de grands crus*. Yet we were stomping through steep, muddy vineyards, holding our customized Cannondale road bikes above our shoulders as we sought out asphalt. This was more my kind of travel, though after a few hours the creamy white Charolais cattle we were passing were beginning to look rather good. After an afternoon climbing over fences, down crumbling, lichen-covered stone walls, and tramping through the orderly rows of vines, we again hit pavement and circled down towards the empty stone village of Fixin. Along the way we passed some folks on one of those commercial bike trips so upscale I expected they would be wearing loafers, and when I glanced at their Vuitton panniers, I saw clearly typed instructions describing in detail every turn and switch to the yard . . . these folks would never get lost, I was certain, and would be on time for repasts. I did not envy them.

Our tour was a private one, cobbled together by Erik Blachford, a former guide for Butterfield & Robinson, now a high-tech exec. Though he gathered the group of friends to retrace one of his favorite routes, he expressively submitted that he was not "the guide," not the hand-holder who would pamper us through the countryside . . . instead, he would facilitate, marking out rough routes each day, and then we could choose to follow or go our own ways. His only instructions as we set out this morning were "Avoid roads with painted lines and roads marked with an 'N,'" which were the thoroughfares.

But I became even more lost that evening when we ventured into the cellar vault of the eighteenth-century Chateau Andre Ziltener in the postcard village of Chambolle-Musigny for a degustation. Beyond the boulevards of barrels, in a cool gravel-floored room dim as a church, we tasted the prized Pinot Noirs of the Côte de Nuits. But, as others took restrained, birdlike sips and *oohed* at the minerally taste distinctions, dove to the deep waters of organoleptic traits, detecting the *goût de terroir* (taste that is unique to the wine from a specific vineyard), I found I couldn't tell the difference between the '95 Chambolle-Musigny and the nearly twice as expensive '96 Bonnes Mares "Grand Cru." I had Pinot envy.

The greatest workout on the trip was exercising our palettes, and we were champions. That night was our fourth in-country, and our fourth four-hour dinner. We found our way to the Aux Vendanges de Bourgogne in the village of Gevrey-Chambertin, and we indulged in a meal so nutritionally incorrect that cardiologists watching would have had heart attacks. We drowned in rich heavy creams, beef, bacon, lamb, game with fur, game with feathers, and duck: breasts of duck, thighs of duckling, duck terrines, foie gras, potatoes cooked in duck, confits de canard. And then the cheeses: plump rounds of goat cheese, runny Brie, a blue *d'Auvergne*, the orange rind Epoisse, Gruyere, Camembert, St-Florentin, Soumaintrain, Chaource, Amours de Nuit, Ami de Chambertin, Citeaux, fromage blanc, all bringing credence to Charles de Gaulle's famous remark that it's impossible to rule a country that makes 250 kinds of cheese.

Even though traditionally the French drink more wine than anyone else—more than sixty liters (sixteen gallons) a person a year, compared with just under seven liters a person in the United States—that night, judging from the dead bottles at the end of the table, we brought the US average up to par.

The next morning, my head doing the postprandial burgundian thrum, I found myself lost in the inscrutability of French plumbing, trying to shower holding the snake-tube showerhead with one hand and the soap with the other. The French excel at technology, what with the Concorde, nuclear power, and the TGV trains, but bathrooms are stuck in another century, designed for maximum inconvenience. If ever there were an excuse for the revival of the guillotine, this was it.

As we saddled up for the day's ride, I decided to split from the tribe, thinking I could make my way with a better chance of getting lost by not following others. So I examined Erik's brief instructions and took off with a whirr of derailleur gears. Of course, I succeeded and promptly found myself going the wrong way on a one-way street in Nuits St. Georges, with Renaults zipping past as though piloted by Alain Prost, drivers screaming at me, one calling me "physical graffiti." So I turned around and followed a French poodle to a bar, where I rolled out my map on a wobbly checked oilcloth–covered table. I ordered a Coke and looked around . . . this was the real Burgundy, the rural France of Marcel Pagnol . . . though it was eleven o'clock in the morning, a line of locals was perched, like a row of amiable buzzards, big bellies to the bar, tippling back clunky glasses filled with *Ricard* (the potent anis-flavored liqueur) and ice water, the drink of Toulouse-Lautrec. I couldn't figure out the best route to our destination, the medieval walled city of Beaune, so I mustered courage and asked a customer, a man in an old shirt, sleeveless vest, flattened hair, a face the color of red wine, a profile that wounded like the edge of a barber's razor. As he banged his glass on the bar he looked as though he could be an assassin . . . but he smiled broadly, baring his nicotine-stained teeth, and then traced a route on my map and pointed at a street out the window. Sure enough, in a couple hours I was on the outskirts of Beaune but had no clue how to find our lodging for the night, the Hotel Le Cep. I wandered about town like a lost puppy until I spied through the crowds a familiar blue and gold biking shirt . . . it was Lloyd, from our group, biking by . . . he had spent the night previous at the Hotel Le Cep, so he knew the way, and I jumped on my bike and weaved through traffic following him home.

That evening I strolled across the way to the Hotel-Dieu (God's House), Beaune's chief tourist attraction. Founded by Nicolas Rolin, a kind of a fifteenth-century Patch Adams who hoped to cheer up the poor and the sick with extravagant architecture, it featured a dazzling roof of yellow, red, green, and black-glazed Flemish tiles. The splendid hall for the ill, the Salle des Povres, with its pastel ornamented and beamed ceiling built to resemble the upside-down hull of a Viking ship, and the stage-set lineup of elegant beds draped in rich fabric, was terribly inviting . . . a home for lost and broken souls, and I was tempted to tuck in for a nap. However, the Flemish polyptych of anguished souls depicted in the painting of the *Last Judgment* showcased the downside of being lost . . . lost souls were being hurled down to Hell.

Afterwards it was time for another marathon meal. But I was leery of more multicourse Olympic eating that left me lagging at the back of the pack, and I felt I was thickening to wine barrel proportions . . . so I begged off and went wandering down cobblestone streets that chimed like metal under my biking shoes, until I found a simple creperie, La Cave A Crepes. There I ordered a crepe filled with hamburger and ketchup, *pommes frites*, and a 1664 beer, and I kept consumption to less than an hour. It was familiar territory, a meal innocent of heroics, but later that night as I met my balloon-bellied friends at the bar, they enthusiastically described their epicurean adventures, and all I could say was that the beer was good, the crepe better than a gourmet burger.

The next day I went to the Athenaeum de la Vigne et du Vin, bought a detailed map of Beaune, and set out with instructions from Erik for a loop ride along the

Cote d'Or (Slope of Gold), clearly marked . . . he even wrote to "carefully" cross the D970 into Geanges. And the day went swimmingly . . . I followed the map precisely, rarely looking up from my pannier, making every turn as instructed. This was the wheel world. And in a few hours, I was happily back in Beaune. But, as we cadged sips of kir royal (a champagne-like sparkling white Burgundy blended with black currant liqueur) on the hotel courtyard, surrounded by sculptured Renaissance stone medallions, and compared notes, I found myself with little to say as others described with glee how they got lost in the hills, took bad turns, and had to retrace enormous inclines and negotiate triple chevrons. Even investment biker Paul described with stiff-necked delight his fall, in which he skidded out on gravel, trashed his bike, and cracked his helmet . . . I had nothing to contribute, save a perfect little tour . . . I never got lost, was never hungry, was on time, and the weather was great. . . . the only pain was champagne. It was all a bit boring.

The following day I set out again on my wheels of fortune with my detailed map and precise instructions and merrily pedaled to the village of St. Romain. Then I did something stupid. Though Erik's map instructed one passage towards Meursault, home of the world's finest white wines, I saw a patch of sunflowers down another, exposing themselves like sacrifices to the sun. I decided to take a brief detour. Everything was fine as I wound down a road lonely as a cloud. I even stopped and admired the rose bushes planted at the end of a vineyard row, and at another spot picked fresh raspberries. And then *SWIisssh* and I shuddered to a stop to discover my back tire had gone flat. Great. I pulled open the repair kit and found a blue plastic wedge to lever out the punctured tube from the frame . . . but as I worked it round the wheel, I suddenly heard a "snap," and the wedge tool broke in half. Really great. Now I was stuck in the middle of no place with a flat tire. It didn't matter I couldn't speak French, as there was nobody in sight. The only sound was the wind nagging through my spokes. In an early email describing the trip, Erik had said if you get a flat, "walk your bike to a café, order a beer, and call a cab." Nice idea, but according to my calculations I was halfway between villages, and the previous one, St. Romain, had nothing open anyway. Above, a buzzard quartered the sky in lazy, graceful curves, its wings barely moving.

Then one of those providential things happens when you're lost . . . a stranger came for help. Seeing my predicament, a bright-eyed Burgundian stopped his Citroen van, inspected my bike, and with a thick farmer's paw made a motion to wait as he drove off. Minutes later he returned and produced a rusted metal version of the wedge, which he immediately jammed into the rim and expertly pulled off my bad tube. As I watched the operation I heard birdsong over my shoulder, the first on the trip, and looked up to see a sky as blue as the Gauloise packet my new friend carried. I felt the hot sun on my face. At last, the stranger flashed a sunburst smile and presented my bike. The steed was ready to ride. I pulled a wad of francs from my fanny pack and pushed them to my Samaritan, but he furrowed his forehead, put his hands to his chest, palms faced to me, and shook them as his head shook no. With a deep tobacco voice he said, "*bonne route,*" then chuffed away, like the Lone Ranger. Rightly considered, this inconvenience was an adventure, and the kindness of a stranger in a strange land was uplifting. The little tumult was an agreeable quickener of sensation. I liked the serendipity of getting lost.

The final day of our bike trip, Erik sketched out a loop that would take us south from the chestnut trees of Puligny-Montrachet through the sleepy hamlets of Remigny, Aluze, and Rully, and then back north through Chagny. The main group split into three clusters of cyclists, and I joined one but changed my own rules . . . I left my map and instructions behind and tooled off in search of civilization *lente* (civilization of slowness). Several times I took the lead, and I made wrong turns and got lost . . . but each time, I stopped and looked around and saw the scenery, soaked in the rural beauty, felt the warmth of the breeze, and smelled the parfum of baked earth, calla lilies, and lindens. Like a good environmentalist, I often had to recycle the same ground, but with each pass I saw new things. Traveling this way, I regretted the invention of the car. At one point we passed another Tiffany organized tour, and I watched the clients glide by with heads hunkered over their instructions as a beautiful hot-air balloon flew over a field aside them. Even the guide didn't notice, the bland leading the bland. And I pedaled onward, drinking in that youthful feeling of freedom that comes when there are no schedules, no plans, and no routes. After years of guiding European bike trips, Erik really had discovered the best way to ride, the joie de vivre of roving, the art of lost.

Somehow, we found our way to Chagny, and to our final grand bouffe at the Michelin three-star restaurant Lameloise (one of twenty-nine in all of France). The room was long and elegant; the tablecloth pulled tight, the cotton napkins double starched, the Baccarat shimmered even in the subdued light. An endless train of waiters, rigid with decorum, came and went on silent feet, and there was trace of reverence in the air. Erik ordered several bottles of the Bourgogne Blanc "Les Setilles" from the cellars of Olivier LeFlaive, and we could hear the moist creak of corks being eased from the glassy necks. The menu was so impenetrable that Erik's wife, Maryam, offered to do an interpretive dance. I was lost among the sprays of the Rabelaisian feast put before me, such as Assiette de Saumons prepares par Nous-Memes Fume, Mi-Cuit et Marine, and Sandre dore sur sa Peau Spaghetti aux Herbes a l'Emulsion de Tomates. I was at sea with the cheese. I was giddy with the parade of desserts that included such as Dentelle Craquante Caramelisee aux Fraises des Bois Feuillete aux Poires Caramelisees. It was a case of tart imitating life. I was deliciously lost in a potent but elusive pageantry of gastronomy and relished every bite.

When I returned home, we put together a brochure dedicated to bicycle trips and sent it to our client base, and we even took out a few ads announcing our new offerings. But almost nobody signed up. So we went back to rawer adventures.

CHAPTER 38

NEWFOUNDLAND AND THE NEVER-ENDING MUTTERING OF THE SEA

The real is only one realization of the possible.
—ILYA PRIGOGINE

ONE PURSUIT THAT HAD ALWAYS INTRIGUED WAS SEA KAYAKING. I LOVED RAFTING. But a raft has the lines of a well-fed cow. It doesn't cut through the water like a kayak, knifing romantically along. It just plows. So I decided to give the conveyance a try, in Newfoundland.

Its rivers run clean and clear; its air spins with the breath of honeysuckle. Its forbidding interior is a land without litter. Its craggy edges and joints are lodged with deeply religious Protestants and Roman Catholics renowned for their charity and moral excellence. On a sunny day, the place seems like heaven. Yet the never-ending mutterings of the sea, the frigid waters, have snuffed countless lives, and a pall of violence forever hangs. The people here are children of their beloved enemy, the sea. They move with the fizz and riot of the natural world. Often characterized as optimistic fatalists, they are a thick-skinned and gentle stock who exterminated the Beothuk Indians, hunted a penguin, the great auk, to extinction, and brought the pilot whale to the brink. For 450 years the economic mainstay was a seemingly inexhaustible supply of saltfish. Now the stock has been reduced to a slim fraction of the glory days. Not long ago, chief livelihoods included clubbing young seals to death. Presently they include mining, damming wild rivers, and felling trees. Despite these intrusions into its wilderness, few places survive with such environmental integrity and harmony; yet the urban-based environmentalists of the planet have painted The Rock as a house for eco-bandits. The island is Newfoundland.

I wasn't looking where I was going. Instead, my eyes were sweeping the sky, caught in the sight of seemingly endless skeins and clouds of flickering pinions. It was a world of wings, millions of them—arrow-swift murres, Pillsbury dough-bird puffins with their clown-colored beaks, great-winged gannets flying arabesques betwixt and between until the sky seemed alive with flight. I continued to paddle as I ogled the phalanxes, until suddenly I heard a thud. It was not more than a tap, really, with the force I imagined a Newfie sealer used when clubbing the nose of a whitecoat. Looking down I saw I had bumped broadside into Gerald's kayak, and my heart sunk as I saw him teeter back and forth; and then, in a slow-motion roll, he poured into the deep indigo waters of the icy North Atlantic.

The words of our guide suddenly spun with my paddle: "A person can only function for five minutes in this water; then he goes numb, helpless." I positioned my kayak next to Gerald and reached to him as he grabbed the edge of my boat, almost turning it over in panic. This was not right, I thought, and rocked my hips to maintain balance. We were both saved with the command from our guide, Jim: "Richard, move out of the way." I dug a few strokes, towards the spume of a humpback whale several hundred yards away, but pulled my eyes back around to watch as Jim and his protégé, Young Doug, with cool, quick professionalism, lined up on either side of the overturned kayak. Placing a paddle between the upright kayaks as a brace, they pulled Gerald's boat from the water, drained it, flipped it over, and positioned it in the water between them. Then Jim instructed Gerald to pull himself on board as the guides stabilized his craft. In four and a half minutes Gerald was back on board, the rescue a barnacle clinging to the underside of memory. And we all continued our paddle to Great Island.

Those who live here call it The Rock or the Granite Planet. The explorer Jacques Cartier christened it "the land God gave to Cain." None does it justice. A garden of wildflowers, a sanctuary for moose and caribou, host to the greatest fish pastures in the world, a landscape of tall trees and hard splendor, Newfoundland is much more than a slate stopper thrust into the bell-mouth of the Gulf of St. Lawrence. It is the tenth-largest island in the world. More than a thousand miles northeast of New York City, it is the most easterly land in North America. It turns its back on the Canadian mainland, barricading itself behind the three-hundred-mile-long rampart that forms a western coast as tattered as an old fishing net. Its other coasts all face the grim ocean and are so slashed and convoluted that they present more than five thousand miles to the sweep of the "Big Pond," a favored Newfie name for the Atlantic. Newfoundland is of the sea, and so I felt there could be no better way to explore the narrow gaps bitten in its foreshore—its coves, bights, inlets, reaches, runs, and fjords—than by sea kayak. So it was I found myself traveling through the glacially scoured scapes that define an old land that some insist has yet to be found.

Our weeklong sojourn started on Friday the thirteenth at Lower Lance Cove on Random Island off the serrated southeastern coast of Newfoundland. The first thing Jim Price, our guide, did was go through our gear and winnow out 75 percent to be left behind. "This is not a cruise or a raft trip." His eyes crinkled at the corners as he spoke. Besides, as I later discovered, he wanted as much premium space as possible to pack Margie's (his wife's) cooking, and for good reason.

When I was properly shaken down to a single change of clothes, I slipped on my spray skirt (backwards at first) and slid into the percussively sleek twenty-foot blue and white fiberglass Seascape tandem kayak. This craft had come a long way from the driftwood and animal skin version devised by Eskimos four hundred years ago. I would be sharing the boat with Pamela Roberson, photographer for our expedition. This was my first time in such a craft, and for the first few minutes I felt like a goose among swans. Finally, though, I got my sea legs and arms, and we were off, the bow shedding waves as we paddled east down Smith Sound towards the North Atlantic.

The boat was remarkably stable yet agile, cutting through the water like a slim missile, and after an hour I felt as though I'd been born into this boat. The vexations of the urban, managed world washed away with the water that fell from my paddle blades, and I expanded my chest in the big cold freedom of salty air.

The scenery was exquisite. We cruised along a ripsaw coastline marked with black spruce, stunted fir, and gaunt granitic walls, past the occasional lobster pot. Arctic terns by the hundreds sailed their sharp chevron wings above us. A tiger swallowtail, Newfoundland's largest butterfly, fluttered across the bow. After a few leisurely hours we turned around a barb in the land, Hayden Point (after the captain who wrecked his schooner here), and paddled into a small, protected bay called Gabriel Cove. We were at Thoroughfare, a once busy outport, now abandoned. All that remained was a pelt of tawny grass swept with wild irises, purple lupines, tall meadow-rue, marsh marigolds, daisies, and buttercups.

Here we set up shop and hiked into the birch and tuckamore to the ruins of a once active merchant post that served the "thoroughfare" tickle through which boats traveled to and from Smith Sound. Today, picking through the planks and woodchips, we could identify just two former structures: the town sawmill and the steeple of the church. After the little archaeological dig, we washed and collected soft water from the little spring that trickled down an alcove just across the inlet from our campfire, and after a dinner of fresh salmon and cod tongues fried in batter, we made an early retreat to bed.

The next morning, after a nursery-colored sunrise and the alarm clock of a robin singing near my tent, we sat down to a breakfast of fried pancakes, sausage, and thick coffee. With a second helping, we looked up to see what appeared to be a black-bearded pirate approaching in a white kayak. It was Mark Dykeman, Jim's partner, just in time for the second pot of coffee. Working as a construction manager in St. John's, he could take only the weekend off, so he had left at 4:00 a.m. this Saturday and kayaked the nine miles to meet us for breakfast.

By midmorning, under a sky painted with gray slashes of clouds, we were off and paddling across the tickle towards another, smaller island, Ireland's Eye. To get there we had to leave our protected cove and round an exposed stretch of the island, a stretch lashed by the waters of Trinity Bay. For a moment I felt we had dialed back a thousand years and were part of that small band of Norse explorers steering high-prowed longboats up to the New Founde Land. But my Viking fantasy lasted but a moment. Just as we broached the mutinous waves, my feet slipped off the pedals controlling the rudder. I squirmed around inside the boat, trying to reposition my legs and feet, but couldn't make the purchase. I was sinking through the thin ice of my composure. Pamela began to yell at Jim, who was paddling merrily along a few hundred yards ahead. After several screams and some frantic paddle waving, he saw us and sprinted back to our bobbing boat, which had turned into the wind and was weathercocking. In a flash he ripped off my spray skirt, reached into the bulkhead, readjusted my rudder pedals, and resealed my skirt. His face wrinkled up in a cocky grin as he motioned we should follow, and off we went.

After a few miles we turned into the snug harbor that once served the town of Ireland's Eye. It was called such because a hole in a rock faced towards the Emerald Isle, and legend held that on a clear day a viewer could spy the ancestral home through the hole.

Negotiating this harbor, it appeared we were paddling into the seventeenth century, which is when the town first appeared on maps. Big chimney-potted clapboard houses with mansard roofs and curved dormers perched the cliffs on both sides. Directly in front of us, at the end of the bay, stood a large, white, wooden neo-Gothic Anglican church. But the windows had no eyes here; the pews gave no songs. Ireland's Eye was a ghost town now. The only living creature we saw was a great bald eagle who swooped over us, glowering with amber eyes, signaling, it seemed, that he was now the mayor and constituency of Ireland's Eye.

The day turned "mauzy." We parked in front of a blossoming lilac tree, and under an oblique rain Jim brewed a pot of tea and cooked up a pithy stew packed with pieces of a moose he had shot months before. After a dessert of Margie cookies (best I'd ever tasted; I wished I'd left even more gear behind and made more room for Margie's baked delights), we trudged up a dripping wet overgrown path across a landscape that seemed to have risen overnight from the sea, to explore the burg of Ireland's Eye. The town was one of 148 communities in the Random Island area resettled in the 1960s by the government to centralize population in "growth centers" where public services such as transportation, schools, and medical care could more readily be provided, and the island could be recast into an industrialized principality. More than twenty thousand people were promised new jobs and a better life as they were coerced to move as part of this program that saw Newfoundland turning its back on the ocean and becoming a neo-Detroit. By and large the jobs were made of air and sea-foam, and the new life was one of psychic and spiritual havoc.

Now the town is most famous for its drug bust. In August 1988, a local fisherman, suspicious of high-speed boats zipping in and out of Ireland's Eye, called the Mounties, and Canada's largest hash bust took place. Sixteen tons, with a street value of $200,000,000 Canadian dollars, had been stashed inside the cavernous church, which is where we now stood, admiring the chancel and apse, and wondering how it could ever have been forsaken. Then we hiked back behind the church a few hundred yards through a thick alder grove and stepped through a spindly white fence to the graveyard. Woodland mushrooms lined the raised edges of the graves. The tombstones, slanted with the settled soil, were decorous affairs, carved in white marble, and I could clearly read inscriptions that told of people born more than two centuries ago: "Edward Cooper, died May 6, 1868, at the age of 87." I wondered of his life and of life in his time and felt certain it was little different a hundred years later when his relatives were forced to relocate and abandon their heritage.

That evening, after a dinner of fresh mussels, Newfie steak (fried baloney), onions, and baked potatoes, Jim changed to his roll-necked Guernsey and pulled from his haversack a bottle of Screech, an imported Jamaican rum so named for the reaction its potency tends to produce. After a few swigs, Jim and Mark loosened and told a little of why they entered the outfitting biz. Jim insisted it was "just for the halibut," while Mark confessed his goal was to someday turn outfitting into a full-time profession, though for now the motto of their tiny company was "Don't quit your day job." Both were keen kayakers and had met seven years ago boating some of Newfoundland's wild rivers. They continued to spend weekends and vacations together exploring new waterways, and once even kayaked to France. Well, they kayaked the fourteen miles to St. Pierre, the French territory just off the bony Burin Peninsula, a southern finger of the hand-shaped island. Now both in their mid-forties, they've decided to see if they could make a business as one of a handful of adventure tour operators on the island, and we were members of one of their first commercial tours, investigating the possibilities of offering their product through Sobek.

On the way back from Ireland's Eye, Pamela's eye noticed a moving brown speck on shore. We paddled closer, and the fuzzy shape sharpened to a distinct form: a young moose. It was one of the seventy thousand or so who now roam Newfoundland, a non-indigenous species introduced to the islands in 1878. It didn't acknowledge our presence and continued to munch on partridgeberries, even as we parked the kayaks on shore just a few yards from his lunch spread. It was only when Pamela stepped on shore to get a close-up shot that the moose decided to move back into the boreal forest, back into the interior to places still unknown by reasoning animals.

The sun shimmered as though dipped in a bowl of crystal as we packed the following day, but it belied the task ahead. It was a grueling five-hour return paddle to Lower Lance Cove. When at last we pulled our boats on shore, we met two plucky white-haired women, Blanche Ivany and her cousin Martha Stone. In a burr rich as Irish cream, they told me why they were there. Blanche, a widow, was born in Ireland's

Eye in a four-square, two-story house in 1931, and lived there with her fisherman husband, Lambert, until 1963. Then the government withdrew funds for the post office, the school, and the government store, and residents were inveigled to move. She and her husband were given nothing for their land or home; just $600 in expenses to reestablish within Trinity Bay. But once moved they could find no work, so Lambert would use his dory to make the long trip back to his old fishing grounds at Ireland's Eye. He died, she said, in 1987 at the age of sixty-one of a broken heart. Now, every Sunday she and her cousin, who was also a victim of relocation, come down to the shale beach at Lower Lance Cove and look across the water towards their old home.

The next day we were paddling off the windswept eastern coast of the Avalon Peninsula, as far east as a paddler can get and still be in North American waters. We were in the Witless Bay Ecological Reserve, on our way to Great Island, one of the world's largest puffin rookeries, when I bumped into Gerald's kayak, sending him into the brink. Gerald took it all in stride, but I couldn't help but feel he hoped for some sort of revenge. It came minutes later, as we paused in a clangorous cove at Great Island to gawk at the wheeling masses of beer-bellied puffins, black-legged kittiwakes, stubby-winged guillemots, cannon murres, and yellow-headed gannets, Newfoundland's largest seabirds. I had never seen such a sight, the sky blazed with wings, and as I looked skyward, I inadvertently opened my mouth in awe, and immediately felt something foreign drop in. It was bad enough to think of what had happened, but I hate anchovies, and could tell that's what my bombardier ate for breakfast. As I spat and wiped myself clean, Gerald's laughter rose above the squawks of the fowls of the air, as though he knew the gods were just evening the score.

After circumnavigating the much-guanoed Great Island, poking into a sea-carved cave Jim named the Dragon's Throat for its esophageal rumblings, running through a natural sea arch, we paddled back to the mainland, towards the town of La Manche, another abandoned outport, but this time not because of political gerrymandering, although there had been government pressure to move. In January 1966 a tidal wave washed away all the boats and stores of La Manche, and most of the homes. It was as though God was siding with the government, so the residents of La Manche capitulated and agreed to be resettled.

We beached, however, at the wharf at nearby Bauling East, an active fishing community with a knot of confetti-colored houses. Leaving the protected bird sanctuary behind, I paddled with a feeling that Newfoundland was perhaps now sailing with the right environmental tact. Then, as we pulled our boats onto the dock, I couldn't help but notice the stench mingled with the iodine tang of kelp. Dozens of dead puffins, their already dumpy figures looking even more bloated, were floating in the tidewash. They weren't the victims of insecticides, oil spills, or poaching. Rather, the cod fishermen's dragnets, which were spread over such a distance that when hauled in they invariably captured a few of the puffins floating on the surface.

For the final leg of our kayak exploration, we moved to the other side of New-foundland, to the 450,000-acre Gros Morne (Big Gloomy) National Park on the primordial coast of the Gulf of St. Lawrence. Named a UNESCO World Heritage site in 1988, the park has been called the "Galapagos of plate tectonics" because of its exposed expanses of the Earth's mantle and various stages of the Earth's evolutionary history. The park also highlights Newfoundland's land conservation policies at its best: an extraordinary wilderness where moose, caribou, and black bear can wander completely protected and people can explore a backcountry without crowds and trash bins. The park is even willing to trial-balloon new policies that could help maintain the park at a savings to the government. Before getting back in our kayaks, we took a hike up one of the park's more popular trails, Berry Hill, a rock knob that was an island during higher sea levels just after the last ice age. At the trailhead was a deep box filled with gravel and a sign inviting us to participate in "an experiment in reducing costs while maintaining quality." Then it gave directions, asking hikers to fill the can with gravel, carry it to the top of the hill overlooking the park, spread the gravel on the trail as an erosion preventative, and then return the can at the end of the hike. It was an idea brilliant in its simplicity. The only problem was there was no can; it had been stolen.

It was a two-mile peat-bog trek to the put-in at Western Brook Pond. Along the way we passed several insect-eating pitcher plants, the somehow appropriate provincial flower. Once there, the clouds slammed shut across the sky like the door of an observatory dome. The wind began to wail, and the water whipped itself into whitecaps. This did not look like pleasant paddling weather, and even Young Doug, who had recently placed seventh in the flatwater kayaking competition in the Canadian Games, wondered aloud if the "white horses" (whitecaps) might be too rough for our planned trip. But Jim, fearless as a snake charmer, would hear nothing of it. Bubbling with boyish optimism (a result of Margie's cooking, I was certain), he had us launch and begin paddling against the cutting wind up the famous pond.

Western Brook Pond is not really a pond. In typical Newfie understatement most any lake or large body of water is called a pond. "To a Newfie a lake is hole in your boot," Jim told me. But this was more of a rock-girt fjord, looking like something out of Norway or New Zealand. Ultimately it didn't matter what you called it; pond, fjord, lake, at that moment it was a combing sea of spindrift, and I was paddling in fear of a capsize. Yet, as I paddled towards its gates, mind fogged in fear, I couldn't help but look up and be stunned by the scenery. The cleft in the mountains ahead looked as though it had been split clean by a giant ax. It was like paddling into a flooded Yosemite Valley, one with no hotels, no galleries, no Laundromats, no glancing tourists. Just rearing glacially scrubbed granite cliffs, 2,200 feet high, beckoning, and I responded, not just for the view but because between those protected cliffs I could see the water was a lot calmer.

An hour later I pulled off the poogies (elbow-long neoprene gloves); we were in the sheltering arms of the beetling cliffs, the wind now at our backs, and the water, while not Formica smooth, was at least forgiving. From here the ride was a pure delight. I even tried sailing, furling my life jacket between the blades of two paddles, but the irregular wind made it a tricky and tiring endeavor, so I abandoned the technique for more traditional locomotion. We passed the dramatic spill of Blue Denim Falls on the left; gneiss hanging valleys on the right. Then Wood Pond Falls on the left, a cascade falling more than 1,500 feet. The dark color of the water beneath us was an indicator of its depth . . . some 540 feet, and the water was Arctic cold, forty-nine degrees Fahrenheit. On the right, with a squint, we could see the red granite seams in the face of an ancient mariner etched in the cliff top; a very old man indeed, probably around six hundred million years old, if the geologists are correct. We stopped at a rookery of great black-backed and herring gulls, perched saucily on the cliffs and taking flight as they scolded us for disturbing their day. I was careful to keep my mouth shut while admiring their aerobatics. Then, with a few more strokes, the canyon made a scimitar turn and we were faced with the piece de resistance of the park, Pissing Mare Falls, the longest and most spectacular falls in Canada, dropping 1,850 feet from the canyon rim.

After ten miles of paddling, we pulled into the pebble beach at the west end of Western Brook Pond. Not surprisingly, we were the only campers in this quasi-paradise. Quasi because though the beauty was nonpareil, the experience was a bit tainted by the blackflies . . . thousands of the pesky biters, always ready for a piece of exposed skin, or a ready orifice. But we discovered the cure . . . Screech, in large doses, taken internally. After a few applications we didn't feel a thing, until the next morning.

It was late morning by the time we started up the trail. The plan was to hike to the rim of Western Brook Pond, where one of the grandest (and least seen) vistas in all Newfoundland could be savored, and then return in time to kayak back before dark.

I decided to start out ahead of the others so I would have time to take photos. This was unlike any trail in any national park I had ever seen. A rotting hand-carved sign pointed westward, the wrong way, from our campsite with the simple designation: "Trail." It would be the last sign, sure or otherwise, of our whereabouts. Just a few yards from camp the path vanished in the spongy tuckamore, but it wasn't cause for alarm, as there could be only one way to go . . . up the U-shaped valley towards the Precambrian walls of the Long Range Mountains (the northernmost extent of the Appalachians). Behind was the pond, and on either side the sheer walls, sharp and sudden as the side of a box, defied negotiation. So, swatting through the brush, climbing up the boulders, wading through the muskeg, I continued upwards.

It was an intoxicating hike. Waterfalls materialized out of riven rock, and the views became grander with every step. This was July, yet commas of snow lit up the gray fans of scree in cirques. Then, after a couple of hours scrambling up a recent rockslide, I was faced with a decision. To the left was a side canyon that looked as though it offered a passage to the top. The alternative was to drop back down a saddle into a second streambed and climb up the other side of the main canyon to a slope that appeared gentle enough for a summit attempt. I chose the closer route, the left ravine, and began my assault.

It was quickly apparent I was on the wrong route. The vegetation became theatrical; plants forgot their manners and behaved like trees. The only way to move forward was to claw upstream through a runnel of birch and springy juniper. It was grueling, sweaty work, but I gritted and kept going, feeling it the wisest course, believing I would be above the tree line soon, and then just a dash away from the top.

After an hour of hand-to-hand combat with the goblin forest, of scratching through a tangle of larch and alder, I emerged above the tree line onto a glacial drumlin and surveyed the landscape. It didn't look good. The gully I had hoped to scale narrowed into a dark chimney, and the final pitch of one hundred feet or so was slippery and sheer, impossible to traverse without ropes and pitons. I had successfully climbed to a dead end. Then I heard Jim's voice echoing from across the canyon: "Where are you?" I yelled back and thought I could see a rustle of trees about a mile down the abrupt valley. "Come down!" Pamela's voice now reverberated. But I was exhausted and needed a few moments before I could move, so I sat down on a lichen-covered rock and pulled a Mirage chocolate bar from my pocket. As I unwrapped it, I looked back down the valley for the first time in a couple hours and was stunned by the sight. Some blessings, I knew, came from Nature, unbidden and unplanned, and this view was one. I imagined it the sort of landscape the Maritime Archaic people who made their way here along the edge of retreating glaciers ten thousand years ago must have beheld. To my left was the misty veil of the great falls, and above a bald plateau where I could make out a small herd of barren ground caribou cooling off on a snow patch. I could gaze all the way to the end of the snaking pond and beyond to the Gulf of St. Lawrence, the waters infamous as the killing fields for millions of baby seals. It was tranquil now, deep blue, no sign of the red tide, the blood of countless seals that so recently stained these waters. And, as I sat there watching a scene of unmitigated calm, I munched my Mirage bar and reviewed the lineaments of this odd island. When I finished the candy, I bunched up the wrapper and began to stuff it in my pocket. Then I stopped, balled the wrapper tighter, and tossed it against the cliff. Somehow it seemed the thing to do, like Ed Abbey's insistence on throwing beer cans along the highways that dissected his sacrosanct desert landscapes. But this wasn't out of anger. It was to defy the immutable morality of the environmentalists who had never visited this place but had so heartily condemned it. I knew the simple act of leaving trash in a wilderness would incur the wrath of anyone with green leanings, and I counted myself in that troop, yet in this case it didn't warrant it, or so I rationalized. I was probably the first human to ever stand on this perch . . . even the Beothuk Indians wouldn't have been stupid enough to try this route; and likely no other human would for many years to come. By that time, the rain and storms and severe climate would have long obliterated the paper wrapper. If a tree falls in the woods and nobody is there to hear it, is there sound? If a wrapper is left where nobody ever sees it, is that trash? Perhaps. But the small act also seemed in some way to express my frustrations with the ecological invective hurled at this island and its people. There seemed a singular cohesiveness of culture and society here, and a consciousness of unity with the natural world. I deeply admired the Newfoundlanders' famous traits, traits worn on the sleeve of Jim Price: self-sufficiency, adaptability, daring, absolute endurance, unbounded hospitality, a rare concern for fellow man, an appreciation of wilderness, and an evergreen good will that triumphs over the futility in life. The history of the people here is one of foreign exploitation, of interference in the modest goals of feeding and sustaining a healthy family. For centuries they caught or killed what the biblical Great Waters offered as their currency with the world: seals, whales, and codfish; but then the world turned against them, condemning the hunting of seals and whales. Simultaneously, foreigners were employing high-tech vessels with sophisticated radar to beat them in the fishing game. In 1986 when Spain and Portugal joined the European community, they blithely ignored the voluntary fishing allocations and every year have taken five times their quota from the shallow waters just beyond the 200-mile Canadian limits. The fall in fish stocks forced the Canadian government to cut its own quotas by enough to throw three thousand Newfoundlanders out of work, and scientists insist quotas will have to be cut far more deeply if stocks are to revive. This in a province where the official unemployment rate is 17 percent (privately some told me it was closer to 30 percent), the sales tax is an ungodly 12 percent, and incomes are only two-thirds the Canadian average. In recent years many former sealers, whalers, and fishermen turned to logging, but now a vocal band of outsiders is again jeering the destruction of a limited resource. Now everything seems to be running short except hard-luck stories. Nonetheless, the resourceful are turning to new sources of income. I couldn't help but notice on my journey that the island highways are lined with cheap motels, gas bars, waterslide parks (when there are less than sixty hot swimming days a year), and tacky tourist shops selling mock cans of Moose, ceramic Newfoundland dog decanters ("produced entirely by local craftspeople"), lobster parts glued together to look like a fisherman, "In Cod We Trust" posters, and Newfoundland in a can. In 1988 the government invested more than $17 million Canadian in a cucumber greenhouse scheme that quickly went bust. And while I was there the Economic Recovery Commission announced it was going to invest in an ice factory for the exportation of Newfoundland ice. And then Jim and Mark have their kayaking adventures.

There is no pat answer. As components of a vulnerable living fabric, we cannot allow the destruction of any species, but it is too bad the human side of the issues are rarely adequately addressed. Greenpeace, Brigitte Bardot (who made a well-publicized trip to an ice floe in 1977 to protest against the annual seal pup hunt), and animal rights author Farley Mowat ("Hardy Knowit" is a favorite nickname) are practically national enemies in Newfoundland; they portrayed the good people of The Rock as biocidal Darth Vaders, when in fact they are decent and in many ways extraordinary folks simply trying to eke out an existence in ways honorable just a few years ago. The key is to find viable alternatives, and the environmental groups would do better to back off the personal censure and castigation and work with the Newfoundlanders to build a better life, something beyond the Rod and Gun Waterslide Park.

I took one last gaze at the Mirage wrapper, re-weighing my decision. I decided to fetch it, and bring it out. But then a gust blew across my shoulder, picked up the wrapper, and sent it sailing into a pine tree. Soon after another cold current funneled up the canyon, slapping my face, which had been sweating from the reflected July sun. It was a tingly combination of hot and cold, like a Baked Alaska. A storm was on its way, blackening the sky, chopping off the heads of peaks. I buttoned my coat, turned, and began the long slog back down the mountain.

Three hours later we were re-congregated at camp, battening down the hatches. A squall had grabbed my Eureka tent and tossed it into the hemlocks, and other bits of raiment and light gear were scattered with the wind. The waterfall above us was being blown upwards, so the water seemed to be running upside-down. On the plus side, even the blackflies had been blown away. The pond that looked so composed just a few hours earlier was now a stark and wild inebriate. "We've got gale-force winds; we can't kayak. We're stuck," Jim announced in a sober tone that was completely unfamiliar to this point. It looked as though we would have to hunker down for the night and wait out the storm, when around the bend appeared the *Westbrook 1*, the forty-two-foot-long skiff that regularly carries tourists up to the end of Western Brook Pond. Pamela took out a white windbreaker, attached it to the top of her paddle, and waved at the tour boat.

Skipper Charles Reid steered his pitching vessel towards our encampment and then announced over his loudspeaker that it was too rough; he couldn't make it in; we were on our own. It was daunting news, but then the russet-faced skipper turned the boat around and somehow backed into our little cove. Quickly we threw on our kayaks and camping gear and were soon sailing back to safety at the eastern end of the pond.

As the *Westbrook 1* cruised amidst the skirling wind and waterspouts, I climbed topside to take a last look at this uncommon landscape. The canyon was filled with blue tendrils of fog, and icy water sprayed across my glasses, but for a moment the mist cleared, and the slant sun shone through, lighting up the brooding cliffs and the grand falls, turning its spray into a brilliantly wavering spectrum of color. It was a magic moment, and I couldn't but think that the entire scene looked like a mirage.

CHAPTER 39

PATAGONIA BENEATH THE HORNS OF A DILEMMA

The day breaks and asks me: "Do you hear
the lingering water,
the water,
over Patagonia?"
And I reply: "Yes, I hear it."

—Pablo Neruda

IN FARAWAY PLACES, THERE ARE ALWAYS FAMILIAR FACES. I THOUGHT I RECOGNIZED his movements, the nape of his neck. Hesitantly, I walked across the floor of the Carlos Ibanez Airport in Punta Arenas, the sandy point at the tip of South America on the Strait of Magellan. He turned and, yes, it was Frenchy, a veteran adventure guide, one I had recruited into the fold so many years ago. We gave each other a guide-hug, one filled with hearty slaps and exaggerated gestures, and then extended the Sobek handshake, simulating snapping crocodile jaws with our palms and fingers. Then we simultaneously asked the same question: "What are you doing here?" He had just completed a trek through Western Patagonia; I was just arriving for same. "Did you hear the news?" he asked. "The boat that crosses Lago Grey just sank; thirty people almost drowned." At first I was alarmed, but then I felt a twinge of resentment. Just a few days before, Leo LeBon, the seasoned Patagonian explorer, had unrolled a map in his Berkeley living room. He pulled his finger across Lago Grey and announced that with the new boat one could reach the famous Grey Glacier in minutes, rather than the several days it took on foot. That was good news, I felt, as I had less time than I wanted to explore this landscape on the cone of the southern continent, and the boat would allow me more terrain.

While I was still digesting the news, the boarding call for Frenchy's flight came, and as he pulled on his pack he said, "I would never cross that lake on a boat. It's too dangerous." And I thought the words odd, coming from a Sobek adventure guide, one who had rowed some of the biggest rapids in the world for his job.

I walked to the parking lot, stepped into the back of a Ford Club Wagon, and started up the Carretera Austra. Though the van was barely three months old, the front windowpane was cracked and scratched from the hard driving here. The ride was rough, the steppe-scenery bleak and monotonous, and I managed to nod off, awaking almost three hours later as we reached the halfway point, the fishing village of Puerto Natales, on the shores of Seno Ultima Esperanza (Last Hope Sound). Black-necked swans were gaggling in front of the ocean-side cafe where we parked. Inside, a bespectacled, pony-tailed piratical figure sat hunched over the table. He was Arian Manchego, twenty-eight years old, half Peruvian, half-Belgian, the chief guide for the Hotel Explora Patagonia in Torres del Paine National Park, the half-million-acre park and UNESCO biosphere reserve that was our ultimate destination. I sat across from Arian, and over an avocado sandwich asked if he had heard anything about the Lago Grey boat. He bellowed the laugh of a big-bellied bartender, spermy and swole, but then suddenly went graven, and the blood seemed to drain from his face. He was there. He went on to describe in detail the events leading to the accident. It happened Sunday, January 30, three days before. It was his first charter on the boat, which had just started service the week before. He was guiding a group of twenty-four seniors . . . he guessed the average age to be sixty . . . who had just completed an Antarctica cruise and were enjoying a rest day before heading home. It was to be a two-hour cruise, and while returning from Grey Glacier, the winds picked up, the lake was chopped with five-foot-high whitecaps, yet the captain continued to gun the boat as though it were gliding on a glassy pond. Worse, someone had neglected to tie the bowline, which somehow uncurled under the boat and caught in the propellers of the two outboards. At 12:30 the boat did a brick-wall stop and dove like a missile into the trough of a wave. The glacially cold water washed in, and the boat almost went over, in the middle of a 250-foot-deep lake. For the next few hours, the boat drifted . . . both outboards were shot, and there were no backups. Several times the boat almost capsized, but finally it drifted close to the southeastern shore, and there Peter Metz, an escort for the Antarctica group, made a heroic leap into the water, fully clothed, rope in hand, and swam to the jagged shore. There he managed to secure the line, and as the boat crashed against a shoreline cliff, he and Arian helped the passengers to shore. At 9:30 p.m., nine hours after the ordeal began, the last passenger staggered into the Explora Patagonia lodge. "I will never go on a boat in Lago Grey again," Arian announced at the end of his tale. I believed him, but again I was a bit surprised at the severe reaction . . . after all, this was the wilderness, and the only thing predictable is that the unpredictable will happen, and the only adventure is the well-planned itinerary gone wrong.

It was after dark when we arrived in Torres del Paine National Park, and as I exited the van, I met the frigid, fire-hose-force wind for which Patagonia is so renowned. This was latitude-with-an-attitude weather, fifty-one degrees south,

Torres del Paine, Patagonia, Chile. PAMELA ROBERSON

blowing north from Antarctica. It slapped my face, stung my hands, and I had to bend at a 45-degree angle to push a walk. Some months previous I had figured I had spent about a quarter of my adult slumber life in a sleeping bag, and I had always assumed when I came to Patagonia, I would do the same. But now, as I slipped through the double doors of the Explora Patagonia lodge, I was happy I wasn't setting up a tent. And as I entered the lobby, it was like going from the tornado of Kansas to Oz.

The Hotel Explora Patagonia was a marvel. Warm, clean, luxurious, its panels were all hand-tooled, finely polished, and in the hall, smooth-sloping curves, which produced a delicate scent of cypress. Though there were just thirty rooms in this lodge, there were forty staff members, and one immediately led me down a Swiss sisal carpet to a sacrament of rich Chilean red wine waiting alongside pickled partridge, pork terrine, and a grilled lamb, all set on British porcelain. A buffet proffered scallop mousse, *pastel de choclos* (Chilean chicken-corn casserole), corvina fish with tarragon sauce, salmon carpaccio, baked rabbit, stuffed artichokes, Roquefort-spinach ravioli, and papayas stuffed with kiwi. This was a cry from my usual freeze-dried camping fare. And after dinner, I collapsed on a soft bed plumped up with a white piqué bedspread covering goose-down pillows and crisp cotton Barcelona sheets. It reminded me, I was long overdue in taking my sleeping bag to the dry cleaners.

But it was morning that made the impression. I awoke to a choice austral summer day and the finest double-glazed window view I had ever seen, in real life or in the pages of *Condé Nast Traveler*: an unencumbered vista of Lago Pehue, a lake the color of a tropical lagoon; of Los Cuernos del Paine, the angular gray and black Paine Horns, sculpted by twelve million years of ice and wind; and the Torres del Paine, the impossibly vertical spires after which the park is named. Not only was the panorama from my bed something from a Middle Earth felicity of imagination, but the architects of the hotel, Germand del Sol and Jose Cruz, had cleverly cut a hole through the bathroom wall so I could relax in the Jacuzzi bath or sit on the toilet and be visually regaled as needles of granite pierced icy skies.

The view was so compelling I was late to my appointment in the lobby. There, in front of a giant fireplace, I met Alejandra Manalla, my guide for the day, and something about her struck me immediately. She was tall, thin as a camel's neck, a bit gangly, with glasses and big lantern eyes. She was eighteen-and-a-half years old and working as a guide during her summer away from college, where she was studying to be a writer. Pablo Neruda, the great Chilean poet, was a role model for her, and I told her he had influenced me as well, and in fact I had made a pilgrimage to his Santiago house just a few days previous. As we discussed this, we were trundling down the road to Guarderia Lago Sarmiento, and during one bump I suddenly recognized something . . . she reminded me of me. I, too, was eighteen-and-a-half years old when I first became a guide, I was studying to write, and I was tall, spectacled, lanky, and quite unsure of myself. She seemed more confident than I my first season, until I asked her about a series of scratches and wounds on her hand and wrist. She turned guillotine pale and then told me she had scratched herself while hiking through a tangle of calafate plants. But red abrasions across her skin belied that explanation. I asked again. She bored soulful eyes into mine and made a protean switch. She revealed she tore her skin trying to climb from the Lago Grey boat as it was crashing against the cliff. She went on to describe her version of the events of the Sunday before. She had nodded off before the boat first crashed into the trough, but then she found herself in the role of guide and did all she could to keep the clients unafraid, though she was more scared than she had ever been and thought she was going to die. When she finished her account, she looked at me and said with some authority, "I will never go on a boat in Grey Lake again. Never."

As if to punctuate Alejandra's conclusion, something with a furry version of a Loch Ness Monster neck skipped across the road on spindly legs: It was a guanaco, the wild cousin of the llama. I was excited with the sight and asked if we could stop to take a photo, but Alejandra insisted I be patient. She told me male guanacos like to surround themselves with harems, and as such there would be greater numbers ahead. She was right, of course. A few minutes later we passed a knot of three guanacos; then a group of a dozen; then a herd of twenty or more. Suddenly, they were everywhere, like 250-pound gremlins. Occasionally, one would stare directly at me with its long lashes and Bette Davis eyes, and I felt I could fall into the camelids. They ensorcelled me, reminded me of Alejandra.

At Guarderoa Lago Sarmiento, we exited the van and started to hike among the guanacos. We walked north, toward Guarderia y Refugio Laguna Amarga, following a wire fence separating the park from an estancia (a large ranch). Every now and then we'd find a cinnamon-colored *tulango*—a baby guanaco—caught in the wire, formless as a pricked balloon, yet stiff with rigor mortis. The fence seemed an inhumane intrusion, until Alejandra explained that just a few years ago there were fewer than three hundred guanacos left in the region. The ranchers in the area had shot

Guanaco in Patagonia. PAMELA ROBERSON

the guanacos, who overgrazed their sheep ranchland. But with the establishment of Torres del Paine National Park, fences were erected, and the population within swelled so that now an estimated three thousand guanacos roam freely in the shadow of the Torres del Paine.

At one point I lagged our group, trying to photograph the silhouette of a woolly guanaco against the palatial cluster of ice-clad peaks and granite teeth. Then a Patagonian red fox waved his glossy tail in the tall grass just a few feet from my camera, and I lightly stepped over for a closer look. I was so close I could feel hot breath before it scampered away. Where else, I wondered, did wild animals grow up with such an underwhelming fear of man?

After the fox trotted, I heard a tremulous cry from up on the hill. It was Alejandra, calling me to catch up with the group. Her voice sounded tentative, plaintive, without the authority I associated with guides. But it was effective. I stashed my camera and hurried to catch up. When I arrived, I told Alejandra a story about how I had been in a capsize of a raft on a river in Africa in 1973. I had been the oarsman and made a misjudgment. A man drowned. I was so devastated by the accident I swore to give up guiding, and I did, for a long year. But finally, the art of the wilds I so enjoyed while guiding overwhelmed the carpings of reason, and I stepped back onto a raft. And I found a valence in the river that had never rung before. Alejandra looked at me with big guanaco eyes.

As the oblique, orange light of evening bathed the celebrated towers, I returned to the Explora Patagonia, where I met Peter and Shirley Metz, the escorts for the Antarctica group that had taken the ill-fated cruise across Lago Grey. I had heard Peter was the hero in the epic, in that while the Chilean crew panicked, he kept a cool head, kept the others calm, and when the boat drifted close to shore, he leapt into the water with a painter, swam to the bank, climbed a cliff, and secured the line. Finally, he stayed to assist all the passengers in exiting the boat and then saw them safely to a pickup point on Lago Pehue. This wasn't the first time Peter had acted as the hero. He was on the tarmac in Puerto Williams in February 1991 when a chartered LAN-Chile British Aerospace 146, carrying a group of Antarctica-bound tourists, overshot the runway and crashed into the Beagle Channel. Peter was in the plane in minutes, pulling out survivors, and bodies. Of the seventy-two on board, nineteen died. And when a Society Expeditions Zodiac capsized in the Tuamotus of French Polynesia, killing two, Peter was there and helped get the survivors to shore. Though it appeared Peter possessed an Homeric catalogue of heroism, he was dangerously close to a grim reputation of attracting disasters. Over a salad I asked Peter about the Lago Grey incident. He didn't want to talk about it. "But," I protested, "there are lessons here. You did the right things. Others didn't. Don't you think we could all learn by hearing about this?"

"No. I don't believe anything good can come from talking about such an incident. It would only give more people pause before visiting this region. It would be bad for business." I noticed then there was more than a soupçon of vinegar in the salad dressing. And even though we talked and drank deep into the evening, Peter sponged up the possibilities of gaining his perspective. And I didn't feel regret that Peter wouldn't be joining me for the rest of my exploration.

The following day I found myself hiking up to the base of the Torres del Paine with Arian, Alejandra, and several hotel guests. These would be my first steps into the Cordillera del Paine, the thirty-mile-long range adjacent to but geographically separate from the Andes. Like Yosemite, the Paine range was shaped by glacial action during the Pleistocene epoch. In geological terms, it is an upthrusted batholith, a gigantic bubble of once-molten granite that rose from the center of the earth and was later covered with huge glaciers stretching from the continental ice cap. When the glaciers retreated, they left behind deep gashes in the "bubble" and an uproar of wild peaks that rise like postmodern monuments from the grassy lowlands near sea level.

It was an odd but satisfying hike as we followed the south bank of the cascading Rio Ascensio upwards, across bogs of primordial muck where Alejandra's tiny feet would leave an impression the size of a bear paw. The name Patagonia was not meant to designate a political unity, but a land of big-footed Indians, the Patagones, as Antonia Pigafetta, chronicler of Ferdinand Magellan's 1520 voyage, named them when he found giant prints near their winter camp. I couldn't help but wonder if the mud here may have been the cause of those first impressions, and ultimately the name for a fifth of a continent.

Arian bounced between the four women clients, yet Alejandra kept pace with me, interpreting the natural history, pointing out the hundred-year-old *lenga* trees, the gnarled Magellanic beech, the pale tresses of "Old Man's Beard," and the "mountain guanaco," while nodding her head at Arian and his flirtations. "Mountain guanaco?" I played the straight man. "That's Arian. He always has a harem." She smiled like a phosphorus fire. Even though this was just her second pelt up this path, it was evident Alejandra knew a lot. She loved what she was doing and confessed she couldn't believe her buttered luck to have this job. In some archaeological way, I remembered feeling that way.

After crawling over the crest of a steep scree slope, I lifted my eyes to a sky full of mountains: Torre Nord (7,400 feet), Torre Sur (8,200 feet), and Torre Central (8,100 feet), looking like colossal crystals growing side by side just across a small alpine lake set in a white-streaked cirque. With the simple expedient of standing still, they dashed any hope of traverse. The microclimates of Patagonia showed their range and speed, with one moment bright as new paint, the next dark and blustery, the striated spires perforating boiling black clouds. I took several photos of Alejandra, who looked lofty as her backdrop. A silence deep as an iceberg swept in and remained, hovering around her. And her eyes seemed to reflect all the wonder of a new world.

Saturday, I signed for a horseback ride. I had expected Arian, but he took the day off, pleading neurasthenia. This time my guide was Giovanna Raineri, from Santiago. She had worked the year before in the Chile Pavilion at the Universal Exposition in Seville, and there met the owners of Explora, who invited her to come join the staff as a guide. She had the adamantine look of an outdoorswoman and exuded confidence as we rode along the lapis-tinted Paine River. We passed wind-twisted trees, zigzagging *nandues* (flightless ostrich-like birds, also known as Darwin rheas), *liebres* (European hares), a *cingue* (Patagonian skunk), and a sparkling spring, where the water tasted like swamp juice. At one point I asked Giovanna if she had been in the notorious boat, and a panicked look sped across her face. "Yes, I was there. It was the most frightening episode of my life. I will never step on a boat on Lago Grey again," she replied as she kicked her heels into the side of her steed and galloped ahead, the wilderness guide turning a back on wildness. No one, it seems, is more trapped inside the armature of signs than the signmaker.

At lunch, over a Magallanes-style lamb and vegetable barbecue cooked over glowing beechwood coals, Alejandra showed up at the *quincho* to help. After a couple of pisco sours, I asked if she would join us for the afternoon ride. She said she didn't really know how to ride, but sure, she would love to. After a quick lesson, Alejandra mounted her steed and trotted alongside. We rode to a small waterfall and scrambled up some slippery rocks to a ledge above the main pool. Alejandra told me that just a few days before, the Explora's chief driver, Pedro "The Silver Fox," had jumped into the pool, not knowing how to swim. He flailed around for a bit, but he made it to shore and emerged smiling. Alejandra seemed impressed, as though she had witnessed the tintinnabulation of a new spirit, one that collaborated with the pageant of forces at the bottom of the world.

The following day, we made arrangements to visit the Valle del Frances, an enclosed sanctuary deeply incised into the Cordillera del Paine. But to get there we would have to take a boat across Lago Pehue; then we would ride horses for several miles, to the Italian Camp, and finally hike the final pitch to the foot of the French Glacier. I had hoped Alejandra would join, but she wasn't in the lobby, and I wondered if it was just too soon for her to cross another lake. This time my guide was Pepe Alarcon, and of course, as had become a circadian rhythm, I expected to hear his personal reactions to the boating accident. But as we loaded the launch, I asked Pepe about the incident, and he turned to me and said he had no reactions . . . he wasn't there. In fact, he was in the Explora Patagonia helping to coordinate the rescue by radio.

Just as the outboards kicked, Alejandra came running down the pier and jumped on board. She was barely breathing hard through her crinkly smile, despite the hundred-yard dash, and I told her I admired the streamlined fitness of youth. She looked back at me, exploring my face through her glasses, and said, "But you know, I really like wrinkles." And I imagined I had the look of a crustacean with its shell off.

The crossing was easy. Someone had turned the Patagonian fan off, and the lake, which has no fish, was flat as a griddle. Soon, we were saddled up and loping our way into the mountains. This time Alejandra seemed at home on her horse, and she trotted ahead, leaving me in the rear, but always looking back to check my progress. We parked our horses at the Italian Camp, enjoyed a picnic lunch, then took off by foot to reach the high vantage. As we arrived at the crest of the walk, a lime-green *cachana* (Austral parakeet) zipped over my shoulder, and the mountain began to tremble. If the flap of a butterfly's wing in Osaka can affect the weather in Kansas, imagine what a parakeet can do in the beefy wind of Patagonia. The bird may or may not have contributed, but several loud noises boomed across the valley. I turned my head and watched a series of avalanches spill from the upper reaches of the French Glacier, which flows from the Paine Grande Massif (10,600 feet), the highest point in the Paine fretwork. The glacier itself was a spectacular mass of ice and snow, splintered with deep canyons and jagged pinnacles, a bristling blue. I turned again and looked up into the smooth-walled Gothic Towers, and another quarter turn and I looked down on the pearl-colored waters of Lake Nordenskjold. It was all savagely beautiful.

On the way back, a williwaw hit, and the tableau of sharp relief we'd enjoyed on the ride up was now a canvas of gray vagueness. I slouched in my poncho like Lee Marvin in *Cat Ballou*, bringing up the rear, sometimes getting lost. I'd call out Alejandra's name, but the wind would suck it up and toss it with the rain towards the Towers behind me, which, wrapped in clouds, now looked bent, like huge mourners at a funeral. Then I would see an orange blaze painted on a tree or rock, and I'd be back on track. Once we got to the shores of Lago Pehue, the wind cranked up its battering, the rain its lashing. Whitecaps whipped across the lake. Several Andean condors, the world's largest flying birds, traced curves across the leaden sky, like spirits slipping by. We boarded the boat and set out for the forty-five-minute crossing. As we plunged through the gray-green swells, the boat pitched and reeled, and Alejandra sat across from me, looking stern beyond her youth and deep in thought. Then at one point, her face lifted like a balloon, her eyes darkly bright, and she threw a weather-burned smile: "You know, I think I would go back on a boat on Lago Grey." And I knew then that somewhere in the mountain landscape of this woman there was a magic glass into which she stepped as a human and came out a guide.

CHAPTER 40

THE CIA AND ADVENTURE TRAVEL

Spies are a most important element in water, because on them depends an army's ability to move.

—SUN TZU

THE YEARS FROM 1976 TO 1990 I SPENT ROAMING THE GLOBE, EXPLORING WILD rivers and landscapes, all under the Sobek imprimatur. Sobek had some fifty first descents to its name, from Cuba to Swat, Sulawesi to Western China, even the first descent of the Congo . . . actually, it was a ride called Congo River Rapids in Florida's Busch Gardens, and some PR flack had recruited John Yost, myself, and George Plimpton to make an Electric Cowboyish "first descent" in front of the evening news.

We were not seeking new partnerships at this point, but an unexpected one showed at our door. I had just finished a raft descent of the Kilombero River in Tanzania, a lively course ferocious with Nile crocs and hippos, both of which bit our boats. I had been following the news about the emergence of Black-majority rule in Zimbabwe (formerly Rhodesia), ending its fourteen-year war that saw blood and guts spilled in the Zambezi River corridor that separated then-Rhodesia from Zambia, where many freedom fighters were based. The free and clear elections meant that the Zambezi was no longer a war zone and might be open to a raft exploration.

So I flew from Dar es Salaam to Livingstone, Zambia, and hiked the Zambezi canyon for miles downstream of Victoria Falls. The hike presented a luminous tableau, rarely photographed, seldom considered, as beautiful as any water passage I had ever seen. The Zambezi, one hundred yards below, purled a serpentine green, a bright ribbon forever vanishing around hairpin turns. This was the ingress to one of the last great unnavigated major river corridors, the eighty-mile section of the Zambezi from the base of the largest curtain of falling water in the world, to the head of Lake Kariba, Africa's second-largest man-made reservoir.

First descent of the Zambezi River below Victoria Falls. BART HENDERSON

David Livingstone had canoed to the lip of Victoria Falls (called *Mosi-oa-Tunya*, "the Smoke that Thunders," by the local Batoka villagers) on November 16, 1855. His plan to find a river route to and from the interior of Africa was instantly thwarted, and he portaged the next hundred miles. So I imagined an expedition that began where David Livingstone left off.

On return to the United States, I went to see John Wilcox at ABC and convinced him this was an epic first descent that deserved to be filmed. He bought in and quickly recruited Levar Burton as on-camera talent, seeking his roots in Africa. I visited National Geographic and persuaded coverage, and the magazine retained budding adventure photographer Nick Nichols, who had lensed our first descent of the Indus in Pakistan. I called Doug Thompkins, founder of The North Face and Esprit, and he signed on as a kayaker. When the word of the expedition began to spread, I received a call from the CIA. The company was concerned about the new regime under Robert Mugabe and wanted to position one of their own to gather on-the-ground intelligence. I was reluctant, arguing that we were apolitical globalists, celebrating the diversity, equity, and inclusion of the varying cultures of the world and hoping to spread the seeds of peace and understanding through travel. I also had a personal animus. My father had suffered a series of nervous breakdowns while working for The Company, and my mother speculated it was because his strong moral code did not match his employer's.

But The Company countered that we would be doing a service for the region, helping to ensure the peaceful transfer of power. We grudgingly agreed, and Tim

O'Dell (not his real name) joined our ranks and set up a Sobek office in Lusaka. As part of the project, we were asked to devise an escape plan if Tim were somehow exposed while in Zambia. So we took one of our Sobek rafts, kitted it with all the necessary gear, including frame, oars, life jackets, a pump, bottled water, and freeze-dried food, and paid a local farmer to store it in his riverside *tukul* (a grass hut that looks like a hairnet on stilts) about a mile upstream of Victoria Falls. This would be Tim's exit route if he was found to be doing more than planning and selling Sobek trips.

On the morning of the launch, the president of Zambia, Kenneth Kaunda, showed and asked if I would write a speech he wanted to deliver before smashing a bottle of champagne on one of the rafts. I had brought my then girlfriend, Joanna Taylor, on the expedition, but I had been so busy prepping the project I had hardly seen her for a week. When I entered our hotel room and shared I needed to write a presidential speech, she made a stand. Either forgo the speech and ceremony to give her needed attention, or she would leave. What a spot! I had to write the speech and be present at its delivery.

On a lawn near the falls, the president mouthed my words, saying repeatedly, "One Zambia; One Sobek," to great applause from the Sobek crew, save Joanna, who had gone missing. When at last we carried the boats, with much help from the nearby Nakatindi villagers, down to the Boiling Pot, just below Victoria Falls, Joanna showed and climbed into my raft. I pushed off first.

The raft buckled and dipped as I dug the oar blades deep in the first rapid below Victoria Falls. Kenneth Kaunda; the ambassador from Zimbabwe; a row of photographers, videographers, and VIPs like birds on a power line; and Tim O'Dell watched from the bridge as my raft canted up a large wave. I was piloting the lead boat on this media-overloaded first descent of the Zambezi.

I could feel the raft rising sideways and saw a black wall looming. I pulled my oars mightily, but the right one clawed only air. I dropped the oars and hung on. The raft hung sideways for a long second. Through the wash of white I could see Nick Nichols, camera pressed to his eye, still clicking. Then the boat plunged over, dumping Nick, Joanna, and me into the roiling mess.

I popped up on the far side of the rapid and looked around for Nick and Joanna. After a few tense beats they buoyed up, Nick's face still pressed against the camera, Joanna cursing the last straw. President Kaunda watched the whole drama from above and turned to Tim and asked, "Is that the way this is done?"

We continued downstream, running large, complex rapids and portaging one monster. When we reached a beach candidate for camping, an Alouette helicopter dropped down on a rock ledge five yards from us. Out stepped three Zimbabwean army sappers who were being loaned to us to clear our campsites, lunch spots, and rapid-scouting routes from leftover land mines. We were used to savage rapids, to aggressive crocodiles and hippos, but land mines were a new intimidation.

The rapids were consistently gnarly, and in one, Levar Burton and longtime Sobek client Grant Rogers, issued from the boat like spawning salmon. They tumbled through the next set of rapids and were swept downstream. Levar emerged unscathed except for his grin; Grant broke four ribs and was whisked away by the Alouette to the Wankie Colliery Hospital for recovery.

The expedition continued with capsizes and close calls. But the kayaks seemed to fair well with their sleek mobility. Levar was curious about the crafts, as he had never been in one, so he asked if he could give one a try. He slipped in, attached his spray skirt, and began paddling cheerfully with athletic grace. A few minutes later I was rowing the raft behind John Yost when a ridged snout lunged from beneath and exploded a tube on John's raft. John reacted with characteristic cool and started slapping the croc over its head with an oar.

The croc made a second lunge and then dove and disappeared. Levar watched the episode slack-jawed from his low-in-the-water boat, and when the croc didn't resurface in several tense seconds, Levar dug his paddles deep, speedboated to shore, leapt out of the kayak, and ran up the beach to producer John Wilcox, who was holding a walkie-talkie. Levar called the helicopter pilot, and a few minutes later the Alouette landed, Levar jumped in, it flew off, and we never saw him again. Joanna left at trip's end and moved on to a more stable and safer relationship.

The rest of the trip proved the Zambezi a world-class raft run, and Tim's Sobek office started to take regular bookings. In not much time it became one of the most popular adventure tours on the continent, with lines of clients and new companies cropping up to fulfill the demand. Victoria Falls became known as the "Adventure Travel Capital of Africa."

With more and more people wanting to experience the Zambezi, Sobek needed more qualified guides. We had been hiring young men from nearby Nakatindi Compound, a subsistence shantytown, to help as porters and "highsiders," human ballast who would throw weight against a rising tube in a hole or wave to punch it down to prevent a capsize. With this local success Sobek Zambezi River manager Charlie Ross cast a wider net and began recruiting from other villages in the region: Siyachilobe, Nsongwe, Machinje, and Mukuni. All the highsiders came from places of poverty and poor education, but they were eager and enthused with the work.

One of the senior Sobek guides, Bob "Big Water" Meyer, began the Zambezi Whitewater School, with Alick "Kulu" Banda, Saimon Sakala, and Elias Sakala as freshman students. Sobek brought Alick and Saimon, who showed great promise, to the United States to attend a summer whitewater school and then sent them and three others to Siberia to represent Zambia in the first International Whitewater Championship competition. From this point on, the young villagers around Victoria Falls had a new, well-paying, exciting occupation opportunity. A measure of prosperity, and sense of worth and dignity, came to the region. There are now schools and good roads that did not exist before.

Today we have the first Zambian-owned rafting company. The owner, Enoch Labisi, was born in Mukuni. He started as a porter and worked his way up to being a guide. He gradually realized he possessed the traits and skills to operate his own

company. He overcame the preju-
dice against Black ownership, and
with determination, confidence, and
moxie he built his company. Trip-
advisor currently lists his company,
Maano, as the number-two whitewater outfitter in Livingstone. He is
an inspiration to other Africans who
dream of success.

   This is one of the legacies of
Sobek of which I am so very proud.

   Tim O'Dell ran the Sobek office
in Zambia for the next three years as
a part-time job, and not a few guides
and clients wondered aloud how we
could afford such a thing, especially
since the kwacha, the Zambian currency, was soft and we could not
easily turn monies from local clients
into dollars. The transfer of power to
Black majority rule in Zimbabwe was
fairly seamless, and many politicians
and pundits around the world saw
Robert Mugabe as an enlightened
new leader, a hero for Africa. In time,
that would change, but not during

Helicopter support from the film crew. The
producer and director would fly out of the
canyon each night and camp in a luxury hotel.
JOHN KRAMER

Tim's watch. When Tim's tour of duty was up, we closed up shop, thanked our
sponsors, and set out to be the fully independent outfit that had been the aspiration
from the beginning. We never heard from the CIA again and were thankful for it.

   Sobek was now pretty established, at least in the small world of adventure travel,
as one of the top-two adventure companies. Sobek was peerless in the international
river-running realm, and Mountain Travel dominated trekking, though we each
offered overlapping product.

CHAPTER 41

WHEN EXPLORERS MERGE

The shell must break before the bird can fly.
—ALFRED TENNYSON

BY 1990 SOBEK AND MOUNTAIN TRAVEL WERE COMPETING HEAD-TO-HEAD FOR the same adventurous clients, with many of the same itineraries. There were incidents when we both had departures for the Inca Trail in the same week, but both departures were only half full and barely profitable or worse. We would compete each year to create the largest, thickest, and most alluringly colorful catalogues of our offerings, and we each battled for the best guides. We both offered trips to the North Pole, and the Seven Summits, climbing the highest peak on each of the seven continents, and we used elite guide Scott Fischer while Mountain Travel used equally proficient Rob Hall (both perished on the infamous Everest expedition in May 1996, memorialized in Jon Krakauer's *Into Thin Air*).

The year previous Sobek had run into some financial shoals with a stupid acquisition I authored. We had found windfall profits with some films, commercials, and events we were asked to undertake: the multimillion-dollar Camel Trophy we produced in Indonesia and Brazil; several ABC adventure specials in such places as Malawi, Sumatra, and Sulawesi; stunt work we did for some features, such as *The River Wild*, *Dream West*, and *The Pursuit of D.B. Cooper* (I doubled for Robert Duvall in a raft-chase scene over a waterfall); and a Folger's rafting commercial with celebrity photographer Bruce Weber. With extra cash in our coffers, I decided we should open a Bay Area office for better access to these types of opportunities. I found a beautiful property in Piedmont, a tony suburb in the East Bay, owned by a law firm, and we bought it, with John Yost and me putting up our homes as collateral. It seemed a safe bet with real estate prices on the rise, and we spent lavishly to remodel and post a large sign on the lawn that read "Sobek," with the crocodile logo. We had arrived, or so I thought, until the neighbors, who imagined us as a cult, complained to the city that we were conducting business in a residential neighborhood. The law firm before us had kept a low profile and nobody was the wiser. But now the neighbors became activists and wore buttons that had a ghostbusters-type red circle and slash, only with a crocodile where the ghost was. The city sued us. I had hired Russ Daggatt, a great friend and brilliant Harvard law graduate who traded in his law career for adventure travel. A phrase he bantered about, "Happiness is reality minus expectations," was much needed as my expectations for the Sobek mansion were being shredded. Though Russ was officially our VP of marketing, he rolled up his sleeves and brought his expertise to our defense. It was a lengthy and costly battle that we finally lost. We were ordered to sell the property at a huge shortfall (we bought it at a premium as a commercial building; were forced to sell it as residential). Our cash reserves were drained, and we could not pay off the loan to the bank, which threatened to call in the home collateral John and I had signed. We were on the brink of losing our company and our homes. I called my father-in-law, a successful D.C.-based lawyer, and asked for his help. He said no. I began to call high-net-worth past clients, but everyone I approached passed. Finally, Ken Jarkow, who had dogsledded with me in the Arctic and had joined Sobek first descents down the Alas in Sumatra and Yangtze in China, agreed to lend us the monies needed to become whole. His one condition: we retain his son Adam, who was going through a rough spot, as a guide for the next season. It was agreed, and Ken wired the monies, we paid the bank, and we got back to business. In a year we paid Ken back in full, with interest. To this day I count Ken as a true friend, and the man who saved Sobek.

We were motoring along once more as one of the two top adventure brokers in the world. Everything changed with Iraq's invasion of Kuwait on August 2, 1990, the start of the First Gulf War. By the time Operation Desert Storm was launched in January of 1991, the State Department issued a strong recommendation that Americans not travel abroad. We were suddenly swamped with cancellations and refund requests. Our Galapagos program, one of our most successful, with departures every week of the year, required we pay in full the lease fees for our boats in advance for the calendar year, our most expensive up-front expenditure. With all the cancellations, we were, for the first time, in a scary cash position. We furloughed staff, tightened belts, and wondered how to survive. I took out a loan against my house to cover payroll, but as the war dragged on, and no cash came in, I wondered once more if I might lose my modest home to the bank. I finally decided to give Dick McGowan, the president of Mountain Travel, a call. I expected he wouldn't take it, after all the bad blood over the years. But when he picked up the phone and I suggested that perhaps we should explore working together in this challenging environment, he asked with the dry sighs of a desert breeze, "Can you come over and talk?"

It turned out Mountain Travel was also in a cash crunch. They had invested heavily in the construction of a ship that could carry passengers to Antarctica and other waters, and it was partially finished when the effects of the war hit the travel industry and the company had to walk away with empty pockets. I proposed a merger, but with both shops bleeding monies and with little new business on the horizon,

Richard on first descent of the Great Bend of the Yangtze. JOHN KRAMER

how to finance? We turned to past client Fred Krehbiel, CEO and co-chairman of Molex Inc., a Fortune 500 company. He had taken a trek to Nepal, and it was transformational, firing an appreciation for adventure and nature that would stay with him for the rest of his life. He had expressed interest in investing after his trek, and now this was the opportunity. Along with friend and traveling companion Tom Lee, he bought out all the partners in both Mountain Travel and Sobek, save me, and loaned the monies needed to make the merger work. A year later it was done, with Tom, a brilliant businessman and keen adventurer, now chairman of the board. We were then Mountain Travel Sobek, today streamlined to MT Sobek.

We were now a nation where the true religion was adventure. With the combined states, I was increasingly interested in new ways to evangelize our message, to expose what we did, which was so life-affirming and nature positive, to the widest possible audience. Even with our combined lists and marketing, we were reaching only a tiny sliver of potential travelers who I was convinced would treasure an adventure travel experience. This quest took me on an exploratory of a different stripe.

John Kramer being thrown from oars on first descent of the Yangtze. RICHARD BANGS

CHAPTER 42

GOING DIGITALLY WHERE NONE HAD GONE BEFORE

As for me, I am tormented with an everlasting itch for things remote. I love to sail forbidden seas, and land on barbarous coasts.

—HERMAN MELVILLE

DURING THE PREVIOUS FEW YEARS, I HAD BEEN PLAYING WITH NEW MEDIA, dynamic digital representations of traditional static print media. It had always been a point of frustration over the years when I set out to convince the uninitiated that adventure travel was a good thing, with alchemic transformational qualities and positive consequences. The universe of adults, though, who would leave the comfort zone and step off the beaten path into the wildness of adventure was small, ridiculously small. Over and over, I met with glazed eyes as I tried to describe the delight and aperçus that came from my latest foray into the field. I felt it was a question of accessibility . . . to most, rafting the Zambezi or trekking in Nepal seemed like something mythopoetic. I wanted to communicate the message that adventure was for everyone . . . unless you craved concrete and enjoyed seeing the air you breathe.

For years John Yost and I did this by producing the annual Sobek catalogue of adventures dripping with gorgeous photos of everyday people in exotic locals, challenging themselves, having fun, interacting with people from distant cultures, and with wildlife rare and beautiful. And, to a degree, it worked. Sobek grew and, while it didn't exactly prosper, it allowed us to pursue the mission of adventure, our passion. The catalogue concept never really realized its potential. We would spend the better part of a year creating the catalogue; we would print and distribute 200,000 copies and would attract 3,000 clients. Part of the problem, I subliminally assumed, was the basic shortcomings of a print publication. Because of space and cost considerations, we could use only one or two thumbnail photographs to illustrate all the diverse sights and sensations of a three-week trek in the Himalaya, or a two-week rafting run down the Bio-Bio. Somehow that seemed a travesty. And one of the most compelling facets of an adventure trip—the sounds, the ethnic music, the wildlife calls—could never be properly portrayed . . . try as I might, I could never describe the rainbow qualities of the gamelan of Indonesia . . . one had to hear it to grasp it, to appreciate it. The same with the hunting cries of the Masai, or the haunting wail of a gibbon.

When I read about the coming age of New Media, I became enthused, and jumped in. In 1993 with Kodak as a partner, I produced, with my friend and Sobek editor Christian Kallen, the first travel Photo CD of adventure travel, featuring the original photographs (restored in Adobe Photoshop) of Ed Hillary and Sherpa Tenzing Norgay's successful first ascent of Mount Everest in 1953, replete with narration from Ed. It also featured dozens of high-quality photos of our key trips and full-bodied, digital stereo sound. You could hear the lions and the Kecak dance, waterfalls thundering and glaciers calving. In my mind, it was a huge leap forward in grabbing an audience and conveying the wonders of adventure travel; in motivating the next step. We bundled the CD in the back of 100,000 copies of our annual catalogue, with hopes that our well-healed and qualified clientele was so enthusiastic about the subject of adventure they would go out and buy the necessary proprietary $200 Kodak Photo CD players that attached to TV sets like VCRs. The theory seemed sound . . . our clients were proven explorers, early adapters, photography lovers. It didn't work. Once again, I was out exploring the sharp outer edge of the curve, but this time I was working in what would become a Betamax format. . . . Photo CD players never caught on. As far as we could tell, only about fifty people actually saw *The Adventure Disc* in their own homes. They made great coasters, however.

But a side effect was brewing. In 1994, because of my early efforts at exploring New Media applications for marketing and selling adventure, I had been asked to emcee a travel and technology conference in New York City. But it was in early December, and Pamela was pregnant with our son, Walker Taylor, who was due about that time. So I bowed out of the emcee slot but volunteered that if Walker came early, I would be happy to fly out and make a presentation.

As it turned out, Pam went into labor November 17, 1994, while I was in the middle of a speech in Washington, D.C. When informed by an aide, I made a hasty excuse to the audience, ran off the stage, and my elder sister, Patricia, rushed me to the airport, where I caught the last flight back and arrived in time for the birth, in the early morning of the eighteenth. I was hooked up to the internet, so I broadcast his arrival to the wired world.

With Walker's early arrival I was able to make the conference and showed *The Adventure Disc* to great fanfare. Afterwards a young man approached me in the back of the room and slipped me his card: Richard Barton, Travel Product Services, Microsoft. "We should talk," he suggested.

And we did, periodically over the months and weeks that followed, exploring different ways Microsoft might work with my company. By this time, I had produced several CD-ROMs and realized their own shortcomings: long development time, static content once created, and ultimately limited space (although, with six hundred megabytes, CD-ROMs held room for the equivalent of several hundred catalogues).

I had read about a new interface/application on the internet, the World Wide Web, which would allow multimedia presentations and cross-linkage to pages anywhere on the internet, anywhere in the world. This seemed the ultimate application for travel, with near infinite space and the ability to update information at any time. I read about a pioneer in this space, Tim O'Reilly, who had invented something called GNN, the Global Network Navigator, one of the first internet browsers. I gave him a call, and he invited me up for the weekend at his place in Sebastopol. We hit it off, and with his help I jumped in and produced the first travel site on the World Wide Web, an interactive, multimedia version of the Sobek catalogue that even featured electronic postcards. It was pioneering of a new sort for me, a whole different exploratory, but in some ways not unlike running unrun rivers. There was no road map, no marker for what lay around the next bend.

The website was a hit, receiving notices in national magazines and newspapers, and Rich Barton increased his phone calls to me. He even flew down to my offices, and we spent a couple hours talking of ways our companies might work together. Still, nothing concrete emerged.

Richard with son Walker sailing in Marina del Rey. CINDY BANGS

Richard rowing and son Walker in bow on the Skykomish River, Washington. ALLAN KEARNEY

CHAPTER 43

ANTARCTICA REAL AND VIRTUAL

I have come to the conclusion that life in the Antarctic Regions can be very pleasant.

—Robert Falcon Scott

THEN A NEW IDEA DAWNED IN EARLY 1995. WHY NOT TAKE THE POWER OF THE World Wide Web into the field and allow virtual travelers to join an expedition, follow it, and participate from the portals of their digital screens, be they at offices, schools, or homes? I was scheduled to travel to Antarctica in December to escort an MT Sobek commercial expedition. Why not make that a trial run for a virtual expedition? I enlisted the help of four key players: Jonathan Chester, author, filmmaker, photographer, Antarctic explorer, mountaineer, and recently a fanatical web citizen, would be the field producer; Christian Kallen, who had collaborated with me on several books, films, and recently the CD projects, would be the project director and editor at Mission Control at our offices in El Cerrito; Gary Schumacher, a VP at World Travel Partners, a top-ten corporate travel agency looking to explore downstream possibilities with the internet and willing to invest in crazy ideas such as this one; and Kevin Twidle, a research fellow in computer science at Imperial College outside London and co-owner of 7-E Communications, was our communications wizard who could make all the satellite equipment buzz and sing. Christian and Jonathan brought in a fifth key player, brilliant web designer Brad Johnson, who took the site and made it transcendental. We called our enterprise TerraQuest.

Just before I flew to Antarctica, Gary Schumacher and I visited the Microsoft campus for an attempt at a deal. We described in detail what we hoped to do with TerraQuest and invited Microsoft to license the concept, offering several virtual expeditions a year. We presented a budget, and Rich Barton and his confrere, travel product unit manager Greg Slyngstad, seemed to think it reasonable. We left the meeting with a handshake and a promise that Microsoft would send a letter of intent before I departed for Antarctica.

The letter never came. But I was almost too busy to notice, putting together the ambitious Antarctica project.

The Antarctica trip would depart from Ushuaia, Argentina, at the southern tip of South America. Ushuaia. The name rolls around the mouth as though full of marbles. A few months earlier MT Sobek donated an Antarctica trip to a celebrity auction to raise monies for Education First, a nonprofit that buys books for underfinanced schools. On the appointed evening I flew to Gucci's in Beverly Hills and vainly tried to mix in with the vainest of crowds. Vanna White was the auctioneer, and before she got up on stage, she desperately pulled me aside and asked how to pronounce the city of embarkation. For ten minutes I attempted to teach the world's most famous woman of letters how to say "Ushuaia," but when it was time for the auction, Vanna mumbled something that had the audience retorting in unison, "God bless you."

Miraculously all the gear arrived in Ushuaia, Argentina, intact, and we set sail to the White Continent wired to the world. Every day we would send back dispatches and digital photos, answer email, and engage in Live Chats, wherein any webizene could converse with us via text. It was a successful exploratory, and mentions of the project made *Newsweek*, the *Wall Street Journal*, the *New York Times*, and many others. One man in Israel who had religiously followed the trip sent a post-expedition email: "Thank you, thank you, thank you. I am a paraplegic, and this was the closest I will ever come to visiting Antarctica, and it was wonderful." And the project didn't go unnoticed in Redmond, on the sylvan campus of Microsoft.

CHAPTER 44

MELINDA GATES, MICHAEL KINSLEY, AND ME

Placed on this planet since yesterday, and only for a day, we can only hope to glimpse the knowledge that we will probably never attain.

—Horace Bénédict de Saussure

With our Christmas return from Antarctica, I was set to start organizing the Tekeze, which at this point would be a commercial exploratory with a Turner Network Television crew on board to document the descent. Turner didn't have the resources to pay all the expenses for a private exploratory, so we agreed to sell seats to proven Sobek clients to help underwrite the project. The response was overwhelming, and before we turned around a dozen clients had signed.

At the same time, I wondered why we never heard from Microsoft and called Rich Barton. He said he was sorry, but there had been a "major re-org" at the company, and he would have to get back to me in due time.

In February I got a call from Rich Barton, suggesting I come up for a meeting with Nathan Myhrvold, whose name I recognized as the chief technology officer, a former colleague of Stephen Hawking's, and the co-author of *The Road Ahead*, the best-selling book mapping out Bill Gates's vision of the digital future. Rich also said Melinda French would join the meeting. Who was Melinda French, I asked. "She's Melinda French Gates, Bill's wife," Rich informed me. This sounded like a serious meeting.

At the meeting it was explained that on December 7, Pearl Harbor Day, Bill Gates had announced a major reorganization of the company, revamping his corporate starship to "embrace and extend" the Web. Microsoft, theretofore a software company, was going to commit its vast resources to developing "content" for the internet. One of the first deals the company made was signing Michael Kinsley to come to Redmond to create an online political policy magazine, which became *Slate*. Now Rich Barton and company were asking if I would come up and create an online adventure travel and exploration magazine. "But this is a full-time job," Rich reminded me. "You'll have to leave Sobek behind." "What about TerraQuest?" I asked. "We'd rather have you, and own the magazine."

It was the offer of a lifetime. I struggled a bit, having spent twenty-three years in the adventure business in my own company, and being excited about the prospects of TerraQuest, owned equally by MT Sobek and World Travel Partners. But this was too much of an opportunity, a chance to give birth to a twenty-first-century magazine with deep pockets behind me. Now I could create my own vision of a geographical and discovery magazine, a publication using tools that would make the stories come alive in a multimedia and interactive way. And I would not only contribute words and photos, sounds and video, but would edit as well.

I would retain ownership in MT Sobek, sit on the board, but would leave the day-to-day of commercial adventure travel behind. And TerraQuest would be purchased by World Travel Partners, to run a couple more virtual adventures before being parked as an archive site, a marker stone for the beginnings of virtual expeditions. I didn't dwell on the velocity of history, though. I was training my field glasses on a new species.

Melinda sent me the offer letter, which was small in salary but generous in stock options. There was a glitch, however. After I signed the offer letter, a huge mudslide poured into the house I had just purchased in Orinda, California. I called Melinda and said I felt I had to bow out because it would take months to repair and then sell my home. She listened, expressed empathy, hung up, but then called back minutes later. She said Microsoft would purchase my home at full price if I took the job.

The other qualm was wondering how the job would affect the Tekeze, a trip I knew I could never miss. I suggested to Rich Barton and Greg Slyngstad that if I joined up, I could devote the first issue to the Tekeze, partnering with Turner and making it a live, interactive expedition from the bottom of the deepest gorge in Africa. I had no idea if the satellite equipment would work from such a depth, surrounded by mile-high walls, but I threw out the concept. They loved it. I moved into my Redmond office April Fool's Day 1996. The first thing I placed in the windowsill was a skull I had found in a cave on Easter Island some years back, with a small hole in one temple and a large chunk of its occiput missing. The tiny hole was where a bullet had entered, the big one where it exited. But I knew nothing more of the fate of this man. I kept the skull as a reminder of the impermanence of all things living, and of how we all ultimately become anonymous. It also was a great conversation piece in a world of emails, software, code, and killer apps.

This twist put the Tekeze into a whole new light. I had been hoping the expedition might be a chance to reunite surviving friends of the 1973 Baro and Omo expeditions, as we had all vowed back then to run the Tekeze. But a commercial

Easter Island, Chile. PAMELA ROBERSON

exploratory concept wouldn't allow such a reunion . . . it would be too expensive. Now, however, with Microsoft and Turner on board, we could organize a dedicated expedition with no commercial clients, just the reuniting five, four professional rafting guides, the Turner film crew, and a production crew from my newly named webzine, *Mungo Park*, after the eighteenth-century Scottish agent of empire who disappeared while exploring the Niger River in West Africa. For *Mungo Park* there would be Jonathan Chester and Kevin Twidle, who had made the Antarctica expedition such a success, and *Mungo Park* in-house producer Steve Lee, as well as my friend David Roberts, as a co–field correspondent who would file regular dispatches from the expedition to the *Mungo Park* website. I had known David for years, had traveled through Yemen with him in 1980, and had made the first descent of the Waghi-Purari River in New Guinea with him in 1983. The latter always impressed me, as David could not swim, and I cottoned to his keening spirit of adventure. David was a great writer, with many books to his credit, and he had been doing some virtual correspondence for Discovery On-line. So I figured David would be our guy.

Trek to put-in for first descent of the Tekeze River, Ethiopia; Richard in center.
BART HENDERSON

My good friend Pasquale Scaturro would also join. More than anyone I had met, Pasquale was the embodiment of Goethe's maxim, "Whatever you dream you can do, begin it. Boldness has genius, power, and magic." Pasquale had reservations, however. Two months after we returned from the scout, his seventeen-year-old son, Adam, broke his neck while wrestling at high school and became paralyzed from the waist down. Pasquale wondered if he should join an extended expedition under the circumstances, but I urged him on. "I've been there. It's good to go." And he said yes. We also had a translator, Daniel Mehari, and a Turner production manager, Jackie Frank. That put our total to twenty-three people, huge by exploratory standards. And just two days behind us would be the commercial exploratory, led by Conrad Hirsh, also with twenty-three people. My offering of the Tekeze to veteran clients as a first descent some months earlier had yielded an overwhelming response, and somehow we needed to accommodate the commercial explorers. So we devised a tricky plan that would allow the Turner/Microsoft expedition to launch first, but only by a couple of days, so that everyone could claim to being on the river during its first descent. It was all outlandish, bordering on being unmanageable, and was very risky. But I committed to go forward, knowing that the Tekeze would go from a million years of solitude to being a media phenomenon in one fell swoop.

CHAPTER 45

MUNGO PARK

I do not know much about gods; but I think the river is a strong brown god—
sullen, untamed and intractable.

—T. S. ELIOT

WE MADE THE EXPEDITION DOWN THE TEKEZE TO GREAT MEDIA FANFARE, UPLOAD-
ing videos, stills, and dispatches from the muzzle of the deepest gorge in Africa, conducting live chats, and bringing down Microsoft servers with the traffic. I returned
and Bill Gates invited me to his home to show him the results of the expedition. And
I took the helm of the online magazine *Mungo Park*. Across the hall was Michael
Kinsley, who was editing *Slate*. I brought in my longtime content co-conspirator
Christian Kallen and talent from *Travel & Leisure*, *National Geographic*, and others.

For the next couple years, we blazed trails sending personalities to pursue
passions in the far-away. It was a heady time, with little in the way of budget
restraints. We sent Tom Clancy to cover the *Atlantis* space shuttle (STS 81) launch
and wired up the astronauts for the first live chats from space (and had the crew
call *Car Talk*, asking how to lessen the noise on their vehicle). We conducted the
first underwater live chat with Jean-Michel Cousteau; we sent Lyle Lovett on a
motorcycle trip the length of Chile; we sent Dr. Ruth to cover the sexual rituals of
the Trobriand Islands, the Islands of Love off the coast of New Guinea; we sent
Stephanie Powers to report on the caribou migration in Labrador. I flew with the
Blue Angels, and while I did not pass out at high Gs, I did vomit, caught on their
lipstick camera used to embarrass journalists.

I loved pushing the envelopes with what technology could do with travel. I
had long been a Hemingway fan and had been transported to Spain with his first
book, *The Sun Also Rises*, which features Pamplona's San Fermin Festival and the
Running of the Bulls. At the time of the book's publishing, 1926, it was a small
event wherein young men would run alongside six fighting bulls from the Santo
Domingo stables, through the city's narrow cobblestone streets, and into the bull-

ring. At least five hundred years old, the festival had evolved into a manhood ritual so that to win a bride one had to survive a run with the bulls. With the book's acclaim, the festival began to draw an international audience—and more casualties. Scores of lives have been lost to the bulls in the last hundred years, the latest a sixty-three-year-old hometown participant who had been running with the bulls since he was fourteen years old. And with every casualty it seemed more people showed up to run. I was one of those people.

The run takes place every morning throughout the eight-day festival (July 6 to 14 every year), and I arrived on day four to the news that four people had already been gored and several others trampled or injured. I teamed up with a twenty-three-year-old Divino, or Divine One, a local who had mastered the art of BR (bull-running) survival. His family had run for four generations, and he had been running since he was fifteen. He told me he still got scared, and that his strategy was to run down the middle of the road, as there were fewer people to trip over. He was disappointed there were so many foreigners—he guessed two thousand—and blamed them for most of the injuries. "Don't touch the bulls," he advised, as though that might be high on my list.

My plan was to broadcast live to a global internet audience my running narrative, something never before attempted. I practiced running around the Microsoft campus fully wired, giving commentary along the way to make sure the technology worked. It worked fine in Redmond.

Richard and the Microsoft *Mungo Park* team, Mount Si, Washington. PAMELA ROBERSON

Now that we were on-site, the crowd intimidated me and I thought I should do a practice run. The festival continues for eight days with bull running each consecutive day; I planned to run on day six. So I thought I should position myself strategically on the day-five run so I could get a good sense of how I would report for the actual run. We walked the road where the run takes place, and I found a scalloped doorway about three-quarters of the way through the route and figured that would be the ideal spot to watch the event up-close.

The morning of the fifth run I positioned myself in the doorway and waited, camera in hand. The canon made the starting boom, and the wave of runners approached, and then scooped in like a flooding river and pushed me out into the middle of the crowd. I found myself running with a thousand other legs the final stretch to the stadium, and there I found a flat spot and collapsed in exhaustion. At least I had some sense of what to expect the next day.

On the day of our scheduled broadcast, which Microsoft was heralding as a must tune-in experience, we passed a Red Cross station near the starting point; some two hundred volunteers were stationed along the route to assist the fallen.

I took my place at the start and did a sound check with my producer, who was stationed on a balcony above the mêlée. Everything was fine. I had memorized a few clever sound bites I intended to toss in as I did my running commentary. Then the canon fired, and I was off in a blizzard of bodies. I looked over my shoulder and a bull was right behind me, maybe four feet away and gaining, his bobbing horn pointed at my back. I forgot about the commentary and started pumping legs as fast I could.

I made it to the end of the run—into the bullring—white pants and shirt stained with sweat and dirt, but no blood. About 10 percent of the runners get there before the gates shut behind the last bull. Two teenage girls in hiking boots beat me through the gates. Still, I was lucky. Thirty-seven others were injured during my run, bringing the week's total to 127. Since late 1924, first year of the run, around fourteen runners had died. It was a bit like Spanish roulette, only the odds go up each passing year, with more and more people pressed into the narrow streets as the bulls run.

I stumbled into the street and found my producer, Bill, who shook his head and asked, "What happened?" I was too spent to answer, and he continued. "The audio was three minutes of you screaming. No commentary at all. But millions tuned in and stayed with the broadcast. It went viral." Then he showed me a photo he took from the balcony, a zoom lens image of a bull in full gallop, head down, horns up, with one point just inches from my back.

In *The Sun Also Rises*, Hemingway depicts a generation lost as it wanders through the fiesta of Pamplona looking for some sort of center or heart. Only one person in the novel knows the way unwaveringly: Romero, a Spaniard who faces the bulls without fear.

With more tourists in Pamplona spinning down the streets; with animal rights groups picketing the bullfights; with matadors booed as politically incorrect; and teenage girls proving as macho, or macha, as the rest, it seemed doubtful this tradition would endure. In the end, the sun also sets.

CHAPTER 46

THE BIRTH OF EXPEDIA

If you wish to advance into the infinite, explore the finite in all directions.
—JOHANN WOLFGANG VON GOETHE

AFTER RUNNING WITH THE BULLS, I SENT MARIEL HEMMINGWAY, GRANDDAUGH-
ter to Ernest, to Cuba to search for his lost Noble Prize medal (unsuccessfully),
and Shari Belafonte to Costa Rica to report on the leatherback sea turtles hatch-
ing, and then I enticed Martha Stewart, the apostle of cozy and quaint, to take a
sea kayak trip to Newfoundland. We didn't pay the talent on these projects, but
rather covered all expenses, including air, and guaranteed millions of viewers, not
dissimilar to talent appearing on talk shows gratis as the platform helped promote
the brand. Martha had an unusual request . . . she would not fly commercial, even
though the flight was about two and a half hours. So I got the okay and chartered
a Honda HA-420 HondaJet and had it waiting for her on the tarmac. Her arrival
in Newfoundland had taken on some significance, and the prime minister brought
an entourage as a welcome party and hired a band and local dancers to receive her.
The St. John's runway was packed with fans hours before her scheduled departure.
But at 8:30 a.m. Seattle time, I received a call from Martha. She was livid. The jet
was too small. She refused to take the trip unless I found her larger transport (she
had decided to bring along a film crew and several friends). To no avail I argued
and asked her not to leave the airport but to give me a little time. The upgrade was
very expensive, beyond our approved budgets, so I called Greg Maffei, CFO of
Microsoft, and asked his blessings. He knew that Charles Simonyi, the billionaire
and superstar early Microsoft exec, was dating Martha, and understood the larger
fallout if we did not accommodate Martha's request. He gave me the nod, and I
sourced a Gulfstream V, and Martha and friends flew to Newfoundland and had a
super time, reporting throughout via *Mungo Park*.

Mungo Park sailed for another eighteen months, and we devised and produced
all sorts of cool live multimedia, covering paleontologist Jack Horner on a dig in

Alberta, sending Robert Scheer back to Vietnam, retracing the route of the Three Wise Men from Iran through Syria and into Bethlehem. We engaged some of the finest writers of the day: T. Coraghessan Boyle, Bill Broyles, Tim Cahill, Deepak Chopra, Nelson DeMille, Annie Dillard, Gretel Ehrlich, Dr. Sylvia Earle, Tama Janowitz, Edward Hoagland, Dr. Donald Johanson, Jon Krakauer, Barry Lopez, Ziggy Marley, Jay McInerney, Redmond O'Hanlon, George Plimpton, Mary Roach, Tom Robbins, David Roberts, Martin Cruz Smith, Oliver Stone, Robert Stone, David Rains Wallace, and many others.

It was a heady experiment, breaking new trails in media and travel, something far ahead of the social media postings that are so common today. But it didn't make money. We brought in income from sponsors, tourism boards, and Kodak, but not enough to cover the burdened costs of operating within Microsoft, a company used to extraordinary margins in software. Parallel to *Mungo Park* was an effort to tap into the GDS (Global Distribution Systems) databases to offer online booking for airlines and hotels. It was losing more money than *Mungo Park*, and at one point after I closed a large sponsorship, I met with Rich Barton, then the marketing manager for the travel unit, and boasted *Mungo* was bringing in more than the travel agency efforts. "Just wait," he said. And he was right. *Mungo* was eventually shut down, and the online travel agency took off, and I was asked to help make it work. It didn't have a consumer-friendly name at first . . . it was just Microsoft Travel, which didn't ring with a wide public, especially since the company was embroiled in antitrust accusations by the Justice Department, and a popular nickname for Microsoft was "The Darth Vader of Tech."

So we hired San Francisco–based Lander Associates, a branding company famous for reimagining Federal Express to FedEx, to research and suggest a consumer-facing name. I was on the deciding team. After a few weeks of research and testing, the branding team came to Redmond and made its presentation. They explained that words with hard consonants and two or three syllables were most likely to become brand earworms, such as Exxon and Kodak. They laid out a dozen names that had come from brainstorming sessions and focus groups and then revealed their top choice: the empty-vessel word "Expedia." I hated it. I immediately wrote a memo to Bill Gates complaining that it suggested an excommunicated priest who had sex with little boys. Bill came back and said we paid a lot of money to the experts, and we were going to run with it. And more so, it would be up to me to make the brand known and respected.

I spent the next several months sponsoring events using the Expedia brand, from bike races to wrestling matches to the Marathon des Sables, the 156-mile ultramarathon that crosses the Sahara Desert, and dispatched Greg Slyngstad to run and represent us. I sponsored a PBS series, *Smart Travels with Rudy Maxa*, and *The Savvy Traveler* on NPR. I opened a series of Expedia cafes offering free internet in airports and launched *Expedia Travels* magazine in partnership with Ziff Davis.

The branding efforts seemed to work, and Expedia found traction and was soon generating a cash flow larger than any brick-and-mortar travel agency. Rich Barton and Greg Maffei saw an opportunity and filed to take Expedia public, and with underwriting from Goldman Sachs on November 11, 1999, EXPE premiered on Nasdaq, now a separate company from Microsoft.

I continued with Expedia for the next few years, with the title editor at large, creating and sourcing travel content and working to grow the fledging company. And I took time to continue exploring and enhance the fortunes of MT Sobek. I led a trek with MT Sobek to the Inca Trail and Machu Picchu with several Expedia colleagues and Patty Stonesifer, head of the Gates Foundation. I put together a trip to Antarctica for Bill Gates and his father and son. I organized adventures for Jeff Bezos, Barry Diller, Dara Khosrowshahi, and other tech pioneers. And I headed north for a canoe adventure with my friend and colleague Erik Blachford, who was now the director of marketing for Expedia, with Rich Barton bumped to CEO. We both needed some chaos after the Rhadamanthine strictures of technology.

CHAPTER 47

CANOEING DOWN THE CRAZY RIVER

Everyone must believe in something. I believe I'll go canoeing.
—HENRY DAVID THOREAU

THE PRIMARY RESPONSE WAS ONE OF EXHILARATION, THE SPLENDID FRISSON THAT comes with gliding by the edge. The river was fast here; the paddles swallowed yards with each stroke. We stretched to pull into an eddy but couldn't make it. Even though we had spray covers over the seventeen-foot red canoe and had just bailed the boat dry less than ten minutes ago, water was splashing about my knees and the canoe was reeling, like a sailboat in a squall. "We've got a leak in the boat," Erik yelled from behind. But there was no time to ponder that information . . . just ahead the river roiled, and we needed a quick decision. To the right a waterfall; down the center a washboard running with white ribs of foam; to the left a narrow channel between an anvil-shaped rock and the shore. "To the left," I screamed back to Erik while turning the bow. We lined up and slewed a good line to make the chute. Zen and the art of canoeing: I could feel my arms connected to the water and my mind to Erik's strokes behind me, and I instinctively knew what to do. The entry seemed perfect, gliding towards the chute as though on a track, slipping down the drop as though by design. Then a hidden hand seemed to reach down, grab the boat, and push us back towards the rock . . . I dropped my paddle, braced against the gunnels, and *bang* . . . we crashed head-on into the Paleozoic stone. It stopped us cold, and the canoe shuddered and then wobbled back into the mainstream, miraculously upright, skidding on a crackling surge of spume. I could see two new holes in the bow. Water was swishing around my belly. We tried to keep the canoe straight as we headed into the tail waves, but it was like steering an overflowing bathtub. Instead of riding over the crests, we plowed through them. When we spotted our guide, Bart, downstream, we wagged our paddles like semaphores, but he was too busy negotiating his own boat through the quicksilver to notice our distress. We were on our own.

Somehow, we made it to a shallow eddy by the cobblestone bank and jumped out into the icy water with numbed feet in our Tevas. The air was dank as an oyster. Clouds, dark as plums, filled the sky and sealed us off, enforcing a sense of claustrophobia. A short way up the loamy shore was a blanket of snow, and beyond cliffs that soared a half mile high. We had no patching material, no detailed maps, food for only a few days, and the sun was beginning to fade behind the brooding peaks. Ours was the last trip of the short season, so no chance of someone paddling to our rescue. Our life jackets were little more than sports bras, a size too small, good to ninety pounds, which we were not. We couldn't camp here, as we had been warned by an earlier trip that there had been a "caribou kill" by a grizzly nearby ... if we pitched in the vicinity we might become "bear pops." As we bent to bail the canoe, Erik and I exchanged a stern look ... there was an ancient silence, as unbroken as the flow of the river, and I felt a bead of fear in my gut ... but suddenly we both snapped to a smile. "I can't think of any place in the world I would rather be," I offered to Erik. "Yup. . . . We're canoeing!" he practically sang as a hosanna.

There is nothing quite as satisfying as messing about in a canoe, and it gets better as the setting gets wilder, and warmer as the flame of risk burns brighter. When the late Bill Mason, Canada's quintessential riverman, said that nothing was quite as perfect as a canoe, he of course meant that perfection is attained not when there is no longer anything to add, such as in a rich man's yacht, but when there is no longer anything to take away, when a craft has been stripped down to its nakedness. But now, with our boat stripped of some of its skin, were we on a vessel beyond apocatastasis?

We were on a river so remote it didn't appear on most maps, the Blackfeather, a tributary of the Mountain River, deep in the Mackenzie Mountains of Canada's Northwest Territories, about a hundred miles south of the Arctic Circle. These were wilderness waterways in the truest sense. The courses had no impoundments, no diversion projects, no bridges, no roads, no homes, no people, no pollution. The Mountain Dene people once hunted and trapped here, but they long ago moved to villages on the Mackenzie, and now the only remnant was a void. These rivers flow, as they have since time immemorial, in balance with themselves. The Blackfeather and Mountain, and every rill that feeds them, are in unmodified natural states. If they belong to anyone, they belong to the wildlife, superbly adapted to this inimical region: moose, wolf, wolverine, Dall sheep, mountain caribou, beaver, and grizzly bear. While just three in our party, including our part-time male model guide Bart, who was making his first descent, we were planning to catch up with four others—two brothers, Peter and Paul; Erik's dad, John; and master guide Tim, at age twenty-two a veteran of many northern river trips. Tim also had duct tape, which can patch almost any hole in a canoe. Because of schedule conflicts, they had launched the day previous, but in our current condition, the prospects of catching up didn't look good.

To get to our river we first flew commercially to the oil pipeline community of Norman Wells on the Mackenzie River. From there we boarded a Swiss-made Pilatus PC-6 Porter, a STOL (short takeoff and landing) floatplane, often called the

Un-canoeing the Seal River, Manitoba, Canada. PAMELA ROBERSON

"Jeep of the air." The high-winged, angular black and yellow Porter took us farther north and east into an intermontane basin in the Mackenzie Range, over a spot of water that looked like a human eye brooding. It seemed to mirror the soul of the landscape. We splashed down on Willowhandle Lake, at about four-thousand-foot elevation. The air is usually the first sign you are someplace different . . . but here, as we stepped off the pontoons, it was the light . . . soft, diffuse, and intense all at once. The air, too, made its point . . . it was autumn cold, and I looked to the south for a piece of last warmth before the sun made its last horseshoe pass around the margins of the sky.

We took off, sliding across the glass-like lake, all silent except for the periodic calls of loons echoing across the canyon and the swish of water as it broke across the hull. At the far end, we hoisted the canoes and kits on our heads and backs, began a mile-long portage along a faint track littered with fresh grizzly tracks, and camped at a creek called Push-Me-Pull-You. As we turned our canoe over to become our makeshift dinner table, I saw the bottom scored with a matrix of scratches and dents, the scars from a season in tough waters.

The next day, we loaded the boats and proceeded to push and pull them down a water passage not much bigger than a garden hose rivulet. It was backbreaking work, in stinging-cold water, that lasted all morning. Eventually, the trickle conflued with the Blackfeather, and there was at last the thrill of a live vessel beneath us riding high over brawling water . . . until the boat began to crankle as though drunk, and our misadventures began.

Now, as we bailed the last gallons from the bilge, we assessed our predicament. "Maybe we could tap some sap from the spruce trees and use it to patch the boat," Erik wondered. I loved the idea and suggested we camp and try to fix the canoe, bears be damned. But it would probably take a full day to make such a repair, which would cut the chances of catching up with our group to near impossible. Erik insisted we make as much distance as possible during daylight and then explore the options. A part of me was drawn to the notion of trying to negotiate through this wilderness on our own, on a mission of survival, no itinerary, no planned meals, no accoutrements to weigh down the soul . . . just a clear, present reason for going forward, for being. But I knew Erik held out hope for meeting his dad and the others, and it was the right thing to do.

We relaunched, and the clouds covered us like a cork. It started to rain. I looked around. In the way that beach stones are more colorful when wet, the rain brought out the colors of the land, and for a minute I was entranced. The limestones and dolomites were buff and cinnamon; the shales a shiny black; the siltstones green; the sandstone maroon. Above, a golden eagle whooshed like a prehistoric bird. Then I plunged back into the reality pudding . . . the canoe was full again, rolling like a three-ton log, nearly capsizing at every turn. We stopped and bailed, paddled for fifteen minutes, and then rinsed and repeated again and again. The wind was whipping the rain around like wet string. It was so cold my whole body was shivering, and whenever a shot of water met my face it punched my breath away. Then, just as I found myself surveying the cliffs for an exit trek, we turned a corner and the Blackfeather made its final adjustments, like a settling stomach, and merged into the murky waters of the Mountain River . . . there, across the channel, was an orange and white tarp, rigged like a sail, with men milling about beneath . . . our rendezvous, our Deliverance. My feelings were mixed. . . . It would be exciting to be with fellow adventurers, and to get to know Erik's dad; and it would be a comfort to be with an expert guide who knew the river and had all the tools to make the rest of the trip ideal. But for half a day, as Erik and I made our way with our leaky red canoe down a river of rapine lightening, there was a sensation, an alertness, a primal freedom that comes with reducing existence to its core in the unavailing wilderness, challenging it on its own terms, and being a bit scared. It was sublime. Looking back at the needles of light flashing off the Blackfeather, I knew that we were leaving the uninvited guest of fear behind. In a 1757 essay, "Of the Sublime and Beautiful," Edmund Burke argued that the sublime began with a proper sense of dread; only terror "is a source of the sublime; that is, it is productive of the strongest emotion which the mind is capable of feeling." And even though each final stroke of the day was dissipating to shining ether the solid angularity of our earlier predicament, I locked it to memory and let a wave of joy wash over me. And I patted our canoe on its cheek . . . it had such a lovely place to run, and all downhill.

CHAPTER 48

OUTWARD BOUND, MSNBC, *SLATE*, MSN, AND YAHOO

It is not down in any map; true places never are.
—Herman Melville

In 2001 the head-hunting firm Spencer Stuart recruited me to be the president of Outward Bound, based in Garrison, New York. I was going through a divorce, and my future ex proposed that if I took the job, she would move nearby with our seven-year-old son, Walker, so we could raise him together. With much reluctance I gave notice to Expedia and headed east, settling into the Outward Bound mansion on the Hudson River. Much of my job was lobbying for donations from private equity, hedge-fund managers and bankers based in Manhattan, and one Monday in September I was touring for an apartment to rent in the financial district to eliminate the long train commute. The next day was 9/11, and it spooked Pamela, who had been house hunting in Garrison. She threw her belongings into our Land Rover, grabbed Walker, and announced she was driving back to Redmond. From that point on my heart was not in the job, and I terribly missed my seven-year-old son on the other side of the country. After some attempts at cross-country commutes to spend time with Walker on weekends, it was evident to me the arrangement would not work. So I gave notice and headed back west, where Scott Moore, now a senior executive at Microsoft, welcomed me back in the fold and gave me the support to launch digital travel products for MSNBC.com, MSN, and *Slate*.

Scott was then recruited to head up the media division at Yahoo based in Santa Monica, and he asked me to join and create a product that would celebrate the transformational power of adventure travel. I made the move and launched Richard Bangs' Adventures with Purpose on Yahoo in which we traveled the world to seek out and communicate local solutions to universal issues.

Nagaland with Richard on the left and Avinash Kohli, the godfather of adventure travel in India, on the right. LAURA HUBBER

Peter Greenberg, travel editor for NBC's *The Today Show* and longtime travel guru, decided to throw a welcome party for my move to Southern California. At the soiree at his home in Sherman Oaks (appointed with furnishings acquired from many of the great hotels of the world), I met the editor in chief of his newsletter, Laura Hubber, who had lingered beyond business hours because she heard there would be free food. My divorce from Pamela Roberson had been finalized, and it turned out Laura had just left a relationship. I asked her out and learned she was a Harvard-educated reporter for the BBC World Service, and an audacious traveler, having trekked through Myanmar, Bosnia, Afghanistan, Kurdistan, Russia, and other dark and magical places. After a courtship, she moved in with me, we had a son, Jasper, and married. And she became a television producer.

The Yahoo exercise did not go unnoticed, and after a couple years in the digital space I was approached by the producer of the original Rick Steves series and asked if I would take the concept of Purpose Adventures to PBS. I agreed and spent the next few years hosting and producing *Richard Bangs' Adventures with Purpose* on public television, with Laura as co-producer. Together we explored the hidden keys in Egypt, New Zealand, Switzerland, Morocco, Norway, Costa Rica, Greece, Hong Kong, Macau, Guangdong, Peru, Chile, Brazil, Ecuador, Assam, Nagaland, and more. In Egypt the television special was *Quest for the Lord of the Nile*, a deep dive into the backstory of Sobek, the crocodile god after whom I had named our adventure travel company. Along the way we picked up not a few awards, and two Emmys.

Shooting the PBS special *Adventures with Purpose, Quest for the Lord of the Nile.*
LAURA HUBBER

As much as I enjoyed creating media that hopefully influenced its audience, I was hankering for another exploratory, and the chance to design a new adventure for MT Sobek. I had heard the Fish River Canyon in Namibia called the Grand Canyon of Africa, though it was clearly not as deep as the Blue Nile or Tekeze. Nonetheless, I could find no account of anybody floating the Fish River, so decided I should scout the possibilities. I called my friend Pasquale Scaturro, who led the Everest expedition that put the blind climber, Erik Weihenmayer, on top, and he, always hungry for new adventure, and I joined forces. Together we recruited nine friends, including Peggy Dulany (née Rockefeller, daughter of David Rockefeller), and headed to Africa.

CHAPTER 49

NAMIBIA, CLOUDS IN THE CANYON

From a certain point onward there is no longer any turning back. That is the point that must be reached.

—Kafka

The Fish River runs only a few weeks a year, in the Namibian summer during the short rainy season. The canyon is ninety-nine miles long and seventeen miles wide. We were attempting this reconnaissance during the rainy season, when there are occasional killer flash floods and the temperate soars to 120 degrees. An email from a South African outfitter warned: "During the summer months and the rains it is lethal to get trapped in the canyon. The river can (and often does) go totally berserk and there is no way out of the canyon for more than 60 miles. I've been crazy (so everyone tells me . . .) for more years than I care to remember, and it scares the bejesus outta me just to think about it!" A thirty-two-year-old Frenchman, Francois Roger, tried to hike the canyon a year ago January, fell and broke his leg, and fried to death in the heat.

The caveats set my blood racing. There was something vitally appealing about braving an interdict.

In the jigsaw puzzle that is Africa, Namibia is the piece that got left behind. The barren state, larger than Texas, lies north of South Africa's western border, and most of its eastern edge abuts Botswana. Like Papua New Guinea, Namibia was a German colony until the end of the First World War, when the League of Nations entrusted South West Africa, as it was then known, to South Africa as a mandated territory. The country gained independence in 1990 yet remains one of the least-explored domains on the continent.

With Pasquale and friends, we made our way to Windhoek, the mile-high period piece of a capital awash in arbors of bougainvillea, sprawled in the shadow of the Eros Mountains. At the shiny Windhoek Country Club & Casino, our palace for a single night in the city, the cobwebs of the kaiser's colonial presence had long blown away, and ample glasses of single malt blew away ours.

In the morning we wheeled south into the vast, rocky ocean that is the Namibian desert, an endless retreat of buttes and ravines, ridges and terraced escarpments, the compacted age lines of the earth as deep and hard and revealing as the dark weather-carved face of an aged German miner. We trundled south beyond the Tropic of Capricorn, south past running ostriches, baboons, and goshawks, down past flat-topped acacias and euphorbias with stems vivid as trails of fireworks. The bare, rocky bones of the earth showed through the road-edge soil. In the distance sharp crests of rock rose above the surface like dorsal fins of giant fish. For hours, the road cleaved an arrow path across raw territory, among the emptiest on Earth. The land felt drained of life—cracked and brittle, like a piece of old leather. A landscape, this was, cruelly lacking in sentiment.

Our host was Louis Fourie, a former South African wine farmer of corybantic energy and sun-pinched eyes who had a dream when he was fourteen years old to own land where he could not see the borders. Prodigal with his plans, he purchased thirty-six thousand acres, including the upper Fish River Canyon, for a song some nine years before. He had fashioned a modest lodge, which served as our base camp. The plan was to spend a few days hiking the upper canyon on Louie's land and then do a trek into the main canyon in the national park, and then a couple flyovers for aerial recces. Our timing seemed spot on, as until a few days before all the canyon had seen were what Louis calls "bankruptcy clouds," the high wispy, rainless streaks that cause a waiting farmer to go under. But by the time we boarded the plane stateside, it had started to rain, the first water in the canyon in ten months. "The river floods this time of year," Louis warned. "It can get up to 250,000 cubic feet per second." This seemed a bit of a stretch, as that would be more than twenty times the flow of the Colorado through the Grand Canyon, which drains the western slopes of the snow-coated Rockies. There was no snow in Namibia. He also said we could drink the water untreated, but it seemed he was traducing the canyon, and none of us took his word on that.

Our tires crackled into Louie's hardscrabble oasis midafternoon, a former farmhouse his wife, Riette, had decorated with her own artwork, heirlooms, and cozy appointments, a green salad in a brown bowl of tabescent cliffs and tors. We started to pack for our first foray into the canyon the next day. Our team included *Outside* magazine editor at large Tim Cahill; Dr. Seth Berkley, president of the International AIDS Vaccine Initiative; Peggy Dulany, chair of the poverty-fighting institute Synergos; Lisa Conte, CEO of Shaman Pharmaceuticals; and several other rogues and scalawags. Louis's garrulous mother, Gerty, flew up from South Africa to be our cook, and she grilled up tasty servings of klipspringer and gemsbok, which we washed down with Windhoek lagers, supposedly brewed to German purity rules. As the sun fired a gorgeous sunset against an oxide-red cliff, we took to swimming in a pond fresh from the rains. Then we sat on the porch talking and sipping fifteen-year-old GlenDronach whiskey. At one point a giant scorpion, looking like the creature in *Alien*, scuttled across the floorboards, and Riette jumped on the table and screeched. It was a wind scorpion. "Lots more of those in the canyon," Louie spoke gently in a tone of obscure reproof.

That night the gibbous moon poured into the bowers a flood of violent light. A hard time I had sleeping.

It was Sunday morning, and the sun shot up and decanted a vast, hard light. We decided to do a shakedown hike, an eleven-mile tramp in which we would drop into an unnamed fissure, climb out the other side, and then descend into the Lion River Gorge, which disembogues into the Fish River Canyon. We would then hike downstream several miles to the first-night camp, accessible with a four-wheel-drive vehicle, and Louis would arrange to have our tents and bags trucked around, along with iced drinks, steaks, tiki lamps, plastic chairs, and a box of Cuban cigars. All we would need for the day would be water and a day pack. Nonetheless, I stuffed my Osprey day pack with extra shirts, shorts, socks and shoes, snacks, rainwear, my knife, matches, three Nalgene water bottles, iodine tablets, sunscreen, bandanas, a medical kit, a compass, a whistle, two flashlights, extra batteries, pens, a journal, and a book on desert survival.

"You taking the sat phone?" I called to Pasquale as we loaded into the trucks, referring to the Inmarsat mini-M satellite telephone Pasquale brought for emergencies. "Nah . . . it's just a day hike. I'll have it shipped around to camp."

"Makes sense," I agreed. It was heavy, and this was just the warm-up, a chance to test our hiking boots; to acclimatize to the heat, and to set our paces for the next several days. We would not even need our 1:50,000 topo maps or GPSs.

Louis decided to manage the moving of our gear to camp, so Riette volunteered to be our guide, though she had never done the hike. Nonetheless, she instilled confidence just with her attire . . . while we were decked out in candy-colored REI wear and brand-new Leki poles, she wore a tennis suit and sneakers, as though this was a stroll to the courts. And she bobbed down the trail, not so much hiking as sailing.

The hike began simply, down a mountain zebra path into a cut in the crust of the desert. Mud crisped into a lattice of curved flakes crunched under my feet. The landscape was dotted with quiver trees, weird aloes that look like hangovers from a Dr. Seuss book. The Bushmen used their hollow branches to hold arrows. I stayed with Riette in the front, who described some of the plants and rocks as we tripped into a canyon blindingly bright and untarnished by time. We saw klipspringers, the tiny-horned wraiths that make silent, serpentine leaps along the blistered cliffs. We saw heart-shaped leopard paw prints; dark beads round as pearls, the scat of a kudu; and the dried carcass of a rock dassie. We hied past looney bushes, succulents, and desert annuals, blooming after the rains. A pair of green parrots, local love birds, flitted across a frowning canyon wall. Then we ascended the other side and gained the shadows of a wall, where we stooped on pieces of shale and gulped water and chewed springbok jerky, which though tasty sat like rubber in my belly. Already we were feeling the heat, and we lingered longer than we should have. Across from us a kestrel rose from a lookout rock and wheeled with motionless wings ever higher and higher on the thermals.

We climbed out of the small canyon and worked our way across a wind-scored plateau dotted with daisies and a more delicate, butter-yellow flower crouching low to the ground. There were golden blazes of another flower, glaring in the sun like an exotic starfish. Delicate pink blooms nodded from wispy stems, and blue wildflowers studded the ground like discarded sapphires. If not so hot, this would be a lovely place.

Then we began our plunge down a Precambrian staircase, a flight of a billion years or so, down the stratigraphy of sedimentary, metamorphic, and igneous rock, to the Lion River. In the mists of geological time, a seabed was lifted miles above the level of the ocean and weathered into ranges of table mountains. Then some five hundred million years ago, a fault opened. Widened by glaciation and altered by more faults and wind erosion, canyons within canyons were formed until, fifty million years ago, a river began to flow.

The canyon was steep and narrow, and the rocks loose. Some stones were sharp, others slanted off into slabs, still others had been scalloped by flood-borne pebbles into smooth potholes slippery as ice. "What do we do if it flash floods?" Lisa asked. "We'll have time," I offered, remembering flash floods down tributaries of the Grand Canyon when I was a river guide. "There is warning . . . it sounds like a freight train coming. Then we head for high ground," and we all descried the steep walls to map a route upward.

The experience of our group ranged wide, from Everest vet to outdoor tyro. Shannon Rutherford, an elegant glass of fashion who lived in Las Vegas, had never been camping, never gone on a multiday hike. But when several times offered the chance to back out of the adventure, she insisted she wanted to give it a go. And a trooper she was. But by midday she wasn't feeling well and stopped to vomit. Jim Laurel, the photographer, turned his ankle on some wobbly rocks and was limping a bit. Russ Sach developed a rash. When we all pulled off our boots to jump into a limestone pool to cool off, about half the feet were angry with blisters.

After the dip I felt energized and found myself in the front of the pack with Riette and Peggy and a couple others. We crossed a layer of red-brown quartzite, intersected the Lion River, and began to make our way down towards the Fish, when suddenly we heard the bright blade of Russ's voice as he raced towards us. "Hold up! Hold up! Seth broke his ankle!"

At first I thought Russ was joking, but his tone was too severe. So I turned to Riette, exchanged glances, and then took off running back up the trail with a couple others. But I hadn't been watching too closely on the way down, and I came to an intersection of two canyons and couldn't remember which one we descended. I yelled. My voice echoed up the canyons, but nothing returned. I called a few more times and finally heard Pasquale's voice up the right canyon: "We're up here."

We scrabbled up the scree and came to a sandstone shelf. There sprawled Seth, his shirt stained with tramlines of sweat. Tim Cahill was crouched over his left foot, firmly holding it in place. Seth described his fall, wherein he stepped off a ledge, twisting his right ankle, and then fell hard over onto his left, which made a shattering sound. His left foot was turned in a ninety-degree angle dangling with no support on the medial side, likely a multiple fracture with torn ligaments. He had called to Tim, hiking a few paces in front. Following instructions from Seth, Tim held the twisted foot in a viselike grip, and Seth turned to reset it.

Hot snakes of pain ran around Seth's legs. He refused painkillers, citing the increased possibility of shock and wanting to keep a clear head. We had a SAM splint, or pocket cast, and Pasquale and Dan Kohn formed it to the bottom of his leg ankle, and foot . . . but Seth's ankle needed side support. We looked around for something flat . . . a branch, a stone . . . but could find nothing. Then Tim Cahill did something beyond the ken for a journalist . . . he pulled out his two elongated notepads, just the right size, and offered them . . . even though they had his thoughts and scribblings of the last few days, the currency of his livelihood, he sacrificed them for the sake of Seth.

With his left ankle stabilized, we had to get Seth out of the canyon. The sat phone was at camp, so we had to try to carry the 200-pound man out. We couldn't go back up the canyon—it would be too hard to lift him—so that left downward, and it was another five miles or so to camp. Pasquale, the Everest climber, the strongest member of our team, was the primary carrier, with Seth's right arm slung over his shoulder, while three others switched turns with his left arm as we tried to work Seth down the canyon. It was slow going, as his other ankle was also injured, and he couldn't manage much weight on it before unbearable pain fired through.

Slowly, slowly we limped down the widening canyon. We tried various ways to carry him . . . the lifeguard carry; the fireman's carry; hoisting by his belt . . . nothing worked for more than a few yards at a time. And it was now midafternoon, the sun at its zenith, the temperature more than one hundred degrees. The entire sky was like a metal dome grown white with heat. "It may be hot, but at least it's steep," Pasquale quipped in his signature mode of positive pessimism.

Seth's rush of adrenaline in the aftermath was gone, and he was hanging like a rag doll. It was very hard to carry him more than a few feet at a time without respite. So we stopped beneath a camel thorn tree with a top like iron filings drawn skywards. Its branches, more gray than green, shined with a metallic glister and gave little shade. I put my day pack under Seth's neck as a pillow, and we propped his leg on another. It was clear we couldn't carry him all the way out in a timely fashion; it would take days at this rate. "I've got a plan," Pasquale offered. "We leave him here for ten days until he's 110 pounds, then we come back and carry him out." It was exactly the type of irreverent comment Seth needed, and he smiled for the first time in more than an hour.

We looked around to see if we could fashion a stretcher from tree branches and our packs, but the insect-like vegetation wasn't sturdy enough for poles. The sun was merciless and personal, staring like a snake's eye. We were on the edge of the muddy, fulvous Lion River, hot as tea, and were running through drinking water almost as fast as we could filter it. We needed a solution, and quickly.

Lisa Conte, a marathon runner, volunteered to jog to camp and fetch the sat phone . . . five miles each way over ground as inhospitable as the moon, three hours at best in the poisonous heat. The exercise had the potential to feed oxygen to the firestorm of the accident with yet another. But when Seth said he thought he had just a couple hours before gangrene might set in, a strong light burned behind Lisa's eyes. Nobody else in the group could run as fast as Lisa. I give her the go-ahead. . . . We needed to try something. As she took off, a troop of baboons barked and a flock of Egyptian geese flapped up the canyon, as though alarmed by the craziness of the hothouse run.

The air was hot, dry, breathless. The canyon walls, smooth as monument stone, had the washed-out glare of too much heat trapped in too little space. Seth lay in the scant shade of the thorn tree and fell into an eschatological funk. "I might lose my leg. I could die here," he mumbled aloud. Then he held his breath, as though the least movement might snap the thread of his being.

At 4:00 p.m. I looked up canyon and followed the contours lacking in any curves or cambers. Something waved into view: a desert mirage, the likeness of something jinking towards us, like a klipspringer. I watched transfixed as the image grew from a blur to something with features . . . it was Louis, carrying a black bag . . . the sat phone. Not far behind was his assistant, Peter Brandt from the tribe of Nama, carrying fence posts, rope, and a tarp to fashion a stretcher.

As it turned out Peggy, Riette, and Chris Haines had continued to camp, and Chris remembered the sat phone, dug it out of a pack, and gave it to Louis. Louis knew the fastest way to the bottom of the Lion River was from the rim, so he picked up Peter, had Riette drive to the rim, and he and Peter hiked down.

Now we had options. Pasquale, Louis, and I unpacked the sat phone and started climbing up the cliffs, up towards the canyon swifts, to find a clear view of the Atlantic satellite, while Dan and the others put together a stretcher with Peter's materials.

Phoning a rescue helicopter from the Fish River Canyon on a Sunday evening was no easy task. It took an hour just to lock into the satellite, and then Louis tried calling various friends and neighbors who might find the number of a medevac service in Windhoek. Nobody could. We tried calling friends and relatives in the United States. . . . Pasquale called his wife and had her search his computer, to no avail. I called the operator and got a reedy woman's voice in London. "We're in Namibia and have an emergency." "I never heard of Namibia," she replied and hung up.

As we were making phone calls, we watched the battery indicator bars reduce, and we watched the silent movie of the team below attempting to use the stretcher.

They carefully moved Seth onto the makeshift gurney and lifted him up ... but they moved like a lumpy, viscous liquid. They struggled to carry him over the rocks for a few yards and then stopped and rested. A couple times they almost spilled him. Then they gave up and looked up to us as though seeking answers nobody had. At one point Shannon moved to the base of our scarp and started prancing around with her hands curled down, performing curvets with one leg. "Let's get horses," she caterwauled. Pasquale and I turned to Louis, and he shook his head no. "There are no horses nearby," he yelled down the cliff. But Shannon dismissed this as tosh and stomped off. Tempers were running high, as they often do with deracinated plans. The fading sun was turning the canyon walls blue-black, menacing, and separate. Pasquale headed down the hill to tell the group to head to camp, to race the darkness. In the last light I watched a fish eagle float down the canyon without moving its wings, looking for a last snack.

The sat phone battery died. We slipped in the spare. Seth had given me Patty Stonesifer's cell, so I called her, and while on hold she called Bill Gates, who said he could send his private jet and would await further instructions. That would take too long, I replied. Louis connected with a neighbor who found the number of a helicopter pilot in Windhoek, and we dialed through. He said he would try to find a chopper, and that we should get back to him with our coordinates. But our GPSs had been sent around to camp. We described our location ... five miles up from the confluence with the Fish River. That wasn't good enough, he said, as it would be a three-hour flight from Windhoek, and it would be dark soon. The pilot said he might try a midnight rescue but would prefer the coordinates before an attempt. Louis said he would get back. The second battery was almost dead, probably enough for one more call. Louis decided to call his mom and ask her to find the coordinates on a map and then call the pilot. But as soon as he got Gerty on the phone, she started to chatter, dominating the conversation. "Shut up, Mom, and listen," Louis yelled into the phone ... but it went dead.

It had gone almost dark, and the river below ran copper, like an ember alone on the hearth. It was hard to pick our way down the talus to where Seth lay waiting in a heat-drugged stupor on his abandoned stretcher. Tim Cahill, Jim, and Pasquale stayed behind while the rest of the group headed for camp. Even though the shutters of the day were nearly closed, Louis volunteered to head down the canyon, as he knew the way and could then take a vehicle to his lodge, where he could use a landline to coordinate ... if he were lucky, he would arrive by midnight.

Louis borrowed a pair of socks from Pasquale and struck out into the night. Letting Louis go was like throwing away the compass, an act of shared self-marooning. We were on our own now, five Americans and our day packs in the pit of an African canyon, distant and unconnected from the world.

We figured we would make a series of campfires and use our flashlights to wave in the helicopter if it made the midnight run. Tim, Pasquale, and Jim picked through their packs to look for matches but couldn't find any. Not to worry, as I had a stash in my pack. But when I went to fetch my pack, it was nowhere to be found. I retraced my route back up the canyon to where Seth was lying using my pack as a pillow, but there was no sign. Somehow the group hiking to camp must have picked up my pack, leaving me with nothing but the shorts and shirt I was wearing. Another layer gone.

We moved Seth to a level spot in the lee of a large granite rock far up from the river, near a cluster of sacred datura. Since we couldn't make a fire, we spread out on the sand and watched the stars and talked. I recounted a Danish Dogme film recently seen, *The King Is Alive*, with Jennifer Jason Leigh, in which a group of tourists gets lost in the Namibian desert and decides to put on a performance of King Lear to distract from their fates. Pasquale regaled with stories of his White House visit after climbing Everest. Down by the river the frogs started to sing, and Seth moved into a remarkably good mood, helped in part by the two-milligram tablets of Dilaudid he finally swallowed. He told brittle jokes and then pondered his own catalogue raisonné, his life's meshings and unmeshings. Fireflies spun about, and every now and then I lifted my head to see if one of the bugs was really an approaching rescue light. About 11:00 p.m. we stopped talking. Jim next to me was snoring. I curled up in a snail circle and watched the silver pinpoints of the Southern Cross.

An owl swooped over our makeshift camp, opening and closing wings as a flower in bloom. Then a dry, warm wind began to scuffle up the canyon. At first it was just a breeze, and its night smells seemed to wash us clean. But it grew and I could feel the sting of grains on my cheeks. It began to blow away the stars, lightning flashed in the distance, and there was that indefinable smell of tension that precedes rain. I stood up, gritted my teeth. "A storm's coming. No helicopter tonight."

I checked on Seth, shone the flashlight on his face, and he looked scared. He had a prison pallor and a web of hairline cracks around his eyes. "What about a flash flood?" he asked. "Nah, not here . . . canyon too wide," I lied. Then I looked about for a flat spot up the sheer walls where we might reposition Seth . . . there was nothing.

The unit of exchange here was a full quart of water, and we were low, so I stepped down to the bank of the river and pumped filtered water into all the bottles and then went back and distributed them to the bodies lying in the sand. Then I noticed a series of caves just above our roost and, borrowing a flashlight, stepped up to check them out. They were tiny, tortured holes, with flinty, sharp-edged rocks as the floor, littered with rat turds. These were probably dens of scorpions, spiders, snakes, blister beetles, and other toxic creatures that have pushed the envelope of adaptability, but they were also shelters from the hostile wind, and a couple were just big enough to squeeze into.

So back I went, checked the tarp that was rolled around Seth, and announced I was retiring to the cave to weather the storm. It was kicking into high gear, and sand was racing along the black earth like rapids, spraying us like BBs, blasting a layer off my skin. "I've got sand up my urethra," Seth yelled. Tim Cahill sacrificed his space blanket to Seth and wandered up to the cave next to mine. Jim sat up against a rock next to Seth and covered himself in two large Glad bags, one up to his waist, the other over his head and shoulders.

I bent into my cave like a street artist folding into a box. Pasquale found an upper entrance and twisted in above my head. Then the skies opened; the rain came down hard. Lightning flashed; thunder rolled. The wind began to make a singular, animal-like howl, and the rain was so loud it sounded like a freight train coming. "No," I said to myself. "It can't flash flood here. . . . Or could it?"

"Dude," Pasquale muttered. But he was talking in his sleep.

I had a clear view of Seth where I was crotched in the cave, and the flashing light made his wrapped form look like a catafalque beneath the gray monument rock. I waited until there was a lull in the rain and then unfolded myself, borrowed Pasquale's flashlight, and ventured out into the sand-laden wind to check on Seth. "You okay?"

"Are you kidding?" he said in a feeble voice, grinding sand between his teeth. "Two broken ankles, sandstorms, windstorms, lightning, thunder, rain, flash floods. What's next, locusts?"

I laughed into the talons of the wind and stumbled down to the river to see if my flash flood nightmare might be coming true. . . . But no, the river had barely changed. I breathed a sigh and headed back to my cave.

Once curled back inside, lying on a bed of broken rocks, the ceiling an inch from my head, Pasquale's foot on my neck, I drew my feet up into a fetal position and listened to a tree outside creaking like an old rope. At least it was dry, I thought. But then the cave began to leak, and rivulets of rainwater poured onto my neck, thighs, and exposed legs. Another round of lightning and long, trembling salvos of thunder, and I closed my eyes for a minute. The whip of the wind outside seemed to celebrate a dark sensation of having attained a new depth of misery. But then I recognized that despite the travails and Seth's misfortune, I was realizing some sort of explorer's solace. Stripped of all my layers; decocted down to an essence, it felt somehow comfortable and real; life was here, not through a window or on a screen. And there was a sense of being unbounded by geography or history. Not reconciled, not resolved. Not free of fretting about Seth. But free of trappings. And if accessories are a species of idleness, then free of sloth. And then I fell asleep.

In the pale, infected light of daybreak I unfolded from my cave and shook my head as sand scattered out. My mouth and throat felt made of tin. The air, doubly still now after the departure of the storm, was like something drawn up from a well, fresh and cool. I stepped down to Seth's stretcher. His face was cracked, like a crocodile's belly, with dust rings around his eyes. There was no helicopter. No rescue party. "That was the worst night of my life, bar none," Seth offered, and he had spent a career traveling to hardship posts. "You didn't have it so bad," Pasquale quipped. "My cave was so small I had to go outside to change my mind," and Seth managed a smile.

"What do we do now?" Seth asked, his voice sounding small in the immense morning air. "I don't know if I can take another day of this heat."

"We wait. Someone will come soon." Already I felt the heat on the back of my neck.

Minutes later we looked across the river to see some sort of mechanical monster working its way down a mesa. With binoculars we saw it was Louis's Unimog, a relic of the South African border war. It ground to a stop several hundred feet up the canyon; Louis hopped out and sprinted on down to the river and then crossed over to us. "Where's the chopper?" I asked. "I don't know. Never made it back to the lodge last night. I just slept a bit, grabbed the truck at camp, and worked my way here."

An hour later a black cormorant near our camp started into the sullen sky. Then suddenly a Bell Jet helicopter whooshed up the canyon. Louis started to cry. But it continued up-canyon, apparently missing our waving red jackets and space blanket. Around a bend it vanished. The canyon filled with a roar of nothingness. Did the pilot give up on us? We waited three minutes; five; ten; and began to vex. The desert seemed to be holding its breath. But then a sound split the silence into fragments: a distinctive *whop, whop, whop* poured down the gorge. After a couple passes the helicopter made a landing, almost twenty hours since the accident. Eddie, a medic wearing a flight suit stitched with a logo that read "Nam Power," hopped out, hustled to Seth, and took control with seigneurial assertion. He pulled out an aluminum splint and, to the great relief of Tim Cahill, replaced the notebooks that had supported the left ankle. Minutes later we were saying goodbye, and the chopper lifted from Seth's battlefield to the meadows of some hospital. Then Lisa and Peggy showed up, having hiked down from the rim with food and supplies. And we resumed our hike to camp, where tents and cold beer awaited, putting back the matryoshka dolls, heading back toward whence we came. But for a nano moment we were as real, as honest, as uncluttered and uncomplicated as one can be in the wilderness, and I felt clean and close to my beginnings, and ready to hike.

CHAPTER 50

FIRST INTO LIBYA; FIRST INTO HELL

Desert is simply that: an ecstatic critique of culture, an ecstatic form of disappearance.
—JEAN BAUDRILLARD

I RETURNED TO REDMOND, AND MY FIRST TASK WAS TO CREATE AN INTERACTIVE travel site for MSNBC.com. I also continued to think about how Sobek could remain on the cutting edge of adventure and wanted to see if I could devise another first, the hallmark of the company. Driving to a TED conference in Monterey, I listened as NPR reported the administration was lifting most of its two-decade-long sanctions on Libya, including the travel ban, as a reward for Mu'ammar al-Gadhafi's pledge to scrap his nuclear arms programs and resolve outstanding claims from victims of the 1988 bombing of Pam Am Flight 103 over Lockerbie, Scotland. Since the late 1990s, Gadhafi had been reaching out to the West in an effort to rebrand Libya, Africa's second-largest oil producer after Nigeria, as an economic El Dorado. As I found once reaching an internet connection, however, the United States continued to list Libya as a State Sponsor of Terrorism. So, at that moment there was no tourism to Libya. I thought I would give it a shot.

Over the next weeks I underwent the process of figuring out how to conduct a tour and how to get visas. Twenty years ago, we had worked with a French concern, Hommes et Montagnes, in the Algerian Sahara. So I contacted the trekking company, which had changed owners in the interim, and indeed they were conducting occasional adventure treks in southwestern Libya for French clients and agreed to outfit a camel safari through the Akakus Mountains, though first warning that the temperate season was over. If we insisted on going now, we would be into the Saharan summer, not for the meek. I pushed for going forward, knowing that if we waited until fall, the landscape would already be changing, and boatloads of Americans would be scrambling to the shores of Tripoli.

272

Visas were a different challenge altogether. Belgium was the official intermediary between the United States and Libya, so I tried contacting the Libyan embassy in Brussels. But I could never get through. I had the same experience with Libyan embassies in Ottawa, Paris, and Malta. Finally, I sourced a visa company in London, Horizons UK, which promised delivery. I invited a group of friends, and within a few days we had a full complement of sixteen folks ready to join me for a first foray into Libya. Photos, passports, and visa applications were sent to London, where they were translated into Arabic; plane tickets were procured, and we each went and purchased desert survival gear.

But a week before departure, no visas had been processed. No explanation. The paperwork had supposedly been sent to Tripoli, but approvals had not returned. We wondered if we had a shill amongst us, a spy or unfriendly journalist or someone on a blacklist. But pleas to Tripoli went unanswered.

I scoured the internet, firing entreaties to every Libyan I could find with an email address. (Libya is quite wired; internet cafes abound. One of Gadhafi's favorite words was "virus," as in "Viruses today are much more stronger than cruise missiles.") Then, the day before flying to London, I received a call from Mr. Solieman Abboud, owner of Tripoli-based Sari Travel. He said he was also a customs official in Tripoli and that he indeed could get us into the country. All we had to do was meet his associate, Ms. Naziha Hassanyeh, in London, hand over our passports, and she would make magic.

A few weeks later I was sitting in the Polo Lounge at the Heathrow Radisson with nine intrepid fellow travelers; down from sixteen just a few days ago, with a wait list. There was yet no Libyan People's Bureau (Libyan for embassy) or consulate in Washington, D.C., so to obtain the all-important entry stamp for the Great Socialist People's Libyan Arab Jamahiriya, Americans had to apply through an overseas mission. After failing in other European capitals, we settled on London, where a visa expediter promised delivery for an upfront fee of $150 each. But a week after the promised authorizations, we had nothing. Our nonchangeable, nonrefundable tickets from London to Tripoli had a departure fourteen hours past. We were pinning final hopes on a heteroclite Lebanese woman we met just yesterday. She took our passports early in the morning and flew to Bonn, where through some mysterious connections on a weekend she claimed she would return with visas duly rendered that evening. She promised to meet us at the hotel at 8:00 p.m. It was 8:45. If she didn't show, we would turn around and go home, though we'd have to get temporary passports at the US embassy.

Libya's swath of the Sahara, with its mountains boiled out of the earth and skein of wide wadis, had long been on my wish list, but Billy Carter's little adventure in 1978 ("The only thing I can say is there is a hell of a lot more Arabians than there is Jews" in Libya) and former CIA agent Edwin Wilson's conviction for selling twenty tons of C4 plastic explosive to Gadhafi had put the destination off-limits for Americans.

So those of us willing to roll the dice were at Heathrow sipping G&Ts and happily paying with credit cards, hoping these might be our last such transactions for a fortnight, as Libya enforced a permanent ban on gambling and alcohol and accepted no credit cards. Then around 9:00 p.m., Ms. Naziha proudly sashayed through the door and opened our passports to the pages with blue and red eagle-logoed stamps covered with a round, dark blue seal. We were good to go.

No American carrier was allowed to fly into Libyan airspace, but British Airways had launched a new Airbus A320 service, and we were at the airline counter two hours before the nine o'clock departure Monday morning, where the agent scrutinized our passports and visas. "There is only one country that's harder to get a visa for," the agent said. "America." Then she waved us through, and soon we were Libya-bound.

As we began our descent into Tripoli, the "The White Bride of the Mediterranean," I watched clouds scud over the landscape and saw the runway wet from a morning rain. At the warehouse-like terminal, we funneled in to meet Solieman Abboud, sucking a Rothmans, on the arrival side of Customs and Immigration. He collected our passports and disappeared between a cinema-size poster of Gadhafi in his Aviator Ray-Bans and a sign that said "Partners Not Wage Earners," a bumper-sticker aperçu from Gadhafi's Green Book. A few minutes later, Solieman reappeared and led us past an empty immigration booth, and inside Libya we were at last. I opened my passport once in the bus and noticed the Libyan visa had smeared. I looked closer and noticed it appeared to have been hand-drawn.

We stayed at the spanking, $125 million Corinthian Bab, at the western end of Tripoli's cornice, the only five-star hotel in Libya. With two soaring crescent towers it looked like a Buck Rogers intergalactic version of a hotel, featuring Kenny G Muzak in the elevators, *Buffy* on the room TV. It had all the accoutrements of a resort—heated pools, spas, vast buffets—but the glaring difference was that at the various lobby bars and restaurants we could not order a whiskey or rye, only tea, instant coffee, soft drinks, nonalcoholic beer, and "mocktails."

The hotel was just yards from the Barbary Coast, where freebooters looted commercial ships in the seventeenth and eighteenth centuries. In 1805, Thomas Jefferson sent American marines across the Egyptian desert to this coast, giving rise to the line in the U.S. Marines' anthem, "From the halls of Montezuma to the shores of Tripoli."

We first explored the adjacent medina, and then down a serpentine passage hissing with intrigue, I exchanged US dollars with a gold merchant for dinars, the local currency, derived from denarius, the most common Roman coin. Every few minutes there was a popping sound, like gunfire, and I instinctively looked for a place to duck and hide. But they were just firecrackers, set off by children at play. The Prophet Muhammad's birthday was in a few days, and it's like Chinese New Year in that the streets snap and smoke with fireworks. This was just a preview.

Later we made the ninety-minute bus ride east to Leptis Magna, the ancient port city that kept Rome supplied with slaves for its gladiator arenas, wild animals for circuses, and women for concubinage. Under Lucius Septimius Severus, who ruled the empire from 193 to 211 CE, the three great cities of the Libyan coast—Leptis Magna, Oea (now Tripoli), and Sabratha to the west—rivaled Rome in splendor, architecture, wealth, and decadence. Sacked after the Romans withdrew in the seventh century, Leptis Magna was abandoned and then buried under the sands until the early part of the twentieth century.

We wound along the coast down a wide road financed by petrodollars, first passing rows of Soviet-style apartment buildings, each with an oversized satellite TV dish attached to a window or porch, then orchards of date palms, orange groves, and silver-gray olive trees whose flexed arms looked as though ready to punch passersby. We were stopped a few times at security checkpoints, but once we presented our heavily stamped paperwork, we were nonchalantly waved through. There were no English signs; Gadhafi banned such in 1970, along with all Italians, Jews, and the American Wheelus Air Base, then largest in the world outside of the United States. We saw only one Western logo in the journey: the red-white-and-blue Pepsi swirl, but without a word of English.

At an inconspicuous driveway, we turned in, parked, and filed into the largest and best-preserved Roman ruins outside of Italy, perhaps most remarkable for its absence of hawkers, freelance guides, beggars, and American cruise ship tourists. Leptis Magna lived under the shadow of Carthage until the Romans transformed the modest trading port into a site of imperial magnificence, prodigiously endowing the city with steam baths, forums, theaters, villas, basilicas, lighthouses, markets, marble toilets, triumphal arches, and an amphitheater that could seat twenty thousand folks. Even one colonnaded street, marked by an etched penis, led to the Roman version of the red-light district. As we wandered the cobbled streets and posed by marble monuments, we reveled in the Trumpness of it all.

For dinner we made way to Al Murjan (Red Coral), themed with anchors and sails and an oil of Gadhafi dressed in a white captain's uniform. Between courses of shawarmas and squid, we swilled Beck's nonalcoholic beer and bitters, toasting Solieman for his visa sorcery. We ended with rich espressos, legacies of a colonial misadventure, which began in 1911 when Italy "liberated" Libya from Ottoman rule and ended with the liberators' defeat by the Allied Forces in 1943. During the occupation, almost half the indigenous population was killed, including Gadhafi's grandfather, as Italy attempted to tame its "fourth shore."

We made the long walk back to the hotel after dinner, through the night market, past hundreds of vendors along a crowded Omar al-Mukhtar Street. Outside speakers blared 50 Cent and Sting, and the great garage of Libya was for sale, from Gadhafi watches to little live gazelles to pre-strung polyvinyl chloride Christmas trees. A series of tiny shops were selling foot-high hamburgers, and when a couple meat vendors discovered I was an American, they gave thumbs-up, a far cry from the moment in 1986 after the United States bombed Gadhafi's residence, killing his infant daughter, when he declared it was legal to eat American soldiers since they had been revealed to be animals.

The next morning, in the volant lobby, readying for the airport transfer, we met our lead French guide, Bastien Stieltjes, a ringer for Hank Azaria as Claude in *Along*

Came Polly. Bastien sported sun-streaked hair down to his shoulders, a Hawaiian shirt fashionably ripped across the back, and a desert finish from a season guiding in Algeria. But as we learned, this was his first time to Libya. His assistant guide, Ludovic Bousquet, had been to Libya before but never on this itinerary, so indeed this was an exploratory, as nobody had seen this route through the Akakus Massif. We were also joined by Al-Mabrouk Ali-Alzalet, a taciturn shadow from the Department of Security. We were not sure if he was with us to ensure our safety or to spy on us.

On a venerable Libyan Arab Airlines Fokker 27 we swooped southwest, into the Fezzan, Libya's great desert province, down toward the ancient entrepôt of Ghat, near the Algerian border. Ghat (pronounced "rat" by Bastien) was a trading center for the great camel caravans of lore, bringing ivory, gold, salt, and slaves from the sub-Sahara, and rumors were it still trafficked in human contraband. It was a long flight, almost three hours; Libya is larger than Alaska. As we began the descent, I could see the sea of sand out the window, long ridges that butted and intersected and overlapped in complex patterns, a network of ridges and dips, crescents and curls, that from above resembled the whorls of gigantic fingertips. In the distance were the Akakus Mountains, which seemed to have punctured the planet's skin, leaving giant scars; and then there were the wadis, stony gashes snaking into hidden vaults.

At Ghat International, we stepped off the plane into the Saharan sun. It was not as hot as anticipated, and a few in our group commented they could easily handle this temperature. To the south we saw the palisades of blue, blunt mountains, our destination. Certainly, it would be cooler inside their rocky chambers.

In Ghat, a desultory, dusty way station, we paused for a brief wander of its labyrinthine medina, where in a mud-and-dung alcove souk merchants were hawking heavy filigreed silver jewelry, desert tapestries with designs of grizzly bears and poker-playing dogs, and small flasks of saccharine-flowered fragrances in a place where perfume is easier to come by than a shower. I bought a pair of lightweight Tuareg pantaloon-type pants with brocaded hems (*akerbai*), thinking these must be the right desert attire, even if they were a tad on the small side.

At the Anay campsite just out of town, we slipped under a tent and sat cross-legged on Berber rugs. We sipped mint tea from shooter glasses and munched on olives, dates, and tuna salad Niçoise, all under the watchful gaze of a watercolored Gadhafi in a camel-hair sash and oversized sunglasses. Here, the Tuareg host handed out long turbans, or *sheshes*, and showed us how to wrap them securely around our heads. Centuries ago, so says lore, the Tuareg tribesmen donned veils to trick enemies into thinking they were women. Today, we were told, the Tuareg women, unlike other Muslims, who generally cover their heads in public, do not wear *sheshes*, though we couldn't confirm, as we never saw any local women. The other, more believable theory was that the *shesh* humidifies the mouth and nose in the dry desert air and filters blowing sand. Then we tucked into four Toyota Land Cruisers, one with Barbary sheep horns strapped to the front, two with goatskin bags, called *guerbas*, filled with fresh water hanging from the roof racks, and thumped and hurtled into the heart of the world's biggest desert toward a 120-mile-long basalt maze, the Jebel Akakus. When we reached our first sand dune, a sensually shaped honey-colored ridge, we spilled out and leapt around sand soft as talcum, as though in our first snow. The Tuareg scratched their *sheshes* in amusement.

At the eastern end of a giant crescent-shaped sand dune, in the belly of the Tadhintour Wadi, the Land Cruisers halted and Bastien announced camp, a sand spit called Tan Garaba. The cars would return to Ghat, leaving only camels as our conveyance for the next five days. We were just three miles from the Algerian border, some thirty miles northeast from Djanet, where thirty-two European tourists were kidnapped last year by an Islamic extremist group believed to have ties to al-Qaeda. The camping gear was arranged in a giant U shape, pointing toward Algeria as though a trench against invaders, including the *ghibli*, the fierce blowing sands from the south.

Here we met our Tuareg guides as well as the *adogu*, or leader, Mama Eshtawy, black as a crow with gimlet eyes; Acrwof Adhan, head cameleer with a jiggy personality and a Jeff Bezos laugh; and Kadar, the steadfast cook, quiet as smoke in his *gandoma*, a long robe that swept the ground as he walked.

Four women were on the trip, yet all were faced with a challenge, as there were no trees or bushes near this camp, only the ruffles and flutes of sand dunes, and there

John Canning with Tuaregs in the Libyan desert. RICHARD BANGS

was no toilet tent. Bastien warned the Tuareg were extremely conservative in regard to showing skin, especially arms and legs, and as such we should avoid revealing our casings beyond hands, feet, neck, and face. In the nineteenth century, a young Dutchwoman, Alexine Tinne, exposed a bit too much and had her arm hacked off by one of her Tuareg escorts and was left to bleed to death. So the far slope of a dune marked with a water bottle became the sacred place. Until Mabrouk marched up the dune with his prayer rug to recite his nightly prayers.

We dined on liver wrapped around the suet of a freshly slaughtered goat cooked in its own fat and sipped sugared tea into the night. Water was scarce, so no showers, and we washed our dishes with the fine Saharan sand. The Tuareg gathered round a small campfire and chattered in Tamashek, a language that sounded like the squeaking of bats. Under the moonlight, the adjacent dune looked like sleek suede, the sort of storybook scene Antoine de St. Exupery evoked. My altimeter showed we were at 2,913 feet, and it was still 87 degrees Fahrenheit at 11:00 p.m.

We awoke to the sounds of old men snorting and humphing—our camels had arrived and were grazing some sere scrub a few yards from camp. I walked over to greet our ships. They were very tall, with impossibly long knobby legs and a cavalier look. All were male and hobbled with thick ropes between their front legs. The Tuareg loaded them with all our gear and six hundred liters of water in plastic literjohns, and they took off down a long-vanished watercourse.

We began our trek with a clamber up the 400-foot-high dune, rose-red in the morning light. Mama slipped off his camel-leather sandals and climbed barefoot, moving up the hill like a ghost. For the rest of us it was tough climbing in the deep sand, the opposite of walking on sunshine, more like walking underwater. Each movement of an arm or leg was a ritualistic gesture, like a benediction without a recipient.

First American trek across the Libyan desert. JOHN CANNING

After laboring for half an hour, we edged noses over the sharp crest of the ridge and gazed down into Algeria and then back toward the vermilion cliffs of the Akakus, a tableau of frozen violence through which we were supposed to hike. It was already 90 degrees Fahrenheit at 9:00 a.m. as we descended the sand billow and began our tramp in earnest.

For several hours we trekked, up over the 4,000-foot Aogeraq Pass, while the temperature wheeled to 104 degrees. Not far from here, at Al-Aziziyah in Libya, the highest temperature in the Sahara was recorded, 136 degrees Fahrenheit. Frank Headen, a veteran adventure traveler, picked up pieces of fulgurite, fused particles, like silica glass, formed from lightning striking the sand. I plucked a pottery shard from a footprint. We passed rocks etched with fossils, left over from the shallow sea that lapped the Sahara in the long Tertiary period (65 million to somewhere around 1.6 million years ago). Then in the distance we spied a lone acacia tree in a tongue of sand, our lunch goal. Two camels with saddles wrapped around their ungainly backs had been stepping with us, their wide, padded feet making no sound on the soft sand. Mama used his long staff to halt the camels and offered rides to the group. Cheryl Sulima, a bank analyst for the Federal Reserve, had a swollen eye from a pesky sand particle that blew in, and Frank was suffering from an upset stomach, so they accepted the offer to ride, though the camels protested with sounds like Wookies in heat as they mounted. With saddles creaking, the two-toed animals plodded off, throwing off little puffs of white sand. The camel was not native to these parts. It was introduced from Arabia probably around the third century, long before the Arab invasions, but it quickly became indispensable. In the peak of the Saharan summer, a camel can endure up to five days without drinking anything. A man, other than a Tuareg, can last but one.

Water is necessary in the Sahara, but shade is a miracle. At 1:00 p.m. we staggered into the scant shade of the thorn tree, leaves torn by camel tongues, and collapsed. We were spent and thirsty from this first hike, and we spread out like dead eagles on the mats. John Canning, media Sherpa and photographer, and I unrolled the Brunton flexible solar panels to charge our batteries.

For a couple hours, we rested in the canicular heat, then Bastien asked for volunteers to help dig a path for the camels over the sandy Tafaq Pass. Ann Duncan, a Seattle portfolio manager, and I decided to offer, and off we went with Bastien and Mama to another huge dune that divided two oueds. As we zigzagged up the dune, we used our tin dinner plates to shovel a path the camels could step along. This was hard work in the superheated air, and I had to stop and swig from my Nalgene every few minutes.

On the far side of the pass, we faced an otherworldly panorama of mock Gothic cathedrals, medieval castles, moon mesas, McDonald's arches, and Disneyesque spires of balancing rocks, splashed with red and ochre, all seemingly baked into the landscape. We made our way down to camp, arriving as the sun was finally setting. It had been a tough day, and my one-size-too-small Tuareg pants had been chafing my groin, which now had a painful rash.

After the mats were unrolled, John plugged his laptop into a solar-charged battery and gave a slide show of the day's photography, with a Lenny Kravitz soundtrack, to the Tuareg, who watched the wizardry through the gap in their *sheshes*, dark eyes so wide they seemed to be devouring the future. We supped on lentil soup, couscous, and goat stew, with a dollop of cool Crème Mont Blanc from Bastien's bag poured over dates. We finished the meal, as every repast, with Tuareg champagne—a triple serving of strong green tea boiled over a wood fire, poured from a height to make cappuccino-like foam, then reheated and deliquesced into small glasses. After tea, we laid out our sleeping bags. It was too warm to tuck in, too warm for even a sheet, so I sprawled naked under the Saharan stars and slipped into sleep.

Although he had never been through these mountains, never been to Libya, Bastien consulted with the Tuareg and reported that the day was to be an easy trek, a short hike to Oued Babou, our lunch spot, where we would also camp for the night. Spirits heartened, and we took off after lingering in camp until well after the sun had punched in.

After an hour's trek, we came to our first canvas of prehistoric rock art in situ: a giraffe, a hippo, a bullock, wildlife that prospered in a greener, gentler Sahara, when the climate was kind, before it turned into the arid sandbox it is today. There were some thirteen hundred sites scattered like teardrops through the Akakus, dating back twelve thousand years. It was an astonishing book of hours.

Then out into the hard sun, rambling down a dry streambed to Oued Babou. We dropped into a deflation basin, an oval lowland scoured by constant blowing. We wandered through a forest of "ventifact," rock polished by sand and carved into far-fetched shapes. Now it was really hot: My portable thermometer read 110 degrees Fahrenheit. The heat radiated back from the ground, creating little eddies of convection turbulence. It was like walking on a griddle beneath a heat lamp. We were beginning to wobble. Heinrich Barth, the German explorer who passed through here in the mid-nineteenth century, noted, "It is indeed very remarkable how quickly the strength of a European is broken in these climes." At one point we stumbled up to a rock ledge and took a short rest in the shade. Cheryl's left eye was swollen shut. Frank's shirt was crusty and stained white with what looked like a skin of ice. "I'm saltier than a country ham," Frank said with a grimace. After a few minutes, though, Bastien pushed us back out into the sun, saying we needed to continue.

We were then into midday, and the heat seemed nuclear (the French tested thirteen nuclear devices in the 1960s not far from here). We were not suffering from an overabundance of shade. All talk had dried up. Some were getting low on personal water, and the extra water was with the caravanners, who took a different route. About 1:00 p.m., we crested a ridge and saw another lone acacia in a wadi . . . that must be camp. But Mama said no. We would take a right at the tree and head into a side canyon, perhaps half a mile away. The goal seemed attainable, like a fish shimmering beneath the surface of shallow water. So we tripped across the hyper-arid landscape (Sebhah, at the other edge of the Fezzan, is credited as the most arid place on earth). We marched over a level plain of lag gravel cemented by gypsum deposits and dotted with black slablike stone. It was like skulking through a graveyard. At the head of the canyon, John Canning and I took a respite in the shade of a boulder, and I applied some aloe jelly to my groin, now ablaze in pain. I had to walk like a cowboy to keep from chafing further. Then back into the full power of the sun, and we slouched deeper and deeper into the recondite canyon. My temples felt as though they had been bound with rope pulled tight; my head felt both too big and too brittle, as though it might crack open like an egg in boiling water. Sweat sprang from my face like shower water, but my skin was dry. Finally, about 2:00 p.m., I reeled into camp, utterly exhausted, in an ecstasy of thirst, with most of the group still behind. The camels were already grazing the sparse provender, having arrived on a shortcut earlier. As the last of the team collapsed in the shade of an overhang, there was discontent. "More like a forced march than an adventure," someone grumbled. "Paris–Dakar without the cars," griped another. "Marathon des Sable without water," bellyached one more. After a partial recovery with long pulls of water and a rest, a group meeting was called. Five of the ten Americans announced they would like to abandon the trip and fly back to Tripoli. Cheryl's eye looked worse, redder and puffier, and she seemed delirious from heat exhaustion. The others simply submitted that this was hotter and harder than they had anticipated, and they would prefer to exit than continue to suffer.

I couldn't argue. The Sahara was not a place for the timorous. And I was suffering my own private hell with my rash. So we pulled out the Iridium satellite phone and called in a couple of vehicles that would meet us for lunch the next day, pulling out the coalition of the unwilling. The remaining five would be Frank; Ann Duncan; John Canning, another adventure travel vet; Hugh Westwater; and me.

With lines redrawn in the sand, the afternoon was relaxed. We played a version of desert boccie ball, using gourds as balls, and watched as the Tuareg, puffing on Camel cigarettes donated by Hugh, played their version of checkers (*al-karhat*), using camel pellets as pieces. As we unrolled our sleeping bags, Bastien warned not to camp close to rocks, as scorpions hide in their nooks and crannies during the day and come out at night and will naturally seek out the warmth of a sleeping bag. I ignored his advice and camped in the lee of a boulder, to avoid the spitting sand that was beginning to whip, the lesser of the evening's evils.

CHAPTER 51

LIBYARATED

The desert wears a veil of mystery. Motionless and silent it evokes in us an elusive hint of something unknown, unknowable, about to be revealed. Since the desert does not act, it seems to be waiting—but waiting for what?

—Edward Abbey

I AWOKE TO A BLACK SCARAB ON ONE SIDE OF MY BAG, A PALE LOCUST ON THE other. Footprints of a Rüppell's desert fox and a Dorcas gazelle crisscrossed camp. John's sleeping bag, however, was encircled by the tracks of a legion of scorpions that seemed to soldier to the edge of his bag and then scurry away, perhaps, he conjectured, from the smell. As I stood up bowlegged, my inner thighs were so chafed they bled. I considered applying the cool Crème Mont Blanc as an ointment (it's a dessert topping; it's a salve) but instead elected to abandon my Tuareg pants for a pair of cotton shorts. Others had gone to shorts, and the Tuareg seemed to take no offense. In fact, Ann later revealed that while each of the women had received a marriage proposal, the Tuareg voted my pale, water-rich body the sort of physique they most admired, if only I were a woman.

It was another hot toddle, four hours under a sun hissing like a blowtorch rather than the promised two, to the lunch spot beneath a long rock brow, where the vehicles were to rendezvous. We chewed on Laughing Cow cheese and pâté smuggled in from France by Bastien, our own South Libyan Beach diet. We lounged, did crossword puzzles, read Jon Krakauer, and sang show tunes. Ann knitted a sock. At home, we often wished for a whole afternoon with nothing to do. Now that we had it, most were restless. At 3:00 p.m. I set my thermometer in the sand in the sun just beyond our sanctuary, and when I checked a few minutes later it read 136 degrees Fahrenheit.

Late in the day, two Land Cruisers came roaring over the sand. It was too late to head back to Ghat, a six-hour drive, so they instead ferried those evacuating to the next camp, while the rest of us hiked across a field of black bony rocks, a former lava flow, and then down into a sand gully. We were a small group now, the sun was low, and the mood merry. Acrwof started singing and dancing alongside the swaying camels, occasionally breaking out in cascades of silly laughter. He hardly seemed a descendant of the Tuareg people who massacred Paul Xavier Flatters's French expedition not far from here in 1881.

Camp was in the middle of a wide wadi called Anteburak spotted with scratches of grass. While Bastien rolled a cigarette, the camels rolled around in the sand. When the camels unkneeled and stood back up, they were so covered with Saharan sand they blended into the dun-colored cliffs as to almost be indistinguishable—camelflage. Mama caught a black lizard from a tuft of grass, which he said the Tuareg ate as a cure for hepatitis. He also kicked aside several tufts in his way and challenged us with a Tuareg riddle: What wears out if you don't use it? We were stumped; he grinned and pointed to the ground: a trail. Bastien said these tufts were favorite hangouts for deadly sand vipers, and we should avoid them. But again, the susurrating wind was kicking sand, and I bunked down behind a large grass tuft, which emitted some sort of clacking sound as I drifted off.

After morning tea, hugs and addresses were exchanged, and the group split as half headed back to Ghat, along with Ludovic, to catch a flight back to Tripoli, then home, Libyarated at last. The five remaining started out for the next camp, but after a short way, stoic Frank began to complain about a double pain in his side. He seemed imbalanced and flushed. We put him on a camel, but he was delirious with pain, and Mama walked alongside to make sure he didn't fall off.

We finally made camp, in a beautiful tributary gateway, Tin Talahat, around noon, and we spread Frank out beneath a shady rock balcony. He struggled to his feet several times to slump behind a rock and vomit. I gave him a painkiller, and he

Coaxing our camels over the sand dunes of the Libyan desert. JOHN CANNING

confessed he was convinced a kidney stone was trying to pass. This had happened to him before, once in China, and he knew the feeling too well. I called a US-based medical evacuation service on the Iridium and spoke with a doctor, who confirmed it likely a kidney stone, which is sometimes stimulated by heat and exhaustion. It also could turn deadly. So we called in another extraction vehicle and waited. A black-and-white mula-mula bird flittered by, which Mama said was good luck. The Land Cruiser finally arrived at sunset, too late to return that night. We made a bed for Frank, fed him more painkillers, and hoped for the best.

Frank left at 5:00 a.m. in a Land Cruiser, with Bastien along to assist. Of the original sixteen signed for this trip, four remained, including Ann, who had, to date, two marriage proposals from the Tuareg. We now had no French guides, and none of us spoke Arabic or Tamashek. And Bastien took my satellite phone. We were alone in the Great Nothing, the sea without water, the Libyan Sahara with our Tuareg guides and a dozen camels.

We spent the morning exploring galleries of rock art—the amazing displays of Tin Tagaget, including ostriches, elephants, rhinos, chariots, and even Jennifer Lopez as a stick figure with a big head and giant behind. There may be truth to theories that these ancient artists were depicting visitors from outer space.

As we lumbered back to camp, the wind began to whisk the sand like flour. The sky turned a hazy yellow, blurring the sun. Suddenly sand filled ears and noses, lungs and pores. It gritted teeth, turned eyes the color of fermenting beer. We were in a sandstorm. The dunes were smoking; the wind made a scratchy drumming sound, caused by the piezoelectric properties of crystalline quartz, the same way a needle on a phonograph translates vibrations into sound. The full Sahara seemed to be shifting, migrating. The Tuareg drew their *sheshes* across their faces and cast eyes downward; the camels squatted, backs to the wind, and closed their long-lashed and double-lidded eyes. We climbed into a cave, but it was more of an eddy, and the whole of the Sahara blasted through. We were finally getting, it seemed, our just deserts. All we needed now to complete the experience was a plague of locusts. We finally climbed up the back side of an inselberg, an eroded pillar from the Akakus remnant bin, and found a bit of a reprieve from the storm. There, we played Hearts into twilight, awaiting our own vehicles for the final return to Ghat. At sunset, Hapip Khlil Abulkharim, a radio controller at Ghat International, swung his Land Cruiser into camp. He apologized for arriving so late, saying he took a circuitous route: "This is an open area, a dangerous area. There is a lot of smuggling through this region, arms to Algeria, and people from Niger and Mali." In 2001, a lorry broke down in untracked sand carrying undocumented immigrants from the south. Ninety-six passengers were found dead. "It's a big problem here, so I took the safe route."

—◡—

For six hours we ground toward Ghat in the midst of a *harmattan*, a wind the Tuareg call the Hot Breath of the Desert. Sand beat on the car metal with a sound like heavy rain. It was too hot to close the windows, but with them open it felt like a row of hair dryers pointed at us on full blast. Along with a little teddy bear, a prayer from the Koran asking for safe travel hung from the rearview mirror, and Hapip fingered it throughout our journey. Nevertheless, we had a flat tire, and the spark plugs began to misfire. Finally, the car conked out, and we switched to another and limped into Ghat in the late afternoon. We checked into the flat-roofed Ghat Hotel, an unlovely affair with a gleaming cappuccino machine that belonged in a Paul Bowles bildungsroman. Out back was a mud-walled camel stable, with a very low door, making it difficult for camels to wander out. For a thousand years, these low doors have been called needle's eyes, explaining why it is easier for a camel to go through the eye of a needle than for a rich man to enter the Kingdom of God. We first called to check on Frank and learned he had not one but two kidney stones, both of which passed without incident. We celebrated with potato chips and guava juice. Then after spraying our beds for bugs and kneeling to shower under feeble hoses, we headed down the street to a hookah bar, where we smoked ornate, waist-high *nargilahs*, puffing fruit-flavored tobacco through long flexible hoses, and watched *Arab Idol* on TV until 2:00 a.m.

Back in Tripoli, we were invited to a final dinner hosted by a prominent Libyan businessman, a friend to the Minister of Tourism. We arrived and were ushered into a living room, where a Berber band dressed in black fezzes, red sashes, and white skirts performed a wide dervish-like performance, spinning about the house; leaping on furniture; balancing vases, apples, and bottles on heads; and bending over guests like lap dancers so that dinars could be stuffed into their hats. One band member played an oboe-like *gheeta*, another a drum made of skin stretched over a mortar (a *tende*), a third a lovely sounding flute called a *nay*, and the last a reed and goatskin bagpipe called a *zukra*. The music was called *mriskaawi* and was performed mostly for weddings, and that evening, our host explained, was a marriage of East and West. Then, as a plate of fried camel was passed, to our surprise, our host offered us his version of home-brewed tequila, or *bokha*. This was a very dry country, and we were a bit shocked, wondering if this might be some sort of setup. But the band members were kicking back shot glasses of this juice, as were others at the party, friends of the host. So we gave it try. It tasted like some combination of bad grappa, anise, and arak. But then someone appeared with a couple of bottles of Tunisian wine, and someone else produced a bottle of Beefeaters, and then a bottle of Ballantine's. We paused when our security guy, Mabrouk, walked in . . . certainly he would arrest us kafirs, depraved unbelievers. But he stepped over to the table with the multiplying bottles of alcohol and asked for a sip, confessing he had never tried such. He then proceeded to swizzle back several glasses of wine, then some scotch, then gin . . . then he started mixing wine and whiskey in the same glass. After a time, he was up dancing around the room with the band, a college kid at his first frat party. Finally, we fed him into a taxi and sent him to a hotel, not his family, where he slept off the night.

On our last morning, Solieman Abboud arranged for an interview with the Minister of Tourism. I had written a letter before departing home requesting the interview, and in the letter I outlined my background, saying I had worked as an executive at Microsoft and had founded Sobek. In Tripoli, the letter was translated to Arabic, and apparently some of the language was transposed. As I walked into his ornate offices, His Excellency Ammare Mabrouk Eltayef extended a firm handshake and said, "It is a great honor to meet the founder of Microsoft." I did not disavow him of the notion but listened respectfully as he said he wanted to send the message that Libya was ripe for tourism investment, from hotels to golf courses to beach resorts. He blamed our visa imbroglio on the US government, saying if America had allowed a Libyan embassy (née People's Bureau) in Washington, we would not have had our problems. And he said that the new tourism initiatives came from the top, from the Great Leader Gadhafi himself.

As we passed through customs, I was pulled aside and asked to explain my solar panels to a group of skeptical baggage handlers. I assembled it in the baggage backroom of the terminal and showed diagrams of how it worked, and they finally let it pass. Then, as the last of us filed down the walkway to the plane back to London, there was a beaming Solieman Abboud waiting, wishing us goodbye. "See if you can return the favor," he asked. "I would like to be the first Libyan tourist to America."

CHAPTER 52

FIRST INTO NORTH KOREA

A Dragon rises up from a small stream.
—Korean proverb

Where once I crackled down unrun rivers, and then plumbed new territory in digital media, now it seemed I was turning stones in places George W. Bush described as the "axis of evil."

It had been sixty years since the end of the Korean War, and for most of that time Americans had been prohibited from visiting North Korea by its government. For many years I canvassed any contact I could ferret about securing visitation, but for naught. Until an old friend, Jack Wheeler, who worked in the Reagan White House on basement intelligence matters, found a way in.

I rendezvoused with twenty-three friends in Beijing, and the first indication that we were entering a Twilight Zone was when a plastic bag was circulated at the airport before boarding the Air Koryo flight . . . in it we deposited our cell phones and any books about our destination, as they were not allowed in the DPRK. We were, however, permitted to bring cameras (with lenses less than two hundred millimeters), laptops, Kindles, and iPads, as long as their GPS was inactivated. There was, of course, no public internet access in-country.

On board the Russian-built Tupolev Tu-204, instead of Muzak we were soothed by the national anthem, the newspaper distributed was the *Pyongyang Times* (in English), and on the video monitors were dramatic re-creations of World War II, as well as a tourist video that evoked Disney documentaries from the 1950s. Immigration and customs were easy, faster than most first-world airports, and they did not stamp our passports, so you just have to take my word that we were there.

We were greeted by guides Mr. Lee and Miss Lee (no relation), who ushered us onto a Chinese-made luxury bus called King Long, where we rolled down spotless extra-wide streets by willow trees and tall apartment buildings as ponderous and morose as unabridged dictionaries. We rolled past heroic posters and photos of Kim Il-sung, the country's founding leader, and his son Kim Jong-il, who died in December 2011, leaving third son, Kim Jong-un, in charge. We drove through the Arch of Triumph (larger than the Paris version) and into downtown Pyongyang, the capital. Along the way Mr. Lee shared, in enunciation occasionally untidy, some information . . . the country had twenty-six million people; three million in the capital. It is 80 percent covered by mountains. From 1905 to 1945, the Japanese brutally occupied it. The Korean War (known as the Fatherland Liberation War by the DPRK) lasted from 1950 to 1953, and during that time there were 400,000 people in Pyongyang, and the Americans dropped 400,000 bombs on the city.

We crossed a bridge to an island in the Taedong River and pulled up to the forty-seven-story Yanggakdo International Hotel, with one thousand rooms, a revolving restaurant on top, a lobby bar with Taedonggang, a very good beer, and room television with five channels of North Korean programming and one featuring the BBC.

As day bled to night, we headed to the Rŭngrado May First Stadium, largest in the world by capacity. We parked by a Niagara-size dancing colored fountain to which Steve Wynn could only aspire, walked past a line of Mercedes, BMWs, and Hummers, and up the steps to prime seats (where Madeleine Albright once sat) at the Arirang Mass Games. The Games (there is no competition, just spectacle) are a jaw-dropping ninety-minute gymnastic extravaganza, with meticulously choreographed dancers, acrobats, trapeze artists, giant puppets, and huge mosaic pictures created by more than thirty thousand sharply disciplined school children holding up colored cards, as though in bleachers at the world's biggest football game. The London Guardian called the Mass Games "the greatest, strangest, most awe-inspiring political spectacle on earth." The Guinness Book says there is nothing like it on earth. One hundred thousand performers in every candy color of the spectrum cavorted, whirled, leapt, and capered in perfectly choreographed unison. A thousand Cirque du Soleils. Ten thousand Busby Berkeleys. It all made the opening ceremonies of the Beijing Olympics look like the opening of the London Olympics. Finally, we poured from the stadium, past the vendors selling posters, DVDs, and memorabilia, exhausted and in overstimulated wonderment.

Early the morning next, we drove back to the airport, during the world's quietest rush hour. One estimate is there are fewer than thirty thousand vehicles in the whole of the country. We passed seven cars, several hundred single-gear bicycles, and perhaps a thousand pedestrians walking the edges of the streets. There were no patisserie-shaped people in this parade . . . all looked fit, clean, and healthy.

There was no commercial air service to where we were headed (and no Lonely Planet guide), so we chartered an Antonov 24, during which the hostess wanted to practice her English with us. Good thing, too, as I noticed the sign at the emergency exit: "In case of stepped out of cabin, attract handle."

Ninety minutes later we landed at Samjiyon, near the "sacred mountain of the revolution," Mount Paektu. At 8,898 feet, it is Korea's highest peak, and legend has it is where Korea's first founder, the mythical Tangun, is said to have descended five thousand years ago.

The drive from the airstrip to the base of the mountain was an ecologist's dream—preindustrial, rice fields cultivated by hand, lush, green landscapes, clear streams, and unlogged forests of white birches. As we rose in elevation, the trees shrank into the soil until we were in a moonscape, the flanks of the stirring volcano, Paektu (white-topped mountain). This was the sublime hill, the most celebrated in North Korea, and we chevroned to the summit in our Chinese bus. From the caldera rim we could look down to a beautiful blue crater lake, and across the lip . . . to Manchuria. There we saw Chinese tourists waving back at us. This was also the spot where Kim Il-sung (Dear Leader) and his son Kim Jong-il (Great Leader) stood, with backs to the caldera, looking commandingly at the camera, offering up enlightenment and guidance. The image was re-created in vivid posters all over the country, so it was a delight to be here, like visiting the setting of an epic film.

There was a gondola that carried visitors down to Lake Chonji, Heaven Lake, alongside a steep stairway. It was five euros each for the ride, but I was tempted by the exercise, and forty minutes later met the group by the frigid water. When Kim Jong-il died, it is said the ice on the lake cracked "so loud, it seemed to shake the Heavens and the Earth."

We took some photos, walked the verge of the lake, and then readied for the gondola ride back to the rim. But the cables weren't moving. The power had gone off, and nothing moved, even us. The prospect of climbing up was too grim for many in our group, including one woman, I will call her Ilene, who said she had shrapnel in her leg from a recent visit to Syria. "What?" I asked. The trip roster said she was a retired schoolteacher from Little Rock, Arkansas. She said she would explain later, but for now the only way she would get up the volcano was on my back. I shivered at the prospect, as she was not suffering from undernourishment. Then, suddenly and gratefully, the catenaries of the tram fired off brilliant blue sparks, the power lurched back on, and the gondolas opened their doors for the ride to heaven.

The afternoon presented a personal surprise . . . we drove to The Secret Camp, where Kim Jong-il, our guides told us, was born in Japanese-occupied Korea on February 16, 1942. His birth was foretold by a swallow and heralded by the appearance of a double rainbow across the sky over the mountain and a new star in the heavens. The simple log cabin (with roebuck deer hooves as door handles) of this auspicious birth stands near a stream called Sobek, spilling from its eponymous mountain. It turns out Sobek means "small mountain" (compared to Paektu). Our hosts were excited with my connection to Sobek, however tenuous.

Clouds painted black brushstrokes over the stars as we entered the cavernous Baegaebong Hotel, which could be the set for *The Shining*, though we were the only guests. Nearby was the wide Rimyongsu Falls, spouting gemlike from a basaltic cliff, and there was a ski slope next door. But this was fall, so the assumption was we were off-season, or tourism hadn't lived up to expectations yet.

The next day we visited the Revolutionary Regional Museum, fronted by ectype Siberian tigers, which still roamed these mountains and were traditional symbols of a unified Korea. Inside, the displays celebrated the North Korean victories over Japan and America, including a video of such shown on a Toshiba monitor using Windows XP.

Then off to the Samjiyon Grand Monument, featuring a giant bronze statue of a young, stiff-backed Kim Il-sung in military regimentals, flanked by squads of oversized soldiers, backdropped by Samji Lake, dotted like snowflakes with egrets. Revolutionary music played from discreetly placed speakers. I was urged to buy a bouquet of flowers to lay at the base, and then we all lined up, sans hats, and made a respectful bow. Photos were allowed, but only of the entire statue from the front, not parts or backsides.

After lunch (the food was always hearty, plentiful, and included meat of some sort, always kimchi, soup, rice, potatoes, and beer, but never dog, which is a summer dish), we made a forty-minute charter flight to the Orang Airport, not far from the Russian border, landing next to a line of MiG-21s. From there we drove three hours to Mount Chilbo, "Seven Treasures," a national park, and applicant for UNESCO World Heritage status. Along the way we passed tobacco and corn fields, cabbage patches, trips of goats, and lines of oxcarts carrying goods somewhere. We paused beneath a 200-year-old chestnut tree at the Kaesimsa Buddhist temple. ("America bombed the churches and Buddhist temples," Mr. Lee told us, "but they missed this one.") It was built in 826 and served today as a repository for important Buddhist sculptures, paintings, and scriptures. The monk had us gather in the temple, below images of flying apsaras, where he tapped a gourd and chanted. He said he prayed for our good health and happiness, and that we would contribute to the peace of the world. Then he suggested we contribute to the donation jar.

It was a short hike to Inner Chilbo, an astonishing vista of wind- and water-sculpted turrets, buttes, mesas, masts, cathedrals, and temples, a stunning combination of Yosemite, Bryce, and Zion National Parks. Mr. Lee, in a North Face jacket and Prospect running shoes, plucked some pine mushrooms off the path and shared them with the group, saying these were delicacies in Japan, sometimes selling for $100 a stem.

After a few short hikes, we bused into a box canyon and checked into the closest thing North Korea has to an eco-lodge, the Outer Chilbo Hotel. The accommodations were spartan (plastic buckets filled with washing water outside the doors), but the setting—high cliffs on three sides, wooded grounds, a clear singing creek—was something apropos to an Aman Resort and may yet someday be.

The following day we hiked to the Sungson Pavilion, a high platform that afforded 360-degree views of Outer Chilbo, grand vistas of the serrated mountains and sheer cliffs that encased the park. And then we unwound the mountain and trundled to Sea Chilbo, a last sigh of igneous rock that poured into the East Sea of Korea (Sea of Japan on most Western maps). The coastal village through which we passed was dripping with squid, hanging like ornaments from rooftops, clotheslines, and every exposed surface. The permeating parfum was *eau de cephalopod*. Past the electronic fences (to keep potential invaders out), on a wide beach, a long white tablecloth was spread, and we settled down to a picnic feast of fresh calamari, crab, yellow corvina, anchovies, seaweed, and beer, just before the rain set in.

The dirt road to Chongjin was outstanding in the number and quality of its ruts. It was lined with magnolias (in the north of North Korea we experienced almost no pavement), and a richness of no billboards or advertising of any sort. We passed hundreds of soldiers, part of a million-man army, in olive drab striding the highway. Mr. Lee forbade us from taking photos of any military presence, or of the popular rickety trucks with furnaces on their flatbeds where wood was fed for fuel. Despite the warning I noticed Ilene had a small camera in her lap, and when the Lees were not looking, she lifted it to the window and made several snaps. I assumed Ilene had just not heard the interdict and made nothing of it.

It was evening as we wheeled into the steel and shipbuilding town, generously lit with streaks of neon (Hong Kong without the brands). We stopped at the Fisherman's Club, which was playing a video of launching rockets and enthusiastically clapping crowds as we ordered up Lithuanian vodka and something called "Eternal Youth Liquor," which had a viper curled up inside the bottle, like a great tequila worm.

We staggered into the Chongjin Hotel, past a pair of Kenwood speakers playing a stringed version of "Age of Aquarius," stumbled up the stairs beneath a poster of "The Immortal Flower, Kimjongilia," a hybrid red begonia designed to bloom every year on Kim Jong-il's birthday, and into rooms where the bathtubs were considerably pre-filled with water to use to flush the non-flushing Toto toilets.

Motivational marshal music cracked the day. We couldn't leave the hotel compound (some power-walked the driveway for exercise, looking like guests at the Hanoi Hilton), but several of us gathered at the gate and watched the beginnings of the day. The street was being swept, folks were walking and biking to work in their shiny synthetic suits, children were being hustled to school, and a woman in a balcony across the way was videotaping us as we photographed her.

North Korea's got talent. The highlight of the day was a visit to a primary school, where a troupe of red lipsticked, costumed children between ages four and six sang, danced, and played instruments as though maestros. They strummed guitars, pounded drums, tickled a Casio organ, and plucked a *gayageum*, the traditional Korean zither-like string instrument, with one outstanding student picking as though Ravi Shankar.

By late afternoon we were back in Pyongyang, and on the way to the hotel we passed the first billboard we'd seen, featuring the Peace Car, a handsome SUV the result of a joint venture between Pyonghwa Motors of Seoul, a company owned by the late Sun Myung Moon's Unification Church, and a North Korean govern-

Richard on the Sobek River
in North Korea. JACK WHEELER

ment-owned corporation that also works on nuclear procurement. Several of the
slick vehicles were lined up in the hotel parking lot, alongside Mercedes, BMWs,
and the occasional Volga.

The next day, after a breakfast of scrambled eggs, toast, potato chips, and
instant coffee, noshed to the tune of "Those Were the Days, My Friend" (it was
originally a Russian song, called "Dorogoi dlinnoyu"), we set out to tour Pyongyang, a city that could be called Edifice Rex, for its complex of outsized compen-
sation monuments. We took the lift (five euros each) up the 560-foot-tall Juche
Tower, named for Kim Il-sung's blended philosophy of self-reliance, nationalism,
and Marxism-Leninism. We wandered the base of a ninety-eight-foot-high statue
of the holy trinity—a man with a hammer, one with a sickle, and one with a writing brush (a "working intellectual"). We paraded through the city's largest public
space, Kim Il-sung Square, akin to Red Square or Tiananmen, featuring giant
portraits of President Kim Il-sung, as well as Marx and Lenin. We bowed again
and placed flowers at another giant bronze statue of the Great Leader, president
for life even in death. We paid homage to the Tower to Eternal Life, with its stone
inscription: "The Great Leader, Comrade Kim Il-sung, Will Always Be with Us."
We admired huge statues in front of the Art Museum of Kim Il-sung and Kim
Jong-il blazing some battlefield on horseback, while two weddings took place near
the hooves. And we passed scores of oversized buildings, from the library to museums to the notorious 105-story, pyramid-shaped Ryugyong Hotel, the dominant

skyline feature, unfinished more than twenty years after construction began (it seemed, from some angles, to list a bit, like the Tower of Pisa).

The metro, deepest in the world, was designed to withstand a nuclear attack. If it were much deeper it would come out in the South Atlantic Ocean near Argentina, its antipode. The stations were named after themes and characteristics from the revolution, and we took a five-stop run from Glory Station (festooned with chandelier lights that looked like celebratory fireworks) to Triumph Station, lined with socialist-realist mosaics and murals.

And we finished the day with a step down to the Taedong River and onto the USS *Pueblo*, or, as the North Koreans said without variation, "the armed American spy ship, *Pueblo*." It was a rusty bucket at this point, more than four decades after the incident, and the guides, in navy togs, showed us the crypto room packed with teletypes and ancient communications gear, the .50-caliber machine gun on the bow, the bullet holes from the North Korean subchaser, and the spot where a US sailor was hit and died. We watched a short video featuring Lyndon Johnson alternatively threatening and claiming the ship a fishing vessel (not true), and then his apology, which allowed the release of the eighty-two crew members exactly eleven months after they were captured.

The final day of the trip we turned south, to the DMZ, the two-and-a-half-mile-wide swath near the 38th parallel that separates North and South Korea, perhaps the tensest border in the world. The paved road was wide and flat, big enough to land an aircraft in an emergency. And scattered every few miles were "tank traps," concrete pillars that could be pushed over to ensnare an armored vehicle heading north. We passed through several military checkpoints along the way, but never with incident.

Once at the DMZ we were ushered into Panmunjom, the Joint Security Area where the armistice was signed July 27, 1953, pausing a war in which almost 900,000 soldiers died (including 37,000 Americans)—and more than two million civilians were killed or wounded. "We were victorious," the guide, who wore three stars on his shoulder, shared, and added, "We have very powerful weapons. Though you in America are very far away, you are not safe . . . but don't be nervous." Then he pointed out a display case with an ax and photos of an incident in 1976 when two American soldiers tried to cut down an obstructing tree on the wrong side of the line and were dispatched by the North Koreans.

With the beat of placed feet, we filed through several gates, and our guide pointed out a flagpole fifty-two stories high, heaving a six-hundred-pound red, white, and blue North Korean flag; beyond was the South Korean version, not nearly as high. Birds and clouds and cigarette smoke crossed between the two, and little else.

At the white dividing line, cutting through the center of three blue negotiation huts, we looked across the barbed wire to our doppelgangers, tourists snapping pictures of us snapping shots of them. We were not allowed to shout, but I made a small wave, and my mirror image waved back.

On the way back we stopped at the Royal Tomb of King Kongmin, a four-teenth-century mausoleum with twin burial mounds, looking like giant stone gum-drops, surrounded by statues of grinning animals from the Chinese zodiac. Inside were the remains of Kongmin, thirty-first king of the Koryo Dynasty (918–1392), and his wife, the Mongolian princess Queen Noguk.

Miss Lee, exquisite in improbable high heels and frilly blouse, pointed to a mountain across from the tomb and said it is called "Oh My God." She then told the story about the place. When Kongmin's wife died, he hired geomancers to find the perfect spot for her tomb. Upset when everyone failed, he ordered that the next to try would be given anything desired with success; with failure, he would be killed immediately. When one young geomancer told him to review a spot in the mountains, Kongmin told advisors that if he waved his handkerchief, they should execute the geomancer.

Kongmin climbed up to review the site. Upon reaching the top, exhausted and sweaty, he dabbed his brow with his handkerchief, while pronouncing the place per-fect. When he found that the geomancer had been executed because of his mistaken handkerchief wave, he exclaimed "Oh, my God!"

Before heading back to Pyongyang, our guides took us shopping at a souvenir stop in Kaesong, North Korea's southernmost city and the ancient capital of Koryo, the first unified state on the Korean Peninsula.

Outside we were greeted by young women in bright traditional tent-shaped dresses. The glass door sported a "DHL Service Available" sign, and inside was a cornucopia of temptations, from statuary to stamps, oil paintings to jade to silks to pottery, to stacks of books by The Great Leader and Dear Leader, ginseng to cold Coca-Cola, to propaganda posters similar to what American student Otto Warmbier stole off a hotel wall. I could not resist a series of dinner place mats of North Koreans bayonetting Americans with the saying "Let's kill the U.S. Imperialists."

On the last night, sharing a beer at the lobby bar, when asked, our guides insisted there was no prostitution in North Korea, no use of illegal drugs, no homosexuality, no homeless, no illiteracy, and no litter. Everything was clean. There was universal health care and education. It was a perfect society. And it was the same messaging I received when visiting the People's Republic of China under Vice Premier Teng in 1977.

Once through security, in the bleak waiting hall for our exit flight, I asked Ilene about the shrapnel in her leg that prevented her from hiking out of Mount Paektu. "I work for the State Department," she half-whispered. "They send me to troubled places to take photos. I photographed Saddam Hussein from a helicopter as he was pulled from the spider hole. And I was on assignment in Syria last month when I was hit." I was stunned. She was in her late sixties. She was overweight. She wore thick glasses. She looked a female version of George Smiley. I looked around the room, and nobody seemed to hear our conversation. And I took a deep breath when the plane bound for Beijing finally took off.

CHAPTER 53

ISN'T IT IRANIC?

I sent my Soul through the Invisible,
Some letter of that After-life to spell:
And by and by my Soul return'd to me,
And answer'd: "I Myself am Heav'n and Hell"
—OMAR KHAYYAM

THE TAPROOT OF THE TREE OF CIVILIZATION, IRAN. WHILE THE UNITED STATES IS an entity less than a quarter of a millennium young, Iran's recorded history bows back five thousand years. At its height, about 500 BCE, Persia controlled more than 2.9 million square miles of land spanning three continents—east into India, south to Egypt, westward to Greece. It reigned over roughly 44 percent of the world's population, making it the largest world power ever by population percentage.

Yet the ebb and flow of time saw the region conquered by Alexander the Great in the fourth century BCE, by Arabs during the great expansion of Islam in the eighth century CE, and by the Mongol Empire in the thirteenth. Every time, it has risen again to create another borderland with a deep and unceasing identity. When it comes to putting today's international squabbles into perspective, Iran takes the long view.

I first visited Iran in 1978, stepping off a Pan Am 1 flight to a city that seemed little different from ones in the West. Women wore miniskirts and jeans, discos blared, and every hotel had a lobby bar. The Shah of Iran, Mohammad Reza Pahlavi, was in power, the result of a coup in 1953 orchestrated by the CIA that removed the duly elected prime minister Mohammad Mosaddegh. My father, a new recruit to the CIA, was part of the team that overthrew the government, an exercise that haunted him for the rest of his life.

In 1978 the gap between haves and have-nots was Grand Canyonesque, and just a year later there was snap that ousted the Shah and ushered in the Islamic Revolution.

MT Sobek signed a deal to conduct trips to Iran for a new program called the New York Times Journeys, and I was anxious to get back and see the changes since my first visit. I was a bit leery, however, so I called my old friend at the CIA and asked if I might be on some blacklist for my father's doings. He said he could find no intelligence that said as much, but he warned I could be arrested, and, if so, there would be little he or his company or any US agency could do to help. He said the wise choice was not to go.

Hence, it was with no little unease I stepped to the Immigration desk at Tehran's Imam Khomeini International Airport.

I tensed when the officer took my passport and pulled me aside. I was left alone at a separate desk while my passport and visa were inspected and cross-checked in a computer. I could feel the sweat bead on the back of my neck like the lick of a ghost. But then, with a beaming face, my passport was returned, and I was waived through. Nobody checked my luggage, which was purposely innocent.

It was nighttime, and the hour drive from the airport passed Khomeini's tomb, a sprawling gold-domed architectural piece that cannot be called humble. Covering some fifty acres, it is one of the largest monuments in the Muslim world, and one of the holiest, and therefore a target. In 2017 ISIS attacked the mausoleum, killing one official and wounding a guard. Later we passed the iconic Azadi Tower, its four giant latticed feet thrusting towards the stars, a monument to the late Shah's vaulting ambition. Its image is well known to American audiences of a certain age who were glued to the screen during the hostage crisis of 1979–1980.

I was leading a group of eight Sobek clients, and the mix was not unusual: Robert Wright, a successful plumber who had traveled with me to Libya, a recovering lawyer, a former marine, a divorcée, a couple of retired academicians, and one woman who seemed to be frozen in marmoreal stillness and who seemed to have no backstory. I will call her Norma.

After checking into the Laleh Hotel, named for a tulip, a national symbol, and adjacent to Tehran's version of Central Park, we ventured out to get an overview of the capital's chaotic, mosaic-like layout. We took a series of chairlifts into the Alborz Mountains, to the Tochal ski mecca at 11,500 feet. It was a bit disorienting to watch parties of women in hijabs, some draped in black manteaus, riding the teleferiques, but hiking, skiing, and snowboarding are big sports here for the many. The other distinction was the number of bandages on noses, both men and women. Nose jobs were in vogue in Iran, and it was a badge of honor to wear the post-op bandage to telegraph the transformation. Surgeons of all stripes are distinguished in Iran. Hadi, our guide, said that one tour group gave him a heart attack, but he was saved by a local heart specialist. I could relate. I had a similar saving grace at Cedars-Sinai in Los Angeles. It was a brilliant Iranian cardiologist who pioneered a procedure that corrected an atrial fibrillation I dealt with a couple years back.

While in line a grinning young man reached out to shake hands and congratulated me for being an American tourist in Iran. Several others joined in for an orgy

Richard leading an American trip to Iran. RICHARD BANGS

of handshaking and earnest welcomes. Then a woman in a chador asked, "Why do you think we are terrorists?"

At the summit we wandered about and gawked at the high dry landscape, which could be somewhere above the tree line in the Rockies or the Alps, and gazed down at the labyrinthine riddle of fourteen million people below. It was windy and a bit nippy, so after thirty minutes we cabled back down to the temperate city to tour its museums, mosques, carpet shops, a couple of the Pahlavi palaces, and the buzzing Central Bazaar. I passed the "Nest of Spies," the former American embassy where the hostages were held for 444 days. Today it is a museum displaying left-behind spying equipment, alongside pieced-together shredded documents marked "Secret." Diplomatic relations were severed during the revolution of 1979, but wherever we went in today's republic, Iranians sought us out, shook our hands, welcomed us to their land, and asked to take pictures with us. Only Norma refused to be in any photographs.

For lunch Hadi suggested a popular local eatery, Moslem, but it was across the street from where the bus let us off. This was a problem, as the most dangerous part of a visit to Iran is crossing the street, mad with cars, buses, trucks, and motorbikes (all Iranian made). Hadi told the story of an American who couldn't cross one swollen river of traffic, and after two hours he called to an Iranian on the other side: "How did you get there?" The Iranian called back, "I was born here."

Hadi showed the way. He stepped into the motoring craziness, held up his hand like a traffic cop, and then waved for us to run across. The line for the restaurant went around the block, beneath strings of patio misters that kept the wait tolerable. Inside the door the line continued, coiling up narrow stairs to a packed room with long tables. I ordered *tah-chin* (saffron and yogurt rice, served with chicken and barberries), *chelo* kebabs, flatbread, and Istor beer, alcohol-free as all public brews, and we dined as a musician played a gourd-bagpipe called a *neyanban*. During the repast, and after repeated queries, with the shy glance of a deer, Norma shared that she was "on the run."

"From whom are you running?" Robert asked.

"They are after me. They want to kill me."

"Who wants to kill you?"

"The United States government," she murmured like a thief.

None of it made sense. Iran seemed an unlikely place to hide from the US government, and a guided Sobek trip even more outlandish. She said she did not want to answer any more questions and wrapped a scarf around her head and face so that we could see only her dark eyes. The rest of us took it in stride and agreed to leave her alone for the duration.

After the revealing lunch it was back again to cross the street, to a bus headed downtown. The ride illustrated the alternative universe that is today's Iran . . . every type of modern shop and restaurant lined the milling streets . . . this could be any Western city, except for one notable difference. There were no recognizable brands . . . no food or clothing or retail franchises, no Starbucks, Gold's Gyms, UPS stores, Supercuts, Kumon, or any products we know (there were a lot of pirated iPhones, however). Western credit cards weren't accepted. The signed Iran nuclear deal in 2015 called for the removal of economic sanctions against Iranian banks, but the United States never lifted them. Then on May 8, 2018, the United States withdrew from the agreement, so hope of Westernization vanished. That meant it was difficult to buy Western products, so Iran, with the world's fourth-largest oil and the largest natural gas reserves, turned inward to create a parallel world of goods and services. Want to buy a Romex watch?

As the morning light spilled down the slopes of the Alborz Mountains, we made the drive along the jagged edge of Dasht-e Kavir, a great salt desert distinguished by its distant hills of biblical proportions. About six hours later we pulled into the brick and pisé outpost of Yazd. With a history that dials back seven thousand years, Yazd qualifies as one of the oldest living towns on earth. It is here the Zoroastrian religion found its first followers, promoting a dualistic concept of heaven and hell, and in time influencing the tenets of Judaism, Christianity, and Islam. It also advocates that hospitality is fundamental to a spiritual life.

Just outside of town we hiked to the top of a Tower of Silence, a circular raised structure where the dead were taken to be picked apart by birds of prey, similar to the Tibetan Sky burials. According to Zoroastrian beliefs, a body becomes impure at death, when evil spirits, or *nasu*, arrive to attack the flesh and soul of the deceased. By contaminating the corpse, *nasu* also threaten the living. Sky burial is considered a clean death because it prevents putrefaction—vultures can eat a body down to the bones in just a few hours. Hadi said the towers were still used until about forty years ago, and he knew a woman who was walking nearby when a bird dropped a human finger on her.

Afterwards, we trekked to Saryazd, bladed with afternoon light. The village claims to hold the world's first bank deposit vaults, a series of small rooms in a protected adobe citadel where folks stored precious personal belongings. This was once part of the Parthian empire, whose army mastered a technique in which retreating horse archers would turn their bodies back in full gallop to shoot at the pursuing enemy. This was the origin of the term "parting shot."

Mosque prayer time, Iran. RICHARD BANGS

In the midmorning heat of the following day, we stood in mud-brick rooms beneath the cooling breezes of wind towers, *badgirs*, ingenious ancient systems of natural air-conditioning designed to catch the sky currents and direct them downward to the lower floors. We visited the Lari house (Khan-e Lari in Farsi), the mansion of a wealthy merchant family, built in 1860. Through its elegant archways, past the prinked garden, we entered the artful bedroom of the teenaged son, who plastered his ceiling with portraits of beautiful young Western women, not unlike many male dorm rooms in mid-century America wherein *Playboy* centerfolds once adorned the walls and ceilings. Some notions are universal.

To wind out the day we made the long gritty trundle to Pire Sabze Chak, the holy pilgrimage site for Zoroastrians. It was a long climb up a barren cliff face, a thousand steps to the grotto that serves as the reliquary, and inside are three flames, meant to be eternal, like the Zoroastrian Fire Temple in Yazd, where a flame has been burning since 470 CE. Fire represents the goodness and purity toward which all should strive.

Once properly consecrated, temple fires should never be allowed to go out.

There were several priests, keepers of the flames, drifting about, and I stood back and admired the hallowed scene. Then a woman stepped in with her young son, maybe nine or ten years old. When she wasn't looking the boy leaned into the flames and blew them all out.

The priests rushed to re-light, and my guide, Hadi, a man who seemed to keep the heat of the desert at bay with his natural coolness, exploded in anger and scolded the mother. A few minutes later, everything was back to eternity.

Another day, another devastatingly beautiful drive, and we pulled into Shiraz, the most liberal of Iranian cities, and once the wine capital of the region. Many of the women rakishly wore their scarfs towards the back of their heads, and the young used a filter app to access the forbidden Facebook, Twitter, Instagram, and TikTok.

There were black banners strung throughout, and stalls selling self-flagellation chains, as we arrived during the annual Ashura celebration. It is a time of remembrance, as Prophet Muhammad's grandson, Husain Ali, was brutally massacred along with his family and followers in Karbalā', now across the border in Iraq. The Day of Ashura is highly mourned by Shia Muslims, with a Passion Play reenactment and flagellation by male Shias. Whips, often with sharp ends, or even small knives, are used to make backs bleed to commemorate the pain of martyrdom. We witnessed the scenes on the street, but our driver hastened past.

Here we visited a glazed tiled pavilion surrounded by fragrant rose gardens, water channels, and orange trees: the marble tomb of Hafez, the fourteenth-century mystic and Persian poet whose works are supposedly in every Iranian home. I have *The Gift* at my bedside, and when in college his verse was fireside fuel for romance, along with Rumi, Omar Khayyam, and Ferdowsi, author of the *Shahnameh*, the longest work of epic poetry ever written, some sixty thousand verses.

The story goes at the splendid age of twenty-one, Hafez, who was short and ugly, worked in a bakery and delivered bread to a wealthy ravishing beauty. He fell hard in love and penned timeless verse to her. But she married a prince, so his love remained unrequited. But his poetry lives on, and the scores of couples here intoxicate (in the nonalcoholic sense) and fall in love with his verse.

At the hotel that evening, an Imam approached and asked where I was from. He was delighted I was an American. We bantered for a bit, and he shared he had three wives. "How does that work in the household, in the bed?" I asked. He shook his head. "They each have a separate house. It would never work under the same roof," he explained, and then he asked if I would like to come to his home for tea. "Which home?" I asked.

"Why, the home of my youngest wife, of course."

With regrets I declined, as we were off to Persepolis.

The lavish ceremonial center of the Achaemenid empire, Persepolis is just forty miles from Shiraz, rising from a dry plain that looks like parchment. It was perhaps the most stunning ruin I had ever seen, surpassing even Leptis Magna in Libya. But it was scarred by graffiti. . . . I looked aghast at the defiling scrawls, until my eyes popped at a signature: "Stanley, New York Herald, 1870." This was Henry Morton Stanley, the African explorer who found David Livingstone the following year. Now I was truly impressed.

For two hundred years the kings of Persia ruled from here and buried their royalty in elaborate tombs. It was a city of tolerance, testified by the well-preserved bas-reliefs showing guests from the many nations of the empire arriving at the palace bearing gifts. But, as always, those who own the newspapers own the story.

Persepolis was burned to the ground by Alexander the Great in 330 BCE in an act of drunken destruction, but the columns, gates, monuments, and ghosts that remain were humbling.

We also stopped at Pasargadae to pay tribute to the tomb of Cyrus the Great, founder of the Achaemenid empire, the largest the world had ever seen, the first superpower. He is celebrated as an advocate of human rights and respect for the customs and religions of those he conquered. He rescued the Jews when detained in Babylon and guaranteed safe passage back to Palestine, and for that he is still lauded in the place perhaps most adversarial to modern Iran: Israel. Today about thirty thousand Jews call Iran home, the biggest grouping in the Middle East outside of the Holy Land.

For many years I was on the board of International Rivers Network, a Berkeley-based nonprofit that fights big dams. One was the proposed Sivand Dam, which some believe could flood Pasargadae and that the humidity from the reservoir would speed up the decomposition of Cyrus's tomb. The dam was finished in 2007, flooding some 130 archaeological sites, and I could now see the valley where the waters were stilled. But to date the lake has not been filled far enough to reach Pasargadae.

At breakfast Norma sat next to me, and I asked how she slept. Not well, she answered. An agent had checked into the room next to hers and was stalking her, she claimed. I let the conversation fly away and went back to my *guilan khagineh* (Iranian sweet omelet) and feta cheese and bread and tea.

As the sun sharpened the sky, we began the long drive through the Zagros Mountains, passing the occasional nomad family traveling with sheep and goats to fresh pastures. We arced over a pass and down to the gardens of Isfahan, a city known in the seventeenth century as "Half the World," as to visit was to experience that much of what the planet offered. It was insanely opulent and beautiful, even with its signature Zayandeh River bone dry.

We began with a tour of a seventeenth-century Armenian church, Vank Cathedral, which features all the overpowering architecture of grand European cathedrals. But it was a small museum showcasing the 1915 Armenian genocide, with photos, film, and personal effects, that was most affecting. It was an enlightened policy to showcase this, a shameful episode in the region, but to acknowledge it in such a powerful way was an attempt to persuade that it not happen again.

A walk away was the famous Royal Square (Naqsh-e Jahan), the second-largest public square in the world, more than five football fields long and once the main polo ground and ancient equivalent of the Mustang Ranch for the Safavid kings. Hadi said they once used the heads of enemies as polo balls and the two hundred second-story apartments were pleasure retreats for indulgence in opium and the velvety folds of wine and concubines.

It is today a pleasant fountain-filled park with couples strolling and children skylarking. Along the middle rim is the Sheikh Lotfollah, the first ladies' mosque in the Islamic world, accessed from the seraglio via an underground tunnel. And at the far end of the square is the magnificent Blue Mosque, covered in an ocean of blue tile work. But what distinguished the grounds today was that we were visiting during Sacred Defense Week, an annual commemoration of the 1980–1988 Iran-Iraq war, during which there were as many as one million Iranian casualties. Lined up in front of the mosque were aging tanks, antiaircraft guns, rocket launchers, and artillery used in the eight-year conflict.

It was an ominous sight, but perhaps more disconcerting was a huge banner strung across the end of the square that said in English and Farsi: "Down with America. Down with Saudi Arabia. Down with Israel." It felt so reminiscent of the hostage period, when every day on television we saw students and banners yelling, "Down with the Great Satan." But the sentiment belied all the welcoming and warmth I experienced throughout Iran. Without exception, everyone I met was curious about me as an American visitor and thoroughly welcoming, extending hands, planting kisses, inviting me for tea in their homes, smiling, and sometimes offering gifts.

As we neared the end of the journey, we passed Natanz, the once secret uranium enrichment site that may or may not be hibernating. At our final stop in the oasis of Kashan, we walked down a garden path near a group of women on a picnic. They all smiled and waved, and then one came running over and offered us slices of moist cake. Even Norma took a bite, before bidding the group goodbye, saying she had to head early to the airport. Nobody asked where she was headed. She disappeared in a poof, not heard from again, a riddle wrapped in a mystery inside an enigma, like so much of this land.

Legend has that it was from Kashan the Three Wise Men, the Magi, set out bearing gifts for the newborn Christ. It was a route I covered when I was running *Mungo Park*, though I managed the trip from my air-conditioned offices in Redmond, Washington. The native generosity seemed not to have waned. For a people with a long, fiery tapestry of rebellion and revolution, invasion and occupation, assassination and unrest, the one constant has been the proud Persian art of hospitality.

Later, I walked down an alley, and an Iranian-made Khodro sedan pulled up alongside. The scarfed woman driver rolled down the window and held out a bowl of olives and pistachios to me. I accepted and popped an olive into my mouth. "This would never happen in America," I said to Hadi. The driver nodded, smiled sweetly, and pulled out into the main street, a stranger vanishing into a strange and lovely and singularly hospitable land.

I traveled the width and length, and I can now say with authority, Iran disarmed me.

CHAPTER 54

SAUDI ARABIA, 2017

BEFORE THE STORM

No man can live this life and emerge unchanged. He will carry, however faint, the imprint of the desert, the brand which marks the nomad; and he will have within him the yearning to return, weak or insistent according to his nature. For this cruel land can cast a spell which no temperate clime can match.
—Wilfred Thesiger

Now that Sobek had pioneered trips to Iran, I wanted to explore its nemesis, Saudi Arabia, which had been closed to Western tourists for decades (with the notable exception of Hajj travelers). In 2017 there were no tourist visas available, but Brid Beeler, who ran a partner travel program we had put together with the Discovery Channel some years earlier, had contacts in high places. She had lived in Yemen and Saudi Arabia and had access few Westerners enjoyed. So, through a princely contact, she managed to secure a series of business visas for a group I put together to tour the country, another first for Sobek.

On the first hours in Riyadh, a woman shrouded in black niqab and ankle-length abaya floated towards me. Behind, her friends were firing salvos of cell-phone photos, as though we foreigners were exotic beasts in a zoo. She stopped and, through her veil, in perfect English, asked, "Where are you from?"

"California."

"What city?"

"Los Angeles."

"What part?"

"Venice Beach. Your English is quite good. Where did you learn it?"

"From American movies. I watch them on my computer at home."

"What's your favorite American movie?"

"*The Devil Wears Prada*."

This was the scene on my first day in Saudi Arabia, and somehow it seemed evocative of a kingdom at a crossroads, theological tradition crashing against the rocks of modernity, a seventh-century purity crossing swords with twenty-first-century internet use, and it was utterly fascinating to be there at that moment. This seclusive culture may be as different from Western versions as can be found on the planet. In 2017 women could pilot a plane but still could not drive themselves to the airport. Or play team sports. Or swim at a community pool. There were no beauty contests (unless you count the Miss Camel Competition, which judges full lips and long eyelashes). No alcohol. No public dancing. No churches, synagogues, or temples. No philosophy (all was Allah's word). No Teslas. And no tourist visas. This was the hardest place for non-Muslim travelers to visit in the world. I spent sixteen years, and a thousand cups of tea, trying to set foot here. It was worth the wait.

I was escorting a group of ten Americans who responded to my invitation to join the first adventure travel outing to the Kingdom. I was surprised to see that Ilene, who had been on my trip to North Korea, was in attendance, but under a different name this time. I pulled her aside and asked that she be very careful on this expedition and not photograph anything forbidden. "We could all be arrested," I warned. "Don't worry," she said. "I have an ocular camera implant that allows my handlers back in America to see what I see. If we get into any trouble, they will send in a rescue team ASAP." Not a little comfort that allowed.

As we approached Riyadh from the air at midnight, the desert out the window looked like an ocean of ink. And the capital, largest city in the Kingdom, zapped the darkness like an island Oz.

After a short night we began our tour with a visit to the state-of-the-art National Museum, which explores the epochs of the peninsula from the dinosaurs through the pre-Islamic period of waywardness, to Mohammed's revelation and the Muslim conquests, to King Abdul Aziz's stitching together of the tribes to create the current Kingdom, to development since the discovery of black gold, the high-grade crude that paid for these galleries.

Our erudite guide, Ali, as colorful as any exhibit, challenged the Saudi code of humility and reticence. In his flowing white *thobe*, he had a dash of Omar Sharif about him, and he confessed his goal was to marry a rich, old American.

Then we headed over to Diriyah, a sunbaked complex of mud-brick houses, ramparts, grassy parks, and cafes that had the feel of a Phoenix mall.

It was Friday, the day of rest in Arabia, and the lawns were filled with family picnickers sprawled beneath the shade of date palms. This respite alongside the shaded Wadi Hanifah is the birthplace of Wahhabism, the rigid doctrine that radiated outwards and rocked the Arabian Peninsula, laying the foundations for the House of Saud. But now, everyone carried a cell phone, and most were using Snapchat (with images and messages conveniently vanishing) and WhatsApp and Twitter, and kids with ice-cream cones were riding hoverboards through the snaking alleys. Sixty percent of Saudis are younger than age twenty, and most are as connected as a Silicon Valley teen. At the Jarir Bookstore, next to the Holy Koran and between picture books of Arabia, was *How to Get Your Own Way: Who's Manipulating You?*

In the gradient golden light of late afternoon, we took pictures of the old mud settlement, Turaif, a UNESCO World Heritage site across the dry riverbed. Then we ducked into a restaurant just before prayer call, when, in accordance with the law, doors are locked for half an hour. We took off our shoes and sat cross-legged for a late lunch of Najdi-style cuisine, including the national dish, lamb kosha, served on a bed of long-grain basmati rice, which I washed down with a nonalcoholic Moussy beer. As a waiter poured coffee from a beaked spout three feet above the small handleless cups, a group of young women in abayas drifted in to take our pictures. Two scrambled over to my side and whispered through gauzy black silk, "I love you," as their friends giggled and snapped and posted away.

We took the night at the Radisson Blu, where "Stormin' Norman" Schwarzkopf based during the First Gulf War, overseeing Operation Desert Storm. It looked like any major chain hotel in the world, except there was no bar in the lobby, no disco on the top floor, and there was a prayer rug in a drawer in my room. There was also an arrow pointing towards Mecca.

In the fresh heat of morning, we headed to the center of the city, to Fort Masmak, looking like a movie-set facade. Surrounded by sand, this squat fortification was built around 1865 and was the site of Ibn Saud's fabled 1902 raid, during which a spear was hurled at the main entrance door with such force that the head still lodges in the doorway.

Outside the fort we passed a large public space ringed with palms, formally called Deera Square, but which Ali calls Justice Square, and which expats chillingly call Chop Chop Square, for reasons easily imagined.

Then it was time for a desultory stroll through the Souq Al Thumairi, which smelled of oud, the dark resinous heartwood that perfumes the stalls between the carpets, copper pots, sandals, silver daggers, and bling-bling.

I bargained for prayer beads; some of the women in our group haggled for Red Carpet–worthy abayas; and Brid, who lived in the Kingdom for many years and knew quality, bought a box of gourmet Bateel dates. We all felt richer for spending our riyals.

Later we transferred to the airport (the only concourse I have seen where men and women enjoy separate security lines) and boarded a Flynas flight to Ar Rub' Al Khali, the great sand sea of the Empty Quarter. As the Airbus A330 took off, a James Earl Jones–timbered voice recited a prayer for safe travel through the on-board screens.

When we landed, the American women in our group changed from the shapeless abayas into form-fitting safari wear. We were met by a fleet of Toyota Land Cruisers and took off, south of nothing, west of nowhere. The lead driver was named Metab, which means "The Exhauster," a holdover from when tough names were adopted to scare off invaders. His long white thobe was immaculate, his black agal headband perfectly in place, but he seemed to live up to his name, veering off the road at high speed, lashing in the dark towards the void. How did he know where he was going? He had no GPS; no maps; there was no cell service; there were no tire tracks. He steered his wheel like a captain in a storm. Then, at last, a spot of light burned a hole in the darkness, and we came upon camp, a simple goat-hair Bedouin tent in the crook of a dune with a campfire out front. Scattered around were individual zip-up Mabeet tents (Mabeet is the twelfth night of the Hajj) for each member of our party, to keep out the snakes, scorpions, camel spiders, and sand from the persistent wind.

There were no showers or toilets . . . this was camping as the Bedouins have always done, and with the early light I climbed a rusty dune for morning ablutions. My footfalls sent cascades of powdery sand down the steep sides with the fluidity of water. Once over the crest, there was nothing but an horizon so far off it eluded comprehension, and a blessed moment of privacy.

After a breakfast of sticky dates, flat *masali* bread, and Laban yoghurt, the guides handed us *ghutras*, red and white head cloths that can protect the face from sun, wind, and sand. Then they deflated the tires from 35 psi to about 11, better for traction along the roar of fine sand. Finally, in the pale oblique light of midmorning, we struck out into the desert, an area of vacancy the size of France, and even more hostile. Our vehicles were packed with water and spare gas (cheaper than bottled water), ready to trace the routes blazed by last century's leathery rusticators Wilfred Thesiger and Bertram Thomas.

We stopped first at the site of the Lost City of Qaryat Al Fau, the pre-Islamic capital of the Kindah kingdom, which prospered from the first century BCE to the fourth century CE as a key stop on the frankincense, spice, and silk routes. But when the Romans converted to Christianity, frankincense was no longer in great demand, and the silk and spice trade was moved to the Red Sea, boats being faster, cheaper, and more reliable than camels. And Quaraiyat Al Fau faded into the drifting sands. The Holy Koran has another explanation, though, for the disappearance of many of the once-great trade-route cities: "All these cities, too big with pride, we did destroy. Against some we sent a sandstorm, some were seized by a great noise. For some we cleaved open the earth, and some were drowned."

Then we poured straight into the field of dunes. Our driver, at first, flirted with the ridges and dips, the crescents and curls of sand, and then slammed on the gas pedal, rocketed up an unmarked crest, and flew over the top. Airtime! Grips tightened. Hearts lurched. He then plunged down the far side of the wave of fine grain, as though about to somersault, and ground into the brown belly of a salt flat. Here he Tokyo-drifted along the pan and hurtled up another steep dune for a traverse along the face, angling the vehicle so it was on the edge of capsizing, spitting sand like a broken blender dispatching flour. Trust Allah, but buckle your seat belt.

At the crown of one dune, the drivers halted so we could step out and feel the hot breath of the desert. The dunes seem to be shifting, migrating. We were in the heart of what Thesiger called "this cruel land."

Bedouin teatime, the Empty Quarter, Saudi Arabia. Nobody had ever heard of
Donald Trump. RICHARD BANGS

Though hired by the Middle East Anti-Locust Unit to search out locust breeding
grounds, Wilfred Thesiger pursued a personal quest across the desert, a quest inti-
mately related to the nomads with whom he lived: He hoped to "find peace that comes
from solitude, and among the Bedouin, comradeship in a hostile world." The spirit
of the Bedouin, he wrote, "lit the desert like a flame." He at first felt like "an uncouth
and inarticulate barbarian, an intruder from a shoddy and materialistic world." After
five years in the desert, Thesiger emerged hardened by heat and thirst, and for the rest
of his life (he died in 2003) he felt himself a stranger in "civilized" company. He had
found what he was looking for in the desert, and it had transformed him.

Back in the car for another rumble, fishtailing over the poured geometry of
silvery drifts, surfing the back side of others, Metab cut the wheel hard to the left
to avoid rolling. He continued carving tracks in the loose sand, until the landscape
resembled the whorls of gigantic fingertips.

As the dunes turned rose-red, tea was served. Camels shuffled by. The Arabic
language contains more than a thousand words to describe camels and their various
breeds and states of maturity. The Bedouin call the desert *sahel*, "ocean," and camels
are the ships of this desert.

Midday the world took on the fishlike translucence of a man who doesn't see
much sun. It was as though Nature had exhausted every tint in her paint box. We
came across a group of camel herders relaxing in the shade of a Land Cruiser, and
in the Bedouin custom of unconditional hospitality, they invited us to sit and share
some frothy camel milk. They were six brothers, plus a twenty-two-year-old Sudanese contractor, who stared big-eyed at the women in our group. When asked, he
said he hadn't seen a woman in eighteen months.

"Do you get any news from beyond the Empty Quarter?" I probed.

"No." He shook his head after Metab translated.

"Have you heard of Donald Trump?"

"No."

Our group applauded. At last, an outpost beyond the reach of Western media.

We camped in the sand again, fine as the grains in an egg timer, but with dots of yellow spotting the landscape. They were desert lemons, which looked tasty, but Metab warned not to touch, a commandment not to be disobeyed, as exposure causes diarrhea. One of our group picked up some yummy-looking nuts and asked if they were edible. "Camel dung." Metab grinned through expressive eyes. A vulture circled overhead. Rain clouds gathered like smudged charcoal, and the wind picked up.

The storm hit in the middle of the night, rippling the tents like flags, lashing the fabric with fat raindrops. But with the dawn, the sky had been scrubbed free of clouds, and the sun was glancing over the dunes. Everything wet was dry in minutes. Breakfast was *khader* (maize, milk, and sugar), mixed generously with blown sand.

After striking camp we rode a landscape more sky than soil, as the light changed the sand from beige to pumpkin to scarlet and the shadows formed ever-shifting patterns and textures, akin to abstract art. The high dunes, or ergs, are migratory, like the nomads they host. They were crescent-shaped with gentle wind-ward slopes, up which the grains slowly crept and settled. They had steep leeward faces, down which grainy avalanches sometimes cascaded. The dunes multiplied into ever-more-dense colonies and eventually linked to form sculptured chains perpendicular to the prevailing winds.

In the soft blue light of our last afternoon in the Empty Quarter, the terrain turned pointillist, to flat lakebeds flagged with sharp, dark stones. All around, mountains loomed like dry bones through the thin air. After journeying some five hundred miles, we stopped at an oasis with a tanklike watering hole, into which all the drivers immediately plunged, fully clothed. We followed suit, swimming with Saudis in the largest sand desert in the world.

We took a late lunch of peanut butter and hummus on hard rusk at a wadi, dappled with water from the recent rain. In the slanting light the pools sparkled like jewels in a necklace . . . this could have been Sindbad's Valley of the Diamonds. I found a bleached camel hipbone just a few feet from a pool . . . he almost made it.

We began the long drive back, from the gritty badlands to postmodern Riyadh. Once we hit pavement, there were camel-crossing signs, sandstorm warnings, petro pipelines, and gaudy gas stations lit like Vegas casinos. We stopped at one, and inside I couldn't resist buying a bag of Lebnah and mint potato chips, as tasty as it sounded.

In the city of Al Kharj, second-largest oasis in the Kingdom, we stopped to overlook one of the huge ancient water wells (now mostly dry from over-tapping the water table), and then motored by the massive King Abdulaziz Palace, built by the Bin Laden family. The heat was like a wall here, until we steered into a private resort behind iron gates that sported freshly mowed grass, waterscaping with artificial cascades, cool vapor misting from shade umbrellas, and, inside, air-conditioning, cold sodas, and a farraginous assortment of foods.

Just outside of town we struck out on a quest to find Mukabir Farzan, a field of some five hundred tumulus tombs, built before the pyramids of Egypt. But we couldn't locate them. I tried Google Maps, MapQuest, Waze, even Siri, but nothing. At last, behind a rough fence and up a hillside, we came across the unexcavated, unprotected, unmarked necropolis. Nobody was here but us, and the mud pie–like mounds were all empty, long ago looted for gold and treasure. It seemed we were looking into wells of unknowable time and dimension. Here men wandered thousands of years ago, origins and ends untold. The dead lay thicker than the living on this hill.

Back in Riyadh we inched through heavy traffic, past sand-colored mosques, minarets, Pizza Hut, McDonalds, and a Starbucks, before pulling into Prince Al-Waleed's Kingdom Centre Tower, tallest in the city. It was also known as the Bottle Opener Building for reasons evident from the street. We rode the escalator to its sleek shopping center, where on the fourth floor the most popular stores were Victoria's Secret and La Senza Lingerie (featuring "Trendy Panties, 7 for 119 Riyals").

At the skybridge, a glassed inverted parabolic arch on the forty-first floor, the city below looked aflame with flashing colors and the vectors of the future. A sign in English read: "In case of Emergency Allah Forbidden: Do not use the elevator; Do not crowd; Do not panic."

After breakfast we were in the airport concourse when a man wearing sandals, wrapped in white towels, with one shoulder exposed, walked past. Not the sort of attire I expected in a modern airport. He was, Brid shared, a man on *umrah*, a pilgrimage to Mecca that can take place any time of year, as opposed to the scheduled and more expensive Hajj, largest religious gathering in the world.

We flew north to the oasis town of Al Ula, about three hundred miles from Jordan's Aqaba and a key staging area for T. E. Lawrence's campaigns. After exploring the walled ruins of old Al Ula, once a robust stop on the caravan route between Oman and Rome, we made our way to our accommodations at Madakhil Camp, a solar-powered luxury glamp, in the high-end-safari style pioneered and perfected in East Africa.

Enveloped by the high-sandstone cliffs of Al-Hajar, the tents were zhuzhed up with simple Arabic motifs; soft, indulgent beds with Arabian horse-hair blankets; electric lights and outlets; and a jeweled chest with a prayer rug inside, in case a guest left his at home. Camels roamed around outside, and the canyon walls turned gold in the twilight hour and were painted by klieg lights after dark.

There were two long common-area tents flooded with deeply napped carpets, one where cups of tea and dishes of sugary dates were served, and the other where breakfast and dinner were taken, the latter, in our visit, including a mandi, in which chicken, lamb, and vegetables are baked in a sand-covered oven for eight hours before serving on the long, low table. When walking back to my tent after the savory repast, I looked up and realized this was a million-star retreat.

But it was the location that made this stay uncommon. It was just a few minutes from the UNESCO Cultural Heritage Site at Madain Saleh, a sprawl of 140 monumental tombs spread over ten miles. They are reminiscent of Petra in Jordan, which made sense, as they were connected to the same Nabatean empire of around two thousand years ago. Imagine Petra without the tourist hordes, camel rides, and artifact mongers, but instead the relics of a vanished civilization set in a surfeit of buttes, mesas, spires, slot canyons, and phantasmagoric formations that make Monument Valley look like facial pimples, and you have a picture of what this offered at that moment in time. Since then, it has been developed into a gaudy, otiose mega-resort, bearing little resemblance to the site in 2017.

We made a steep switchback drive to the top of the escarpment, to the Haratawerth Overlook, where groups of Saudi women, like crows on a wire, were enjoying a view quite like the South Rim of the Grand Canyon.

Then we did some more dune-bashing with Yusuf as our driver. I felt safe, as he had a pendant hanging from his rearview mirror that featured ninety-nine names for God (he said his mother gave it to him for luck and safety when he did the Hajj). Yusuf roared us up Ragasat Canyon, past congeries of rock pillars called the Dancing Ladies, into sinuous passageways beneath curved cliffs and ancient rock art.

We rolled in for tea in the shade of a mushroom-shaped rock of pink sandstone topped with the red stains of iron ore deposits and then caterwauled some more through the ungentle dunes.

Evening was the best time to view the tombs of Madain Salih, carved in the sides of the smooth, rounded red-stone formations that dotted the desert floor. We walked into the empty chambers of many, some with slots carved into the walls to

Haratawerth Overlook, the Grand Canyon of Saudi Arabia. RICHARD BANGS

shelter the bodies of a family. I put my hand on one tomb and talked to whomever lay inside, but with discretion, as I did not want to wake them.

On the exterior pediments the heads of eagles had been cut off, and there were bullet holes around the carved roses and snakes, defacements by devout sects that believed any icons are forbidden by strict interpretation of Islam. We ducked into a large room carved from the rock, a *Diwan*, a religious gathering place where animals were sacrificed; and we could trace a complex viaduct system that ran along the outside walls. The Nabateans were master hydroengineers, manipulating rain runoff and aquifers to allow human flowering in the desert.

The most imposing of the tombs was Qasr Al Farid, carved from a single sandstone monolith, from the top down, which we faced without another traveler in sight, as though we were with Charles Doughty, the British explorer who came across this treasure in 1876.

Opening the tent flap the final morning, the sunlight filtered through the canyon, bringing colored life to the cliffs and sand. We made way to one of the stations on the Hijaz Railway line, opened in 1908. The narrow gauge linked Damascus to Medina, designed to carry pilgrims on Hajj, cutting travel time from six weeks to four days. Station forts were built every 7.4 miles along the 808-mile route to protect the railway from bandits. During the first World War the Ottomans sided with the Germans, while T. E. Lawrence helped orchestrate the Arab Revolt, blowing up trains and tracks. The railway closed in 1918 and never ran again.

From here we drove three hours north, with a police escort, to Tabuk, home to the Kingdom's largest air force base. We were behind schedule, but Yusuf never exceeded the speed limit, as speeding tickets are assessed directly to the car owner's cell phone, and if not paid, the government blocks the phone, an effective fillip. But we made it in time for a quick dinner, some Saudi champagne (apple juice and Perrier) to toast our trip, and caught the last flight back to Riyadh. Then we each boarded connecting flights to the United States, to a world even Sinbad could not have imagined, leaving behind, however faint, the imprint of Saudi Arabia, and its sophrosyne grace of custom and hospitality, its correspondence between belief and place.

CHAPTER 55

IT'S DJIBOUTIFUL!

Over the gloomy sea the sky grew red. Quickly the fire spread among the clouds and scattered them. Crimson burned to orange, orange to dull gold, and in a golden glitter the sun came up, dribbling fierily over the waves in little splashes, as if someone had gone along and the light had spilled from her pail as she walked.
—T. E. LAWRENCE

FOR YEARS I WAS HAUNTED BY TWO EPISODIC QUESTIONS: WHAT HAPPENED TO OUR broken rafts when we shipped them to Djibouti? And what was at the finale of the first river Sobek ran, the Awash.

Finally, I had the chance.

The triggering event was the opening of a direct flight to Djibouti on Qatar Airways. I could fly from LAX nonstop to Doha, wait a couple hours in perhaps the most luxurious airport lounge in the world, and then connect to Djibouti.

I called my friend Scott Siegler, who had traveled with me through Bosnia the year before. Scott was a former studio head who would rather trek into the heart of darkness than date an actress, and before I could finish the call he was on board. So, after a smooth ride to the Arabian Peninsula, and then across it, we made a quick transfer to the Sheraton Hotel, right on the glimmery waters of the Gulf of Aden. After a freshly squeezed juice and a swim in the naturally warm pool, we were ready to shatter the glass of Western gentility. The timing seemed good. The *London Telegraph* earlier in the year named Djibouti "Africa's Hottest New Travel Destination."

Still, when I mentioned to friends and family I was heading to Djibouti, I got two responses: (1) Where the #!@* is Djibouti; or (2) Why? Isn't that the middle of the Hot Zone?

On our second night in the country, we had dinner with the US ambassador, Tom Kelly, at the Café de la Gare, the best restaurant in Djibouti.

The ambassador was unequivocal: "This is the safest city in Africa." He pointed out that Djibouti is the only country on the continent never involved in a war. It is, of course, a strategic location, a sort of back door to the universal truths of the region, and as such hosts a posy of militaries. There is a major US base (largest in Africa) with some 4,500 Americans. Some call it the Global Assassination Center, as a great many of the US military drones used throughout the Middle East to target terrorists are housed and serviced here. There is a German base, a French base, a Japanese base, Italian, Spanish, and others. Seal Team Six is based here. The Chinese are a major economic presence and are building a new port, their largest outside of mainland China, as well as new roads, a new railroad, and a major resort on the Red Sea to service Saudis and other high-end tourists.

I also met the director of tourism, Mohamed Waiss, who scryed that Djibouti would soon become "The Singapore of Africa." He touted all its assets, especially its whale sharks, and boasted he had introduced the first World Whale Shark Festival. He gave us "I Love Djibouti" gift bags when we left.

There had been a bombing two years earlier by an Al-Shabaab woman in a downtown restaurant that killed a Turk. This was, of course, a big deal, but it was cited as an exception that might have happened in any European or Asian city. Al-Shabaab is a Somali organization and was not a meaningful presence in Djibouti.

Nonetheless, all the restaurants had entrance screeners and security guards, and a new police station had been erected a few yards from the restaurant. We took lunch at the modest eatery and sensed no trepidation (except for the salmon, which traveled a long way to get there). No American or tourist had ever been harmed by a political/religious group in Djibouti (there was no Arab Spring, and the president was democratically elected).

Tom Kelly pointed out that the Djibouti Muslims were fiercely moderate and proud of it. Djibouti was also a relatively expensive place, so it had not attracted the masses of refugees who flooded elsewhere. A few successful Somali pirates had moved here and purchased expensive cars and condos overlooking the water. The Sheraton had a number of exiled Yemenis, but they received no discounts and were of the moneyed class, mostly doctors, lawyers, and prosperous businessmen, waiting to return when the dust settled. There was a UN refugee camp to the north of the country, but it was far away from the city and was apparently well-managed, and it brokered its displaced to willing countries around the world.

The global effort to eradicate the Somali pirates was based here, and Tom Kelly said the united effort had been successful, a rare example of a coalition on a mission that could claim victory. With constant air surveillance and preemptive strikes, there had not been a pirate incident in two years.

We walked all about the city, day and night, and drove and explored much of the countryside, and never felt anything less than warm welcomings and open arms. Djiboutians are very grateful for the US presence, generally embrace Americans, and, if possible, would love to marry one and move to Minnesota.

It turned out there were French and Djiboutian firms operating tours, but only one American company, a boutique operation called Rushing Water Adventures, owned by Ken Gradall from Wisconsin. His primary offerings were whale shark excursions, paddling in the Gulf of Aden, snorkeling among the remarkable coral reefs (Jacques Cousteau claimed them as the best in the world), hiking, and trips to the salt lakes. Ken was a former health care worker in Somalia and spoke fluent Somali, the lingua franca of the Issa, the dominant of the two major clans (the Djiboutian 100-franc coin features the outline of two camels, one standing above a kneeling other . . . Ken said the standing one represents the Issa; the supplicant the Afar).

Ken picked us up in his Mitsubishi truck at the airport and transferred us to the Sheraton, distinctive for its hookah bar, the razor wire around the pool, and the stray green parrots. We promptly hit the sack to mitigate the jetlag of a ten-hour time differential. By noon, though, we were ready to rock.

As if to prove the peaceful tone of the city, Ken took us to lunch at La Chaumiere, the site of the 2013 bombing. The menu was as full and varied as the crowd, with Chinese, Mexican, Italian, Ethiopian, and American burgers, but nothing too spicy.

Afterwards, Ken showed us a bit of the town. The main road was lined with graceful old buildings once the haunts of seigneurial merchants. But the pink and cream facades were now faded, the stuccowork entablatures and rosettes cracked and stained. At a section called the Blue Doors, flamboyant fabrics, slingshots used to air-strike weaver birds, amber necklaces, and curved double-edged daggers were hawked. Ken pointed out the aged mosques with curvaceous ogee arches and the shiny new foreign-funded versions (including one where former US Secretary of State John Kerry spoke). We rolled by qat kiosks, a bay full of listing dhows, and the factory that claimed the highest per capita consumption of Coke in the world. Djiboutians like to chew qat, a social custom involving a shrub with amphetamine-like qualities, and the preferred mouthwash is a warm Coke.

Unlike in the more fundamentalist Muslim countries, where most women are covered in black abayas and hijabs, here the majority dressed in vivid rainbow wraps and scarves. "This is the Paris of Africa," said Ken. "Just look at all this fashion," he added and pointed to a row of women money changers so vibrant in the cast of their clothes I told them to keep the change.

Ken parked on a hard beach near the airport, and we launched our New Zealand–made kayaks for an hour paddle out to Turtle Island, floating the seam where the Red Sea and the Indian Ocean meet. Once at the shoreline, we stepped out of our boats into the shallows and watched as hundreds of blue-spotted stingrays exploded from the sand in front of our footsteps and scurried through the clear water. We passed a lone fisherman waist-deep on a sandbar unfurling his net, who recited an impromptu poem for us. In a land with little literacy (less than 1 percent), storytelling, songs, and poetry are vital to keep history, culture, and the deep subsoil of traditions alive, and from fishermen to politicians, skills of oratory carry more weight than any written accords.

We slid back onto our boats and feathered towards another island, a sacred ibis rookery, and as we got close the sky became a high shifting roof of wings. Then, from the horizon at a cliff at shoreline emerged the largest bird I had ever seen. It was black, and silent, and it sailed purposely over our heads and across the sea towards Yemen. "It's an MQ-1 Predator drone," Ken said. Its mission unknown.

Oblivious to the aerial show were scores of turtles: loggerheads, hawksbills, and greens, who popped up in front of our bows for a quick look-see, then dove back down into the UN-protected waters. One of the visual delights of the equatorial desert is twilight, and we paddled back to shore into a dazzling cocktail of orange and red.

The next day we picked up a bag of almond croissants at La Djib House, the neighborhood patisserie, and drove inland, past troops of baboons, the occasional gazelle, and acacias with goats in the top branches, chewing the long, thin thorns contentedly.

About seven miles out we passed the "Who Died Market," which sold heaps of used clothing. We trundled past dragon blood trees, black lava fields that sucked the color from the sun, and bundles of bony firewood for sale by the side of the road. We steered by herds of biscuit-colored goats, scrawny camels with ribs in bold relief, egg-shaped portable huts, and tall, dark nomads wearing *sanafils*, the signature light cotton skirts knotted at the waist that billowed like parachutes in the wind. How did they survive in this slag heap? "They must eat rocks," Scott conjectured.

We passed capsized trucks and Maersk shipping containers in the dry wadis. We stopped at the overlook for the Grand Canyon of Punt, where venders offered to sell us geodes, local honey, porcupine quills, sin-black obsidian knives, and plastic water bottles filled with salt.

We resisted the temptations (and the one that plagues me . . . the desire to hike into any canyon I come across) and continued the drive down, down into the depths of the Danakil Depression, the Valley of Hell, hottest place on earth. At last, it revealed itself, the brilliant white face of Lake Assal, lowest point in Africa, third lowest in the world, the salt sheen spreading like a white ink stain across the water. Beyond, the lake turned into the most seductive Caribbean turquoise color, but nothing lived in this basin. Even the vultures avoided it.

"It is Djiboutiful," exclaimed Ken.

We parked and hiked up the *source d'eau chaude*, a clear tributary, with hot springs spilling into the waters at fracture points. I dropped my Nalgene, filled with ice water, into one of the springs, and it came out tea. Scott pulled a bag of salted potato chips from his pack, which he said he brought to replenish body sodium leached out by the heat. But he was bringing coal to Newcastle; we were in the salt capital of the world.

At the upper end of the canyon there was a clear pool, looking very much like swimming holes in the Grand Canyon. I had not brough a swimsuit, but the water stirred some ancient urge to shed civilized skin, so I stripped and dove in, with Scott and Ken right behind, for a cool hour of soaking. There were hundreds of little fish nibbling at our feet, a free fish spa that would be a pretty peso in Cancun.

Danakil Depression, the hottest place on earth, Djibouti. Ken Gradall on left, Scott Siegler on right. RICHARD BANGS

At one point a group of Japanese arrived at the edge, and I asked what brought them here. They were from the Japanese base, and that brought my next question: Why do the Japanese have a base in Djibouti? Because of the Somali pirates, it turned out. The shipping lanes through the Red Sea and Indian Ocean from Europe to Japan are vital, and so the base exists to help keep the passage safe.

We then crunched across the broad, hyper-white expanse that is the salt flat of Lake Assal. This is the saltiest body of water in the world, far saltier than the Dead Sea, or the Great Salt Lake, ten times that of the sea.

For centuries the Afar, who claimed to be descendants of Noah's son Ham, trekked across the largest salt reserve in the world to load their camels with sacks of the crystalline mineral and then caravan to the highlands for trade, mostly wheat, but also perfumes and spices. It still happens.

A couple of Afars, standing bolt and erect on the edge of the lake, tried to sell us salt crystals and gazelle skulls coated with salt (a bargain at $10, but how to get "it" home?). And there was a memorial plaque to Bernard Borrel, a French judge found burned to death in a burled ravine near here in 1995, a casualty perhaps of the spaces the empire left behind.

While walking the shoreline (it was 110 degrees in the shade, but there was no shade) we came across a group of large men, Dwayne Johnson–sized. They shared they were NCIS-Djibouti, stationed at the US base, taking a day trip before heading back for Meatball Marinara sandwiches at the base Subway, the highest grossing location of the franchise in the world, they said. That pricked our appetite, and we began to head back to the car so we could make it to dinner at the hotel. As we climbed out of the lake basin, Ken stopped the car and had us get out. There was a diagonal crack in the road, like a scar on the face of the landscape, and it ran to the horizon in both directions. We straddled the jagged fissure, and Ken said that we had a foot each on the two great tectonic plates, the Arabian and African, which are slowly splitting the continent, similar to how Madagascar cut away from the homeland 150 million years ago.

I had hoped to make it to Lake Abbe, the terminus of the Awash River on the Ethiopian border, to conclude the trip I had started almost fifty years before. But Ken disabused me of the idea with our short stay . . . it was a two-day trip out and back to Abbe, and we were in-country for just four. But as I looked at the map, and back down to the lowest point in Africa, and the rift that created this sink, I realized that this valley must have once exceeded its frame. The waters of the Awash must have, in an earlier epoch, run farther downwards, as all rivers do, until it reached the bottom. That would be Lake Assal. No water runs between the two lakes . . . it evaporates. But the climate was once milder, the region wetter, so in an earlier geological time, this was the end of the line. In some fashion, I could say, I at last finished my journey down the Awash River.

The next day, under an oyster-blue sky, we set out to Arta Plage, the famous beach where the whale sharks congregate each winter to feed in the rich meeting of the waters of the Red Sea and the Indian Ocean. I had dived with the whale sharks in Cancun, but Ken said that experience was nothing compared to the behemothic banquet found here each season.

But we were early, by just a few days (the season is November to February), and so instead went snorkeling along the most colorful reef system I had ever seen. I had dived in many places, from the Caribbean to the Galapagos to Bali to the Andaman Islands, but I was not prepared for this. I have been colorblind my whole life, but now, Hallelujah, I could see. The reef practically pulsed with HD colors; popped like a Cirque du Soleil, spun like a candy pinwheel, or at least how I always imagined a pinwheel of bright colors looked like. And that was just the coral . . . there were butterfly fish, angel fish, parrot fish, damsel fish, duke fish, surgeon fish, and 101 others I could not identify. I gulped down a whole bellyful of colors.

Across the water from this beach, we could look up to bosky headlands, mile-high volcanic mountains that looked, in their middle reaches, as though scumbled by a painter's brush, though the summit lines were sharp, scraping the blue welkin like an etching knife. I almost expected the sky to bleed.

We made it back to town in time for dinner at Time Out, an Italian/Ethiopian restaurant on the main square, owned by Vittorio Gulla, a friend of a friend who lives in Addis. Vitto said he moved to Djibouti from Addis only recently because he found the coastal environment friendlier. It was a long wait between ordering and serving—the gears here turn more slowly than at home—but when the plates arrived, Scott scooped into some injera and wat, while I indulged in pasta primavera with a St. George beer. We paid in cash, as few eateries or shops in Djibouti take credit cards, and then found the way back to the Sheraton, where an Afar wedding was unfolding, in shimmering costumes and a traditional type of dance, called *jenile*, colorful as a Djiboutian coral reef.

The next day was our final. We had hoped to take the ferry across the Bab-el-Mandeb (Arabic for "gate of tears") strait to the old slave-trading settlement of Tadjoura to check out an eco-lodge, but we missed the boat. Instead we drove a short way out of town to the Decan Wildlife Reserve, an interactive park where you can walk among the animals (at least the herbivores; the predators are fenced). We stepped among zebras, Arabian oryx, porcupines, dik-diks, giant tortoises, gazelles, ostriches, and murders of crows; and we got close enough to cheetahs, caracals, lions, and rogue camels to speed the blood.

On the last afternoon, I asked Ken to drive me to the train station where we once shipped our bitten rafts. However elegant it once was, it had not excused the battle against desert decay. It was shuttered and crumbling, the rail run to Ethiopia a cartouche of memory. The Chinese were building a new rail line scheduled to open soon, leaving the old station to slowly collapse and return to dust.

I made my way inside, where a guard stopped me and said it was unsafe. I asked if he knew where some old inflatable rafts might be stored. He didn't know what I was talking about and shooed me out. I walked around the outside . . . it was a wide building with narrow, lancet windows . . . and there in the back was a rounded Afar hut held together with an assortment of fabrics, like patches on a leaking ship. Inside was a bed, a firepit, a palm-leaf mat, and a block of salt, meant to ward off djinns. But as I looked closely at the dark material draping the acacia skeleton of the structure, I could make out a faded logo: Sobek.

CHAPTER 56

MADAGASCAR, SOMETIMES YOU HAVE TO EAT IT TO SAVE IT!

The ears were large, flaring forward, the eyes limpid amber, in which the pupil floated like a glittering jewel, changing color with shifts of the light: obsidian, emerald, ruby, opal, amethyst, diamond.
—William S. Burroughs

It is *fady* to kill a lemur. The punishment is ill health, and five years in jail.

Madagascar, the planet's fourth-largest island, floats 250 miles off the east coast of Mozambique in the southwest Indian Ocean. The Afro-Indonesian people govern their lives with a series of social taboos, or *fady*. And a longtime *fady*, rooted in the commands of the *razana*, the Ancestors, is that it is wrong to kill the little button-eyed primates called lemurs.

The clocked relatives of monkeys, apes, and humans are found only on this island, rafted away from the vast bulk of the African continent 150 million years ago. Yet even today, in a world of heightened environmental consciousness and recognition of the accelerating loss of species, lemurs are still being killed; sometimes served at the tables of wealthy foreigners who will pay a little extra to have a taste of the exotic. In the 1990 Marlon Brando film, *The Freshman*, the plot revolves around a moveable restaurant that serves endangered species to high-rolling epicureans. In a case of life imitating art, I heard a rumor that a restaurant existed in the Malagasy Republic that served lemur. Adrenaline had once been a primary goal of my adventures; but over the years I discovered I found more satisfaction in travel that somehow made a positive difference. I baked that into the Sobek credo and called these efforts Adventures with Purpose.

When I approached Antananarivo, the 200-year-old capital, on an Air Mauritius Boeing 737, the air was a trippy blitz of thick smoke, the landscape parched and coughing. As subsistence farmers below were clearing crop and pastureland and scorching trees to create charcoal, I struggled to fill out the Customs and Immigration form on my lap. After twenty-five hours flying from Los Angeles, it was not a simple chore on the coarse, brown customs form that seemed made of cheap toilet paper.

While waiting for the baggage in the Ivato International Airport, I visited the men's room and discovered in a world of disappearing species there was yet another. The attendant offered to sell me toilet paper, as there was none in the stall. "There is a shortage in Madagascar," he explained, and I knew why—it was being used for customs forms.

Within an hour I was on an Air Mad flight to a large island off the northwestern shore of the Mozambique Channel, Nosy Be ("Big Island" in Malagasy). From the air there was muscular poetry to the brown, bare landscape, the raw red rivers, like broken veins bleeding to the sea. Astronauts have said the Texas-size island was the only landmass easily identifiable from space, because it is surrounded by a halo of rust-red sea, the color of the lateritic topsoil relentlessly scrubbed off its denuded surface by wind and rain.

The microcontinent of Madagascar is the most eroded place on Earth. Man has grievously wounded this estate. Some estimate 90 percent of the Great Red Island's forests have been destroyed, and it continues to lose 375,000 acres a year, a rate that will ensure a totally bald island within a lifetime. The impoverished farmers of preindustrial Madagascar deliberately torch the rain forests for fuel and agricultural land. After a few seeding seasons, the thin soil is depleted, erosion sets in, the tired, overtaxed land is abandoned, and a new wedge of forest is obliterated, a dangerous cycle that promises to turn the land that time forgot into a dead zone.

In the fifteenth century, Arab traders called Madagascar the "Isle of the Moon." Today the epithet seems prophetic. The protection of the remaining woodlands is a race against starvation, ignorance, and time.

As we began our descent to Nosy Be, bright Ricky Nelson and Roy Orbison tunes playing over the loudspeaker challenged the scene below. But as the wheels lowered, the landscape turned green, and a flock of snowy egrets fluttered from the parasol of a gigantic glossy frond. To further abet the mood change, as I stepped off the plane a lei of fresh frangipani and bougainvillea was placed around my neck by a smiling Malagasy girl. She led me outside to a row of stands where plump, giggling women were selling stacks of vanilla, bottles of mango, and peppers in vinegar.

I climbed into a red, candy-striped two-cylinder Citroen Deux-Chevaux with $100 bill stuck on the front windshield. Looking closer I saw a profile of Madonna where Ben Franklin belonged, and in place of the nation's name were the words "Altered States of Madonna."

We bumped down a sun-roasted road trying in vain to avoid the potholes that are an unstudied endemic species in Madagascar. The edges of the road were lined with kapok and pollarded yellow-flowering ylang-ylang trees from which a perfume essence is extracted. We rolled past vast sugarcane fields and balloon-shaped concrete huts built in 1921 as cyclone shelters. I checked into Les Cocotiers hotel, and on the wall was a sisal fiber tapestry of a village scene, and next to it a lizard I would get to know. He hung on the wall like a bad canvas: Art Gecko.

At lunch I spied another *vazaha*, a paleface, and wandered over to join George Rosemond, a retired surgeon from Philadelphia. In a country that had allowed tourists only since 1984, it now saw about 200,000 visitors a year, and but a fraction were Americans. If George and I had passed each other in Philadelphia, we would have gone by without a nod . . . but here we practically embraced and spent minutes sharing travel hints and tales. We then ordered the local special, a pork stew with sticky rice spiced with green leaves from a flower called *anamalaho*, which leaves tongues stinging as though stuck in an electric socket. This led us to a couple of bottles of Eau Vive, French bottled water. But we soon discovered that beer in Madagascar was cheaper than bottled water, so we switched to hearty Three Horses beer, into which George poured his own airline-size bottles of Canadian whiskey.

Several bottles of Three Horses led George to tell me of his ordeal in getting to Madagascar. A week earlier he had made the same grueling flight I had to Mauritius from the United States, but when he caught his connecting flight to Madagascar, he was unaware there was an intermediate stop. When the plane landed, he followed the crowd, went through immigration, where his passport was stamped, and proceeded to customs. When his bags never appeared, he exited customs to see if the promised travel agent was there to meet him. But there was nobody. So he flagged a taxi and asked to be taken to the Antananarivo Hilton, as described in his itinerary. But the taxi driver, who spoke only French, shook his head no and left. Bewildered, George sought out an airline employee, who courteously listened to his plight and then smiled and explained that George was unfortunately not in Madagascar as he thought. He had stepped off the plane one stop too soon and was on the French Overseas Department of Réunion Island.

Now George had been in-country for ten days and was joining me for an exploration of Nosy Be and its adjacent island, Nosy Komba. To get to the dock we drove through the hot, rickshaw-filled streets of the eponymously named Hellville (Admiral de Hell accepted cession of the island to France in 1841), and among the rosewood canoes we boarded a motorized pirogue named *Pirate*. Madagascar was once a veritable den of pirates, especially during the end of the seventeenth century. With its many hidden coves, ample supplies of lemur meat, fruit, and water, the island provided a perfect base for privateers of every stripe. Madagascar then reverberated with debauchery, violence, and brutality; some argue things have not improved in the stripling years of the twenty-first century.

Woman in Hellville, Madagascar. The yellow mangary
pigment paint is used to improve the skin, not as a
decoration. PAMELA ROBERSON

It was a forty-five-minute sail to the volcanic outcropping called Nosy Komba, and along the way the dolphins leapt at our stern as though encouraging the voyage. Once on the busy beach we waded through women snugly wrapped in *lambas* (technicolored cotton shawls) and warm-faced, barefoot children whistling through bougainvillea blossoms, all chatting in a mellow, polysyllabic tongue related to a language in central Borneo. Behind the main village of Ampangorina, we stepped past an old blind man strumming a resonating tubular bamboo box with metal strings called a *valiha*, and into the black lemur reserve.

Scores of Margaret Keane critters lolled in the crotches of trees, swung from rafter-like branches, bounced lightly through the trees like arboreal kangaroos, and scrambled to human shoulders to beg bananas with big, irresistible, imploring eyes. The males were truly black, sable-furred from head to toe, faces punctuated with wide, inquisitive, lemon-colored eyes. The white-bearded vulpine females sported fashionable golden-furred coats and earmuffs of white Einstein hair.

Diurnal and fruit-eating, these creatures were remarkably trusting of people. Not a trace of fear fogged their translucent eyes, a result of an isolated evolution without predators since the Age of the Dinosaurs. Conservationists say 80 percent of the flowering plants (some ten thousand species) and 90 percent of the beasts on this singular outpost, including the thirty-one species and forty subspecies of lemurs, are found solely on Madagascar and its satellite islands. The area is the most outlandish living laboratory of evolution in the world, far more than the Galapagos. It is, in a way, Sir Arthur Conan Doyle's Lost World.

When the cataclysmic forces of plate tectonics tore the island from the African continent, its cargo of plants and animals merrily evolved on a parallel but separate track from the rest of the Earth's ecology. "It is as if time had suddenly broken its banks and flowed down to the present in a completely different channel," wrote naturalist Alison Jolly in her classic book, *A World Like Our Own*. Because of the island's unequalled levels of endemism, razing a patch of irreplaceable primary forest or poaching an animal can have more devastating repercussions here than just about anywhere. Several new primate species have been discovered in this natural attic in recent years. The rosy periwinkle, the source of a medicine used to treat childhood leukemia, grows here. It's quite possible a cure for the next global virus, or some other scourge, might be in a scrim of forest about to be burned, or in the unexplored DNA of a rare hunted species.

While we disported with the black lemurs, a local guide, Pierrot, told me that the tradition among the Nosy Komba villagers was strong: "If you feed the lemurs, you will be rich; if you kill one, you will become sick and die." I asked Pierrot if he had heard of a restaurant that served lemurs. As far as he knew, no such eatery existed.

Under an old fig tree cabled with lianas we lunched on carangue fish. Not far away a white-necked pied crow waited patiently for our scraps. It was hard to imagine, looking over the curved, coconut-palmed white beach to water like tourmaline glass, that this was an Eden on the edge, with several species already pitched into the abyss.

Some have likened those who hunt lemurs to the Nazis. In 1934 Hitler devised a plan to deport European Jews to Madagascar, where it was hoped they would all die from tropical diseases. But when the British took the northern part of La Grande Ile from the Vichy government, the plan was abandoned. In its place Hitler sanctioned the Final Solution.

The following day I flew back to Antananarivo and hooked up with a guide named Serge, who lost his left eye to an arrow while playing Cowboys and Indians when a small boy. Serge's surname was Harizo, a name he claimed was one of the shortest in the country (the king who conquered and united the highland clans in 1794 was named Andrianampoinimerinadndriantsimitoviaminandriampanjaka). I asked Serge if he knew of the rumored restaurant. He said he had, just recently, but didn't know if it really existed, or where it might be, but he promised he would put the word out and help me try to locate it. In the meantime, he would take me to the special reserve at Perinet, sixty miles to the east, halfway to the coast.

As we bowled down the road that switchbacked off the eucalyptus and pine-lined Hauts-Plateaux of Antananarivo, there was a haze both inside and outside the car: outside from the incessant burning, inside from Serge's cigarettes. Even though Serge had met less than a score of Americans in his guiding career, he had seen enough to make observations, and one is that to Americans smoking is *fady*. I agreed and asked, if out of cultural deference, he might put out his smoke. He did.

The trip took us past gneissic slopes covered with coarse grass and *lavaka*, great fan-shaped erosion gashes in the hillside, looking like fleshy wounds inflicted by some savage giant. And then there was the burning. In the distance the fires were a necklace of streetlights. Up close, the defoliated, barren landscape was much uglier.

Once at Perinet we took a nocturnal walk down the Ancienne Route Nationale Numero Deux, into the protected montane forest. The silence was carpet-deep, and our guide, Laurette, spoke in a cathedral hush as she swept a weak flashlight across the trees. Every few minutes her narrow beam caught the round, hot-coal eyes of the world's smallest primate, the reclusive antigi, or mouse lemur, about the size of a newborn kitten; and those of the fat, brown, greater dwarf lemur, as well as the eye shine of tiny tree frogs and chameleons (two-thirds of the world's chameleons slink on this island, including the biggest and the tiniest).

In the morning I awoke to the strange calls of wild lemurs, and I was quite excited with the sounds, until Laurette told me all I was hearing were chickens. Then, after a breakfast of boiled zebu milk, litchi nuts, and a barnyard egg omelet fried in palm oil, Laurette took me to stalk the wild indris, the largest of the lemurs. We walked over the Sahatandra River, beyond the entrance to the reserve—the river, said Laurette, where her cousin Joseph, the best wildlife guide the area had ever produced, was murdered in a jealous rage by two other guides incensed over Joseph's success.

A flock of raucous black parrots flapped over us, and I watched a malachite kingfisher levitate over the river. A cuckoo shrike with a long, dark tail fluttered nearby. As we turned into a glade of creaking bamboo, a blizzard of butterflies briefly eclipsed the view (there are three thousand species of butterfly in Madagascar, of which 97 percent are endemic). We hiked past a tall, wire-mesh structure, where an attempt was made to keep indris in captivity. The complex diet of the animals includes fruits and leaves from some sixty trees, only a sampling of which grew in the large cage. When several indris died in the coop, the experiment was cancelled.

We stopped next at a thorny-fingered tree from which Laurette plucked a foot-long virulent-green Parson's chameleon from its uppermost branches and poised it on her sweater. As if on cue it blinked and rotated its bulging red eyeballs in independent directions and took on the brown of the sweater. Then she pointed to a native crow-like bird with a deeply forked tail and a silly crest. It was a drongo, which had, she said, a very humanlike wail. Like lemurs, it was *fady* to kill drongos. Legend had that in the seventeenth century, pirates raided the region looking for slaves. When the villagers fled to the jungle, some of the women with babies couldn't keep up, so they hid in the bushes. As the pirates were passing, a baby cried, and they stopped to investigate. Then they heard the cry again but noticed this time it came from a bird. Thinking they were duped by the bird, they turned and left, and the mothers and babies were spared. Since then, drongos have been considered sacred.

Laurette moved with a feline grace through the tangle, and I awkwardly stumbled behind. After we crawled through the damp, orchid-festooned forest for an hour, the air splintered with the spine-chilling, unearthly call of the indri. The sound grabbed me by the scruff of the neck and pointed ears skywards. The word "lemur" is from the Latin for "ghost," and the aural-linked etymology seems clear as the calls seemed to echo from the hereafter. They were loud, eerie, and childlike, sounding to me like some kind of sad human saxophone.

The ghostly symphony lasted only three minutes and then abruptly stopped, leaving behind the susurrant hum of insects and the flatulent honks of frogs, feeble by comparison. Laurette made a loud kissing sound, followed by an exhaled "haaaaa"—the call of love, she explained, and they responded with more fortissimo musical wailing. The indri song, often compared to that of the humpback whale, is one of the loudest sounds made by an animal, one that peals through the forest for nearly two miles. It seemed the plaintive sound of a besieged species.

Laurette called the indri *babakoto* (loosely translated it means "ancestor") and made it clear they were *fady* to eat, as the people believed they were directly related to the animals. But even though it was *fady* to kill these in-laws, and quite illegal, every year many within the reserve were lost to poachers, the "killer apes," who trafficked the meat for the comparative fortune of $1 a pound. I asked if she had heard of an eatery on the island that bought the rustled lemurs to cook and serve to unscrupulous customers. Rumors had spread like a sea fog, she said, but nobody she knew had yet found this awful place.

We finally sighted four of the boy-sized, tailless indris, two of each sex, with panda markings, teddy bear ears, and haunting amber eyes. Their fur was thick and silky, predominantly black, with patches of white on their backs, rust on their tummies, and, slated by gray around the bare, black muzzles. Four stories up, they ricocheted from precious hardwood to hardwood, through a palisade of trunks, one after another, as though catching the same bus to work. At one point the rain forest suddenly seemed to be weeping, and Laurette turned to me with a broad grin across her moon-shaped face. The indris were urinating, something they do in unison, and by schedule, every morning, creatures of habit. Then they were off again, using powerful thrusts of long, agile, black-socked legs to make graceful, acrobatic flings. They looked so cuddly, so human, that it was easy to see why the locals believed indris were ancestors. It was difficult to fathom how they could be hunted for food.

I took the narrow-gauge train, nicknamed *Fandrefiala* after a long, slim forest snake, back to Antananarivo. A poster beneath the steeply peaked, dormered roof at Andasibe (Big Station) proclaimed FOREST, HEART OF MADAGASCAR, a propaganda piece designed to motivate a change in thousand-year-old habits. Yet on the way back the passengers' faces became soot-streaked from the trees burning out the windows, and flakes of forest fluttered through the car like pages of a yellowing book. Outside was a charred, ravaged wasteland, acres and acres of smoldering devastation. Much of the native forest was aflame from farmers engaged in the ecologically disastrous technique of slashing and burning new croplands, mostly to grow dry rice. Others were burning select eucalyptus and tamarind for *charbon*, charcoal. It took about ten trees to create a four-foot-high sack of charcoal that sold for about $1 a bag. "Forest in a sack," Serge called it.

While Madagascar is one of the richest nations in the world in terms of nature and biodiversity (the eighteenth-century French scientist Philibert Commerson called it "the naturalists' promised land"), it is one of the poorest economically, with an average per capita income of just $490. The country had been independent since 1960, yet under an old French law still on the books, contraceptives were illegal in Madagascar, so the typical rural family has eight or nine children. The country posts an alarming 3.5 percent annual population growth—in the last twenty years, the population more than doubled to more than thirty million, threatening to capsize the boat.

To cook the rice necessary to feed so many children, the parents need fuel, and the fuel of choice, because it is cheapest, is charcoal. Thus, for most in Madagascar, environmentalism is a long-sighted luxury that clashes with current crying needs; the next meal is the priority. In 1986 more than forty thousand people died in a famine in the southeast, and out the train window I saw countless children potbellied with malnutrition. But if alternatives to existing practices aren't adopted, the present will be a burnt sacrifice to the future. Incinerating one's own environment is the ultimate self-immolation. HRH Prince Philip, the Duke of Edinburgh, and founding president of the British National Appeal, the first national organization in the World Wildlife Fund family, once watched a flaming forest in Madagascar and said to his hosts, "Your community is committing suicide." But even His Highness could offer no viable alternatives, no ready solutions. It is a tragedy without villains, a war against an enemy with no face.

I spent the night in Antananarivo, and out my window a blue haze of smoke draped itself around the flowering jacaranda trees, the spires of churches, and the roofs of the motley, orange-tiled homes. At breakfast I asked Serge if he had any luck locating the restaurant. He hadn't, but was still trying, and hoped to find it by the following week.

In the warehouse-like airport I lingered at a gift shop featuring belts ($50), wallets ($80), purses ($176), and briefcases ($300), all made from the skins of crocodiles whose forefathers swam from Africa during the Pleistocene. Now crocodiles have been hunted out almost everywhere on the island, except in a few lakes in the north, where they are revered as ancestors, and sometimes as profitable components of luggage.

The next stop on my survey was the southeastern tip of Madagascar. Fort Dauphin, on the opposite end of the island, is 999 miles from Nosy Be. Fort Dauphin and San Francisco are geographical antipodes, the farthest points on the planet from each other.

The flight down the island first passed over a puzzle of emerald-green rice paddy rectangles and then over a faded landscape with a threadbare coverlet of green, the tattered felt of an old billiard table. But as we crossed the Tropic of Capricorn the felt faded to parchment, creased with chasms. The last minutes of the flight we sailed over a lacerated folding desert that poured into the sea at the country's oldest town, named after the Dauphin, the six-year-old prince who was crowned Louis XIV of France just as the first French settlement was being established in Madagascar in 1643.

Once a thriving port, it was now a harbor in an advanced state of decay, and famous for its winds. True to reputation, it was dark and blustery upon arrival, with purple-bellied clouds pressing ozone into my nostrils. I quickly piled my luggage into a white Renault station wagon and headed north for the fifty-mile, two-hour drive to Berenty, just as the last rays of the sun stippled the craggy granite mountains. Driving towards Berenty on a stormy night was like driving through a war zone. With the windows down I could hear the stutter of axes and the steady tears of saws between the peals of thunder. On each side I saw fires lashing at the sooty night, burning to bring up new shoots of grass for goats and humped zebu cattle to graze. The lyre-horned zebu, more than a source of dairy and meat, were talismanic units of wealth, used to pay for marriages and funerals, and there was continued pressure to breed more. These fires were singeing the edges of the wildlife reserve, perhaps burning away species yet to be discovered. When Indonesian explorers first paddled twin-hulled outrigger canoes to the island around 1000 CE, Madagascar was cloaked in virgin rain forest. Since then a pygmy hippo, an aardvark, two species of giant land tortoise, three species of bird (including the *Aepyornis maximus*, or elephant bird, a flightless creature weighing one thousand pounds and more than ten feet tall that gave rise to the legendary giant roc of Sinbad's second voyage, according to Marco Polo, who heard the tale from Arab traders), and fourteen species of lemur have disappeared, their habitat burned for farmland and fuel and overgrazed by livestock, and their doom hastened by overhunting. Lemurs today are the most threatened mammal species in the world. Of the world's 103 different species of lemurs, 23 are now considered "Critically Endangered," 52 are "Endangered," 19 are "Vulnerable," and 2 are "Near Threatened," all clinging to the sides of a shot and sinking ark.

Near "the tree where man was born," a bowl-shaped baobab, we took a right turn onto a pitted dirt track. It was a four-mile trundle through the species-unique spiny desert and across a neatly manicured sisal plantation to the 1,100 acres of private reserve owned by the wealthy de Heaulme family. These gardeners of Eden decided to protect the various species of the area back in 1936. A bony-faced, straw-hatted man wrapped in a blanket and wielding a spear was guarding the entrance, but as soon as he saw my white face, he lifted the barrier and said, "Salaam." I was exhausted, so after dinner and a beer, I retired to a pillow filled with dry grass in my bungalow.

I awoke to a furry little dog face with bright Bart Simpson eyes staring at me from the doorway. It was a ring-tailed lemur. Then I heard the pitter-patter of little footsteps on the roof . . . dozens of them, more ringtails, scampering, tap-dancing, insisting I get out of bed. I pulled on my shorts and stepped outside to an alien panorama. There were scores of cat-size prosimians with long snouts and squirrel-like tails bouncing everywhere. There were three species within a hundred yards of my bungalow. Child-sized, creamy-furred, western sifakas were performing ballet-like sideways leaps across the road; red-fronted lemurs were swinging like circus children from octopus trees; and dove-gray ringtails, velvety tails curled like upright question marks, were frolicking around the grounds, snatching bananas from the accommodating *Homo sapien* visitors. Several had month-old babies clinging to their backs like miniature jockeys. It looked like a scene from the movie *Gremlins*, only here, on Main Street in Lemurville, all the critters were agreeable and nice.

At breakfast I met the Breakfast Club, a group of habituated lemurs who shamelessly seduced visitors into sharing the fare. I also met a group from the Earthwatch Institute (the Boston-based work-study group) on a two-week tour. After the repast, we all headed down to the narrow gallery forest along the Mandare River, an exuberant brushstroke of life on an otherwise bleak canvas.

A researcher explained that the females in the troops are dominant and will win any battle of the sexes. Members

Sifaka lemur in Madagascar. They rarely touch the ground. PAMELA ROBERSON

of a troop of twelve snacked on the bean-like fruits of the tamarind trees, anthropomorphically sunning themselves, performing dazzling acrobatics, grooming one another, engaging in energetic play, marking territory boundaries with scent glands in the base of their tails, and sounding calls of alarm when a harrier hawk swooped overhead. I held a banana to one, who scampered over my shoulder from a bauhinia tree and peeled back the skin with humanlike hands with black fingernails. As he chewed, his round, lustrous eyes stared at me like a little Rodney Dangerfield begging for respect. Though the ringtail was only inches from my face, I stared back across a vast evolutionary distance. Still, there seemed to be a flicker of recognition, and as I wondered how any caring human could kill and eat a big-eyed being who looked like a blood-related baby, the lemur seemed to look back and wonder as well. I reached over and touched the long, prehensile fingers of his little hand, and they were cold.

Towards the end of the day, while lounging in front of a pit crawling with brown-backed radiated tortoises, I asked the woman researcher overseeing the Earthwatch group if she had heard of a restaurant that serves lemur. She scowled. "If there is such a restaurant, I would gladly go and burn the place down," she replied and stomped off towards her quarters.

The next day I was back in Antananarivo, where the morning mango rains had washed the streets but not the air. Serge told me he found the restaurant and would take me there for lunch. It was Friday, when the world's largest open-air market took over the streets, and so it was a slow drive to the Ambodifilao section of town, an area of decaying, pastel Gallic buildings with pointy roofs and second-story wooden balconies. The scene seemed a vaporous watercolor in the smoky, diffused light.

There, on a narrow storybook street, was the Restaurant La Tulipe, subtitled Chez Claudine, with the tagline "Cuisine Chinosie, Specialties Gibiers"—"Gibiers" meaning "game." We were a bit late for lunch, arriving around 2:00 p.m., but there were a few stragglers, all European, finishing meals.

We took seats in the open-air section and studied the menu. It featured *cuisses de Nymphe L'ail* (frog legs in garlic) and *Pigeonneau frits*, but no lemur, or "Tarzan," as the waiter called the animal. At first, he claimed they didn't serve Tarzan. But then, after much insistence, he excused himself to speak to the owner. A few minutes later he returned to ask if we would like to try radiated tortoise, bats, or boas, none of which were on the menu. We said no, that we were really interested in lemur. He apologized and said they were out of lemur, but if we placed an order, they could supply one by next week. That would not do, I complained, as I was scheduled to depart the country the following morning. So we shrugged shoulders and ordered *crabe farci* and zebu sandwiches.

Sometime into the first few bites, the owner, Claudine, appeared at our side. She seemed sophisticated and friendly, a stout, jolly, middle-aged lady with two gold rings on the fingers of her left hand and a gold broach in the shape of Madagascar on her breast. She looked vaguely European. In fact, she volunteered, her father was Chinese and her mother was half French, half Malagasy, and she owned the restaurant with her Chinese husband.

Serge explained that I traveled halfway around the world to taste lemur, and that I was well-connected back in the United States; I could bring other connoisseurs who might enjoy the exotic tastes of her establishment, if only I could sample the wares. She looked at me, searching for clues of sincerity, and suddenly broke into a radiant smile. "I think we may have some lemur frozen in the refrigerator, left over from last week. Would you like to try that?"

Yes, we nodded.

"Would you like it marinated in its own sauce, or with wine, ginger, and mushrooms?"

"Could we try both?"

"Of course." And she disappeared into the back.

A few beats later I asked the waiter how we could tell it was really lemur being served. He vanished into the kitchen and returned with a fellow waiter. Together they proudly unfurled the skin of the red ruffed lemur, an endangered species. It had been killed by Claudine's Chinese brother-in-law, who was, they said, at that moment out hunting more.

After about fifteen minutes the victuals were served, and a decision had to be made. I knew I wanted to track this restaurant down; I knew I wanted to uncover this small, perhaps symbolic, atrocity and send word to the right people of these goings-on. But I had not thought of what to do if actually served the animal. I screwed up my face and then looked to Serge, who stared back with his one good eye.

Then Claudine stepped to the side of the table and stared down at us. *"Bon appétit."* Then, after a few silent seconds, "What do you think?"

I picked up the fork and picked at the tiny ribs. She hovered over us, and I took a bite. It tasted like tough beef, even smothered in sauce. I chewed, then tried the other plate, and Serge joined me. Claudine stood over us for several chews, and we smiled thinly throughout. Finally, she excused herself, saying she hoped I would spread the word of her haute cuisine and send her more tourists. I nodded a promise and continued to chew. When she left the room, I took my camera from my pocket and took a fast series of photos. When it came time to pay the bill, I couldn't help but notice that Tarzan was the heftiest item, more than double any other dish. It was 12,000 Malagasy ariary, about $3 in US currency.

I can't say if it was the lemur or the crab, but I felt ill the rest of the day, especially as we toured Parc Tsimbazaza, the national zoo, and the keeper showed me the red ruffed lemur. He explained there were presently more in captivity than in the wild, as they were being poached so effectively. That evening, after a frosty glass of Three Horses beer, I composed a note to the researcher I met in Berenty, and in it I told of the restaurant at 17 Rue Rabezavana. I told her if she is going to burn the place down, I will gladly supply the match. It is the one place in Madagascar that deserved to go up in smoke.

A few weeks later, I received a note back from the researcher: "It's gone."

CHAPTER 57

ZURVIVING ZANSKAR

(THE THIN LINE BETWEEN LIFE AND DEATH RUNNING A RIVER IN LITTLE TIBET)

There is no happiness for him who does not travel. Therefore, wander. The fortune of him who is sitting sits, it rises when he rises, it sleeps when he sleeps, it moves when he moves. Therefore, wander!

—*THE RIG VEDA*, 800–600 BCE

WALKING DOWN A VACANT ROAD ON THE WAY TO PADUM, CAPITAL OF THE ANCIENT kingdom of Zanskar, about five miles off the river, I passed a Tibetan monk with his distinctive red *kasaya* wrapped obliquely about his shoulders. He stopped, cupped his hands prayerfully, and pressed his fingertips to his lips. In halting English, he asked my age. When I told him, he looked me in the eyes and said, "Ah, you have short life left."

It was a daunting coil of thought, as we were on the roof of the world, close to heaven, and about to enter the Zanskar Gorge, one of the most remote canyons on the planet, eleven thousand feet high, surging with ice-cold water from the Himalayan glaciers that feed this unruly rift.

This was a reunion trip of sorts. It was the first time George Wendt, John Yost, and I had traveled together in the decades since we founded Sobek. Though a team from Sobek first descended the Zanskar in 1978, Kashmir, with its troubled border with Pakistan, soon afterwards closed to foreign travelers, and the river ran wordlessly for more than twenty years. John first rafted the Zanskar in 2007 and has made yearly pilgrimages since. This was his seventh descent, and John invited his old partners, and we brought along a cadre of friends, Sobek clients, and my son, Walker.

This was not an easy place to get to. I flew Turkish Airlines to Istanbul, overnighted, and then continued to Delhi for a total of twenty hours in the air. Then we all flew to Srinagar at the nubbin at the top of India and overnighted on a cedar

Sobek founders George Wendt, Richard, and John Yost on the Zanskar River, Ladakh, India. RICHARD BANGS

houseboat on Lake Dal. Then a three-day hard drive over steep, crumbling mountain pass roads, where a glance downwards sometimes revealed the skeleton of an unlucky bus or truck. We passed through the town of Drass, which seductively bills itself as "The Second Coldest Inhabited Place on Earth," and Kargil, site of the 1999 conflict with Pakistan that saw more than one thousand killed from both sides. Now the town was lined on the northern side with high concrete "shelling walls" so vehicles and passersby could hug the edge and avoid incoming rockets or gunfire.

We passed bearded goats that looked like little devils, pine martens, hyraxes, and the ultimate Scrabble word, dzos, the offspring of yaks and cows.

Before descending into the Zanskar Valley, we trundled over the 14,600-foot Panzila Pass, camped between the snowy tonsure of the twin 23,000-foot peaks of Nun and Kun, and visited various chortens and *gompas*, turning the many prayer wheels, seeking blessings for our endeavor.

We finally launched at 11,930 feet on the Doda, a tributary draining the giant Darang Durong glacier, and which joins with the Tsarap to create the Zanskar (the Zanskar never gets below 11,000 feet), and paddled half a day to our first camp at the base of the Karsha Gompa, a Buddhist monastery that is stacked up the mountain like a birthday cake. It was here I met my monk.

That night John gave his quotidian briefing. He spoke in little archipelagos of thought. "I'm sorry we forgot one of the tables, but we'll think of something. And tomorrow there is a Class V rapid that was created two years ago from a road blast. I'm not even sure we can walk around."

This news worried and riled me. One of the members, a Himalayan high-altitude expert, and his wife approached the bench. "John, if we had known there was a Class V rapid, we would not have come. We expect you will find a way for us to walk around."

John was suffering from some sort of flu and didn't have the strength to argue. "We'll figure something out."

The next day we left the featherbed of civilization behind, carrying everything we would need for the passage, including a half dozen live chickens riding atop one of the rafts. The Nepalese guide for the chicken raft is good, and it glides through the first rapids with virtuoso artistry. It was, from my vantage in the next raft, poultry in motion.

We entered the gorge, dark and sheer. It inhaled the sunlight. The walls swirled with different colored dikes and aplites, discordant swarms of magma that cut through and across strata in patterns that looked as though the walls swallowed hallucinogens. We ran a few chilly rapids and then pulled over at a small eddy. We scrambled up to a dirt road and walked a couple hundred yards downstream, where a deep-throated roar ricocheted around the locked canyon. It was at this point the road builders set off a stack of dynamite that didn't go as planned. It triggered an avalanche that threw a house-size boulder into the river, pressing the flow against the opposite bank and creating a powerful sluice that erupted into a huge, recirculating hole, a potential killer. The blast also buried a bulldozer, and at the edge of the road the yellow frame of the earthmover was partially exposed. A little farther down in the rubble, our guide tells us, is the driver, who was cut in half with the detonation. John named this rapid "Jackhammer."

The road was blocked ahead, ending in a hummock of blast debris, and then an abrupt impassable cliff. But down below, at river's edge, there was a fan of sharp rock behind the giant boulder that would make a hike-around possible, to everyone's relief.

But as the guides tried to line the people-less rafts around the rapid, one flipped, with no consequences; but the bowline of a second raft, filled with gear, snapped, and the raft plunged downstream around the bend, a ghost boat into the maw. That could spell consequences, as there was but one camp in the narrow gorge with enough level ground to hold the group, and it was just a few miles from Jackhammer. The runaway raft held tents, sleeping bags, food, and medicinal alcohol, so the trip could transmute into an ugly expedition if the boat couldn't be retrieved in time. The guides, all young Nepalese, hastily lined another raft around the rapid, and two of them hopped in and started rowing madly downstream hoping to catch the fugitive. All the rest of us could do was scramble over the edged and acicular rock pile, reload with double the passengers squeezed into the remaining rafts, and hope, as we wolfed downstream, that we would rendezvous with the lost boys.

After a few rapids, and a few shadowy bends, we saw the two guides waving frantically from a shoreline rock. How did they get there? Where were the rafts? It turned out they had successfully rescued the runaway raft, pulled it to shore, and hiked upstream as far as possible to let us know.

The evening bled away the daylight as we celebrated at camp, local whiskey and brandy flowing. One of the Nepalese guides played Justin Timberlake on his Samsung phone, amplified by inserting it into a plastic cup. The nearest light we could see was the moon.

With the morning the camp looked as new and shiny as wet paint. We took a hike to the Tibetan village of Nyerag, high up an unreasonably steep canyon tributary. John had been cultivating visits to the twenty-five-family village since he started running the Zanskar, and it made a difference. Tashi Dorje, the village leader, greeted each of us with a vigorous bear hug and then served up Ladakhi tea (barley and salt); yak-butter tea (a septic cocktail); and Chhaang (a barley beer so good it is said the Yeti often raids isolated mountain villages to drink it). Then he rolled out the Tibetan rugs, and we started to buy. He said the rugs were absolutely guaranteed, so if there were a problem, all we had to do was return it to his home in Nyerag and he would swap it out, no questions asked. At the end of the trading, he thanked us and said because of the rafters and their purchases, he had been able to send his four children to boarding school.

Before the hike to the village my elder son, Walker, heard tell that John Yost's eldest son, David, had spent four years traveling the Americas barefoot. He bicycled from Prudhoe Bay, Alaska, to Ushuaia, Argentina, without ever wearing a shoe. Walker was inspired, so he made this climb barefoot, but on the way down he stepped on a series of thorns and a sharp rock that cut deep into his sole. He limped back to camp, bloodied and bruised, and after a round of ointments and bandages, slipped back into his shoes.

The next day dawned cloudy, plunging the air temperature to a notch above shiver, but the morning float was relaxed after the negotiation around Jackhammer. The geology had gone insane, with hoodoos mutating into giant teeth, anticlines morphing into synclines, strata bending, breaking, folding, and spinning kaleidoscopic patterns, and orogenetic rocks performing acrobatics. The canyon here was more stunning than any George Wendt had ever seen; he who had been operating rafting trips down the Grand Canyon of the Colorado for almost half a century.

The rapids were large, but rolling, with long pools between the whitewater. One sported an oversized souse-hole where John capsized a couple years back, but we all made it through unswimmingly, though water went into my ear like an ice pick. Then the river, which had been at times a half mile wide, narrowed to a slot, just a few yards wall-to-wall, and the forced water was a crazy quilt of turbulence, moving boils, whirlpools, eddy fences, and suck holes. It looked as though the river was being fed into a black fog. Our paddle boat was pushed against the left wall, but with some high-siding and tactical paddling, we pulled away. The oar boat behind was not so lucky, and when pressed against the wall, it climbed the cliff like a monkey and flipped. The guide, the cook, and three passengers, all more than age sixty, were in the churning cold water, one pinned under the raft. The kayaks and the other rafts were quick to rescue, and in less than a minute all were safely onboard other rafts, though clearly in shock. The cook and Ollie, a veteran adventurer from Seattle, weren't wearing wet suits, and hypothermia was setting in. Everyone acted fast . . . the overturned boat was towed to the nearest beach, the dunked passengers helped to shore, Walker quickly gathered enough driftwood for a bonfire, and limbs were rubbed and massaged to stimulate circulation. "It was terrifying," said Laurel, who had been stuck under the raft. "But it was thrilling, too." He had lived the Winston Churchill quote: "Nothing in life is so exhilarating as to be shot at without result."

Though the only wounds were psychic, there was the lingering mist that things could have gone differently, perhaps terribly so. We had been unable to observe the basic hygiene of modern communications, as the Indian army, ever alert to Pakistani aggression, allowed no satellite phones, so a severe injury or accident had to be dealt with on the spot. It was not unlike our early Sobek exploratories, when we took a country bus to the place on a crude map that showed a river crossing, blew up our inflatable rafts, and headed downstream into a cauldron of the imagination. Things didn't always work out, but it was an authentic adventure, an unaffectedly nourishing journey of discovery, as this was that day.

That night the darkness was thrown over us like a sheet. After swigs of whiskey and beer, chilled perfectly by the river, we retired to respective tents and collapsed in exhaustion. But sometime in the early morning, rain against the fly woke me, and I crawled out to see the river rising to within a few feet of the camp. I'd been in flash floods before, on the Colorado, in New Guinea, and in Africa, and watched help-lessly as vital gear washed away. Once, on the Omo River in Ethiopia, an ammo box with a camera inside was torn away, only to be discovered on a beach a year later with a bullet hole through the top. Apparently a local found the metal box and couldn't figure out the latch, so took a shot instead. But the camera inside was dry, and the developed pictures were catalogue quality.

I stood at the river's edge watching the river rise, ready to alert the camp if it lapped too high. But the rain stopped, and after a spell the water began to recede, and I tucked back to the warmth of my sleeping bag.

The final day began calmly, floating into a canyon so blunt and stark it looked as though they could have filmed the moon landing here. John assured we were through the worst of the rapids, and it was a sail to our takeout at Leh. But within a few minutes of launching, there was a shrill whistle. The guides all carried whistles and used them during a capsize, a runaway raft, and when approaching big rapids. But with a quick glance to all the guides, it was evident none was holding a whistle to his lips. Then, *kaboom!* It sounded a bomb had been dropped, an avalanche triggered, or Pakistan had attacked. Everyone ducked and then peeked up to see an explosion of rock and dust fly across the river just a hundred yards downstream. It was the road construction team, trying to blast a route from Leh to Padum, to where the down-stream crew stopped at Jackhammer two years before. Not many boaters passed here . . . more people have climbed Everest than have rafted the length of the Zanskar . . . so the blasters did not expect us. But, still, it was a reminder how thin the line runs here, and we all rushed to propel the boats through the settling rock powder to beyond the blast zone.

At the confluence with the Indus, we looked downstream towards Pakistan, where John Yost and I had made the first descent sometime back, with an equal share of close calls. But the border, of course, was closed, so we turned upstream to Leh and clean sheets and hot showers. At dinner we toasted our "zurvival," but then we heard some sad news. A Swiss kayaker, Ian Beecroft, not far behind us, had drowned on the Tsarap, the river that joined us at the Doda to form the Zanskar, just a few miles from where the monk met me on the road to Padum.

CHAPTER 58

MOMENTS OF DOUBT

Grey is all theory; ever green is the tree of life.
—GOETHE, *FAUST*

IF TRAVEL IS ABOUT A COLLIDING OF REALITIES, IT IS NO LESS ABOUT THE BREEDING of illusions: romance, adventure, and promise; greener pastures; secret answers; and peoples more splendid than ourselves. But as I've grabbed more than a fair helping in my career, I've also undergone a quiet erosion of these illusions.

Recently, I traveled through Africa with two scholars, Paul Maritz, who was born in then-Rhodesia (now Zimbabwe) and has invested significantly in ways to improve the lot of Africans, and Dr. Emmanuel Akyeampong, a Ghanaian-born professor of history at Harvard University. As we stood above a palm-fringed quay on the Gold Coast of West Africa, on the fusty ramparts of a fifteenth-century slave castle, Emmanuel talked about how the slave trade stole some of the most physically fit stock, leaving behind the infirm to procreate. He said it forced tribes into hiding in infertile areas, where they grew cassava and other less-than-nourishing foods, affecting the well-being of subsequent generations. Families were torn apart; social mores and traditions were washed out to sea. What remained was a culture of fear. All these led to situations today, where many young Africans do not know the under-history that has shaped their lot, and so they assume a fatalism and ambivalence that self-perpetuates. Young Africans are often puzzled and unsure, their vision of a future flat.

From Ghana we traveled southeast to Mozambique, a country still reeling from its seventeen-year civil war, in which an externally financed movement called REN-AMO set out to destroy the Marxist government and wreak wholesale destruction on the social and communications infrastructure. Schools, clinics, roads, and rail-ways were all ruined. During this period, RENAMO killed an estimated 100,000 Mozambicans in what the US State Department called "one of the most brutal holocausts against ordinary human beings since World War II." Many were killed

Richard with Paul Maritz. BRETT COX

by the land mines salted throughout the country, and still today we could not drive or hike off established routes for fear of being blown to pieces.

Crossing the border into Zimbabwe, which was enjoying over more than 2,000 percent annual inflation. That of course was nothing compared to the fate of my friend Justin Seymour-Smith, whose family for generations had run a quiet farm and wildlife park that featured one of the last populations of endangered rhinos. Under the policies of Zimbabwe's president, Robert Mugabe, Justin's family property was confiscated, much of the wildlife was shot for food, and the Seymour-Smith family was forced to flee with little more than the clothes on their backs.

Then we crossed to Botswana, to a wildlife refuge called Tuli Block, which once harbored some of the greatest populations of big game in Africa. Much of the area was flattened and dry, the shrub and grass cropped close to the ground. "This is a problem," the ranger pointed out. "This park is fenced. . . . We border two other countries, Zimbabwe and South Africa, and the animals can't cross the borders, can't follow their natural migrations. They circulate in containment here, sometimes with devastating effects. Since I've been here, we've lost five plant species to the elephants."

On the way back, I made a road trip through Serbia, Bosnia, and Croatia, and I could not ignore the great disfiguring swaths of clear-cut forest, scars across a green countenance of 100-year-old pines and beech. The political thunderstorms that crashed over the Balkans for millennia have not been kind to these vast natural assets, especially of late. Less than 1 percent of the area is protected, but even that is a dubious designation. The war ended in 1995, but it left much of the region devastated economically and, some would say, morally. In the rush to find a new economy, the land was being skinned at record rates, usually for non-sustainable, short-term benefits, often illicitly. Every hour of the day, belching diesel trucks bearing timber, some of it from irreplaceable primary forest, trundled past me on the way to Italy or to other hard-woods markets. What would be left for my sons, or their own children, to wonder at?

Soon afterwards, I headed to Central America to kayak Lago Nicaragua, host to the only freshwater sharks in the world. But I saw no sharks and found that the lake had become treacherously polluted. Worse, I learned that more than half of Nica-raguans don't have access to basic services for drinking water, a travesty in a land of rain forests, huge natural lakes, and many rivers. When I then returned to Indonesia after an absence of ten years, my old friend Dr. Halim Indrakasuma bemoaned how the environmental integrity of his country had plunged. He talked about a drilling accident in East Java that released a torrent of toxic mud, leveling villages and leaving ten thousand homeless. He said that in ten years, Indonesia, once the cabinet of Asia with its vast forests of hardwood, would have to import timber.

Then, to throw another treated log onto the fire of disenchantment, I took a moment to dive in Fiji, where the coral is etiolating to the color of a bathtub.

I shared many of these moments with my close friend Tom Peirce as he lay in a hospital bed in his hometown of Aspen, Colorado. Tom had started an adventure travel company, High Country Passage, not long after I founded Sobek, and over the years we had shared many, many stories of adventure and the lyric joys of travel. We had compared notes and contacts and insights and shared the canoe in which we ran the shoals of businesses that stirred the waters of wonder. But now Tom was stricken with a most unkind jolt—lung cancer, though he didn't smoke—and he wondered if the onset cause might have somehow been environmental. Tom died a few weeks later while undergoing experimental therapy in Oregon.

George Fuller, my close friend and companion on so many adventures, died of pneumonia in Bali in 2006 while seeking native medicinal cures in the threatened forests. George Wendt, friend and partner in the original Sobek, passed in 2016 from complications caused by Non-Hodgkin lymphoma. George, John Yost, and I were to share a wild river run in Guatemala, but instead John and I held a tearful memorial by the rushing waters not far from Antigua.

Through all this, what gave me solace? The wonder and hope that comes from travel, especially travel with a purpose.

CHAPTER 59

RWANDA, CAN WATER SAVE GORILLAS?

I feel more comfortable with gorillas than people. I can anticipate what a gorilla's going to do, and they're purely motivated.

—Dian Fossey

It all boils down to water.

By some estimates, more than two billion people, a third of the world's population, are threatened by a scarcity of clean, potable water. And in a tiny swath of highland rain forest smack in the center of Africa, the last of the mountain gorillas, about 1,000 in all, are threatened as well.

It may seem enigmatic that gorillas living on the slopes of fertile volcanoes that receive rainfall almost every day could be in jeopardy over water issues. Mountain gorillas don't even drink—they slake from a salad bowl of wild celery, thistles, nettles, and bamboo. But it is the richness of the environment that has preserved this rare primate; and that same richness may be the vital cause of its demise.

Greg Cummings, director of the Gorilla Organization, believes there may once have been one thousand gorillas that roamed the Virunga Mountains. Gentle vegetarians, they had no predators, knew no borders, and lived in tropical affluence, all their needs supplied from the swaddling forest.

That all changed in 1902. A German officer, Robert von Beringe, sighted and shot the first mountain gorilla, setting off an era of trophy hunting. In a rude bit of eponymous taxonomy, the primate is named *Gorilla beringei* for the man who may go down in history as the catalyst for its extinction. By 1925, at least fifty gorillas had been taken and, in a moment of progressive sanity, the Belgian government established Africa's first national park in the Virungas as a sanctuary for the gorillas.

Today that sanctuary is divided into three parks in three countries—Uganda, the Congo, and Rwanda—and is a fraction of its original size. And while today sport

Virunga Mountains, Rwanda. DIDRIK JOHNCK

hunting no longer exists, other more insidious forces are pushing the gorillas to the edge of extinction.

Habitat reduction is the modern *maudit*. The area that butts against the park boundaries in Rwanda is the most densely populated in Africa, with some five hundred people per square mile, and they are desperately poor, living on less than a dollar a day. When I flew over Rwanda, it was like flying over a circuit board, with little delineation between farm plots and cattle ranches, and only the cloud-eating Virungas the exception. When the mists cleared, the volcanoes looked as though they had been draped with ragged green tablecloths, the only uncultivated land in the country. Rwandans have an average of six children per family, and there is no place left to go. In 1958, the park was 131 square miles; by 1995, it was reduced to 48 square miles, the rest lost to the match, machete, and plow. And, as with the people, there is no other place for the gorillas to go. None has ever reproduced outside this unique Afromontane lair; none live in captivity.

Even after the madness of 1994, in which a million people were murdered in one hundred days and another two million fled the country, Rwanda remains Africa's most overpopulated country, with some 8.5 million people in a landlocked tract the size of Vermont. Some accuse the wildlife conservationists of neocolonial myopia. Why make all these efforts to save 1,000 gorillas when millions of people are pounding at the door of survival? Greg Cummings argues that gorillas in fact may be a savior to the disenfranchised. Gorillas have become a major tourist attraction—Rwanda hosted 163,000 visitors in 2019, generating $498 million, and a portion of the revenues went to community-based projects to improve crop yields, education, and health care. Greg's own organization raises significant monies from a raft of American billionaires and funnels the cash to local endeavors that improve lives. "When I first came to Rwanda in 1992, I picked up a postcard that showcased the country's wildlife, and gorillas were conspicuous in their absence," Greg remembered. Few Rwandans had ever seen a gorilla or even an image of one. One of Greg's goals, he said with tongue only slightly in cheek, was to help usher in an "all-singing, all-dancing gorilla-loving nation." Gorillas may be the country's greatest natural resource, and Greg contended that "if people champion and defend the gorillas, their own future is secured. Gorillas are Rwanda's gold."

But the blight on the survival of the gorillas may be the dreaded knell, and in a seemingly oblique way it has everything to do with water. And as we drove through the tropical savagery of an afternoon rainstorm, Greg explained why.

As in much of the developing world, where the human population has burst beyond its seams, people have slashed and burned the forests to plant. With the arboreal root system gone, the rich topsoil quickly washed away, and a natural catchment was gone. Runoff from the rain was immediate, and despite two rainy seasons, villagers found themselves with not enough water to endure. "Today, the greatest illegal human incursions into the gorilla park are not poachers, not firewood seekers, not planters, but water gatherers," Greg explicated. "Every day, villagers walk for hours deep into the park to volcanic sills and streams to fetch water."

But how does that harm the mountain gorillas? Because just as avian flu, Ebola, COVID, even AIDS may be the scourge of the human race, novel diseases are the biggest threat to the survival of the little kingdom of gorillas. The gorillas have few immunities, and exposure to villagers on a water quest can have dire consequences. Not long ago, eight gorillas were lost to measles. Others died of flu, scabies, and other human-borne diseases, far short of their forty-five-year life expectancy. Some seven million years ago, we evolved from a common ancestor of these great apes, whose DNA is 97 percent shared with our own. A mini plague could wipe out the remaining gorillas in a flash, a portent perhaps of our own fate writ small.

The solution? Greg thinks it is providing a reliable source of fresh water to the communities surrounding the park, forestalling water quests into gorilla zones, lessening unsupervised contact (when tourists make the treks, they are screened for coughs and ill-health symptoms, obliged to keep a distance of several yards from the apes, and not permitted to defecate near water in the sanctuary).

The UN designated March 22 as World Water Day, with the theme "Water for Future Needs." In that spirit, my Sobek colleagues and I invested in Greg Cummings's vision for helping the mountain gorillas of Rwanda by building a cistern that would collect rainwater and supply a dependable source of clean water for one of the human communities just outside the park. It was but one coin in a vast and complicated coffer of coexistence and species survival, but like a reservoir that shines like silver, it would be an asset that makes a difference. I invited actress-turned-environmental-activist Daryl Hannah to join me in the long trek to this equatorial outpost, a village that straddled the watersheds of the Congo and the Nile, and she, along with Greg Cummings, hoped to see the water flow not away to giant rivers, not away from the priestly realm of the mountain gorillas, but into the cooking pots and mouths of Rwandans in the mists.

As we made the long, bumpy ride to the headquarters of Parc National Des Volcans, our driver, Alex, wrestled the wheel like a skipper in a typhoon, trying to miss not only the ruts but also the river of people pouring down this track. A great many of them were carrying yellow plastic jerry cans, water jugs, looking for the precious element. Some were on rusted bicycles with as many as ten jerry cans strapped to every available bar. Many were headed into the park on an illegal hunt to find the water that would help feed their families.

At one point, near the Gorilla Nest Lodge and Golf Course, we stalled at the edge of a craterlike fissure caused by erosion, its twisted mouth looking as though waiting for a catch. As Alex shifted gears forward and reverse, a hundred children surrounded the vehicle and pressed their faces against the glass; most were smiling as they reached out, palms up, for some sort of acknowledgment. But others looked angry, as though we were insulting them by driving past, as foreigners do each day, on $1,000-a-day safaris to see the gorillas. I was swept away with disorientation, as though we had veered off into an illusion, and didn't know what to do. I rolled down the window and a dozen hands pushed through as though trying to claw their way out of poverty. I offered a plastic bottle of water, and it was snatched away by one of the boys, as though it were a thousand francs, a fortune in this terribly oversubscribed piece of the world.

There was a constant tug of conscience and imperative here. We came to meet the mountain gorillas and countenance the contours of their plight, but it was impossible not to be affected by the human stories, and there were so many it simply crushed the psyche. It was almost some sort of reverse caste system at work: It was the tiny population of gorillas that got all the world's attention, and millions in donations, while the seething sea of people was, in relative terms, marginalized and ignored.

Once at park headquarters, we met our guide, François Bigirimana, who had been tracking gorillas for twenty-six years and had known the famously misanthropic Dian Fossey. While studying gorillas in the late 1960s to the mid-1980s, she made it a personal crusade to stop the poachers, a campaign that brought world attention and may have led to her own grisly murder when she was macheted six times to the head in her bed just after Christmas 1985.

Just before this trip, I breakfasted with Peter Guber, the producer of the biopic *Gorillas in the Mist*, which he cited as his proudest film in a long catalogue of features. He remembered that when he pitched the movie, the executives at Warner Bros. were skeptical of his conceit. He wanted to film the lead, Sigourney Weaver, in situ with the authentic gorillas for six weeks and then write the script around what transpired. "That's backwards," Guber was told. "We write the script, then hire actors in gorilla suits and film on a soundstage in London. Nobody will know the difference." Guber prevailed, and viewers were awed by the verisimilitude, and the film went on to inspire millions, fund several gorilla conservation organizations, and influence the hosting governments to make efforts to eliminate poaching.

To a degree it has worked. During Fossey's era, the gorilla population shrank to about 250, teetering on the brink of extinction. Now there are more than 1,000, but there is still loss to poachers, who kill gorillas to sell their heads for wall mounts, their hands for ashtrays, and their babies as pets. François said he caught a poacher three weeks ago who had crossed over from the Congo. He had snagged a baby, and François returned it to the forest and put the poacher in jail. The more menacing poacher, though, is the father looking for bush meat to feed his family. He lays snares inside the park to capture duiker and bushbuck, and the gorillas sometimes step into one and end up losing a limb or dying from infection. And then there are the bamboo poachers, who cut down one of the major food sources for the gorillas. François said if caught, bamboo poachers get five years in jail; antelope poachers get ten; and a gorilla poacher goes to jail for life.

After an orientation in a tin hut in the racket of a rainstorm, we began our trek up the volcano in search of the Sabyinyo group of eleven gorillas. It was a slosh wading through forest as dense and green as broccoli, a forest that had never seen an ax, all of us screaming at the stinging nettles as they stuck through pants, shirts, even gloves. We tucked our pants into socks to keep out the safari ants and stopped every few minutes to catch our breath in the thin air. We were at nine thousand feet, winching ourselves upward through a matrix of mud and montane jungle.

After ninety minutes, we lurched over a ridge and practically into the arms of the largest silverback in Rwanda, Guhonda, at four hundred pounds, the alpha male of the Sabyinyo group, who was sucking water from a wild celery stalk. François made a rolling grunt-hum, "Mmmmm," and I repeated, as he said this was gorilla language for "I'm a friendly visitor."

Guhonda loped to a glen where seven members of his group were resting after brunch, and François guided us down to a gallery just a few feet away. For the next hour we watched and photographed with our array of digital cameras as the gorillas did their thing. Two babies, looking like plush toys, tumbled and bit and rolled about just as my sons, Walker and Jasper, used to as toddlers. The mothers patiently disciplined and groomed their charges, while Guhonda lounged in the middle of it all, the king on his thistle couch. Individually they stared at us with their large knowing eyes, and it seemed as though we had stumbled upon a neighborhood of mirrors, or of lenses to a different time in our lives. While below the park the eyes of the young seemed to telegraph a winter landscape in a tropic paradise, the soft brown eyes of the gorillas spoke of an unfallen place and time.

As we tripped down the slippery volcano, Greg Cummings, who had made some fifty treks to the mountain gorillas, summed it up: "You come here with all this high-tech gear and think the gorillas will be impressed; instead, you are overwhelmed by how much we've lost."

When Greg Cummings met Bill Gates Sr. at the Gates Foundation and Bill learned that the fee for an hour's visitation with the gorillas was $375, he balked. "That's more than I got as a lawyer."

Donations and fees to save the gorillas are in the millions of dollars each year. One billionaire benefactor, when told how many gorillas were the recipients of his largess, remarked, "I just gave enough to put up all the gorillas in Claridge's for a year."

The monies for gorilla salvation go to many good works, such as training trackers, clothing and arming antipoaching squads, snare removal, behavioral research, even inoculations. But the Gorilla Organization was devoted to "a holistic solution," one that invested in community development surrounding the park. Greg's theory was that if the lives of the 2.5 million people who live in the shadow of the Virungas are improved because of the presence of great apes, they will come to say to the more shortsighted, "Hell, no. You're not coming into the gorilla habitat. The gorillas are our bread and butter here." And the gorillas' presence is the reason for a local supply of clean water, as we were to witness.

"I think that sometimes environmentalists can be out of touch with the reality of poverty, of the challenges that face people who have just emerged from civil war. Wildlife conservation can't happen in isolation," Greg postulated as we trundled toward the village of Gitaraga, just below the 13,540-foot-high Muhabura volcano, home to several gorilla groups.

Greg's organization employs what he calls gorilla tactics, investing in a number of community projects, such as farmer training for better crop yields, artisan schools so villagers can make handicrafts to sell to tourists, micro-credit loans to entrepreneurs, environmental education, poacher reform, school building, and, especially significant today, the building of cisterns. "We've built twenty-six cisterns, all attached to the long roofs of schools, all within two miles of the park." It's the children who make the long, illegal journeys into the park to fetch water, the children who put the gorillas most at risk with exposure.

And as we ground up the last muddy hill to Gitaraga, it was the children who met us, some fifteen hundred in all who attended this tiny tin-roofed school. They came swarming to our vehicles, a sea of smiles, backdropped by the storybook volcano that looked lifted from a Japanese silk. None recognized Daryl Hannah, who lent her name and energy to this day, and this project. But they made the connection between our presence and the construction that had been going on for the past fifteen days next to their school, a twenty-five-cubic-yard cistern that was in its final moments of fashioning, here in a village with no springs, no source of clean water within five miles.

Out of the ruck of cheering children emerged Peter Celestin Muvunyi, the lead engineer for the building of the cistern. He led us down a path littered with yellow jerry cans, to the new cistern. Peter was proud of this work, built in record time, and it was only the second in the series built with stones rather than brick. "It's more expensive to build with stones, but it is better for our environment," Peter boasted. "The bricks need to be cooked, and that requires cutting down trees to fuel the kiln, and fewer trees mean less catchment."

The circular cistern was a lovely sight, almost elegant in its simple design, bordering on art. A plastic pipe ran from the school-roof eaves, feeding rainwater to the contained reservoir, which then released its bounty through a faucet three yards from the base. It was here the children who used to walk so far each morning, missing school, would now find the water for their families, and that was more beautiful than art.

Like the black space between stars, the effectiveness of one more cistern on saving gorillas was difficult to measure. But at least one star was willing to believe theory over micrometry. Daryl Hannah had flown halfway around the world to participate in the opening of this cistern because she was a supporter of World Water Day, and because the concept of being involved in a project that could contribute to the future well-being of mountain gorillas was irresistible. Daryl had most of her life been involved in saving animals. She grew up on the forty-second floor of a high-rise in Chicago, but even there, when she found broken-winged birds and other small creatures in need, she would take them home and nurse them to health. When she was seven, her family was on a road trip and stopped at a restaurant off the freeway. She wasn't hungry so she stayed in the car, but when she saw a trailer of cattle she wandered over and began to commune with a big-eyed calf. She spent a half hour petting and speaking with the young cow, and when the driver emerged, she turned to him and asked the name of the animal. "At seven o'clock tomorrow, 'Veal,'" the driver replied, and Daryl never ate meat again and became a lifelong friend and savior to animals.

As an adult, Daryl hugged a manatee, swam with dolphins, petted a moose, and was kissed by a wild wolf. Now she took in strays and rescues animals of all stripes—dogs, cats, horses, turtles, tropical birds, even a South American tree frog she found in a Los Angeles swimming pool. So when, just a few weeks earlier, I told her of our project to help finance a cistern at the edge of the gorilla habitat, working with the Gorilla Organization, she volunteered to help. "I've always wanted to see the gorillas!"

Now it was time. It was a preternaturally sunny day in a part of the world usually swirling in mist. There was a ribbon across the entrance to the cistern, and Daryl was presented with a china plate covered with embroidered linen. Inside was a pair of scissors, which she gently removed, and with which she attempted to cut the ribbon, which was stubbornly resistant. But after a few attempts, it fell away, and Daryl, the mayor, the governor, the director general of tourism and national parks, and all sorts of keen parties walked to the basin below the cistern, where a shiny silver tap awaited. Daryl was handed a plastic petrol container, which she positioned to drink, and as she turned the spigot, there was a sound like pumping brakes. All of Gitaraga held its breath; we all sensed an intangible atmosphere of imminence, as though a huge charge of lightning was building up within a thundercloud. Then, a whoosh, and cool, clean, clear water issued forth. The sun struck; the water burst into a million gems . . . it was pure, pure magic. I reached my hand into the cascade and felt the vitality and power as it coursed up my arm, into my chest, and up into my brain. The lives of several hundred families, and perhaps as many gorillas, were at that moment changed, even if by but a bucket's worth in a wide and stormy sea.

CHAPTER 60

GORILLAS IN THE CLEAR

And the gorillas themselves are too shrewd to talk . . . they have a very healthy wariness about people in general and government people in particular. As one of them told me once, "If it got out that we can talk, the conservatives would exterminate most of us and make the rest pay rent to live on our own land; and the liberals would try to train us to be engine-lathe operators."
—ROBERT SHEA AND ROBERT ANTON WILSON, *THE GOLDEN APPLE*

AS A STORM OF PEOPLE GATHERED TO CELEBRATE THE CISTERN, I IMAGINED THE gorillas on the volcano above looking down in amusement, wondering among themselves what all the fuss was about.

More than two thousand Rwandans came to the grounds of Gitaraga Primary School near the Ugandan border to rejoice in the new cistern, some from as far away as the capital, Kigali. There were film crews, photographers, dignitaries, a movie star—this was the biggest thing to ever hit town.

There was a crude PA system with a swarm of feedback; there was an entire Goodwill Store of fashion. There were speeches (they could use the Academy Award rules for duration) and thank-yous and acknowledgments. Failure is an orphan; success has many fathers, and we seemed to have a whole haunt of silverbacks there that day.

The governor, as the mayor before him, cited gorillas as the great natural asset that generates monies for community projects such as this, and he stressed the gorilla habitat must be kept sacred. When the governor asked if anyone still hunted in the forest, a mapped face raised his hand and said he had been culling his subsistence in the park his whole life. The governor asked him to come forward and offered to buy him a hoe if he promised to stay out of the park. The old man was suspicious but agreed only if the governor gave him the money right there, right then; and to the amusement of the crowd, the governor reached deep into his pocket and produced a few thousand francs.

This is an auditory country. There are no movie theaters in the shadow of the Virungas, no video stores, and the few televisions are in hotels for foreigners.

Magazines and newspapers are rare; most people don't even read. The primary source for information is the radio, and it was the radio that served as the critical tool to incite the genocide of 1994, provoking the ruling Hutu to kill neighbors, families, and friends, anyone with rival Tutsi heritage, up to a million in just more than three months. Now the radio is used to spread a different kind of propaganda, that of conservation and celebration of the gorillas, and it has infused itself into school curriculums and the consciousnesses of young minds like the Golden Rule to Western school children.

When the speeches were done, the music and dancing began. There were *ingoma* drums, choruses, and a one-stringed instrument called an *indingidi*, a sisal-snared fiddle, whose sawer could beat Charlie Daniels down to Georgia. All the songs were themed with water as the source of life. There was a kind of Rwandan rap, wherein a young girl from the wildlife club challenged her peers:

"You children what is your plan now?"

"We want to live in a healthy Rwanda with clean water and a protected environment. Conservation is the only way we can protect the sources of life, of water and trees."

"Who told you all this?"

"We are students, and we have our own club. Dian Fossey helped us to learn more about the wildlife of Rwanda."

Then there was a peculiar rendition of "Jingle Bells," with the words altered a bit for local relevancy, but the spirit in some ways the same: "Because the cistern has come there will be no more sleeping without food. Because the cistern has come there will be no water you can't cook. There will be lots of cleanliness now, and everything is going to be fine with the people of the area and of the kids of this school."

Next there was a kind of ballet, simple yet expressive, dignified but provocative, a delicate poem of subtle arm movements, genteel turns, and graceful swoops, arms rippling, supple bodies undulating, a dance full of politeness, all set to customized lyrics, "Come and see. We are happy because we have water." It seemed a refined and elevated art, coming from one of the most remote villages on the planet. It seemed so hard to draw the circle between preserving the gorillas by honoring their habitat through providing alternative sources of water for adjacent communities from monies generated by gorillas, but somehow their music and dance did so elegantly.

The grand finale was the *Ikinimba* dance, a venerated bop that told the stories of Rwandan kings and heroes, with rotating arm movements like rice blowing in the wind and impossible foot moves. I knew, because the Rwandan dancers invited the American visitors to the floor, and most of us looked like The Wild Czech Brothers attempting an interpretive dance of "Flight of the Bumblebee." The exception was Daryl Hannah, who has the long limbs of a gazelle and chose not to attempt imitation, but rather did her own funky pronk that somehow made sense in a place that seemed a physical manifestation of jazz.

We ended our day with a visit to His Excellency Paul Kagame, president of Rwanda. Greg Cummings wore a tie with more gorillas on it than survive in the Virungas; Daryl wore sneakers without shoelaces; and I donned my only clean shirt, a Buzz-Off Ex Officio. Paul Kagame lived in the Virungas for several years when he led the rebel Tutsi forces and made forays back and forth from Uganda. But during that time, he never saw a mountain gorilla. It wasn't until he came to power in 2000 that he made a gorilla trek, a four-hour slog in the rain, but when he saw the gentle giants in their own private DMZ, he found religion. He went on record later that year saying that the nation's two highest priorities were conservation and HIV prevention. So when we asked how he managed to oversee a national

Baby mountain gorilla, Rwanda. DIDRIK JOHNCK

change of conservation consciousness in the midst of so many pressing human problems, a transformation that resulted in a lessening of poaching and encroachment and a significant increase in the gorilla population, he tied it back to the 1994 genocide, to which he had made a harsh-light policy of remembrance, making sure people looked into the face of evil and understood it so it would not happen again.

"When something so horrible happens, it allows people to start over, to reevaluate priorities. Gorilla tourism is our third-largest source of foreign exchange, and we value gorillas now in a way we didn't before the war. We have a unique asset in the gorillas, and by helping them they can help us."

Somewhere up high in the Virungas, I was convinced, the gorillas were celebrating, sucking water from thistles and celery, rolling about the bamboo, exchanging commentary about the humans below. Tomorrow, with Daryl, we would climb to these innocent landscapes and learn what we could from our cousins and their lofty, leafy kingdom of grace.

Baby mountain gorilla, Rwanda. DIDRIK JOHNCK

CHAPTER 61

DARYL HANNAH WOULD RATHER STAY HERE

You may drive out nature with a pitchfork, yet she'll be constantly running back.
—Horace, *Epistles*, Book 1, Epistle 10

VISITING THE MOUNTAIN GORILLAS IS AN EXERCISE IN DEVOLUTION. WE FLEW halfway around the world, drove for several hours to the base of a set of tropic volcanoes, hiked for hours, and then crawled the final steps up into the lair of our ancestral kin.

On the trek toward the park, we passed several wattle-and-daub huts roofed with what looked like witches' hats. They seemed hastily constructed and gave the impression they would get up and leave if they only had the energy, and something did not block their way.

We passed long-horned Ankole cattle, who until recently regularly mowed down gorilla vegetation (Dian Fossey famously shot thirty head at close range in her private effort to preserve the gorilla habitat). But the cattle no longer roam upward.

We waded through a field of what looked like daisies, but they were in fact pyrethrum, a cash crop and natural insecticide. Not long ago, twenty-two thousand acres, roughly half of the protected gorilla habitat, was given over to a European scheme to cultivate an alternative to DDT. But the fields encroached no farther.

All were stopped by a fetial wall. From fees generated by ecotourists, and donated monies from NGOs, a five-foot-high volcanic stone wall had been fashioned that surrounds most of the park. Ostensibly designed to keep buffalo and forest elephants from raiding crops, it served another, perhaps greater, purpose of delineating the park boundary so farmers, hunters, rangers, and antipoaching squads knew the armistice line. Rwanda has a zero-tolerance policy for unauthorized visits to the park, though the mandate is still violated with some regularity. A few days ago, our team followed six young girls on a dangerous water quest into the park, not just because they were at risk of being arrested, but also because the slippery landscape was so severe a fall could be fatal. Unsupervised exposure to gorillas on these quests has the potential to transmit disease in both directions. One villager on a recent water quest was bitten by a venomous snake and lost his leg. But with alternatives, such as the village cisterns now being constructed, water quests may become a thing of the past.

At the zigzag passage through the wall, we stepped over a scattering of porcupine quills—some wildlife still traveled both directions—and began the steep climb up the volcano. We swatted away branches, clung to creepers, slid through muck, and whacked the biting safari ants as we reeled up into the richest ecosystem in Africa. Daryl, who for several years lived in an off-the-grid home at ten thousand feet in Telluride, Colorado, had fewer problems with the elevation than the rest of us, and she was quickly at the front of the pack, eager for first contact.

Somewhere in the middle flanks of the volcano we heard a rustling, and with a few steps a black ball of fur flew from the top of a bamboo stalk. It was Daryl's first mountain gorilla sighting, and her shadowed eyes aroused as the sea waiting for thunder. The gorilla knuckle-walked by us to within a couple feet, and we proceeded to follow. Suddenly gorillas surrounded us, from babies to blackbacks and silverbacks, thrashing about in their own guiltless ways. We listened to a baby whimpering as its mother refused it back passage, an attempt at weaning. We watched as two young males wrestled, fur flying and leaves scattering as they tumbled about the forest. "Monkeying around," Daryl said and laughed, and for a moment one of the gorillas looked at us and seemed to display a toothy smile. Another baby strolled to one of our video camera microphones, covered in synthetic fur as a wind screen, and reached out to touch what seemed a fellow creature. A mother with disproportionately huge eyes stared at Daryl as though she had seen her in some movie but couldn't quite place her, and puffs of condensation steamed from her mouth. Two other apes rose up and thumped their chests with a sound like mallets on wood, and Daryl thumped her own chest back. The sway-bellied silverback watched all the activity dispassionately, with eyes that nature seemed to break through, then fell back to chill on a springy bed of vegetation. When Daryl sat near the lounging ape and began to explain her delight, the silverback seemed to punctuate each sentence with a disapproving grunt. Then when another criminally cute baby wandered by, I asked Daryl, "Don't you just want to take it home?"

"No. I'd rather stay here."

Violence just seemed missing here. At that moment there was not a breath of brutality in these long-haired beings. The vast forest seemed motionless as in a picture, caught in a continuous Now, living in the churns of mists with neither past nor future. Then our hour was up.

As we gathered our packs, we heard another sound that didn't quite fit the milieu. We stopped moving and listened, and a sonance filled the air, as though pouring into a bowl. It was beautiful music, like a small spring singing to itself, and we realized it was the sound of children singing down the slopes, down at the village of Gitaraga, where the new cistern was installed. At that moment there seemed a balance, one that

Daryl Hannah cutting a ribbon for the Gitaraga clean water cistern in Rwanda. Laura Hubber in the rear. DIDRIK JOHNCK

may have existed two centuries back before French naturalist Paul du Chaillu, after encountering a family of lowland gorillas, described them as "hellish dream creatures," an impression that maintained today and was reinforced through cliche and popular film. But in Rwanda, a culture shift was under way, precipitated by tourists, politicians, nonprofit organizations, and local communities. For the moment, the gorilla population was stable and growing; the habitat was mostly protected. Life for the surrounding communities was improving. Hope wafted the air.

Back in 1996, I shared a dinner with Bill Gates, who had recently returned from trekking to see the mountain gorillas. He proclaimed the sight one of the wonders of the world, but he was pessimistic about the prospects. He was aware of the political problems in the region, and the enormous population pressures, and he thought the trend not good. At the end of a lengthy conversation that spiraled through dessert, Bill bet me $100 that within ten years the mountain gorillas would be extinct. As soon as I left the dinner party, I regretted I had not bet differently, such as 1 percent of our respective net worth.

When I returned from Rwanda, I emailed Bill to report he had lost the bet and requested $100 be sent to the Gorilla Organization, the good-works group that had done so much to make a future for the gorillas possible through investment in community projects, such as the Gitaraga cistern. By empowering villagers alongside the volcanoes, the people came to appreciate the asset in their backyard and now made efforts to preserve this breathing, thumping, black and silver currency. And Bill made good on the bet and sent the monies promised, and then some, the next day.

As we reached the buffalo wall on the return trip, Daryl stopped short. "I'm just gonna stay here now. Say hi to my family. I'm gonna go live with the gorillas." And she turned toward the volcano and walked back into the forest, to perhaps a more splendid state, and nature's own infinite but gracious imperfections, the habitat of the mountain gorillas of Rwanda.

CHAPTER 62

SEEKING THE SOURCE

It's not all pleasure, this exploration.
—DAVID LIVINGSTONE, 1873

HERODOTUS IN THE FIFTH CENTURY BCE AND PTOLEMY SEVEN CENTURIES LATER wrote about the "fountains of the Nile," the waters from which issued the greatest river in the world. To locate its source—*Quaerere caput Nili*—was the hope of great captains and geographers from the classical age to the Victorian: Cyrus and Cambyses of Persia, Alexander the Great, Julius Caesar, Nero, and the mid-nineteenth-century rivals, Richard Burton and John Hanning Speke. After dismissing the geographical claims of Speke and Burton (both of whom he disliked, especially Burton, translator of the Kama Sutra, a man he considered morally bankrupt), Dr. David Livingstone set out in 1866 on his final expedition to Africa to claim the prize as the discoverer of the source of the "Father of Waters," the Nile. He was convinced the "four fountains" sprang from swamplands in what is today Northern Zambia, near the Angola border.

Livingstone got it wrong and instead discovered the scrimshaw beginnings of the Congo, second-longest river in Africa, and there he left his heart.

The Scottish missionary-explorer, who spent shy of thirty years seeking "God's Highway" (a water passage into the African interior that would allow colonization, the end of Arab slave trading, and Christian conversion of heathens), died of malaria, dysentery, and melancholia at the age of fifty-nine in the Bangweulu Swamps, desperately clinging to the delusion he was tracking the course of the Nile. His heart was cut from his body, placed in a box, and buried under an mpundu tree, while his body was carried to the coast and shipped to England. One of his last journal entries reads: "Dear God, I am oppressed that this may, after all, be the Congo. Who would risk their life for that dreadful river?"

We would.

Despite touching the sources of several of the great rivers of the world, I had never let my hand swirl the waters of the Congo. So, quite keen I was to see the Coy Fountains. I was traveling with Zambian lodge-owner/guide Chriss Wienand and old friends and African hands Pasquale Scaturro, Justin Seymour-Smith, and Paul Maritz, who was enthusiastic to see *Balaeniceps rex*, a rare dodo-like stork with a wedge-shaped bill known as the shoebill that hides in the swamps.

So we made the two-day drive from North Luangwa to a far outstation of remoteness, the trackless swamps of Bangweulu ("where the water meets the sky"). We wended towards the Muchinga Escarpment, passing herds of buffalo and several hyenas, including a couple courting under a wild gardenia tree (when they loped away, I plucked a bouquet as freshener for the Land Cruiser).

Up a rough track we wound out of this southern branch of the Great Rift Valley to the rim, then across the plateau, flat as a griddle. No more drama; no mopane (apologies to Mary J. Blige). With little notice, the watershed was crossed between the Zambezi and the Congo, and we basked in the hot breeze of a plateau nearly four thousand feet high (by average elevation, Zambia is among the highest countries in Africa). We camped at Kapishya Hot Springs, soaked under arching raffia palms, swam in a crocodiled river, and listened to the eerie whoops of hyenas as we zipped up our sleeping bags for the night. Lions and other cats have been known to attack campers at night, but hyenas are the only animals that assail fairly regularly. Justin had a friend who lost an ear to a hyena while camping in Mozambique; many years ago, I was camping in Awash National Park in Ethiopia where a French tourist had her face bitten off. We built a witch-burner fire nearby and hung the bags together, and I took a spot in the middle.

Sobek the crocodile. BART HENDERSON

In the crisp morning air, we began the long final stretch to Bangweulu. Outside the town of Mpika, which specializes in brokering salt, bananas, and cassavas, we passed the Clinton Night Club ("Your Pleasure Resort") but managed to resist. The Möbius strip of wildlife protection is presented in all its emptiness as we steered west through the miombo woodlands of Lavushi Manda National Park, a barren passage that revealed only a ragged troop of baboons. There were no game scouts, no camps, as there were no tourists. Most of the game had been poached. The circle of nonlife.

As we knocked down the last few miles, we entered a corridor of villages and passed hundreds of children but few adults. The kids waved and yelled and ran to us, hoping we would stop and change their lives. Many were orphans, parents lost to AIDS. Even though this was not a trucking route or crossroads, where most AIDS is spread in Africa, the women here, we were told, perform dry sex, a practice in which the vagina is dried of its natural secretions, supposedly to give more pleasure to lovers. The extreme friction causes lacerations, which in turn make infection to both sides more likely. Add to this the refusal by many to use free condoms dispensed by health organizations and NGOs, believing there is a white man's conspiracy to reduce Black African population with dirty tricks, and you get a region where more than 50 percent of the population is younger than fifteen years old.

Late in the day we traversed a single-lane causeway above the floodplain, the dry-season entrance to the GMA (game management area) that covers the Bangweulu Swamps, and headed for a silver water tower, the only relief under the open sky. We were the only visitors, and Gary Williams was pleasantly shocked when his old friend Chriss Wienand walked through the door. For ten years, Gary owned and operated Shoebill Island Camp, four canvas tents and a thatched dining room catering primarily to trophy hunters. But he sold it last year to the Kasanka Trust, a nonprofit that manages an eponymous nearby park and attempts, with mixed results, to distribute proceeds directly into conservation and development in the park and nearby communities. Gary threw in the towel after the Lusaka government stopped issuing hunting licenses, squashing his main clientele, and with his frustration with the increase in poachers, who are destroying the main attraction, shoebills, not for meat or resale, but to keep tourists at bay so the poachers can hunt mammals without witnesses or interference. Now the camp receives birders in the prime season, November to March, and the odd ecotourist the rest of the year, not enough to make a business.

In the painterly light of the African morning, we headed out on our quest to see a shoebill, a wild stork chase. We drove for half an hour and passed two jackals and a thousand black lechwe, the ergonomically designed, swamp-loving antelope found only here. We slalomed through crowded cemeteries of gray termite mounds, parked at a temporary fishing village, and then began to walk. Sludge was a better word. Quickly we were knee-deep in gloppy mud, and the going was agonizingly slow, the temperature hovering around 100 degrees Fahrenheit. This was not the magnificent source spotting I had envisioned, and there was no transcendence in touching these waters. As for finding the bird, Chriss had mentioned earlier he once had spent sixteen days in the Bangweulu trying to fetch a shoebill for the San Diego Zoo, but all he got was a feather.

Three hours into the trudge we'd seen saddle-billed storks, rufous-bellied herons, various egrets, marabou storks, black-breasted snake eagles, and African marsh harriers, and we'd picked up a few leeches, but no shoebill. Two of our local guides told us to stay put on what might be called a reverse oasis, a spot of dry land in a sea of cloacal mud and water. The guides would go ahead for fifteen minutes and check out the front lines. But forty minutes later, with no sign of the guides, we decided to turn back. We were low on potable water, and the haze of midday heat was kicking us down. The lamination on my hiking boots was gone, and the bill of my shoe was separating. Slowly we slogged back, thirsty, overheated, and tired; the ingredients of a potential epic stew stirring. At one point one of our party folded into a pile on the ground, exhausted with the swamp high stepping under a sun that seemed like thunder made visible. He hydrated, rested, recovered, and we continued through the muck. It felt as though we were walking wrapped in hot towels. Paul practically stepped on a hyena, which scuttled away with angry eyes. Seven hours after starting, we arrived back at the Land Cruiser, shoebill-less. An hour later, our guides arrived back, saying they saw four.

As with good ecotourists, it is the experience of effort, not the goal, which counts, and we retired to the bar.

CHAPTER 63

SLEEPING WITH ELEPHANTS

I have a memory like an elephant. I remember every elephant I've ever met.
—HERB CAEN

IT WAS THE LAST NIGHT OF OUR EXPLORATION OF REMOTE ZAMBIA, AND WE SAVED the wildest place for last, Mandevu Park, a 50,000-acre private game reserve on the lower Luangwa River that had yet to appear on any map. We had supped on a meal Mexican, probably the only tacos and hot sauce in a 500-mile radius and were sipping G&Ts around a mopane wood fire (a hot-blazing hardwood that "burns as long as your passion") as the gibbous moon began its bright sweep across the southern sky. Much of the conversation was about how to deal with African wildlife encountered unexpectedly. Unlike Kenya, Tanzania, South Africa, and other popular wildlife-viewing destinations, Zambia allows "walking safaris" (the concept was invented here by the late elephant control officer, Norman Carr), in which visitors can pad with the animals (other countries allow viewing only behind a layer of motorized metal). Earlier in the day, we had taken a hike, probably the first Westerners to do so, up to the top of Mount Shongon, which means "the place no one goes" in Nyanja, the local language. Along the way we stepped along the footpaths of an array of herbivores and predators. The fireside talk concerned what to do when surprising a beast while wading through high grass or the tangle of thorn trees. Professor Justin Seymour-Smith was the panjandrum on wildlife behavior, and he counseled across the flames: "You never know what a wild animal will do. Meeting you without warning on its turf, it might turn and go away, or it might charge. There are no shortages of tales in Africa of folks who have been on the wrong side of animal whim. But there are some general rules. If you encounter a big cat, never run. Stare it down and slowly back up, otherwise it will chase you like a house cat to a mouse; if you chance upon a gorilla, crouch down and bow your head as though praying; if you bump into a hippo or croc or venomous snake, run like a rat—but you don't have to run faster than the animal, just faster than your friends."

Exhausted from our aggressive wanderings that had taken us from the secluded Busanga Plains in the west to this hidden preserve on the Mozambique border, I announced an early retirement, before the professor finished his dissertation, and toddled to my little North Face Lunarship tent pitched on the high mud banks of the Luangwa River. The others were staying in "chalets," grass huts with beds, showers, and flush toilets, but because I am a world-class snorer, I courteously offered to pitch a tent one hundred yards from the rest. Besides, I liked looking up through the mosquito netting to the Southern Cross.

For some reason, sleep was not forthcoming, and I rolled about in my bag for some time. I felt the cold air from the canyon downstream creep in. I heard the sighing of the river, the whir and chirp of crickets, and, later, the voice of an owl, like a dark brushstroke on the night.

Then about 10:00 p.m., I heard some rustlings upriver. I sat up. The moon showered the desolate glow of a dream onto the scene; the light on the winding river was luminous as a pale shell; and the lineaments of the upstream trees seemed to be swaying. Hippos, I thought. The night previous I had been awakened when a couple of river horses were snorting in the shallows not far from the tent. Hippos graze at night, entering and leaving the river along well-trampled paths, and my little tent was pitched a prudent distance from any such corridor. I rolled over and again attempted to force sleep. But the crackling continued, and it was getting closer, or so I imagined. But after a few turns of the hourglass, the sound abated. Something, though, seemed not right. I sat up again and peered through the mosquito netting. The ridges of the hills were crowned with a moonstone radiance, melting into a profound blue in the shadowy ravines. Everything—the kith of hills, woods, ancient rocks—hung in chasms of blue air; the whole valley was floating veiled in quivering liquid light. Cloud shadows drifted imperceptibly across the sea of trees, deepening the blue to indigo. It seemed I was looking at the ghost of a world, a lost world.

I squinted and scanned the horizon. At first I detected just a gray blur against the dark foliage upstream. It might have been a tree. Or a cluster of bushes. But it moved. It disappeared and reappeared again farther down the bank. At last it lumbered out of the surrounding tangle of shrub and creeper and emerged at the edge of the riverbank. It was no longer just a blur but had shape and form . . . an elephant form. *Loxodonta africana*, a thunderhead of flesh and huge rolling bones with long white tusks flashing in the moonlight. Slowly, almost imperceptibly, it crossed the bank toward my outpost, with pauses now and then to fan out its ears, and perhaps meditate, or dream.

The jumbo tread closer and closer; my heart, already shaking at the cage of my chest, began to throb. Never had I seen a beast so big so close. If life is measured not by the number of breaths taken, but by the moments that take breath away, I was extending my life by a load. About five feet from the entrance to my tent, he halted and stared inside with a look of wildness no civilization could endure. I remained as motionless as I could and looked back into enormous eyes like clear brown water. Then a cramp in my leg developed, so I tried to reposition it without making a sound, but I rubbed against the sleeping pad, which made a squeak. The elephant swung his trunk towards me, and I could see the symmetric ridges emptying, like rained geometry. He sniffed, then stepped back a foot and flapped his ears like the mainsail of a ship, the way elephants do when angry or about to charge, or so I thought from documentaries and picture books. Was he about to charge? I wished I had stayed to hear more of Justin's animal escape advice. Should I try to unzip the tent and run? Should I clap my hands like a rifle shot and see if he will run? Should I shine my flashlight in his eyes? Should I lie down and play dead? I had my Iridium sat phone in my fanny pack. I wished I could call David Attenborough. Or Justin. Or Simon, a professional hunter sleeping on the other side of camp. But I had no numbers to call and was certain the elephant would hear my voice if I did. I just froze in a sitting position and watched as the elephant circled my blue cocoon to the other side and began to make long siphonings on the sausage tree that spread above me. Whew. I relaxed a bit. He was ignoring me. But then I heard what sounded like sawing upstream. I looked and saw a huge acacia swaying in the moonlight, like the treetops in Jurassic Park before a sauropod appeared. Another elephant was rubbing his broad back against the tree on the camp perimeter. Then it stepped from a palisade of thorns onto the campgrounds, following the footsteps of its predecessor, along the rim of the river toward my tent. He was bigger than the last, an animal magnitude from another time, and the glint of his tusks brighter. With smooth, rhythmic strides he moved to the very edge of my tent, and he too stopped and glared inside. His great fanned ears moved slowly to and fro. His breath poured through the netting and pressed down on my shoulders. As he altered his position in the moonlight, the shadows showed the structure of his great body, immensely heavy, slung from mighty backbones, supported by columnar legs. I could not help but think he looked like a baobab come to life.

The Sublime is conceived as a quality of magnitude or natural force that inspires ineffable feelings of awe, wonder, and insecurity in the onlooker. The emotional

An elephant staring into a tent. JOHN CANNING

response is an overwhelming sense of the power, grandeur, and lusty stealth of nature in its most terrifying of moods.

This was, with little doubt, a sublime moment.

Now one bull was chomping on the tree next to me and another on the other side staring me down, two oversized rolling bags of horror. And my stomach started to growl. The Mexican meal was starting to process, and I couldn't hold back a sound. It piped from my tent, and both elephants turned to glower and flap their giant ears. My God, I thought, I am about to be stomped to death by elephants. Genuinely frightened, I felt my heart fly around my insides. My mouth went dry as a wintert-horn, and my limbs shuddered. I thought about rolling the tent down the bank into the river, but then remembered I had tethered it to the sausage tree so as not to blow away. And besides, the river was filled with crocs and hippos. The tether rope then made me quiver. The first elephant was a yard away; if he moved forward and tripped on the tether, he would fall on my tent, crushing the ingredients. I considered again making a run for it, but then I remembered how much noise the zipper makes and knew it would cause the elephants even more alarm. Then I heard a sound like Niagara by the tree. My bladder was full as well and was beginning to howl. Too many G&Ts. I was terribly tired. But I dared not close my eyes. The thought of being trampled with eyes open wide was bad enough. But I knew if I fell asleep, I would snore, and I could think of nothing worse than a squashing while snoozing. There I sat, stiff as new shoes, as the elephants scoffed and sniffed and chivvied about me. Elephants can eat for twenty hours a day, then rest the rest. A long night this might be. But then, after a couple of hours of munching, the two leviathans lay down in a sandy spot below my tent and went quiet. I took advantage of the respite and also lay down but commanded myself not to fall asleep. But my eyelids were heavy, and my mind wandered about in a haze of unbeing. I heard some crunching, sat up, and looked through the mesh. Did I nod off? The moon had crossed the sky and sunk behind the trees. In the now quite dark landscape, I could barely make out a silhouette shambling back upstream. With an unhurried pace it moved back into the shelter of the trees, entwined itself within branches and leaves, and then it was gone.

There was no other sound, save the litany bird, whose call seemed to cry, "Good Lord, deliver us." There were no more hulking specters. I presumed both were gone at last. But a silent presence still hung in the air. I was about to burst, so I unzipped the tent and leapt outside to relieve myself over the small bluff above the river. Just as I finished, there was a basso profundo bellow that ripped open the night just a few yards below me. I had pissed on the other beast, who was sleeping down the bank by the water's edge. I dove back into the tent, rezipped it, and hurdled into my bag. There was a subtle spark to his tardigrade pace as he clambered up the bank, to the frame of my tent, and fixed a walleyed stare. Our eyes locked, and for a second I thought I saw a display of *avere misericordia*, a hint of empathy for a small, vulnerable creature wrapped in nylon.

Then the elephant turned and plodded back into the bush. And into a deep and anodyne sleep I fell, returning with the dawn to a more managed, if less noble, wild place.

CHAPTER 64

THE REWARDS OF RISK

The true adventurer goes forth aimless and uncalculating to meet and greet unknown fate.

—O. HENRY, "THE GREEN DOOR"

IF THERE IS A COMMON THREAD TO ADVENTURE ACROSS THE AGES, IT IS RISK. AND risk is its greatest asset. At the moment of capsize, the wall clutch, or facing the feral eyes of a forest animal, we are febrile but also unlocked in a way that never happens in the comfort zone, so that the slightest tap makes us shiver to the bottom of our beings. If we survive, it is at this moment that we learn most profoundly, we glug down the liquid lessons of life, and consciousness evolves.

Though risk weaves throughout, the notions of adventure, and the nature of its practitioners, have altered much over the past thousand years. Trying to capture an encompassing definition is like trying to catch a lizard by its tail . . . as soon as you think you've got it, it leaves it in your fingers and grows a new one.

A half century ago I discovered I could fund my global rummagings in the name of seeking out new adventures for an emerging clientele who would follow in my footsteps.

In the late 1960s, after scraping together enough change to make some first rafting descents along rivers of the Eastern Seaboard, I knew that running new rivers would be my lifelong compulsion. . . . I rolled out a map of the world and drooled at all the fresh, turning water that had yet to be navigated. So, with some like-minded friends, I started the trifle of a company we named Sobek Expeditions with peacock ambitions to carom down all the wild rivers of the planet. The formula was simple: Use the company coffers to fund an exploratory rafting expedition; assuming the expedition was replicable (and more than a few times it was not), write up an itinerary, print a brochure, and offer the retracing as a commercial trip, hiring Colorado River guides to run the excursion; use the profits from the commercial tour to fund another exploratory, in a *The Endless Summer* cycle. My narcotic was for the adventure where none had gone before, and I rarely returned for a second descent. Thankfully, others did.

Our first clients were early adopters, alpha-seekers, calculated risk-takers, dilettantes who collected experiences but didn't want to be involved in the fuss of planning and organization, or the extreme danger of being first . . . they wanted to be professionally guided. This type of adventure was invented in the Romantic era, with the first guided trips to Mont Blanc, and perhaps the first adventure travel company, the Chamonix-based Compagnie des Guides, was formed to accommodate these new holiday doings.

One of these doers was Ernest Hemingway, with his guided safaris and fishing expeditions; Sandy Hill Pittman and the late Dick Bass are more modern examples, having paid dearly to have guides get them up the Seven Summits. And there were hundreds others who would pay to follow Lars-Eric Lindblad to Easter Island, or Leo LeBon to Nepal, or John Yost and myself down the Bio-Bio or the Zambezi. These adventurers, who expected discomfort, challenge, and risk to earn their prizes, fueled the beginnings of American-based adventure travel companies, including Mountain Travel, Abercrombie & Kent, and Sobek Expeditions. As outfitters pioneering a new type of travel, we practically guaranteed that something would go wrong. Our place of business was the wilderness, more flux than fixed point, and ever dangerous; routes were untested, infrastructures didn't exist, GPSs weren't around for geodetic bearings, and cell phones, the internet, and ChatGPT weren't available for instant information. But that was okay. . . . Our clients didn't care. When there was a screwup, when we got lost, more often than not there was unearned exhilaration, not damnation.

Rafting the Bio-Bio River, Chile. BART HENDERSON

I fished from my pockets of memory a watershed moment when things began to change. Up into the early 1980s, the adventure travel business was a niche enterprise, a gimmicky subset of the vacation industry catering to the Beta adventurers and not much more. My partners and I pretty much lived hand to mouth, but that didn't matter, as we were traveling the globe and digging up the doubloons of personal adventures. I lived in a bunkhouse near the office, took no salary, and had a passport with so many accordion pages it was fat as a paperback. And the relationship I had with our clients was wonderfully symbiotic and respectful. Though clients were often motivated by the chance to go one better, or at least one showier, than their neighbors, I realized they had a keen conviction that there was transcendence, serenity, and atonement to be found in the wildernesses of the world; a chance to start over in the bosom of raw nature.

One day in the early 1980s a twist of fate with broad downstream effects happened in the road. Curt Smith, a young man with a business background, was driving down California Highway 49 when he made a bad turn in front of the Sobek offices, got into an accident, and had to stick around as his car got fixed. While waiting, he became a guide. A few months later, in the fall of 1983, Curt suggested we have an "offsite" to discuss the future of the company. So, the weekend following, Curt, my partners, some top guides, and I retreated to the cramped Sonora living room of Paul Henry, our accountant, and rolled out our sleeping bags on the floor for two days of planning. Mostly we talked about new places to go and new activities to try. But at one pivotal moment, Curt challenged us and said, "Don't you want to make money?" John Yost was quick to reply: "No! We're in this for the adventure, not for money."

But Curt kept pushing, and by the end of the weekend, we had agreed to a new concept . . . something we would call "soft adventure." The idea was to produce an adventure tour for the masses, and that meant an itinerary that was comfortable, easy, inexpensive, dependable, and accessible. Three months later we began mailing a new brochure entitled "Andean Odyssey: 9 days from just $999—Airfare included!" There were thirteen departures, all identical, all featuring easy walks, a bouncy raft ride through the Sacred Valley of the Incas, and a scenic train ride to Machu Picchu. But unlike adventures past, wherein participants camped, ate freeze-dried or what could be caught or picked food, and pushed themselves physically and emotionally, this iteration sponged up the possibilities of genuine drama and feeling. Participants stayed in inns each night, with hot showers, cold drinks, clean sheets, insect and moonlight free. The offering was wildly successful, and adventure was forever changed. . . . It was commoditized! Born was the soft adventurer, boldly going where hundreds, perhaps thousands, had gone before.

Comfort in the wilds had been around for some time, but it had mostly been for the moneyed class. This offering was among the first that addressed a mainstream audience and relied on low margins and high numbers to become a business. It worked, and the Sobek catalogue was suddenly chock-full of soft adventures, and our intrepid guides were escorting knots of blue rinse, charm bracelets, and natty safari jackets among the glaciers and rain forests. A hundred adventure companies sprung to life with the concept of taking adventurers into the back of beyond with the same consistency and creature comforts as a Caribbean cruise or a European bus tour. Now, if there was an unexpected change in itinerary, or rain when the brochure suggested sunshine, or if the orangutans didn't show their faces on schedule, or the eco-lodge had ants, the soft adventurer asked for a refund. When something went wrong, there was little serendipity; there were lawsuits. Chance, like a bone in the desert, was bleached from the landscape.

Letting the soft adventurer out of the box was a mixed blessing, though. For me, it meant a compromise, watering a pure product down for the hoi polloi, rejiggering my company for a lower common denominator, concentrating more on streamlining current offerings rather than cobbling together exploratories. But it meant better wages for the guides and staff, health insurance, 401(k) plans, and tents with working zippers, and it meant sharing the Obeah of adventure with more people, and that was a good thing.

When Ed Hillary spoke out against commercial climbs up Everest, his words rang with remorse for a season lost to time: "How thankful I was that I was active in a pioneering era when we established the route, carried the loads, all worked together for the ultimate objective. The way things are now, I don't think I would have bothered." Today, with explorers looking backwards we hear the same cry: that those who climbed a mountain or ran an unrun river before the advent of adventure shepherds, GPSs, and connections to the Web were the real pioneers, with a much more authentic experience. Many have complained that Yosemite, the Grand Canyon, Kilimanjaro, and Victoria Falls have lost some divinity because of their manufactured and commercial accessibility, and that the backcountry is no longer so if one can call for help on a cell or sat phone. Some, though, say it is elitist to deny the validity and authenticity of what a softer adventurer may have experienced; imperious to preserve in private sanctuary the epiphany that came with a special effort, time, and place. In my years as a river guide, I escorted blind children, senior citizens, and paraplegics down the Colorado River, and I can testify that the transformational aspects of the experience were as vital for them as for the young, hearty do-it-yourself expeditioners. It may be less of a feat now to climb Everest than in 1953, what with better gear, communications technology, and routes well described, but adventure is a relative experience, one that has morphed through the ages and is interpreted on an individual basis. The sense of exhilaration and achievement is no less for the guided adventurer who stretches her ice ax above the summit of Everest as it was for Ed Hillary. And those same exalted feelings are just as powerful and genuine for the tyro adventurer who pitches his first tent, lights his first campfire, looks his first leopard in the eye, or takes his first canyoning jaunt in Switzerland. All took risks, and if they survived, they reaped rewards.

Besides, it is the novice adventurer who may save the wilderness world for the rest of us, and it is the theater of wilderness where the risk of adventure is played. The ledger is long of wilderness areas gone down because there wasn't a constituency to do the battle. Glen Canyon is the poster child. A basic problem has been that wilderness areas are usually hard to get to, and the numbers who saw them, experienced them, fell in love with them, were too often too small to make a difference.

That's where the companies that cater to the novitiates come in, as instruments of awareness, appreciation, and activism that no feature in the pages of *National Geographic* magazine ever could. When time comes for a call to action to stop the drowning of a wild river, the patronage for preservation is that much greater for the adventurers who have been escorted to the magic places and been touched by what they saw and felt, even if they did expect a flush toilet in the campsite. Several years ago, we lost a fight to save Chile's crown jewel of a wild river, the Bio-Bio, down which George Wendt and I made the first descent in 1976 and which had become a Sobek favorite. The concrete slug of a private big dam quieted it. We got Robert Kennedy Jr., Al Gore, Nany Pelosi, and the local Mapuche Indians behind the movement, but because only a few thousand travelers had

The last descent of the Bio-Bio, Lava South. It's now buried beneath the stagnant waters of a dam.
BART HENDERSON

ever seen the river, the constituency for preservation was not there, and we lost the Bio-Bio. The same happened with the Euphrates and Çoruh Rivers in Türkiye, the Tekeze in Ethiopia, and many others around the world. Today more people raft on a hot weekend than visit the Smithsonian, and that means that many more who fall in love with a wild river, who understand its issues, will lend a hand when it needs many.

According to a US Data Center study, more than half of all US traveling adults have taken an adventure trip in their lifetime. One can become an ersatz Indiana Jones, complete with khakis and fedora, with a click-through to any of a thousand outfitters on the web. The definition of adventure keeps widening and stretching. Indoor climbing walls, often not far from a real rock face, are increasing in popularity. The tyranny of geography can be cut away with interactive virtual adventures, transmitted in real time from the field via the Web, yet experienced in a climate-controlled cube through the portal of a smartphone, computer screen, or VR goggles.

Summit Mount Rainier. Skip Horner back left; Richard center back. RICHARD BANGS

How will people take their adventures in the future? Oculus or other VR head-sets might make Philip K. Dick's vision of buying memories, as envisioned in his short story "We Can Remember It for You Wholesale" possible . . . or maybe you can visit your local travel agency, buy the "Climb Everest" implant, and emerge minutes later with a complete memory of the grand adventure . . . all without a Khumbu cough, pulmonary edema, toes lost to frostbite, snoring tentmates, or any element of peril or fear. Adventure might become a sleight of logic . . . wrinkle-free, washed clean of any speck of risk, nothing more than an inconvenience wrongly considered, nothing more than a myth.

But I don't buy it. Nothing can replace the flame of feeling of the hot sun on your neck, the punch of brisk water on your face, the unwearied thrill of riding a wave or cresting a summit, the wallop of uncomfortably disrupting the familiar. This is the turbulent pleasure, somewhere between fright and admiration, of true adventure, of The Sublime. This makes it my fatality to live.

CHAPTER 65

IN THE WAKE
OF ADVENTURE

I have not told one-half of what I saw.
—MARCO POLO ON HIS DEATHBED, 1324

SO MUCH HAS CHANGED IN OUR THINKING SINCE THE ROMANTICS FIRST ARTICU-
lated the value of the vast. The difference between the scale of a Himalayan peak and
the events of thoughts is so much greater. Our technical language for the huge has
increased as we discover language for enormous events—a light-year, a terabyte, a
megaton—and huge numbers such as a googol (one followed by one hundred zeros)
and a googolplex (one followed by a googol of zeroes), the latter bigger than the
estimated number of atoms in the universe. The size of the universe is estimated in
the region of ten yottameters, where a yottameter is a distance so big that light would
require one hundred million years to travel it. The truly untouched sublime resides
somewhere beyond the heliopause.

But what has not changed is how adventure travel can move us—how these
numbers, concepts, and landscapes can evoke the aesthetics of the infinite and
prompt us to explore, both inwardly and in the physical spaces. The spaces, seemingly
unencompassable, stir up so much more than mere language. Horace-Bénédict de
Saussure wrote: "What language can reproduce the sensations and paint the ideas
with which these great spectacles fill the soul of the philosopher who is on top of a
peak?" The prize for broaching the high spaces is both far sight and insight.

Not long after I published a book on adventure travel in Indonesia, I received
a letter from a solo European traveler who had made his way to the interior of
Kalimantan, on the island of Borneo, to the village of Long Ampung on the Kayan
River. It was his second private tour of this hidden vault of wilderness. The first
time, a year previous, when he hired Dayak porters to carry his gear to Long Uro,
about a four-hour trek, they wanted $1.80/person for the enterprise. In the interim

an adventure tour company had arrived and paid the same porters $3.00 each, and now that was their asking price.

The letter writer was incensed. He could not believe that others might follow in his footsteps on an organized tour, and that they might pay more for what he received so cheaply. Once more, he complained, tourists of this type would corrupt the local culture and ruin the experience for true explorers such as himself.

This is at once a specious and elitist conceit, imperialist in its assumptions, and anti-evolutionist in its expression. The ersatz moral ping that courses through the minds of the mobile rich visiting the inert poor is rarely based in reality. All politics is local, and inevitably the locals want to decide how and when they change, and tourism, more often than not, offers an alternative, a chance to change, to evolve. Later in the same letter, the irate author talks about the high infant mortality rate

Former headhunter, Kalimantan, Borneo, Indonesia. PAMELA ROBERSON

of the region, the absence of medical aid, and comments that a nurse or doctor visits but twice a year. The nexus is missing, but inductively it would seem that if adventure travelers began to arrive in significant numbers, and paid fairly for local services, then monies might become available for hospitals, schools, and social services. It has worked in Nepal with ACAP (Annapurna Conservation Area Project), which exacts a fee from every foreign traveler, and the monies are then turned over to the locals, not only to supplement a miserably poor economy but to help in construction of ecologically sound lodges, and to buy kerosene as a fuel substitute so fewer trees will be cut. Economics is the most potent coin in adventure travel, and to wistfully wish that nobody follows in the privileged footsteps of an explorer so that the less advantaged remain so, and will entertain lone visitations for obscenely cheap prices, is a shameful fancy. Yet, it may be equally shameful to allow the ungraceful degradation from the relatively small numbers of adventure travelers to the call numbers of slash-and-burn mass tourism. The challenge is to find the balance, while defending God's last good acre from non-sustainable industries, such as logging, agriculture, petroleum extraction, and mining, which tend to thresh whatever they finger in a sort of reverse Midas touch.

Cultural issues aside, without economic incentives, habitat preservation will prove an expendable luxury in the increasingly desperate non-developing world. Adventure travel draws much of its potential from a dichotomy of riches: The industrialized world is flush with cash, but the tropical world has the lion's share of the planet's animal and plant species. Adventure travel is a plausible way to apply some of the financial wealth of the developed world toward protecting the biological wealth of inchoate places. Sound adventure travel practices that provide such a currency flow have already proved their worth in a number of noteworthy examples. At the Tangkoko-Batuangas Nature Reserve in North Sulawesi, much of the wildlife, including the rare black macaque, has been poached almost to the point of extinction. But recently tourists have begun hiring local guides from the village of Batuputih to show them the animals that previously were killed for food. The guides' daily fees provide enough incentive for the villagers to stop poaching, and even to join Indonesian park service patrols to reduce poaching by others.

That's an inspirational tale. But let's take this to the next step and look at the visitor, not the visited. The word gets out that travelers can now call on this piece of paradise and see endangered wildlife in the raw. They seek out the Edenic myth, and soon an hibiscus-covered resort is built, with dancers in the lobby, cheeseburgers and imported wine on the room service menu.

Now, as many visitors do not realize, the resort, with its capacity for hundreds, has paved a piece of wildness and created a facsimile utopia that not only upsets the balance but spawns a set of problems stickier than rotted pawpaw. The bloodline of these problems is entwined in Western history, snagged in its culture, in the concept of packaging and selling "paradise," when the inconvenience is that paradise ceases to be when too many pad its trails, when too many dip in its waters.

Though the marketing of Paradise as a construct of adventure travel is a young art, merchandising Eden has a rich legacy. Consider the government tourist officials of the Dutch East Indies during the period between World Wars I and II, whose brochures and magazine advertisements attempted to lure world cruise travelers to

the "Tropical Garden of Eden." This Paradisiacal myth is deeply implanted in Western tradition, with roots in both classical and biblical soil. It was kept alive in the Middle Ages by cartographers, who customarily showed the authentic locations of this antediluvian promised land as in the Orient, between the Tropics of Cancer and Capricorn. The romancers of the Age of Discovery had little difficulty in placing Elysium in the

Dyak woman, Borneo. They begin to stretch earlobes at a young age. PAMELA ROBERSON

exotic lands that curl through the equator, which they would people variously with noble savages, lost tribes, or superior human beings. The early explorers—Columbus among them—gave open support to this kind of thinking. And it is this mindset that persists today in the expectations of tourists who flock to the equatorial islands and other "wildernesses" today, searching blatantly for Paradise.

The tourists' impact, as should be expected, more often erodes than preserves the acreage of Paradise. Resort tourists, even the ones who believe they have registered with an "environmentally correct" property (one that separates the trash), too often see what cannot naturally occur, an idyllic insulated retreat with all the amenities of a

Beverly Hills hotel. It is for these deep pockets that the resorts are built—trees felled, swamps drained, rivers dammed, and villages shoved aside to preserve the "natural feel" of this contrived Paradise. Even more sadly, the villagers themselves may find their traditional livelihoods as fishers, farmers, and artisans supplanted by a resort economy built around touro-dollars; they can find work only in the white-smocked service and support industries, learning new words for new skills, and new vices. The end result of this type of tourism is all too often pollution, both environmental and cultural, and the damage is too frequently irremediable.

The adventurer traveler, however, is generally a kinder, greener visitor who immerses herself in the trackless travel experience and comes back deeply connected, wiser and concerned, educated and motivated. These travelers are the ones who accept what they find, learn to appreciate it on its own terms, and become passionate enough about the magic and magnificence of a place to join in the effort to preserve its life-forms, cultures, and ecological systems. The true adventure traveler seeks out locally owned inns and eateries, uses native guides, visits natural areas, and chooses low-impact transportation, a raft rather than a cruise ship, walking rather than a tour bus, moving across the earth's surface perpendicular to gravity and companioned by time. And, perhaps most profoundly, the adventure traveler minimizes the foreign exchange leakage, spending a significant portion of vacation monies in the local economy, purchasing goods, services, even authentic art directly from the source, giving indigenous populations incentives to preserve.

There are some other key distinctions between conventional travel and adventure travel. To a considerable extent, in conventional travel, the standard of excellence is a predictable, uniform experience . . . "the best surprise is no surprise" epistemology promoted by the chain hotels and restaurants. Adventure travel, on the other hand, celebrates multiculturalism, equity, and inclusion. The goal is discovery, enlightenment, and all manner of personal challenge—intellectual, physical, cultural, even spiritual. This embracing of a polyethnic Earth represents a positive evolution towards a higher consciousness. The first principle of the science of ecology is that uniformity in any system is unstable and unhealthy while, conversely, diversity is the singular attribute of a healthy, stable system. Seeking out and fostering diversity in the natural world and among human cultures is a most significant characteristic of adventure travel. The best way to instill an appreciation of the wonderful diversity of this planet is to experience it firsthand. These experiences can shake us awake. Then, the appreciation becomes more than just academic, but rather emotional, able to stand up to the wind tunnel of rationale. To someone who has truly gained such an appreciation, it is not necessary (or sufficient) to justify protection of wild spaces or endangered archaeological sites in term of discounted net value of revenue flows from tourism versus those from natural resource exploitation. The nonmaterial benefits of protecting these special spots may be intangible (in a material sense), but they are very real—and they are priceless and irreplaceable.

Related to this, conventional travel advocates an ethnocentric, one-way community connection versus the Manichean approach of adventure travel. In the case of adventure travel, hopefully the relationship between the visitor and the visited is such that each learns from the other and neither is forced to conform to the standards or expectations of the other. It is mutually deferential, without the tarnishing and trivializing that were once the calling cards of the ugly American. And there is encouragement to not just respect the foreign or unfamiliar, but to regard its link to everything on the planet, and to fathom the interconnectedness and interdependence of all things, to know that when a dragonfly flaps its wings by the Columbia River, it affects the weather in Kyoto. Also, adventure travelers are active versus passive, in that the traveler takes an active role in creating the experience, rather than just collapsing on a beach or the barstool and being waited upon. In most cases, just getting there requires active participation, such as rafting, hiking, or kayaking. And the active traveler is the traveler most likely to act, to take an issue position once being exposed to a threatened environment, and to dedicate time, energy, money, and voice to saving what now has personal meaning. Such is the moral imperative behind adventure travel. With firsthand experience comes appreciation, acknowledgment of worth and respect, and a desire and a reason to preserve the Earth's bounty. The Colorado River still flows through the Grand Canyon, the salmon still run up the Rogue; Walden Pond still reflects; the wildlife of Tanzania still roams—all in part because of the softly stepping visitors who liked what they saw and experienced, learned about the issues, and subsequently got involved. Where and how we travel is our choice, our vote, and then our opportunity.

As promising as adventure travel is as a tool for environmental conservation, and cultural enabling, travelers—even the most well-meaning—have an incontrovertible impact on the places they visit. It is impossible to visit an environment, a culture, and not exact some toll. The key is to ensure the impact is minimal and better than the alternatives.

It is the larger ledger that must be considered. Every inch of the planet has been charted, inspected, and lusted after by commercial or governmental concerns, and most often, if left alone, unvisited, these places fall to the short-term exploitation of industrial and business enterprises. And in many cases, nobody notices until it is too late. But when the adventure traveler comes around—the active traveler, the rafter, the kayaker, the backpacker—they become an active constituent and a powerful voice for a better way. Monies are imbued into the local economy, improving the woof and weave of life, while at the same time celebrating tradition. Adventurers fight to keep the wild places so, as they have been personally touched by the alchemy and beauty of pristine places and want to return, even if just in memory.

It does no good to wish that travelers not follow in your footsteps and alter what is inevitable. It is better to wish that the visitors, and their guides, travel with a certain consciousness, in a certain responsible and appreciative way.

Someday the Dayak villager might just save enough from the foreign adventure travelers so he can visit our neighborhood, and maybe he'll leave some coins behind: coins of equality, opportunity, and pride.

Richard kayaking with the godfather of ecotourism, Michael Kaye, in Tortuguero National Park, Costa Rica. LAURA HUBBER

Postscript 1: This book began with a recent expedition in Angola, during which I waved to my past and to a group of young explorers preparing to set off down the Lungwevungu River with hopes to prove the true font of the Zambezi ferments in the highlands of Angola. On April 20, 2023, I received this email from Steve Boyes, founder of the National Geographic Okavango Wilderness Project: "We have proven that the real source of the mighty Zambezi is in the Angolan Highlands by 400km, contributing over 85% of the annual flows into the Upper Zambezi."

Postscript 2: The deepest river is the river of intimacy. Soon after I met my future wife, Laura Hubber, I took her on a raft trip down the upper Jordan River in Israel. In the midst of an inconsequential rapid a wave reached up, clutched her torso, and tossed her into the brink. Besides a dollop of indignity, she was unscathed as I pulled her back into the boat, her unpinned hair falling like wet flames over her shoulders. I thought little of the episode. Eighteen years later, last fall, I took Laura rafting down the Colorado through the Grand Canyon, the passage that set me on a blaze that has never been doused. We hiked from the South Rim down the Bright Angel Trail and set off at mile 89.5 on an eighteen-foot NRS raft. We ran Horn Creek, then Salt Creek, without incident. But in the middle of Granite Rapid, where boulders from Monument Creek have constricted the river against the north wall, a massive wave swept over us and seemed to linger, searching for something. When we eddied out in the quiet water below, something felt different along my left hand. I felt my fingers and found my wedding ring was missing, a ring that had never left my hand in a decade. Panicked, I inspected the raft from the bilge through the baggage, but the ring was gone. With an arched smile, Laura volunteered: "The Colorado. Your first love. She's jealous."

Richard and Laura Hubber rafting the Colorado River. JOHN CANNING